Vital Crossroads

A volume in the series
CORNELL STUDIES IN SECURITY AFFAIRS

edited by Robert J. Art Robert Jervis Stephen M. Walt

A full list of titles in the series appears at the end of the book.

Vital Crossroads

MEDITERRANEAN ORIGINS OF THE SECOND WORLD WAR, 1935–1940

Reynolds M. Salerno

Cornell University Press

Ithaca and London

First published 2002 by Cornell University Press

Printed in the United States of America

Library of Congress Cataloging-in-Publication Data

Salerno, Reynolds M.
Vital Crossroads: Mediterranean Origins of the Second World War, 1935–1940 / by Reynolds M. Salerno
p. cm.
Includes bibliographical references and index.
ISBN 0-8014-3772-5 (alk.paper)
1. Second World War—Origins—1935–1940. 2. Second World War—Mediterranean—1939–1945. 3. Great Britain—Foreign Relations—France—1919–1945. 4. France—Foreign Relations—Great Britain—1919–1945. 5. Italy—Foreign Relations—France—1919–1945. 6. France—Foreign Relations—Italy—1919–1945. 7. Italy—Foreign Relations—Great Britain—1919–1945. 8. Great Britain—Foreign Relations—Italy—1919–1945. 9. Italy—Foreign Relations—Germany—1919–1945. 10. Germany—Foreign Relations—Italy—1919–1945.
I. Title. II. Series.
D742.M485352001
940.53'112—dc21 2001006971

Cornell University Press strives to use environmentally responsible suppliers and materials to the fullest extent possible in the publishing of its books. Such materials include vegetable-based, low-VOC inks, and acid-free papers that are recycled, totally chlorine-free, or partly composed of nonwood fibers. For further information, visit our website at www.cornellpress.cornell.edu.

Cloth printing 10 9 8 7 6 5 4 3 2 1

To Jennifer

Contents

	Acknowledgements	ix
	Abbreviations	xiii
	Introduction	1
Chapter 1	"The very midsummer of madness" 1935–37	10
Chapter 2	"The most formidable politico-military combination that has ever existed" November 1937–September 1938	40
Chapter 3	"The natural aspirations of the Italian people" October 1938–March 1939	73
Chapter 4	"Neither an acre of our territory nor a single one of our rights" March–August 1939	108
Chapter 5	"Keep the Allies guessing" September 1939–January 1940	143
Chapter 6	"A drama that will remake the map of the continent" December 1939–June 1940	178
	Conclusion	213
	Notes	221
	Bibliography	253
	Index	279

Acknowledgments

I acknowledge and thank the following organizations and foundations that provided financial support of my research for this book: the John M. Olin Foundation, the John D. and Catherine T. MacArthur Foundation, the Lynde and Harry Bradley Foundation, the Smith Richardson Foundation, International Security Studies at Yale University, and the Yale University Graduate School of Arts and Sciences.

My research on this subject began in earnest in 1994. Since then, I have visited twenty-three private and public archives in four different countries and dozens of university libraries. This research would not have been possible without the generous cooperation and assistance from the staffs of these various organizations. The following institutions and individuals have granted permission for me to cite and quote from the documents in their possession: in the United Kingdom, the Lord Ironside, Lady Avon, Mr. John Simon, the Special Collections of the University of Birmingham, the Churchill Archives Centre of Churchill College Cambridge, the Master and Fellows of Trinity College Cambridge, the Bodleian Library of Oxford University, the British Library, and the Trustees of the National Maritime Museum at Greenwich, London, and the Trustees of the Chevening Estate and the Center for Kentish Studies in Maidstone, Kent; in France, the Centre Historique of the Archives Nationales, the Archives Historique at the Ministère des Affaires Etrangères, the Service Historique of the Marine Nationale, the Service Historique of the Armée de la Terre, and the Service Historique of the Armée de l'Air; in Italy, the Servizio Storico Archivi e Documentazione of the Ministero degli Affari Esteri, the Archivio Centrale dello State, the Ufficio Storico of the Marina Militare, the Ufficio Storico of the Stato Maggiore dell 'Esercito, and the Ufficio Storico of the Aeronautica; and in the United States, the Houghton Library at Harvard University, the

Franklin D. Roosevelt Library, the National Archives and Records Administration, and the Library of Congress. All translations are mine unless otherwise noted.

I am especially indebted to my tireless and patient editor at Cornell University Press, Roger Haydon, who offered wise critiques and counsel. Robert Jervis, the academic series editor, and the anonymous outside reader both provided meticulous and constructive comments on early drafts. My primary adviser and dear friend at Yale University, Paul Kennedy, deserves immense credit for stimulating my interest in this particular topic, urging me to consider a multilateral perspective, and critically reading and actively promoting the project throughout its maturation. The many scholars who have provided observations and recommendations on drafts of various chapters or related articles include Zara Steiner, Sir Michael Howard, Geoffrey Parker, Alastair Parker, Talbot Imlay, Brian Sullivan, MacGregor Knox, Marc Trachtenberg, Martin Alexander, Frank Snowden, John Hattendorf, William Philpott, Keith Neilson, Greg Kennedy, William McBride, Peter Jackson, Rebecca Frerichs, and Howard Passell. Others who provided important guidance and welcome advice along the way are Christopher Andrew, Matthew Connelly, Hervé Coutau-Bégarie, Willard Frank, John Gaddis, John Gooch, Paul Halpern, David Herrmann, Holger Herwig, William Hitchcock, Mark Lawrence, Fred Logevall, Joseph Maiolo, Ernest May, Williamson Murray, Tim Naftali, Michael Powell, Michael Roi, Jennifer Siegel, David Schimmelpenninck, Stephen Schuker, David Stone, Jon Sumida, Maurice Vaïsse, Geoffrey Wawro, Wesley Wark, D.C. Watt, and Robert Young. Susane Roberts of the Sterling Library at Yale University offered generous bibliographic help and Ann Carter-Drier at Yale's International Security Studies supplied essential logistical support throughout the course of my research. I thank both my sister Kempley Bryant and Pascal Geneste of the Service Historique de la Marine for reviewing my note references. Much of the credit for anything this book achieves is due to them, and any errors it contains are mine alone.

There were still others, of course, who were not directly involved in the manuscript itself but whose influence was instrumental. Jan Albers, Paul Monod, Marjorie Lamberti, Nicholas Clifford, and Don Wyatt at Middlebury College deserve credit for instilling in me a passion for history and encouraging me to pursue it at the graduate level. My parents, Richard and Christina Salerno, have provided generous and loving support, understanding, and encouragement in more ways than I can adequately express. My two sisters and brother, as well as my parents- and siblings-in-law, all tolerated far too much talk about the Mediterranean in the 1930s during family holidays. Two cousins, Mark Mathewson and Jay Harrington, graciously allowed me to use their homes in their absence to finish the majority of my revisions.

I completed the manuscript for my three beloved and delightful children, Ryerson, Bailey, and Colt, who wonder why their father spends so much time reading and writing and who always try valiantly to distract him from it. I hope someday they will forgive me for my prolonged absences while they were very young. My greatest debt is to my dear wife, Jennifer, who has suffered patiently through *Vital Crossroads* for the last seven years. Without her, this book would never have been completed or this history come to life. She endured and inspired it. I am deeply grateful, and I dedicate it to her.

REYNOLDS M. SALERNO

Albuquerque, New Mexico

Abbreviations

496AP	Papiers Edouard Daladier (France)
AA	Armée de l'Air (France)
ACS	Archivio Centrale dello Stato, Rome
ADAP	Akten zur Deutschen Auswärtigen Politik
ADM	Admiralty Papers (Britain)
AFC(J)	Anglo-French Staff Conversations
AFI	Archivio Fotografico Italiano (United States)
AG	Archivio di Gabinetto (Italy)
AIR	Air Ministry Papers (Britain)
AMC	Allied Military Committee (Britain)
AN	Archives Nationales, Paris
AP	Anthony Eden Papers (Britain)
AP-F	Affari Politici—Francia (Italy)
AP-GB	Affari Politici—Gran Bretagna (Italy)
AP-I	Affari Politici—Italia (Italy)
ASD	Archivio Storico Diplomatico al Ministero degli Affari Esteri, Rome
AUSA	Archivio dell'Ufficio Storico dell'Aeronautica, Rome
AUSMM	Archivio Ufficio Storico della Marina Militare, Rome
BEF	British Expeditionary Force
BL	British Library, London
BOD	Bodleian Library, Oxford University, Oxford, England
BUL	Birmingham University Library, Birmingham, England
CAB	Cabinet Papers (Britain)
CAC	Churchill Archives Centre, Churchill College, Cambridge, England
CHT	Ernle Chatfield Papers (Britain)
CID	Committee of Imperial Defence (Britain)

CIGS	Chief of the Imperial General Staff (Britain)
CKS	Centre for Kentish Studies, Maidstone, England
COS	Chiefs of Staff (Sub) Committee (Britain)
CPDN	Comité Permanent de la Défense Nationale (replaced HCM in June 1936) (France)
CSDN	Conseil Supérieur de la Défense Nationale (France)
CSG	Conseil Supérieur de la Guerre (France)
CTV	Corpo Truppe Volontarie (Italy)
DBFP	Documents on British Foreign Policy
DDF	Documents Diplomatiques Français
DDI	I Documenti Diplomatici Italiani
DGFP	Documents on German Foreign Policy
DPAN	Débats Parlementaires Assemblée Nationale, France
DP(P)	Defence Plans (Policy) Subcommittee (Britain)
DRC	Defence Requirements Committee (Britain)
EMA	État-major général de l'Armée (France)
EMG	État-major général (France)
EMM	État-major général de la Marine (France)
Eur 30–40	Papiers Europe 1930–1940 (Série Z) (France)
EWD	Economic Warfare Department (Britain)
FDRL	Franklin D. Roosevelt Library, Hyde Park, N.Y., U.S.A.
FMF	Forces maritimes françaises (France)
FNEO	Forces navales dans la Extrême-Orient (France)
FO	British Foreign Office
FP(36)	Foreign Policy Committee Minutes (Britain)
FPC	Foreign Policy Committee (Britain)
FRUS	Foreign Relations of the United States
GM	Gabinetto del Ministro (Italy)
HCM	Haut Comité Militaire (defunct after June 1936) (France)
HL	Houghton Library, Harvard University, Cambridge, Mass., U.S.A.
HMG	His Majesty's Government (Britain)
HNKY	Maurice Hankey Papers (Britain)
IRI	Istituto per la Ricostruzione Industriale (Italy)
JIC	Joint Intelligence (Sub) Committee (Britain)
JP(39)	Joint Planning (Sub) Committee Minutes (Britain)
JPC	Joint Planning (Sub) Committee (Britain)
LC	Library of Congress, Washington, D.C., U.S.A.
MAE	Ministère des Affaires Etrangères, Paris
MAG	Ministero dell'Aeronautica Gabinetto (Italy)
MAI	Ministero dell'Africa Italiana (Italy)
MAI-AS	Ministero dell'Africa Italiana—Archivio Segreto (Italy)

MdAE	Minstero degli Affari Esteri (Italy)
MEW	Ministry of Economic Warfare (Britain)
MGG	Ministero della Guerra Gabinetto (Italy)
MMG	Ministero della Marina Gabinetto (Italy)
MMG-AS	Ministero della Marina Gabinetto—Archivio Segreto (Italy)
MP	Member of Parliament (England)
NARA	National Archives and Records Administration, Washington, D.C., U.S.A.
NMM	National Maritime Museum, Greenwich, England
P-40	Papiers 1940 (France)
PA-AP	Papiers d'agents—archives privées (France)
PD	Parliamentary Debates, House of Commons, Great Britain
PHPP	Eric Phipps Papers (Britain)
PNF	Partito Nazionale Fascista (Italy)
PREM	Prime Minister's Papers (Britain)
PRO	Public Record Office, Kew, England
RAB	Robert A. Butler Papers (Britain)
RAF	Royal Air Force (Britain)
RD-L	Rappresentanze Diplomatiche a Londra (Italy)
RD-F	Rappresentanza Italiana in Francia (Italy)
SAC	Strategical Appreciation (Sub) Committee (Britain)
SAS	Seziόne Altri Studi (della Marina) (Italy)
SHAA	Service Historique de l'Armée de l'Air, Vincennes, France
SHAT	Service Historique de l'Armée de la Terre, Vincennes, France
SHM	Service Historique de l'Armée de la Marine, Vincennes, France
SIA	Servizio Informazioni Aeronautiche (Italy)
SIM	Servizio Informazioni Militari (Italy)
SIS	Servizio Informazioni Segreto della Marina (Italy)
SME	Stato Maggiore dell'Esercito (Italy)
SMG	Stato Maggiore Generale (Italy)
SMM	Stato Maggiore della Marina (Italy)
SPD-CR	Segretaria Particolare del Duce—Carteggio Riservato (Italy)
SWC	Supreme War Council
T	Treasury Papers (Britain)
TA	Territorial Army (Britain)
TCL	Trinity College Library, Cambridge University, Cambridge, England
TCUT	Trinity College Library, University of Toronto, Toronto, Canada
UC	Ufficio di Coordinamento (Italy)
UC-G	Ufficio di Coordinamento—Germania (Italy)
US	Ufficio Spagna (Italy)
USE	Ufficio Storico dello Stato Maggiore dell'Esercito, Rome

USMM	Ufficio Storico della Marina Militare, Rome
USNIP	United States Naval Institute Proceedings
WM	War Cabinet Minutes (Britain)
WO	War Office Papers (Britain)
WP	War Cabinet Papers (Britain)

Vital Crossroads

The Mediteranean Region, 1935

Introduction: Mediterranean Origins of the Second World War

The Second World War started in September 1939 when the German army invaded Poland, provoking Britain and France to declare war on Nazi Germany. The war did not start in the Mediterranean. In fact it was nine months before Fascist Italy intervened and extended to the Mediterranean a war that until then had been limited to the European continent and the North Sea. Nevertheless, the situation in the Mediterranean played a decisive role in the European drama of the late 1930s and profoundly influenced the manner in which the Second World War unfolded.

This Mediterranean perspective is new. Until now, historians have explained the outbreak of the Second World War as the result of an irreconcilable conflict between Great Britain and Germany, a struggle that occurred almost exclusively in Europe. There were good reasons to focus on Britain and Germany: they were the only two major European powers at war continuously from September 1939 until May 1945, and for eighteen months after the fall of France and before the United States entered the war, the United Kingdom battled the Axis powers virtually alone. Nazi Germany was arguably the war's most important provocateur and will forever be known as one of the most ambitious and heinous regimes in history. The war records of the other major European powers pale in comparison. Aside from a short war against Finland during the winter of 1939–40, the Soviet Union remained outside the conflict until attacked by the Germans in June 1941. The French government, after fighting a "phony war" for nine months, fell in June 1940 and was not liberated until August 1944. Fascist Italy did not intervene until June 1940, and its government was driven into exile in July 1943.

These dates and events affirm the importance of Britain and Germany to the history of the Second World War but do not imply that the British and Germans alone were responsible for the *origins* of the war. Many international scholars have allowed the dominance of Britain and Germany *during* the war to influence their study of events *before* the war. Moreover, and perhaps equally important, many of these scholars have tended to interpret international conflicts as rooted in bilateral, East-West antagonisms. This disinclination to recognize complex, multilateral origins and repercussions of international events may reflect the fact that most of this scholarship occurred during the Cold War—a time in which a bilateral conflict overshadowed all other international relationships.

The overwhelming emphasis on the evolution of bilateral Anglo-German relations has resulted in a history that, predictably, attributes almost all the accomplishments and failures of the times to those two powers as well. In general the Allied and Axis relationships have been characterized as profoundly unequal: military and economic weakness condemned France and Italy to be junior partners with Britain and Germany, respectively. Allied strategy and diplomacy have become almost synonymous with British foreign policy, and Fascist foreign policy is most often described as little more than opportunistic. Such interpretations not only trivialize France and Italy but also misappropriate historical responsibility.

The ubiquitous Anglo-German perspective has also emphasized continental objectives and influences at the expense of other global and imperial factors. Much of the study of the war's origins currently focuses on the extent of Germany's continental ambitions, the deficiencies of France's defensive military strategy, and Britain's reluctance to commit an expeditionary force to the continent; the Mediterranean has been banished to the periphery in this history. Yet the importance of the Mediterranean theater during the war demonstrates the European powers' belief that this region had great strategic significance. This fact as well as the immediacy of the Mediterranean to what the great powers coveted most during this period—empires—demands that the prewar Mediterranean situation receive equally scrupulous historical attention.

France and Italy were the European powers with the most at stake in the Mediterranean. Imperial Rome had ruled over the greater Mediterranean region spectacularly and decisively. Virtually every Italian schoolchild was nurtured on a history that revered Giuseppe Mazzini and Giuseppe Garibaldi, nationalists who had fought to unite Italy in the 1860s and to recreate the Mediterranean dominance of the Roman Empire. Italy's nationalists believed that a new Mediterranean empire was a necessary step in rebuilding a great Italian nation. Yet the young Italy struggled mightily in pursuing these goals, failing to win any glittering prizes in the colonial scramble of the late nineteenth century, and badly humiliated when the Ethiopians repelled and destroyed Italy's colonial army as it tried to advance on the town of Adowa in 1896. Thereafter Italy remained outside the European race for colonies until its war against the crumbling Ottoman Empire in 1911–2. Narrowly avoiding defeat, the Italians drove the Turks out of the one remaining part of the North African coast, Tripolitania, not under British or French control. The success in Libya, as the new colony was called, rekindled Italian hopes for a sweeping and spectacular Mediterranean empire.

The Great War offered Italian nationalists an opportunity to advance their imperial aspirations in the Mediterranean. With a modest empire that included only Libya, Eritrea, and part of Somaliland, Italy in 1914 could not claim the elusive mantle of a great European power. The secret Treaty of London of 1915, however, by which the British and French persuaded the Italians to join the Allies against the Central Powers, pledged that Italy would share in the colonial and continental spoils of war. Specifically, it would receive a portion of the eastern coast of the Adriatic, a string of islands in the Aegean, Ottoman territories in the Near and Middle East, and even additional parts of Somaliland. Becoming the most influential European nation in the Mediterranean would allow Italy to augment its population, to acquire desperately needed agricultural products and raw materials for its import-dependent economy, and to stem the "perpetual hemorrhage" of emigrants. Most important, the extension of its Mediterranean empire would satisfy the ambitions of the nation's imperialists and nationalists and finally confer on Italy the status of a great power.

But the Paris Peace Conference denied to Italy much that the Treaty of London had promised. The peace treaty that was signed at Versailles in 1919 granted substantial imperial spoils to the triumphant at the expense of the vanquished. Germany was compelled to relinquish territory and shipping and to accept disarmament and a vast war indemnity. Germany was also stripped of all its overseas colonies. The majority of Germany holdings in Africa were transferred to Britain as mandated territories of the new League of Nations; France received Togoland and Cameroon. In the Middle East, Britain and France shared the remnants of the Ottoman Empire, Britain assuming League mandates over Palestine, Jordan, and Iraq and France acquiring mandates in Syria and Lebanon. In contrast to Britain and France, Italy could not claim reparations from its defeated enemy, for the Hapsburg government now ceased to exist. All Italy received in the postwar settlement were Trent, the Trentino, Trieste, and the Austrian-populated South Tyrol (Alto Adige) up to the Brenner Pass.

Italian public opinion was outraged over the thwarting of Italy's war aims, and the issue of Fiume at the head of the Adriatic Sea most dramatically manifested this fury. Italy claimed the port city, which Italians had settled centuries before, even though it had been ruled by the Hapsburgs until

1918. The Allies denied Fiume to Italy because it would have placed Slavic minorities under Italian rule and thus violated Woodrow Wilson's principle of self-determination. Decrying a "mutilated victory," the poet Gabriele D'Annunzio and some two thousand war veterans seized Fiume by force in September 1919. Although D'Annunzio's occupation provoked international condemnation, it garnered immediate support from a majority of Italians. D'Annunzio was dislodged the following year, but the Italian government took Fiume in 1923, and eventually the League accepted this de facto Italian acquisition.

In his rise to power, Benito Mussolini exploited Italian nationalism and its determination to build an Italian empire in the greater Mediterranean, as well as the political, economic, and social dislocation wrought by the war. Not only had Italy lost close to 750,000 soldiers, but also its postwar economy was burdened by an immense wartime debt, an endemic balance-of-payments deficit, and devastating inflation. The resulting domestic turmoil raised fears of a Bolshevik revolution percolating within Italy's borders. In March 1919 this trepidation coalesced with the sentiments of indignant nationalists and disillusioned ex-servicemen to produce the first *Fasci di combattimento*—Mussolini's paramilitaries, who were driven by a program of revolution at home and expansion abroad. After Mussolini was elected to parliament in 1921, his *Fascisti* terrorized socialists and fomented anarchy, underscoring the feebleness of parliamentary rule in Italy. In October 1922 his Partito Nazionale Fascista, supported by an influential group of industrialists and agrarians, marched on Rome and compelled the king to ask Mussolini to form a new government. By 1925 Mussolini had eliminated all domestic political opposition to his rule and created an ideological, totalitarian dictatorship built around the legend of *Il Duce,* supreme leader.

Rebuilding an Italian Mediterranean empire was a principal element of the Duce's geopolitical agenda. Nevertheless, during his first decade in power he concentrated on creating a domestic ideological consensus for Fascism and entrusted most decision-making in international affairs to liberal Italy's career diplomats. As a result, early Fascist foreign policy strove to consolidate the African empire and to earn the respect of other European powers. Foreign ministry officials attempted to solve Italy's demographic and economic problems by cautiously expanding its empire on the continent and in the Mediterranean through conventional European diplomacy. A policy of negotiation with Britain and Germany and confrontation with France and Yugoslavia was the basis on which Italy hoped to build legitimate imperial power.

Whereas the Mediterranean represented for the Italians the cruel treatment received at Versailles, postwar imperial expansion in the Mediterranean was cause for great celebration in Britain and France. Empire was a principal defining element of nationhood in the early twentieth century.

The democracies perceived their empires as emblems of world power and influence, supporting their industrial and financial strength by providing agricultural products and raw materials for nationally exported manufactured goods. Both nations also contended that their empires would allow civilization to prosper. The British especially believed that their imperial subjects would eventually adopt the liberal culture and political freedoms that Britons enjoyed at home.

Yet the Mediterranean played different roles for Britain and France. It represented the heart and soul of the French empire, providing not only international stature and economic stability but also national identity and continental security. Possessing colonies in Tunisia, Algeria, Morocco, Syria, and Lebanon, as well as throughout West Africa, France saw itself as a great Mediterranean and Moslem power. Most of its principal and essential imports, such as petroleum, coal, manganese, copper, and jute, arrived by way of the Mediterranean—which thus served as France's indispensable imperial communication and trade route and as a source of national pride.

The Mediterranean also directly served French continental security. Since 1919 the French had viewed their victory in the Great War as hollow and tenuous. The Germans had defaulted on their war reparations to France and subsequently succeeded in having their war debts reduced. The 1925 Locarno agreements—which elicited a tacit German acceptance of the loss of Alsace-Lorraine, the permanent demilitarization of the Rhineland, and a promise by the major Western powers to defend the existing borders of Germany, France, and Belgium—left open the possibility of German territorial revision in the East. This fundamental weakness of Locarno, combined with Germany's treaties with the Soviet Union in 1922 and 1926, had led the French to bolster their network of alliances with the new states of Eastern Europe. Those allies, it was hoped, would constitute a second front, a cordon sanitaire keeping Bolshevism out of Europe and Germany within its 1919 frontiers. In 1925–27 the French signed agreements with Poland, Czechoslovakia, Romania, and Yugoslavia, recognizing that the only secure supply route to these new allies was through the Mediterranean.

But all these eastern allies were weak states that France could not defend against a Germany with revisionist aspirations. Therefore, unless Germany had no desire to expand eastward, such alliances would almost inevitably involve France in a war against Germany—exactly what France was trying to avoid. The French, especially the military, recognized this paradox and understood that absent a durable entente with Britain, France could rely on little more than its own military strength for security. For this reason, the French built what became known as the Maginot Line, a defensive barrier of varying degrees of impenetrability that ran the length of the eastern frontier along the Rhine from Luxembourg to Basle. Increasingly, the French also depended on their ability, in the event of trouble on the western front, to transport across the Mediterranean troops raised from the standing colonial army or native reserves in Africa.

Whereas the Mediterranean was thus intrinsic to French and Italian national identity and security, it was perceived as only instrumental to British security. Following the defeat of Germany and Austria-Hungary in 1918, Britain's worldwide responsibilities and power had reached heights never before dreamed of by even the most zealous nineteenth-century imperialists. Having finally quenched their thirst for expansion, the British now approached international diplomacy—including affairs in the Mediterranean—determined to preserve the European balance of power and the integrity of the British Empire. Paramount in this effort was the sanctity of the Far East, the home of the most important jewels in the imperial crown. English capital invested in India, Burma, Malaysia, the East Indies, and China far outweighed even the resource potential in the Near and Middle East and Africa. As a result, in British eyes the Mediterranean served as little more than the shortest path to Britain's most important overseas commercial interests.

Given their strong preference for free and open Mediterranean communication lines and shipping routes, as well as their feelings of guilt over the treatment of Italy at Versailles and their high regard for Mussolini, the British tacitly acquiesced in Fascist Italy's imperial program throughout the 1920s. Following Mussolini's bombardment and occupation of the island of Corfu in 1923, they ignored the League's promise to punish the aggressor and instead took steps to humiliate Greece: they quietly forced Mussolini to evacuate Corfu but compelled the Greeks to pay an indemnity. Soon thereafter the British sought and achieved an entente with Italy that included Mussolini's diplomatic support for the 1925 Locarno treaties. They then avoided intervening when Mussolini challenged France and Yugoslavia in the Balkans and North Africa during the late 1920s, and they rejected outright many French requests for a "Mediterranean Locarno" in 1929–32.

The British believed they were immune to the consequences of an emerging Franco-Italian rivalry. Their perspective on Mediterranean affairs was principally inspired by the rising presence of imperial Japan in the late 1920s. The Japanese invasion of Manchuria in September 1931, and the jeopardy in which it placed British holdings in Asia, effectively brought an end to any substantial British Mediterranean security. The Mediterranean became a training and staging ground almost exclusively: all the fleet exercises that took place there during the early 1930s were designed to address problems pertaining to the reinforcement of the eastern fleet, the development of Singapore as a naval repair and refueling base, and the defense of trade or military convoys passing through the Mediterranean. Britain seriously considered no contingency for a Mediterranean war before 1935.

While the British and French after the First World War strove to retain control of their current borders and possessions, the Italians and Germans aspired to revise the European balance of power. Like Italy's, Germany's political system and society emerged from the Great War with deep, damaging wounds. Germany had been emasculated territorially and abruptly demoted from its great-power status. Most traumatized by the postwar situation was its military. The German army, limited by Versailles to 100,000 officers and men, crumbled in a vast military strike; the German navy, rendered powerless by the treaty's disarmament clauses, mutinied. With no empire to rule, no fleet to project power, and no shipping to build national wealth, Germany was wholly vanquished. The sudden shift in fortunes and the punitive manner in which it was imposed shook German society as a whole and prompted a surge in nationalist violence, particularly among the demobilized and disgruntled soldiers and sailors and the frustrated and military-minded youth. Soon a consensus in German public opinion emerged, asserting that the judgment of Versailles had to be reversed; access to world markets and raw materials had to be regained; and the German empire and national honor had to be returned. Adolf Hitler's National Socialist German Workers' Party embraced these desires, deriding the Weimar "Jew Republic" as the perpetrator of Germany's collapse and promising to achieve mastery abroad and total power at home. With the fervent support of the German military, which had already begun disregarding the restrictions of Versailles in its determination to reestablish German hegemony in Europe, Hitler assumed the Reich chancellorship in 1933.

Hitler's rise to power and Nazi Germany's determination to rearm and to revise the terms of Versailles inspired Mussolini to invigorate Fascist foreign policy and to reconsider his strategy for imperial extension. In 1932–33 he assumed complete control of Italian foreign and defense policy, purging the "old Fascists" who had become too powerful or too independent and appointing Fascist sycophants. As part of this realignment in Rome, the Duce sought to integrate Fascist Italy's ideological motives with its geostrategic objectives. Although Fascist Italy retained its strategic and economic interests in southern and east-central Europe, Mussolini increasingly appreciated that an extensive Italian empire in the greater Mediterranean region could exist alongside a German-dominated continent but would directly conflict with British and French vital interests. The possibility of becoming a strategic and ideological partner with Nazi Germany, which could challenge Britain and France to the north and help Italy achieve its imperial ambitions to the south, steadily emboldened Mussolini. Italy would become one of the world's preeminent powers if it acquired an empire that provided unfettered access to the world's great seas, stretching from East Africa and the Middle East, up the Red Sea, through the Suez

Canal and into the Balkans, across North Africa and the western Mediterranean. By 1934 Mussolini had informed his party that access to Italy's historical and geopolitical objectives in Africa and Asia could soon be achieved through Italian domination of the Mediterranean.

As Nazi Germany had influenced Fascist foreign policy, the maturation of Italy's Mediterranean ambitions motivated a reconsideration of German strategy. The basis of Hitler's foreign policy, which recognized Germany's naval and military weaknesses as well as British and French control over the majority of Europe's overseas colonies, was the concept of *Mitteleuropa,* a central European economic bloc with Germany at its core. Such a living space, or *Lebensraum,* would provide the surplus population and economic resources necessary to reconstitute German power. Initially, Hitler believed that this new German empire could be achieved only by allying with Britain. But Mussolini's Mediterranean ambitions and willingness to challenge Britain and France worked to Germany's strategic advantage: an Anglo-French-Italian tension or conflict in the Mediterranean would facilitate Germany's military conquest of Central and Eastern Europe and alleviate or even obviate the need for a British alliance. For this strategic reason as well as the close ideological affinities between German National Socialism and Italian Fascism, Hitler supported and demonstrated extraordinary loyalty to Mussolini in the years before and during the war. The Mediterranean situation was also an instrumental factor in the evolution of Nazi Germany's ruthless imperial ambitions and the strategy designed to achieve them.

THIS BOOK demonstrates that the international politics of pre–World War II Europe—particularly in the Mediterranean—can be understood only as the complex, multilateral interaction of the foreign policies of Britain, France, Germany, and Italy. Although the military and economic strengths of these countries differed, the relationships between and among them were not strictly bilateral or unilateral. Often, the relations between any pair of them were affected by one of the pair's relations with another country or even by contrasting interpretations of the other pair's motives or goals. For instance, the Anglo-French relationship was influenced at different times by the current state of Britain's or France's relations with Italy or Germany. Simultaneously, the Franco-Italian and Italo-German relationships changed and evolved as a result of British and Italian maneuvering, Anglo-French war planning, and British and French attempts to appease Germany.

The book also shows that the Mediterranean theater—as significantly as the western front—profoundly affected the origins and course of the Second World War. Control of the Mediterranean was a central concern for the European powers in 1935–40, and a fundamental reason why Europe went to war and why the conflict unfolded as it did. The Mediterranean was a strategically crucial theater for Allied and Axis war planning because of the substantial value of European empires in North Africa, the Near and Middle East, and the Far East. In fact during this period the European powers were often motivated principally by their imperial interests and ambitions; they frequently subordinated their continental and alliance policies to imperial priorities.

The Mediterranean was a vital crossroad, allowing the French and Italians to influence and often determine the nature and direction of Allied and Axis policy to an extent disproportionate to their nations' military and economic strength. The intractable differences in British and French Mediterranean policies, and the Allies' failure to adopt a coherent war strategy for that theater, effectively relinquished the initiative in the war to the Axis powers, leading to nine months of "phony war," the fall of France, and eighteen months of peril for the British. At a time when many statesmen in London and Paris dreaded the ability of the German Wehrmacht and Luftwaffe to march across the European continent, they equally feared that the Italian Regia Marina and Regia Aeronautica would strive to fulfill Mussolini's imperial ambitions in the Mediterranean.

[1]

"The very midsummer of madness": 1935–37

The Mediterranean Crisis

The year 1935 started optimistically for Anglo-French-Italian relations, largely as a result of the three countries' shared concern over Germany's growing power. On 7 January Mussolini and French Foreign Minister Pierre Laval signed an agreement that proclaimed the "necessity of maintaining the independence and integrity of Austria." In an Anglo-French communiqué the next month, the British expressed approval of the Franco-Italian accords, and the two states promised to consult with other interested powers if any state menaced Austrian independence or integrity. Following Nazi Germany's first open repudiation of the Treaty of Versailles—proclaiming the existence of an air force, reintroducing conscription, and initiating construction of twelve submarines—representatives of Britain, France, and Italy met in Stresa in early April and adopted a resolution—the Stresa front—that accepted "no unilateral repudiation of international obligations," reaffirmed the intention to consult one another if any power threatened the independence of Austria, and stated that they would actively pursue an air pact. By June the French and Italian militaries had developed plans for joint military operations to defend Austria and to prevent German remilitarization of the Rhineland.[1]

Although these arrangements collectively could have contributed to the creation of a formidable anti-German coalition, their value was damaged by the Anglo-German naval agreement of June 1935 and the subsequent outbreak of a crisis in the Mediterranean. The naval agreement sanctioned the expansion of the German Kriegsmarine up to 35 percent the size of the Royal Navy. Although the British believed the arrangement would limit future German shipbuilding and not jeopardize Britain's ability to defend its interests in Europe or the Far East, the Germans planned to exploit it to facilitate extensive and undisturbed rearmament until a time when the treaty could be safely revoked. The French interpreted the agreement as not only a revision of Versailles but also an open rejection of the Anglo-French communiqué and the Stresa front; Britain had forsaken its commitment to a broader European settlement in favor of national security. Moreover, the naval treaty—and the shift out of the Mediterranean by British and French naval forces that followed it—provided Mussolini with an opportunity to pursue what, in December 1932, he had ordered General Emilio De Bono, minister of colonies, to begin planning for: the extension of the Italian empire into east Africa. On the day the naval treaty was signed Mussolini made specific Italian claims on Ethiopia. Four days later Laval, now the French premier, reaffirmed France's commitment to that part of the January agreement which gave Italy a "free hand" in Ethiopia.[2]

Confident that Britain and France would not resist Italian expansion into East Africa, Mussolini intensified the conflict with Ethiopia throughout the summer and repeatedly rejected British and French proposals for a negotiated settlement. At the end of August, with Italy's designs on Ethiopia evident to the entire world, Britain and France reinforced their Mediterranean defenses and eliminated Italy's naval superiority. Although the balance of naval tonnage in the Mediterranean had suddenly shifted in favor of Britain and France, the two powers did not attempt to forestall Mussolini's drive into east Africa. Facing no military opposition, Mussolini ordered Italian troops to invade Ethiopia on 3 October.[3]

Britain and France also decided not to take up arms to reverse Italy's flagrant transgression of the League of Nations' principles of national sovereignty and collective security. Concluding that a war with Italy "would be a grave calamity," the British Cabinet believed that if Britain committed itself to a naval conflict against Italy in the Mediterranean and especially if Britain lost any warships in the process, the naval balance in the North Sea would tip in Germany's favor, and all of China and Southeast Asia would lie open to Japanese expansion. Yet much of the hesitation to act militarily came from the French, who rejected Britain's request for unconditional French commitments against Italy in the Mediterranean. Laval wished to avoid any hostilities there, confident that an overt Franco-Italian conflict would drive Mussolini into the German camp and further complicate French continental strategy and defense. Along with many other officials in Paris, Laval still hoped that the Stresa front could be reconstituted.[4]

Instead of using force, Britain and France arranged for the League of Nations to impose sanctions on Italy. At Laval's insistence, though, the League excluded the two punitive measures that could have forced Mussolini to reconsider his east African adventure: an oil embargo and the closing of the Suez Canal. Moreover, the Laval government attempted to alleviate the severity of sanctions by delaying their application until late November, refusing to enforce them in French Morocco or in territories under French mandate, and maintaining commercial and financial relations with countries that did not apply sanctions. Even so, the imposition of sanctions on Italy infuriated Mussolini, who had been led to believe by the 1935 Franco-Italian accord and the Stresa pact that Britain and France would quietly acquiesce in Italy's annexation of Ethiopia.[5]

The son of a poor blacksmith and schoolteacher in Romagna, Mussolini became a journalist and newspaper editor as well as the secretary of the local socialist party. Initially opposed to Italian participation in the Great War, he founded a pro-war newspaper, *Il Popolo d'Italia,* and later a political movement, the *Fasci de combattimento,* that advocated for the collapse and rebirth of Italian society and successfully brought him into power. A bald man with heavy jowls, a bulbous nose, and an impressive physique, Mussolini was a voracious reader and an intelligent, vain, callous, and insecure man of strange magnetism and remarkable rhetorical talents who was intoxicated by power. His Fascism lacked a central ideological framework, but as early as January 1919 he had proclaimed that "imperialism is the eternal and immutable law of life." Thereafter, his dream of creating a second Roman Empire through expansion in the Mediterranean, "the sea of Rome," buttressed by an enduring authoritarian dictatorship, became Italian Fascism's ideology.[6] How he would achieve that dream was not clearly defined but became increasingly unambiguous after 1935.

Interpreting France's action during the sanctions episode as treachery, Mussolini in December 1935 started withdrawing the four Italian divisions that he had sent to the Austrian border in July 1934, following the attempted Nazi coup d'état and the murder of Austrian Chancellor Engelbert Dollfuss. Additional Italian troops had been concentrated near the Brenner Pass in August 1935, inciting indignation on the part of the Germans in the South Tyrol and Austria. Italy's decision to reduce its strength on the Austrian border persuaded many in London and Paris to search for a diplomatic solution to the Italo-Ethiopian crisis. But news of a proposal under consideration whereby Ethiopia would relinquish about half of its territory to settle the conflict with Italy—the infamous Hoare-Laval pact—enraged British and French public opinion, scuttling all efforts to conclude the Mediterranean crisis. Then in early January 1936 Mussolini asked Ulrich von Hassell, the German ambassador in Rome, to notify Hitler that Italy was willing to reconsider its defense of Austrian independence in return for an Italian-German understanding. Over the following few weeks Mussolini pledged that Italy would take no action if Germany remilitarized the Rhineland, despite the Franco-Italian military agreement of June 1935.[7]

A fundamental shift in Italian foreign policy had just taken place. The

Italo-Ethiopian crisis and the sanctions episode had compelled Mussolini to reconsider the implications for Fascist imperial ambitions of German rearmament and continental expansion and to begin appreciating the ideological affinities between Italian and German foreign policies. Beginning in early 1936 Fascist Italy would grow increasingly attached to the ambitions of Nazi Germany. Although Mussolini had no intention of being controlled or manipulated by the Germans, he recognized that a new Italian Mediterranean empire could coexist with a new German empire on the continent but would directly conflict with British and French interests. The Fascists would continue to take what they could from the democracies peacefully but believed that the Italian empire would reap greater benefit from Italy's association with Germany than with Britain and France. Mussolini's ideological antipathy for the democracies and his fear of and admiration for the Nazi regime also inspired Italy's maturing partnership with Germany. After 1936 there would only be fleeting opportunities to draw Italy out of Germany's orbit and no chance whatsoever of Italy's siding with the Western powers against the Nazis.

Germany's reoccupation of the Rhineland in March 1936 and Italy's capture of Addis Ababa in May rekindled attempts to resolve the crisis in the Mediterranean. Britain and France did not respond forcefully to the German abrogation of the Locarno treaties because the two powers were unprepared militarily. Moreover, in the Mediterranean they faced a potentially hostile Italy, which had refused to join in any sanctions against Germany. Rather than seek concessions from the Ethiopians, the British and French now began reconsidering their sanctions policy. Initially, the Popular Front, which had assumed the reins of the French government in early June under the premiership of Léon Blum, reaffirmed France's commitment to sanctions. But France's military leaders, who had argued since March that the enhanced German threat made pursuing an alliance with Britain and resolving the crisis in the Mediterranean essential, lobbied for lifting the embargo, recognizing Italy's Ethiopian empire, and signing a "Mediterranean Locarno" with Italy.[8]

Strong British pressure also persuaded the French to abandon the sanctions against Italy. Following the Palestinian rebellion in April 1936, some important members of the British government began to challenge others—such as Foreign Secretary Anthony Eden—who favored an oil embargo against Italy. For Chancellor of the Exchequer Neville Chamberlain, the claim that an independent Ethiopia could still be preserved at this late date by continuing or intensifying sanctions was "the very midsummer of madness." Chamberlain was a tall, thin man with a gaunt face, bristling mustache, and cold, brown eyes. A conservative who came from a famous political family, Chamberlain had served as a businessman for the first forty years of his working life and had gained an appreciation for the economic relationship between the British Isles and the empire, as well as a distaste for communism. In Whitehall, Chamberlain was known for concentration and hard work rather than sociability and charm, earning him many admirers but few friends. On account of his strength of conviction, decisiveness, and straight talk, a friendly colleague described him as a "lucid expositor and a competent defender of departmental policy." But he was also vain and obstinate, and he hated any kind of opposition and criticism. According to another colleague, "He likes to be set on a pedestal and adored, with suitable humility, by unquestioning admirers." By 1935 Chamberlain described himself as "sort of acting P.M.," confident that over the Ethiopian problem he had "as usual greatly influenced policy." Believing that he had "supplied most of the ideas in bringing the French to reason" over the Rhineland crisis, Chamberlain now argued that the new German threat should compel Britain to bring the sanctions episode to a close in order to end the tension in the Mediterranean and rebuild the Stresa front.[9]

The British Admiralty, particularly First Sea Lord Sir Ernle Chatfield, complemented this perspective by persuading the Chiefs of Staff (Sub) Committee (COS) that security for the British Isles and the Empire required a resolution of the Mediterranean crisis and a return to normal fleet distribution. Chatfield was small in stature but known for his keen intellect, austere sense of humor, persuasive disposition, and reverence for the British Empire. As he explained to his colleagues, "We have to divide our fleet and be able to meet the German fleet at home and the Japanese fleet in the Far East." Endorsing Chatfield's recommendation, the COS outlined the strategic motivations for abandoning the sanctions regime: "Our hopes lie in a peaceful Mediterranean, and this can only be achieved by returning to a state of friendly relations with Italy." In June the Stanley Baldwin government proposed an end to the embargo against Italy.[10]

The League lifted the sanctions on 4 July 1936, and within two weeks the British and French fleets had returned to their pre-1935 deployments. The crisis in the Mediterranean had reached its conclusion, but the Anglo-French-Italian conflict in the Mediterranean had only begun. The British and French had refused to recognize Italian sovereignty over Ethiopia and thus had not resolved their difficulties with Italy. In fact the sanctions episode would forever taint Fascist Italy's relations with Britain and France. Even though the French had ensured that the embargo was not imposed stringently on Italy, the Fascist government heaped indignation on the French for not being responsible for reversing the policy. As the new Italian foreign minister, Galeazzo Ciano, stressed to a prominent French publicist, "Italy will always remember with regret that England and not France brought about an end to the injustice of sanctions."[11]

Many other factors besides the conclusion of the sanctions affair contributed to the sudden anti-French sentiment emanating from Rome. Ciano, the Duce's confidant, emissary, and heir apparent, was an unabashed proponent of closer Italian relations with Nazi Germany. Ciano was the son of a highly distinguished admiral and war hero, Costanzo Ciano, who had been instrumental in bringing Fascism to power in Italy and had remained a close friend and naval adviser to Mussolini. After earning a degree in law and working as a journalist, the younger Ciano entered the diplomatic service. Multilingual and highly intelligent, he was recalled from overseas in 1930 to meet the Duce's eldest daughter. The baby-faced, frivolous, ambitious, vain, and arrogant Ciano, with "a high-pitched, nasal voice [and] a flat-footed, slightly comic walk," proposed to Edda Mussolini seventeen days after meeting her and married her very shortly thereafter. But he remained a gallivanting ladies man who, as Mussolini's chief propagandist and sycophant, grew rich passing out political favors to industrialists.[12]

In 1935 Ciano volunteered as a bomber pilot for the invasion of Ethiopia. He left Eritrea and returned to Rome at the end of the year to report to Mussolini on the unexpected Ethiopian resistance. Ciano endorsed the Duce's decision to drench the advancing Ethiopians with mustard gas and then urged his father-in-law to strengthen relations with Hitler. By May 1936 Mussolini had dismissed Foreign Undersecretary Fulvio Suvich and the foreign ministry's *capo di gabinetto,* Pompeo Aloisi, both of whom had favored using the Nazis to pressure Britain and France into making concessions to Italy but whose anti-German attitudes contributed to their rigid opposition to an Italian-German alliance. In their place Mussolini appointed Ciano, who at the age of thirty-three, became Europe's youngest foreign minister.[13]

Aside from his son-in-law's outspoken conviction that the Nazis were ideological kin, Mussolini viewed the rise to power of the Popular Front government in France as evidence that the political left, specifically Communism, had gained a foothold in Western Europe and, if not checked, would challenge Fascism in Italy. Finally, the pusillanimous response of the Western powers to the Rhineland remilitarization and the unhindered Italian seizure of Addis Ababa persuaded Mussolini that he could now realize his long-held dream to build a Mediterranean empire, which could be achieved only at the expense of France. Attaching his foreign policy ambitions to those of Hitler, the Duce in April declined an invitation for staff talks with the Stresa partners and ordered his diplomats to take "a more markedly pro-German line." He and Ciano then facilitated and acquiesced in the Austro-German accords of July, which laid the foundation for a German *Anschluss.* As Mussolini told the prominent Nazi Roland Strunk earlier in the year, "Between Germany and Italy there is a common fate which is becoming stronger and stronger."[14]

The Spanish Civil War

The League's decision to lift sanctions on Italy coincided with the outbreak of civil war in Spain. The emotional, ideological, and strategic aspects of the Spanish affair rent the fracture in Franco-Italian relations that had opened during the Italo-Ethiopian conflict into a genuine chasm. Immediately after the first army uprisings in Spain, the Republican government approached Blum for help. Blum, a Jewish socialist, had always regarded Mussolini and Hitler as dictators whose ideological affinities destined them to align with each other. Blum envisioned the Popular Front as a product of generic anti-Fascism and thus ideologically obligated to support the Spanish Republicans with arms. He also claimed that a Fascist Spain would add a third European front to France's already tortuous security dilemma. Many others in the French government urged nonintervention, however, fearing Comintern influence in France and claiming that French involvement in Spain could lead to a general conflagration in Europe for which France was unprepared. This position was supported by Foreign Minister Yvon Delbos who advocated integrating Italy into various diplomatic schemes, and by those within the French military who believed that a friendly Italy was an essential element of French security.[15]

Added to this contentious French debate over how to respond to the Spanish civil war was the British case for nonintervention. In late July Eden informed the French of the British Cabinet's belief that General Francisco Franco, the leader of the generals revolting in Spain, would quickly overthrow the Republic, and that Anglo-French intervention would delay this inevitable outcome and jeopardize peace in Europe. Despite Britain's perspective, French domestic concerns proved decisive. For the stability of the government, the viability of his social-reform program, and the preservation of civil peace and order, Blum steered a middle course by closing the Pyrenees frontier to French exports bound for Spain, permitting foreign arms and volunteers to move across French borders into Spain, and proposing an international nonintervention agreement. By 15 August the French nonintervention proposal had become Anglo-French policy, and on 9 September France joined Britain at the first meeting of the Non-Intervention Committee to reaffirm their policy.[16]

Before Britain and France had officially endorsed a nonintervention policy in Spain, Mussolini approved a request by Franco to provide the Nationalists with twelve Italian bombers and five Italian tanks. One of Mussolini's motivations for aiding the Nationalist cause was his ideological hostility to the Fronte Popolar of the second Spanish Republic, against which he had financed failed plots in 1932 and 1934. As he explained to his wife, Rachele, "Bolshevism in Spain would mean Bolshevism in France, Bolshevism at Italy's back, and the danger of Bolshevization of Europe."[17]

Yet the Duce provided war matériel to the Nationalists principally to improve Italy's strategic position in the western Mediterranean vis-à-vis Britain and France. After reporting the French and Russian decision to supply arms to the Republicans, Italian intelligence incorrectly claimed that a secret agreement existed between the French and Spanish Republics that granted France special privileges in the Balearic Islands and the Iberian Peninsula. Such an arrangement would give France unassailable control of the western Mediterranean and an overland passage from North Africa to the European continent. By contrast, an Italian-supported Nationalist victory would not only stem the Communist tide in Western Europe but also give Italy the opportunity to establish bases in the Balearics that would threaten French naval and air forces and jeopardize French troop transports from North Africa. Italian occupation of these strategically important islands would also force Britain to abandon both its Gibraltar base and its Mediterranean trade route. Favorable results in the Spanish civil war, Mussolini and Ciano calculated, could effectively turn the Mediterranean into an Italian lake.[18]

A final motivation for Italian intervention in the Spanish affair was Mussolini's admiration for and rivalry with Nazi Germany. In Spain, he sought both to build Italy's relationship with Germany and to prevent a bilateral Hitler-Franco alliance. Recognizing Germany's expanding economic and military strength as well as Hitler's revanchist ambitions, Mussolini strove to emulate the Führer's determination to build a new empire for his nation. At the same time, Mussolini was drawn to Germany out of the fear of being separated from the Nazi regime. In fact he believed it was critical for Fascist Italy to be Nazi Germany's most important ally; otherwise, Italy could find itself subservient to German power. Mussolini was determined to demonstrate that Italy had the fortitude and potency to be an equal, not a dependent, partner with Germany.

Nazi-Fascist relations had gradually matured since September 1935, when the Italian and German military intelligence chiefs met to discuss the Ethiopian affair and to arrange a regular exchange of information. In February 1936 the Führer promised to transfer ten German submarines to the Regia Marina, which would allow the Italians to strengthen their presence in the Dodecanese and the Adriatic. Shortly thereafter, in response to massive Jewish immigration into Palestine, German and Italian intelligence cooperated in Haifa to incite trouble among Arabs, contributing significantly to the April rebellion there.[19]

Germany's first delivery of arms—twenty bombers—to the Nationalists arrived in Spanish Morocco at the end of July, one day before the Italian bombers landed there. The August 1936 airlift by Italian and German planes of more than 6,500 rebels into Spain, flying over Republican-controlled sea lanes, became a stepping-stone for close Italian-German affiliation in Spain and Europe. Within a week of the start of this airlift, the chief of the German *Abwehr,* Admiral Wilhelm Canaris, met in Rome with his Italian counterpart, General Mario Roatta, to start the process of coordinating the two countries' intelligence in Spain and, specifically, their aid to the Nationalists. By the end of August the German and Italian secret services had shipped to Spain thirty-eight bombers, forty-two fighters, and dozens of tanks, antiaircraft guns, machine guns, and rifles. Although Roatta and Canaris had agreed that Germany and Italy would provide Franco with roughly equal amounts of matériel, Mussolini told Roatta that Italy's Mediterranean ambitions required the Italians to do everything possible to limit German influence with the Nationalist camp.[20] In many ways, German engagement in Spain encouraged and accelerated Italian intervention.

Germany and Italy showed disdain for the Anglo-French policy of nonintervention, increased their level of support to the Nationalists, and strengthened their political relationship throughout late 1936. By December the Germans and Italians had delivered more than 280 aircraft, 95 tanks, hundreds of guns, mortars, and pieces of artillery, thousands of hand grenades, and millions of rounds of automatic ammunition. Besides improving the state of Franco's armed forces, Italy had turned the island of Majorca into a well-fortified Italian air base by the end of the year. Ciano's October visit to Germany to launch the Rome-Berlin Axis and Reich Marshal Hermann Göring's January 1937 visit to Rome marked a new degree of Italian-German collaboration. In Spain the two countries granted de jure recognition to Franco's administration, they contributed both matériel and soldiers to the Nationalists, and they demanded of Franco a role in the conduct of the war. Between early November and mid-February 1937, Germany sent the Condor Legion—which included more than 5,000 tank and air personnel—and Italy transported more than 49,000 "volunteers" from the Italian army, militia, and air force. Although the staggering rate of both German and Italian arms shipments and soldier transports to Spain tapered off in the spring of 1937, Italy and Germany remained militarily committed in Spain until Franco's victory in March 1939. In Spain, according to Ciano, Italy was "fighting in defense of our civilization and our revolution."[21]

The events in Spain also served to codify in Hitler's mind the geopolitical value of Fascist Italy. In late 1936 Hitler had become lukewarm about the prospect of an alliance with Britain, contending that it would hinder Germany's plans for expansion in central and southeastern Europe. An Anglo-German alliance, Hitler believed, would undermine Italy's policy in the Mediterranean and force Italy to side with France. Germany's attempt to create a new order in southeastern Europe would be stymied by a Franco-Italian bloc. In addition to the strategic advantages of an alliance with Italy over one with Britain, Hitler embraced Mussolini's outspoken anti-Bolshevism. Among Europe's great powers, only Italy and Germany were in a common ideological struggle against Communism. By the end of 1936 an alliance of two fascist-style militaristic dictatorships that could dominate central and southern Europe had come into existence. Hitler's views on Britain and Italy soon found their way into German war planning, which in early 1937 included for the first time the possibility of a confrontation against Britain with Italy at least benevolently neutral.[22]

German and Italian consensus on the need to support the Spanish Nationalists belied the discord within Italy over the wisdom of a major shift in Italian foreign policy toward cooperation with Germany against Britain and France. General Federico Baistrocchi, chief of the army staff and war undersecretary, complained that significant amounts of the army's resources were already committed to the war in Ethiopia and the pacification of Italian East Africa; massive transfers of Italian arms to Spain would drain what little strength the Italian army still possessed. Despite Baistrocchi's dismissal in October 1936, the army staff did not immediately revise its war planning to reflect an alliance with Germany. Admiral Domenico Cavagnari, the Italian navy's chief of staff, resisted all attempts to sell Italian warships to the Nationalists and complained bitterly about the Germans' attempts in late 1936 to exercise naval authority in Spain even though they had only two submarines in Spanish waters. Marshal Pietro Badoglio, chief of the Stato Maggiore Generale (SMG) and a noted Francophile who had participated in the talks with the French in 1935, lamented that Italy's new foreign policy increased the risk of war with the Western powers.[23] Because the Fascist regime's political and ideological imperatives took precedence over military considerations, however, those skeptics within Italy's military leadership were decisively overruled by the Mussolini-Ciano position of enhancing Italian relations with Germany.

While the French tried to straddle anti-Fascism and noninterventionism in the Spanish civil war as a way to retain Anglo-French unanimity in the Mediterranean, the British reacted to the steadily increasing level of Italian and German intervention in Spain by unilaterally adopting a new policy for the Mediterranean. Arguing that many eastern Mediterranean states now questioned Britain's predominant position in the region, the Foreign Office (FO) advocated signing a defensive treaty with Greece and Turkey and warning Italy against any alteration of the status quo in the Mediterranean. The service chiefs, however, persuasively insisted that it was "most important to avoid any measures which . . . merely tend to further alienate Italy." Britain's lack of adequate naval bases and weak military strength in the eastern Mediterranean would require the British to be on the defensive if

Italy became hostile, regardless of the number of British allies there. A simultaneous war at home or in the Far East would only exacerbate Britain's strategic predicament in the Mediterranean. In September the Cabinet rescinded the diplomatic assurances that Britain had made in the eastern Mediterranean during the Italo-Ethiopian crisis and began searching for a diplomatic accommodation with Fascist Italy.[24]

The opportunity to improve relations with Italy arose when Mussolini, during a November 1936 speech celebrating the formation of the Rome-Berlin Axis, obliquely expressed interest in an Anglo-Italian entente. Britain responded favorably to Mussolini's overture and the two countries in January 1937 signed a declaration—known as the Gentlemen's Agreement—of common but not conflicting Mediterranean interests and a mutual commitment to the Mediterranean status quo. While the British expected that the Gentlemen's Agreement would help them solve their strategic dilemma by bringing the Mediterranean crisis—Ethiopia and Spain—to a close diplomatically, the Italians saw the accord as a way of garnering British recognition of Italian Abyssinia (Ethiopia) and dividing British and French policies in the Mediterranean. On the day that the treaty was signed Mussolini dispatched additional reinforcements to Franco. Then, during the spring of 1937, he fortified the island of Pantelleria and sent a large number of troops to Libya. Despite Italy's apparent disregard for the terms of the Gentlemen's Agreement, the British COS responded to the diplomatic initiative by designating the security of the Mediterranean region as their least pressing military obligation, behind protecting the British Isles, the Far East, and imperial communications. In the spring of 1937 the Cabinet approved the recommendation of the Committee of Imperial Defence (CID) that "Italy could not be counted on as a reliable friend, nor yet in present circumstances a probable enemy," annulling the government's position of the preceding year that war with Italy should be considered a possibility.[25]

Evolving Italian Ambitions

Italy's control of Addis Ababa, the maturing relationship with Nazi Germany, and the continued commitment to the war in Spain inspired a significant change in Italian military planning. Under Baistrocchi's leadership the army in 1936 had reaffirmed traditional Fascist strategy, contemplating operations on the continent against France and Yugoslavia. But his replacement, General Alberto Pariani, outspokenly pro-German and a protégé of Ciano's, argued in February 1937 that "the conquest of Ethiopia has profoundly influenced our military considerations, placing in the foreground the *guerra mediterranea*."

> The battle between us and France will likely originate on the islands of the Italian *antimurale,* that is, specifically on the Tunisian terrain. It is obvious that the front Corsica-Sardinia-Sicily-Pantelleria-Tunisia would partition the Mediterranean, providing tranquillity and security for our action in the eastern basin. It is still more evident that a battle between us and England will unfold in Egypt and the Sudan, regions that, when our organization has developed, we can seize how and when we like.

The time had arrived for Italy, protected on the continent by her association with Nazi Germany, to plan in detail the attainment of her Mediterranean ambitions.[26]

The reorientation of Italian military strategy toward the Mediterranean in early 1937 and the increasing Italian faith in Nazi foreign policy did not indicate a sudden Italian absence of concern for continental affairs. A Mediterranean empire could not exist without a secure Adriatic, which in turn made it necessary for Italy to have an exclusive interest in—if not outright domination of—the upper Balkan Peninsula. As Mussolini explained to his fellow Fascists, "With Germany we can march on the Rhine but not on the Danube." Moreover, Italian influence and control in the Balkans would demonstrate Italy's strength and determination not to be engulfed by Germany's continental ambitions, as well as help provide the foundation for an equal Nazi-Fascist partnership. Specifically, Mussolini coveted Slovenia, Dalmatia, Montenegro, and Albania and envisioned Croatia as little more than an Italian protectorate. Aside from their role in guaranteeing Italian security in the Adriatic, the Balkans could provide the essential natural resources and raw materials that Italy lacked.[27]

Italy took a significant step toward achieving Balkan hegemony when Ciano and Yugoslav Prime Minister Milan Stoyadinovich signed a treaty of friendship in March 1937. The agreement provided for Italo-Yugoslav economic cooperation, temporarily ended Italian efforts to subvert Yugoslavia through Ante Pavelic's Croat terrorists, and pledged that the two states would remain neutral if either was the object of unprovoked aggression. Even though the Yugoslavs, under intense British pressure, refused Italy's proposal for an alliance, Ciano throughout 1937 regarded "the Belgrade Pact as fundamental for our policy. The alliance with the Slavs permits us to look upon the eventuality of the *Anschluss* with serenity." Not only had the treaty with Yugoslavia assuaged Italy's anxieties in central Europe, but also it had shaken the French eastern security system to its core. France, through its alliances with the countries of the Little Entente—Czechoslovakia, Romania, and Yugoslavia—had been the most important great power in the Balkans. The Italo-Yugoslav pact had released Yugoslavia from the Franco-Czech orbit and questioned France's influence in the Balkans. Ciano noted with exhilaration that as a result of this treaty "the French system of alliances has exploded [*saltare*]."[28]

The French perceived this development as a fundamental attack on French security strategy, finally motivating a decisive shift in French policy toward the Mediterranean. France had indeed been indignant about Italy's and Germany's military intervention in Spain and apprehensive about the new Rome-Berlin Axis. When the Italians in November 1936 demanded that the French ambassador in Rome recognize the king of Italy as the emperor of Ethiopia, Blum ordered France's representative home. But early in 1937 most French statesmen and strategists still believed that the security of France was almost exclusively threatened by a revanchist Germany. Italy's new relationship with Yugoslavia, however, represented an overt attempt to install Italian preeminence in the Adriatic region at France's expense. The potential loss of Yugoslavia as a French ally meant not only the sudden evaporation of France's influence in the Balkans but also the beginning of the end for France's network of central European allies and the eastern front—one of the most important deterrents to German aggression. By defecting from the French-sponsored Little Entente, Yugoslavia could indirectly destroy France's relationship with Czechoslovakia and Romania.[29]

The timing of the Italo-Yugoslav pact led the French to attribute yet another motivation to Italy's diplomacy in the Balkans. Two days before signing the treaty the Italians informed the Non-Intervention Committee that Italy would not withdraw any "volunteers" from Spain until Franco defeated the Republicans. The connection between Italy's almost simultaneous actions in Belgrade and London was inescapable. The Quai d'Orsay, France's Foreign Ministry, which since 1924 had ironically endorsed the idea of an Italo-Yugoslav accord, now speculated that the Italo-Yugoslav treaty would allow Mussolini to expand Italy's engagement in Spain and to seek Italian domination of the western Mediterranean. Delbos, in particular, suggested that the Italians were attempting to eliminate their Balkan preoccupations so that Mussolini could confidently "bring his effort to bear on the Mediterranean." This theory became a widely shared conviction in official French circles by early July, when the Comité Permanent de la Défense Nationale (CPDN) studied the organization of French colonial defense, particularly in the Mediterranean, for the first time since the Great War.[30]

While the French had begun to consider the possibility of war in the Mediterranean, most of London's statesmen remained confident that a resolute policy of conciliation would ensure peace in that region. Even Mussolini's almost immediate violation of the spirit of the Anglo-Italian Gentlemen's Agreement did not shake the British conviction that imperial defense depended on a tranquil Mediterranean. At the Imperial Conference of May–June 1937, the British revealed that "our policy must be governed by the principle that no anxiety or risks connected with our interests in the

Mediterranean can be allowed to interfere with the despatch of a fleet to the Far East." The Admiralty planned to send a strong naval force to Singapore soon after the outbreak of hostilities with Japan, even if Britain was already at war in Europe.[31]

Britain's willingness to extend these guarantees to the Dominions at a time of declining British naval strength and escalating international intervention in the Spanish civil war demonstrated the enduring importance of the British Empire and the confidence that any British losses in the Mediterranean could be recovered, whereas those in the Far East could not. It also indicated London's confidence in being able to reach a Mediterranean appeasement with Italy. The French, whose imperial holdings in the Far East were less significant than Britain's and whose continental security was largely dependent on free Mediterranean communications, could not afford to be as arrogant or cavalier regarding the Mediterranean as the British.

Yet among London's military and diplomatic officials there were many lingering doubts about Britain's imperial perspective. Foreign Secretary Eden was the leading opposition voice. Despite his appearance of languid self-confidence, characteristic of the English upper class to which he belonged by birth and education, Eden often worried and doubted. Only forty years old in 1937, much younger than his colleagues in similar positions, he was sensitive to criticism and jealous of his official status and responsibilities. Nevertheless, he was widely respected as truly gifted in issues of international war and peace. He had served in the Great War, winning the Military Cross at the Battle of the Somme and reaching the rank of major by war's end. After being elected to Parliament in 1923, he had excelled in British foreign affairs, rapidly advancing from Austen Chamberlain's parliamentary private secretary at the Foreign Office in 1926 to Baldwin's foreign secretary in 1935.[32]

Together with Sir Robert Vansittart, permanent undersecretary at the FO, Eden claimed that diplomatic cables and intelligence from Rome, Berlin, Vienna, and Paris confirmed that Mussolini and Hitler had reached a "definite arrangement" whereby Italy withdrew her interest in Central Europe so that she could focus on building a "Roman empire" in the Mediterranean. Moreover, the Italian garrison in Libya now consisted of approximately 38,000 European motorized troops and 10,000 Arab troops. Britain was restricted by treaty to no more than 10,000 British troops in Egypt, and Egypt's native force did "not even exist as an efficient fighting force yet." Vansittart emphasized that these Italian troops could have only an offensive purpose—and British Egypt was clearly less well defended than French Tunisia. In mid-July Eden told the Cabinet that Britain should adopt a policy of intimidation by manifesting the progress of British rearmament with military reinforcements in the Mediterranean—both aircraft to Egypt and ships to the Mediterranean fleet. According to Eden, the COS's recent Far Eastern Appreciation supported this position.[33]

By contrast, Sir Maurice Hankey, secretary to the Cabinet and the CID, insisted that Britain and Italy were "fanning each other's suspicions." Seizing on the outbreak of an undeclared Sino-Japanese war in early July, Hankey argued that any refortification of British defenses in the Mediterranean would instigate war rather than prevent it. Instead, a "frank interchange of views" could assure Italy that Britain would not interfere in Ethiopia and bring about Italy's "reasonable" attitude in the Spanish affair. In fact these talks should aim to trade de jure recognition of Ethiopia for a "full return of the Italian attitude to the pre-Abyssinian position." In late July the CID reaffirmed that Singapore and home defense had a decisive priority over ground, air, and sea defenses in the Mediterranean; Eden's request for reinforcements was denied. At the same time Chamberlain, now prime minister, proposed in writing that Britain and Italy start conversations to remove "all causes of suspicion or misunderstanding." Mussolini immediately accepted the invitation.[34] Motivating Chamberlain was both his conviction that a resolute policy of conciliation would ensure peace in the Mediterranean and his concern about the spread of Sino-Japanese fighting to Shanghai, where the value of British investment exceeded that of any comparable area outside the United Kingdom. For the British, crisis reigned in two crucial theaters simultaneously.

Reluctant and unable to prepare for a Mediterranean war, British strategists placed their faith in a Mediterranean reconciliation even if it required acquiescing in the Fascist government's demand for Abyssinia to be recognized as part of the Italian empire. The French, however, in light of Italy's recent actions in Spain and Yugoslavia as well as the direct link between France's continental and Mediterranean security priorities, categorically refused to consider granting Italy a diplomatic victory in East Africa.

The Pirate Submarine Campaign

Only five days after Mussolini accepted Chamberlain's invitation for Anglo-Italian talks, he agreed to Franco's "urgent" request that Italy intercept Russian shipments of weapons and supplies steaming from the Black Sea to Spanish government ports. Franco's intelligence indicated that five Soviet freighters, escorted by three submarines and carrying more than 2,600 tanks and 300 aircraft, had passed through the Turkish straits and were headed for Republican Spain. Even though Italian intelligence could not confirm this Spanish report, which was indeed grossly inflated, Mussolini believed that an Italian naval campaign could precipitate a Nationalist victory in the Spanish civil war.[35] Conducting simultaneous wars in Abyssinia and Spain had strained the Italian military's resources and severely weakened Italy's preparedness for a wider European war. Thus, Mussolini was desperate to bring these two conflicts to a close as soon as possible.

Beginning on 6 August 1937 Mussolini stationed submarines in the Aegean and along the Spanish Mediterranean coast, as well as a naval barrier of cruisers, destroyers, and naval auxiliaries in the Straits of Sicily. In addition to these—almost one hundred naval vessels, representing half of the Italian fleet—Mussolini sent air reconnaissance flights eastward. The Italian naval patrol—unmarked and mostly operating only at night—received orders to attack any Republican ship, any Soviet merchant ship, and any merchant ship under a Republican escort. Before the campaign was halted in early September 1937 the Italian navy had made 438 attack runs on suspected targets and fired forty-three torpedoes at twenty-four vessels, sinking four merchant ships and heavily damaging one Republican destroyer.[36]

Despite an international outcry that included many vague accusations of Italian complicity, Italy publicly denied responsibility for the naval campaign in the Mediterranean. The Soviets were infuriated by the targeting of Russian merchant ships traveling to Republican Spain, but the most openly upset were the French, very few of whom doubted who was responsible for the "piracy." Parisian demonstrators did not need official confirmation before erecting signs of "Boulevard des Inconnues" along the Boulevard des Italiens. Blum viewed the naval attacks as yet another blatant example of Italy's determination to assist the Spanish Nationalists and spread Fascism throughout Europe.[37]

Delbos and many other French officials found Mussolini's speech in Sicily at the end of August, in the throes of the naval campaign, particularly revealing and representative of Italian policy in Spain. In Palermo, Mussolini extolled the "solidarity" of the Axis powers and celebrated the imminent Nationalist victory in Santander, Spain, a battle in which Italian troops had participated. Ominously, he also predicted that the current historical epoch would witness the "foundation of the second Roman empire" with Sicily as its "geographic center." For the French, Mussolini's Palermo speech affirmed the strategic—and not only ideological—nature of Italy's involvement in Spain. Two days after the capture of Santander, Mussolini wrote to Franco that the "intimate fraternity of arms [among the Fascists, Nazis, and Spanish Nationalists] guarantees the final victory that will liberate Spain and the Mediterranean from every threat to our common civilization." The immediate publication of this letter only amplified French anxiety.[38]

In contrast to France's indignation, the British response to the piracy campaign was cautious and conciliatory. At the end of August the British chargé d'affaires in Rome, Maurice Ingram, showed Ciano an intercepted Italian air force report on the movements of British vessels in the Mediterranean and then informed Ciano that a British steamship had been attacked by planes based at Palma. Despite having this information, Ingram, whom Ciano described as a "limp, insincere British official," emphasized that he "did not wish to make the least protest" but suggested that Anglo-Italian relations "should not be troubled by unforeseeable and deplorable complications." Many British officials indicated that they hoped the planned "frank interchange of views" with the Italians would go forward. According to Guido Crolla, the Italian chargé d'affaires in London, the tension in the Mediterranean had reinvigorated Chamberlain's determination to start negotiations with Italy. British recognition of the Italian empire in Ethiopia seemed closer than ever before.[39]

Reliable evidence, obtained by British Admiralty intelligence within a week of the first assaults on merchant ships in the Mediterranean, did not affect Chamberlain's policy. Preoccupied by a potential confrontation with Japan and a need to keep the primary communications line to the Far East clear and unencumbered, the Admiralty disregarded its own intelligence and lobbied for a peaceful resolution of the new Mediterranean crisis. On 12 August the Foreign Office was informed that the British ship *Corporal* had been attacked by Italian aircraft from Palma and the Spanish tanker *Campeador* sunk by Italian surface ships off Tunisia the previous day. Shortly thereafter, with freshly intercepted and decoded Italian naval signals in hand, First Lord of the Admiralty Sir Alfred Duff Cooper told a hastily assembled group of ministers that a "submarine attack upon British ships approaching Spanish government ports was contemplated and . . . might take place at any moment." The ministers quickly approved the suggestion of Admiral Sir Dudley Pound, the commander of the Mediterranean fleet, to strengthen the protection of British merchant convoys in the Mediterranean. Pound specified, however, that unless a submerged submarine was found within five miles of a recently attacked British ship, the Royal Navy should not attack or sink any suspicious vessel but only discern its identity. No action would be taken against hostile surface ships or airplanes, and no attempt would be made to protect non-British merchant ships headed for Republican ports. Such a moderate reaction to the piracy in the Mediterranean allowed British diplomats to continue pursuing the opening of conversations with the Italians.[40]

Italy's naval operation placed France in an extremely uncomfortable position with Britain, the power with which the French most desired a lasting entente and alliance. At the height of Mediterranean piracy, Delbos told American Ambassador William Bullitt that the French were "furious with Eden and Chamberlain for having inaugurated a rapprochement with

Italy . . . [which] should be treated with contempt and disdain as a relatively unimportant jackal." The French chargé d'affaires in London, Roger Cambon, claimed that French merchant ships in the Mediterranean were being systematically followed by Italian destroyers and aircraft. Identifying Italy as responsible for the campaign, the French ambassador explained to the British that France no longer could contemplate recognizing Italian sovereignty in Ethiopia. Yet the British refused to address Italy's recent activities in the Mediterranean at either the next League meeting or the next session of the Non-Intervention Committee. As a result, the French agreed to participate in a conference on Mediterranean piracy at Nyon in early September.[41]

Undeterred by the weak British pleas to discontinue his operation in the Mediterranean and stimulated by the French fury, Mussolini continued the campaign until the Italian submarine *Iride* accidentally attacked the British destroyer *Havock* on 30 August. The British, although not prepared to issue a formal protest to the Italians, indicated that the situation in the Mediterranean had now become "intolerable." After receiving a note from Franco that the Italian piracy campaign had run its course, Mussolini suspended offensive operations in the Mediterranean on 4 September—two days before the Soviet Union officially accused Italy of torpedoing and sinking two Russian ships and almost a full week before the British, French, and Russians met at Nyon to establish an international antisubmarine patrol to stop Mediterranean piracy. So that the Nationalists could continue to discourage Soviet efforts to supply the Republican government through the Mediterranean, Mussolini sold Franco four old destroyers and lent him four submarines.[42]

In London, an emergency meeting of ministers was called on 2 September to address both the deteriorating situation in the Far East and the equally grave crisis in the Mediterranean. First Sea Lord Chatfield argued passionately that if Britain expected to have the option of sending a fleet to the Far East, stability would first have to exist in the Mediterranean. Eden then reported that even though both Crolla and Ciano had recently been warned by British officials that "it was in the highest degree desirable that nothing should disturb the atmosphere which was now favourable to Anglo-Italian conversations," attacks on merchant shipping in the Mediterranean had persisted. In fact an Italian torpedo had narrowly missed a British destroyer in the Mediterranean the day before. Among the ministers present "there was little or no doubt the submarine which had attacked the *Havock* was an Italian submarine." Later that night Chamberlain approved the ministers' decision to bolster the Royal Navy's presence at Gibraltar. Orders were subsequently given for a division of destroyers to leave the Home Fleet the following day and to report immediately to the Mediterranean.[43]

Without waiting for the French and British governments to agree on a diplomatic response to the piracy campaign, the French naval staff in late August instituted a special surveillance operation in the Mediterranean to protect French merchant ships and to patrol French territorial waters. Then, well before the Nyon conference, the French Marine Nationale sought and received funding for the constitution of a fourth cruiser division to carry out these new Mediterranean patrols without a corresponding decline in French naval security elsewhere. Admiral François Darlan, chief of the French naval staff, placed this division under Admiral Jean-Pierre Esteva, commander-in-chief of the Marine's southern division, who shared his chief's conviction that a decisive Anglo-French naval response would both halt the piracy in the Mediterranean and enhance Anglo-French naval collaboration in the region. As it happened, the Marine's surveillance mission significantly influenced the course of the Nyon talks and compelled the British—whose inclination was to do nothing to end the piracy and to avoid any cooperation with the French—to respond no less decisively.[44]

Mussolini's naval operation earned the misnomer "pirate submarine campaign" at the Nyon conference of 10–14 September, where Britain and France agreed to patrol specific zones of the Mediterranean and to destroy any unidentified submarines. Presenting the British before Nyon with an impressive array of intelligence clearly implicating the Italians in the piracy campaign, the French asked that the patrol of the Mediterranean extend to hostile surface ships and aircraft threatening any merchant ships, instead of Britain's plan only to defend itself against submerged submarines. The British Admiralty categorically rejected this French suggestion but acceded to the French wish that each nation would protect all merchant shipping—regardless of nationality—within its assigned zone. The irony of patrolling the Mediterranean for only hostile submarines, so that establishing the identity of those responsible for Mediterranean piracy was virtually impossible, struck the French naval staff as strange indeed.[45]

Privately, the British Admiralty admitted that the objective of the proposed Mediterranean patrol should be neither to initiate hostilities with any other power nor even to pursue aggressively the identity of the pirates. Instead, the patrol was designed to address a political predicament without increasing tension in the Mediterranean. Defending the Admiralty's position, Admiral Andrew Cunningham, the deputy chief of the naval staff, claimed that counterattacks against submarines could "be undertaken with far less risk of hostilities with Italy than if they were extended to surface vessels and aircraft. It is obvious that so long as the attacker is a submarine, the risk of its identity being established is comparatively small."[46]

The most significant British victory, however, followed the conference, when the British persuaded the French to invite the Italians to cooperate in the patrol system established at Nyon. In light of Mussolini's pending visit to Germany and perseverance with the Nationalist cause in Spain, René Massigli, political director at the Quai d'Orsay, suggested that the Nyon powers restrict any Italian participation to the Tyrrhenian Sea in order to preserve a secure Anglo-French route through the Mediterranean. But the Italians demanded "absolute parity" in patrol responsibilities; the British agreed and compelled the French to accept it. Acquiring patrol zones in the central and eastern Mediterranean, between the Balearics and Sardinia, and inside the Tyrrhenian Sea enabled the Italians to continue sending supplies to the Nationalists without detection. The one concession that the French received in return was a supplemental agreement, signed in Geneva on 17 September, that extended the terms of the Nyon agreement to include the surveillance of and, if necessary, the appropriate response to surface vessels and aircraft that attacked merchant shipping. Yet Britain accepted this arrangement only because the addition of Italy to the piracy patrols eliminated the risk of identifying the Italians as pirates. Clearly, the negotiations at the Nyon conference were little more than political grandstanding. Nyon's results benefited only the Fascists, inspiring Ciano to exult: "It is a fine victory. From suspected pirates to policemen of the Mediterranean, with the 'sunken' Russians excluded."[47]

Mussolini's Advancing Mediterranean Agenda

Encouraged by the lack of resolve shown by the western powers at Nyon, Mussolini decided to strengthen Italy's presence throughout the western and central Mediterranean. The Duce had kept only weak bomber units at the Palma base on Majorca since the start of the Spanish civil war to avoid worsening tensions with Britain and France. But in September 1937 he sent twelve bombers to Majorca, including one piloted by his son Bruno, and ordered them to begin regular attacks on Republican ports. By January 1938 Mussolini had doubled both his bomber force in the Balearics and the scale of Italian attacks on port facilities and shipping. Moreover, in September he dispatched three additional army divisions to augment the Libyan garrison. By October there were approximately 45,000 European motorized and 13,000 native troops in Libya; by the end of the year the British estimated that at least 50,000 Italian soldiers were stationed in Libya.[48]

In late 1937 Mussolini had firmly attached his foreign policy ambitions to those of Nazi Germany. His visit to Germany in September 1937 sealed his admiration for Adolf Hitler and paved the way for a groundbreaking "arrangement" between the two regimes in early November. Although he signed no new accord and held no detailed political conversations with the Führer, Mussolini was mesmerized by Nazi Germany, particularly the militarism of its culture and the organization of its people. In October Mussolini told his minister of education, Giuseppe Bottai, that "relations with Germany . . . constitute the strict direction of our policy. We should now consider the Rome-Berlin Axis in a long-term historical perspective." Specifically, the German relationship would enable Italy "to demolish the political-cultural supremacy of France." Even Ciano, who perceived stark racial, cultural, and religious differences between Italy and Germany, understood that the two dictatorships were pursuing unique "national formulas"—"The Germans in racial ideology. We in Roman imperialism."—that set them apart from the democracies and other regimes of the left. In late September Ciano admitted that the "Rome-Berlin Axis is today a formidable and extremely useful reality."[49]

The Nazi regime also now depended on its alliance with Italy. On 5 November Hitler met with his military leadership to explain Germany's need to expand its territory for agricultural production in Europe. Germany had to improve its strength on the continent before it could seek the return of overseas colonies. Hitler argued that Britain and France were implacably hostile and thus Germany's problems could only be solved by the use of force. A sustained conflict in the Mediterranean could soon arise from the protracted conflict in Spain—a war that was in Germany's interest to prolong. In the event of an Anglo-French war against Italy, Hitler asserted that Germany should take advantage of the circumstances to attack Austria and the Czechs without delay. The extent of Italy's Mediterranean ambitions and the vulnerability of the British Empire made Italy a desirable ally.[50]

The outbreak of war in the Far East also served to bring Italy and Germany closer together. Mussolini and Ciano immediately saw in Japan a potential ally with similar enemies. Not only were Japan and Italy both hostile to the Soviet Union, but Japan had aspirations in the South China Sea that directly conflicted with British and French colonial interests. By early October Italy had begun selling airplane equipment and replacement parts to the Japanese, and by the end of the year Italy had stopped all shipments to China and had delivered to the Japanese plans of the British base at Singapore, procured by Italian intelligence. This show of Italian goodwill was soon reciprocated by a German-Japanese invitation for Italy to join the Anti-Comintern pact, which the Italians signed on 6 November. At the end of November Italy recognized Manchukuo and then, after a meeting of the Gran Consiglio del Fascismo that lasted less than two minutes, withdrew from the "moth-eaten" League of Nations in early December.[51]

The conspicuous ideological nature of this arrangement with Germany and Japan disguised its decidedly strategic basis. As Italy's relationship with Germany derived originally from their common European enemies, the new association with Japan arose because the Italians calculated that the escalation of Anglo-Japanese tension in the Far East would either place

Britain at a disadvantage in a war against Italy in the Mediterranean or discourage Britain from challenging Italy in the first place. In the wake of the tripartite treaty, Italy diligently lobbied the Japanese general staff for a military agreement "which alone can resolve the issue with England." Ciano believed that the series of diplomatic events in late 1937 had important consequences: "The alliance of three military empires the size of Italy, Germany, and Japan throws an unprecedented weight of armed strength into the balance of power. England will have to reconsider her position everywhere." In late 1937 Italy's political leaders recognized that an "isolated clash" with the English, whom Mussolini described as "people who think with their asses," was now inevitable. In fact Ciano "confidently" welcomed this eventuality with "perfect serenity" and contemplated "whether it is not up to us to force the pace and put match to barrel ourselves."[52]

Italian military and naval strategy soon reflected the changes in Rome's foreign policy. In November the Italian navy's planning department formally revised Italian naval strategy. Noting that the political situation had recently become "decisively worse," the naval staff decided that the Regia Marina should abandon its existing plans for a war against Yugoslavia and Turkey in the Adriatic and the Aegean and, instead, anticipate a Mediterranean war in alliance with Germany against Britain, France, and the Soviet Union. This strategy shift had been preceded by significant efforts to expand Italian shipbuilding, but it also served as justification for requests to accelerate naval rearmament even further. Admiral Domenico Cavagnari, chief of the Italian naval staff, presented the new plans at a rare meeting of Italy's service chiefs on 2 December 1937, urging the army and air force to reconsider their strategies with the understanding that Italy now had to be prepared to "concentrate her forces against the principal enemy: Britain." As a result of Cavagnari's presentation and the Duce's insistence, the army and air force then adopted a new general directive, Piano di Radunata 12. This directive, which Pariani approved in January 1938, was for the first time based on a coalition war hypothesis that aligned Germany and Italy against Britain and France.[53]

The Italian pirate campaign and the perceptible shift in Italian foreign policy that followed it particularly alarmed the French. Blum, Delbos, and especially Alexis Léger, secretary general of the foreign ministry, believed that Mussolini's visit to Germany in September demonstrated the permanence of the Axis; most likely the dictators had agreed on disparate territorial aims in central Europe and the Mediterranean. Léger was a slim, elegant, dark man who had grown up in the French Antilles. As one of Aristide Briand's favorites, Léger had risen quickly through the French diplomatic ranks, reaching the top of his profession in 1933. Renowned for his spectacular intellectual ability, Léger also pursued a second career as an accomplished poet (pseudonym Saint-John Perse), receiving the Nobel Prize in literature in 1960. His French imperial perspective, combined with his vision for a United States of Europe under French leadership, contributed to his tendency to look with disfavor on Fascist Italy—a bias that became almost vitriolic after Mussolini's defiance of the League during the Ethiopian crisis.[54]

The abrupt dismissal in October of Vittorio Cerruti, Italy's ambassador in Paris, supported Léger's theory that the Axis was genuine. Cerruti had recently warned the French that Mussolini wanted to make war on Britain and that it was the purest illusion to think that Mussolini could be detached from Hitler. Even the new French premier, Camille Chautemps, who had argued the year before that a Mediterranean appeasement should be pursued and that the Italian end of the Axis was more malleable than the German one, now did not conceal his "profound distrust" of Mussolini.[55]

Many in France interpreted the buildup of Italian bombers in Majorca and the coincidental increase in the scale of aerial attacks on Republican port facilities and shipping in the Balearic Sea as an overt Italian attempt to seize the Balearics in preparation for a future war against France. In late September Delbos suggested to Eden that Britain and France either seize Minorca (currently in Republican hands) or demand that the Italians desist their fortification of Majorca by threatening a French reopening of the Pyrenees frontier. After the British rejected both these ideas in favor of a conciliatory policy toward Italy, the Marine Nationale desperately recommended stationing a joint Anglo-French naval force at Port Mahon on Minorca, to do nothing more than demonstrate the West's opposition to Italy's occupation of Majorca. In October this proposal was also dismissed by the British Admiralty as infeasible and unnecessarily provocative.[56]

In addition to reopening the Pyrenees frontier to Republican Spain in October, Chautemps and Delbos tried to persuade their British counterparts that bilateral talks with the Italians would only induce the Germans, suspicious of an Anglo-French drive to break the Axis, to escalate their colonial and continental demands and to promise the Italians broader rewards for their friendship. Unable to shake the British from their resolve to negotiate with the Italians, the Quai d'Orsay nevertheless pursued arrangements in southeastern Europe and the eastern Mediterranean at the end of 1937 specifically to counter what the French believed was an overt Italian threat to those regions. Both Turkey and Greece, although the former had economic ties to Germany and the latter had an oppressive dictatorship, were targeted by the Quai as nations with which to improve relations because of their mutual animosity toward Italy. Despite a weakening of the Franco–Petit Entente coalition, the Quai hoped to counter Italy's association with Yugoslavia and profit from Romania's rejection of direct German influence by sponsoring the creation of a Danubian federation among Romania, Hungary, and Bulgaria.[57]

Even though the French adamantly opposed British appeasement of Italy and relentlessly pursued a policy in the Mediterranean almost directly at odds with Britain's, the Quai recognized that strategically, France had to rely increasingly on an alliance with Britain. The Belgian monarch had announced in late 1936 that he intended to steer an "independent" foreign policy; Franco–Petit Entente negotiations in the spring of 1937 had collapsed; the projected French military conversations with the Soviet Union had failed in June; and the escalating crisis in the Far East increasingly threatened a virtually defenseless French Indochina. Thus, in the interest of re-creating an entente with Britain as well as securing the western front, most French diplomats in late 1937 agreed to work alongside the British toward a series of peaceful Central European arrangements with Germany.[58]

Despite the imperative of building a British alliance, Admiral Darlan was infuriated at Britain's reluctance to recognize the strategic implications of the Spanish war. A descendant of Scandinavian immigrants, Darlan was blond, blue-eyed, handsome, well built, and committed to the French Republic. He had served in the Great War with distinction but had become increasingly Anglophobic following Britain's support for the Washington Naval Treaty of 1922, which had granted Italy capital-ship parity with France. In mid-1936 Darlan had headed a mission to London that argued the Italians and Germans posed a strategic threat to the Balearic and the Canary Islands. Although Darlan's mission failed to persuade the British Admiralty that these islands should be defended or preemptively occupied, Blum in October 1936 promoted Darlan to France's highest naval post over other more experienced admirals because the premier recognized that Darlan "thinks exactly as I do" about the Italians and Germans.[59]

In late 1937, following Mussolini's visit to Germany in September, Darlan argued for a comprehensive and geographic reorientation of French foreign and defense policy. Increasingly concerned that France and Britain could soon find themselves at war with Germany, Italy, and Spain, Darlan suggested that France focus on littoral and imperial, rather than only continental, security. French industry and the eastern-front concept, not to mention supplemental defense for the western front, relied on secure Mediterranean transportation. In the event of war, French strategy should envision first subjugating the western and central Mediterranean and menacing Italy—destroying the Italian fleet and occupying Libya, Spanish Morocco, and the Balearics—while remaining on the defensive in the East, the Northeast, and the eastern Mediterranean. Then, only after Mediterranean communications were secured and provisions assured, France should launch an assault against Germany.[60]

Notably, Darlan did not suggest that French defense policy bolster the security of French Indochina and the French islands in the South Pacific. Both the État-major général de la Marine (EMM) and the Quai d'Orsay appreciated that the level of French investment in the Far East, where France did not have one major naval base, was considerably lower than elsewhere in the French empire. Consequently, the greater Mediterranean region, including East, West, and North Africa, the Levant, and Corsica, was a higher defense priority than French possessions and interests in the Far East. After the outbreak of the undeclared Sino-Japanese war in July, France halted all arms shipments to China through Indochina and sent no additional defenses to the Far East. The increasingly precarious situation in Europe at the time—particularly the Spanish civil war—dictated French caution in the Far East. It was accepted in Paris that the French empire in the Pacific was too exposed to take any action that could risk Japanese retaliation. In 1937 the Quai initiated a policy that pressed for Anglo-French-American cooperation in the Far East and attempted neither to conciliate nor antagonize China or Japan. Thereafter, the French government perceived, with escalating clarity, a rigid distinction between imperial defense in the Far East and the Mediterranean: the former was—should it become absolutely necessary—dispensable; the latter was not.[61]

Despite the consensus in Paris on French policy for the Far East, Darlan's proposal to focus French strategy on the Mediterranean was extremely controversial. The French army and air force argued that such a Mediterranean orientation would either incite the Nazis to attack France through Belgium or Switzerland, or provoke a conflict with Italy that would jeopardize France's network of Eastern European alliances. Even worse, such an alignment could precipitate both of these possibilities simultaneously. French strategy, according to General Maurice Gamelin, chief of the general staff, should not stray from its current emphasis on Germany and the western front: "A conflict with Germany will mean a long struggle. Everything will depend on our ability to hold the frontier and to profit from our natural resources and those of our allies." Preoccupied with improving French security vis-à-vis Germany, Gamelin and General Joseph Vuillemin, the air force chief, argued that France should attempt to reestablish the Franco-Italian "alliance."[62]

General Gamelin was a military intellectual of medium height and stocky build who was always calm, courteous, and elegantly dressed. He impressed his colleagues as "the picture of self control" whose dominant personality trait was that "he has time." As one of the heroes of the French defensive success on the western front in 1914, Gamelin instinctively defined French security according to the German threat across the Rhine. By 1935 he had become the senior serving officer in the army, the preeminent service in France, and had developed amiable personal relations with many of France's most important politicians. Yet as a political conservative, monarchist, and devout Catholic, Gamelin's loyalty resided more with France than with the Republic.[63]

Even though Gamelin served as chief military adviser to Defense Minister Edouard Daladier—a relationship that became increasingly one of mutual dependence—Daladier never completely trusted Gamelin and often disagreed with him. In this case, Daladier reasoned that in contrast to the western front, both Britain and France were vulnerable in the Mediterranean. Daladier had grown up in a village in Provence, in Mediterranean France, and had received an advanced education in modern French and Italian history. After returning from his service on the front lines in the Great War, he embarked on a career in politics. His political base became the Provençal town of Orange, where he served continuously as mayor throughout the late 1930s and into the war years. Small, portly, tough-looking, and neither an intellectual nor a prosperous bourgeois, Daladier appealed to the ordinary Frenchman. As a member of the centrist Radicals, he quickly rose through the ranks, gaining a reputation for expertise in defense policy and brokering coalitions among the many factions in the Chamber of Deputies and the Senate. When Socialist Party leader Blum formed a Popular Front government in 1936, he had asked Daladier to enter the cabinet as one token of Radical support.[64]

Daladier's Mediterranean roots and academic background influenced his perspective on Italy and his conviction that France had something significant to offer the British to the South: French troops in North Africa and a formidable French navy that controlled the western basin and important Atlantic trade routes. Moreover, the Mediterranean gave France a sea route to eastern Europe that could bypass hostile continental powers. The Mediterranean provided not only the basis for building the coveted Anglo-French alliance but also a viable alternative to the stark, unpleasant choice of relinquishing eastern Europe or confronting Germany. By late 1937 Daladier had persuaded both the army and the air force that French strategy could no longer focus only on Germany. "While in a position to face an attack from Germany and to pin down its forces to the extent necessary in order to allow action by us or our allies, France must remain ready to pursue eventually, as a matter of first urgency, the defeat of Italy."[65]

In response to both the defense minister's concerns and new intelligence that emphasized Italy's hostile intentions, the air force staff added to its war plans attacks on air bases and fuel and munitions depots in Italy, Sardinia, Sicily, and Libya. The army staff also began considering air and amphibious attacks on Sardinia and Sicily, land offensives across the Alps, and a drive against Libya.[66] At the end of 1937, months before the *Anschluss,* many important elements of the French government perceived a genuine Italian threat in the Mediterranean and identified the Mediterranean as the centerpiece of a future Anglo-French entente.

THE ESCALATION of the Sino-Japanese conflict in late 1937 motivated the British to reach conclusions about Italy and the Mediterranean in direct opposition to those favored by France. Skeptical about the ability or willingness of the United States to send a fleet to the Far East in the event of trouble, Chamberlain argued that the British and Americans should pursue conciliation in that region. Since a confrontational policy against Japan was unacceptable as long as tension existed in the Mediterranean, he again pressed for granting Italy de jure recognition of Abyssinia and ensuring a peaceful Mediterranean.[67]

Eden and Vansittart countered that Fascist Italy's decisions in late 1937 to withdraw from the League, to recognize Manchukuo, to adhere to the Anti-Comintern pact, and to continue to expand its military presence in both the Balearics and Libya compelled Britain to strengthen British defenses in Egypt, to accelerate British rearmament, and to discard a Mediterranean appeasement. Not only would granting Italy de jure recognition of Ethiopia, made independent of the League, face opposition from British public opinion; it would also lead potential friends in the Near East to lose faith in Britain. But Chamberlain resolutely resisted these suggestions and instead relied again on Maurice Hankey. In November Hankey argued, "We have our danger in the West (Germany) and our danger in the Far East (Japan), and we simply cannot afford to be on bad terms with a nation which has a stranglehold on our shortest line of communications between the two possible theatres of war. . . . [de jure recognition of Ethiopia is] *vital to the existence of the Empire and of the United Kingdom as a first-class Power.*"[68]

The crisis in the Far East provided Eden with another opportunity to press for a change in British policy in the Mediterranean. In December 1937 U.S. President Franklin Roosevelt proposed a blockade and quarantine of Japan in an attempt to persuade the Japanese to end their aggression against China. Roosevelt hoped that Britain would send cruisers, destroyers, and submarines to the Far East for this purpose. Eden endorsed the idea and fought hard for it in London, indicating that Britain would have to coordinate closely with France in the Mediterranean if the Royal Navy sent forces to Singapore. Besides countering the threats posed by Japan and Italy, an alliance with France would help address the British navy's anticipated weakness between May 1938 and August 1939: three capital ships were undergoing reconditioning; none of Britain's new construction would be complete; and both Italy and Germany would launch more new capital ships than France during this period.[69]

Chatfield, however, opposed both a dramatic peacetime redistribution of British naval forces to the Far East and any close association with the French

Marine. The Admiralty, and eventually the service chiefs, believed that any discussions with the French would jeopardize Britain's efforts to reach an accord with Italy. In addition, sending a naval force to the Far East would require the Royal Navy to abandon Malta and Cyprus; Britain's presence in the eastern Mediterranean would then be limited to ground forces in Egypt. Britain would either have to strengthen its defenses in the Mediterranean or reach an accommodation with Italy before sending the fleet to the Far East. In the absence of either achievement, the fleet should remain in the Mediterranean. "Imperially," wrote Chatfield, "we are exceedingly weak because we are so vulnerable. If at the present time, and for many years to come, we had to send a fleet to the Far East, even in conjunction with the United States, we should be left so weak in Europe that we should be liable to blackmail or worse." Chamberlain agreed that it was "a most unfortunate moment to send the fleet away and I would therefore take no immediate action which would involve us having to do so." The prime minister rejected Roosevelt's proposal and concentrated on achieving a Mediterranean appeasement. British domestic politics and public opinion, as well as French opposition to imperial concessions to Italy, prevented the British from openly bribing the Italians into a permanent friendly relationship with Britain. But Chamberlain reasoned that he could trade Britain's de jure recognition of Ethiopia for an Italian promise to reach a Mediterranean settlement.[70]

The service chiefs then composed a strategic appreciation that endorsed the prime minister's Mediterranean–Far Eastern policy. According to the COS, in a war against Germany, Japan, and Italy simultaneously "our naval forces in the Mediterranean would be reduced to a few submarines and light surface forces. This would mean that Italy would be able to control the sea communications in the eastern Mediterranean, subject always to any action which the French navy might be able to take." Such an eventuality, even if Britain were allied with France and Russia, would "place a dangerous strain on the resources of the empire." Britain could not contemplate war in either the Far East or the West until after the Mediterranean had been secured. The obvious political implication of this appreciation was that cooperating with the Americans was less important than arriving at a diplomatic arrangement with Italy.[71]

Notably, those same British statesmen who argued that British imperial interests in the Far East justified a Mediterranean appeasement policy also rejected Roosevelt's suggestion for a naval concentration at Singapore. To redistribute its forces in this manner, Britain would have had to cooperate with France in the Mediterranean and the United States in the Far East. But these statesmen believed that relinquishing Mediterranean security to the French would jeopardize British attempts at reconciliation with Italy. They also feared that the entire operation would expose Britain's global weaknesses and vulnerabilities. Finally, a blockade and quarantine of Japan would increase the likelihood of conflict erupting at a time when the British were unprepared strategically and militarily for war. Declining Roosevelt's proposal allowed Britain to continue pursuing a Mediterranean appeasement policy and promoting the fallacy that it could secure its vast empire through conciliation. According to the British, stabilizing the Mediterranean by negotiating with Italy provided the best chance for an enduring European peace.

Even though Eden had few allies in London who agreed that Britain should abandon efforts to reach an understanding with Italy and instead collaborate with France and the United States, he relentlessly campaigned against negotiations in the current international atmosphere, describing Mussolini as "the complete gangster [whose] pledged word means nothing." In his desperation, Eden even asserted that since Britain should be striving for a deal with Germany, any concessions to Italy would damage Britain's reputation in Hitler's eyes and jeopardize the prospect for a favorable Anglo-German arrangement. This new argument may have been inspired by Delbos, who in January argued that it was unwise to embark on conversations with Italy and that the Axis could be weakened only from the Berlin end. Delbos then claimed that Mussolini had recently said that Italy would soon annihilate the British fleet and reconquer Savoy for the king. Gamelin also admitted that France had improved its defenses along the Libyan-Tunisian border and reinforced its garrisons in Tunisia and the Tibesti region. Eden accorded these reports great significance after British intelligence wildly speculated that an Italian offensive against Britain in the Mediterranean during the spring of 1938 was a distinct possibility.[72]

Many in the British government, as well as their service advisers, were also reluctant to respond to these Italian threats and Fascist Italy's unsettling behavior in late 1937 because they had begun to recognize that, as William Strang of the FO succinctly summarized the situation, "the worse our relations with Italy, the closer we must be to France." The service chiefs were particularly conscious of Strang's truism and acted to ensure that close cooperation with the French would not be necessary, recommending in January 1938 that Britain neither improve its existing defenses nor provocatively deploy any military or naval force in the Mediterranean. Britain could not contemplate war in either the Far East or the West if tensions existed in the Mediterranean. As Chatfield wrote, "It is essential that we should make friends and not enemies when we have so much valuable property to be attacked and while our defence position is still weak." The Cabinet soon endorsed the service chiefs' plans, insisting that any provocative British military response in Egypt would disrupt the regional agenda of the prime minister, who believed that the "only way we can maintain our moral position is to make [de jure] recognition [of Ethiopia] part of a general scheme for appeasement in the Mediterranean and the Red Sea." The guiding principle for British defenses in the Mediterranean remained "no obtrusive measures."[73]

Fear of cooperating with France does not entirely explain the service chiefs' motives for avoiding provocative action in the Mediterranean. Early in 1938 the Treasury continued to obstruct the services' attempt to accelerate British rearmament. In February the services revised upward their rearmament estimates for the period 1937–41. But Minister for the Coordination of Defence Sir Thomas Inskip and Chancellor of the Exchequer John Simon claimed that this proposed level of expenditure would "impair Britain's economic stability," which would ultimately be a better deterrent to aggression than would military prowess. Inskip recommended a five-year defense program of only 1,570 million pounds—more than 18 percent less than the three services had requested for their least substantial rearmament program. Again Inskip pleaded for a change in European diplomacy rather than a search for financing alternatives to meet the existing situation: "The burden . . . is too great for us. I therefore repeat with fresh emphasis . . . the importance of reducing the scale of our commitments and the number of our potential enemies."[74]

Despite the Treasury's arguments and restrictions, Eden interpreted the service chiefs' reluctance to fortify the Mediterranean as a blatant political act designed to satisfy potential enemies, particularly the Axis powers, and offend probable friends, especially France and the United States. Had Britain, Eden asked, reversed its priorities? "I cannot help believing that what the Chiefs of Staff would really like to do is to reorient our whole foreign policy and to clamber on the band wagon with the dictators, even though that process mean[s] parting company with France and estranging our relations with the United States." Nevertheless, Chamberlain and the Cabinet on 16 February accepted the expenditure recommendations of the minister for the coordination of defence. The navy, in particular, had to scale back its shipbuilding plans for 1938, from three capital ships to two and from two aircraft carriers to one. Anticipating that the battle over rearmament had not ended, Simon warned the Cabinet that even the current allocation would place "a very heavy strain indeed on national finances, which could not in any event be exceeded on the review in 1939 save [in] the most compelling circumstances."[75]

[2]

"The most formidable politico-military combination that has ever existed": November 1937–September 1938

THE *ANSCHLUSS*

Early in 1938 Hitler replaced dozens of Germany's highest-ranking military and diplomatic officials, including Field Marshal Werner von Blomberg, General Werner von Fritsch, and Foreign Minister Baron Konstantin von Neurath—all remnants of the old conservative ruling class. Hitler assumed personal control of the military and appointed General Wilhelm Keitel to head the military staff and Joachim von Ribbentrop the Foreign Ministry. Both men were committed Nazis. Then in early February the Austrian prime minister met Hitler in Berchtesgaden to receive a confirmation of the German recognition of Austrian independence. Instead, Hitler declared his intention of absorbing Austria.

Chamberlain immediately looked to Italy to avert this crisis. After receiving reports from British officials in Rome that events in Austria had stunned Italian officials and that Ciano now sought an early conclusion to an Anglo-Italian treaty, and from Italian Ambassador Dino Grandi that Mussolini would try to restrain Hitler from violence against Austria if Anglo-Italian talks began, the prime minister directed the Earl of Perth, the British ambassador in Rome, to meet Ciano officially. Eden, who suspected "some kind of arrangement between Rome and Berlin" and like Vansittart feared that Mussolini "may be playing us along," opposed any British negotiations with Italy. He resigned in protest on 20 February.[1]

But Chamberlain found strong support for his Italian policy in Lord Halifax, his new foreign secretary. Halifax was a tall, gangling, unattractive man who has been described as "a living caricature of a north-country peer." Aristocratic and Anglican with a speech impediment common among male children bred to the English upper class, Halifax was an avid fox hunter. He was also brilliant, having taken a first in modern history at Oxford and been elected a Fellow of All Souls. A conservative who disguised disagreement and avoided blunt language, Halifax was generally sympathetic to Germany and Italy and had a reputation for despising all Frenchmen. Shortly after assuming his new post, Halifax told the Cabinet that, despite the steady deterioration of Austro-German relations, there was "reason to believe that Signor Mussolini was annoyed with the Germans" and he emphasized the "importance of the conversations with the Italian government."[2]

London's important decision-makers were unwilling to accept that Mussolini was irrevocably committed to opposing Britain. To do so would have placed British statesmen in a terrible political and psychological bind because they lacked the military and financial strength to confront the German, Japanese, and Italian threats simultaneously. Acknowledging a genuine Italian menace in the Mediterranean would have required the British to begin war planning with the French. Yet an alliance with France remained an unacceptable consideration at this time. In addition to the strain such an alliance would place on limited British resources, it would reveal both Britain's inability to secure its own territories and the failure of British foreign policy. The Cabinet endorsed Halifax's position on the need for talks with Italy, desperate to believe that he was right. Chamberlain's path for a Mediterranean appeasement finally appeared clear. Only days later, on 12 March, the Germans invaded and annexed Austria.

The British believed the *Anschluss* would provoke a full Anglo-Italian reconciliation, but in fact the German assault on Austria did not motivate the Italians to pursue a treaty with Britain. Nor did it surprise or upset Italy's political leaders. Although the Germans had not informed the Italians exactly when the *Anschluss* would occur, the Italians had long known that it was inevitable. Mussolini had told the Germans in January 1936 that he was no longer committed to defending Austria's sovereignty; Italy had acquiesced in the Austro-German accord of July 1936; and Ribbentrop had alluded to an eventual German *Anschluss* at the signing of the Rome-Berlin Axis in October 1936. Moreover, Ribbentrop and Mussolini had discussed the topic in detail on 6 November 1937. On this day that Italy signed the Anti-Comintern pact, Ribbentrop, Ciano, and Mussolini discussed a wide range of international issues at the Palazzo Venezia. Before the meeting's close, Ribbentrop inquired about Italy's perspective on the future of Austria, indicating that Germany planned to settle this dilemma soon. Mussolini responded candidly that Austria

> is a German country of race, language, and culture. The Austrian question should not be considered as a problem between Italy and Germany. . . . Aus-

> tria is a German state. . . . The Italian interest today is not as lively as it was a few years ago because of Italy's imperialist developments, which have now converged Italy's interests on the Mediterranean and her colonies.

But the Italian *voltafaccia* on Austria was not offered without strings attached. Mussolini explained that the development of an Italian Mediterranean empire, with Sicily as its geographic center, was now the principal goal of Italian foreign policy. Germany had to acknowledge Italy's imperial ambitions in the Mediterranean as Italy had accepted Germany's plans to incorporate Austria. Without hesitation, Ribbentrop assented. That very evening Ciano wrote in his diary that Italy now "is at the center of the most formidable politico-military combination that has ever existed." Two weeks later Ciano compared Ambassador Pellegrino Ghigi's mission to Vienna to "a doctor who must give oxygen to a dying man."[3] The fate of Austria had been set, and the Italians were not only forewarned of but also confidants to the German crime.

On the subject of Austrian independence, Ciano was extremely evasive and deceitful with his colleagues from Britain and France. After reports of Schusschnigg's visit to Berchtesgaden, Ciano opined privately that "the *Anschluss* is inevitable" and immediately urged Grandi to accelerate talks with the British: since Italian "policy may be permanently aligned against the western powers" after the *Anschluss,* Italy had to reap every concession possible from the British before Germany's action tainted Italian diplomacy. In Rome, requests by both Perth and French Ambassador Jules-François Blondel to speak with Mussolini and his foreign minister on the eve of the *Anschluss* were denied; Austria was not a subject that the Italians were willing to discuss in early March 1938. The immediate official Italian reaction to the *Anschluss,* contradicting what Ciano had admitted to Perth two days before, claimed that Schuschnigg failed to inform the Italians of the results of the Berchtesgaden meeting. Describing the German incorporation of Austria as a fait accompli, the Italian government expressed its resolve not to interfere with the internal politics of Austria.[4]

These public affirmations of Italian lack of concern for Austrian affairs disguised the genuine effect that the *Anschluss* had on Italian foreign policy. In the first place, the ease of Hitler's annexation impressed the Fascists and drew them closer to the Nazis. Hitler wrote Mussolini a long letter on the eve of the *Anschluss* that explained Germany's action in Austria and thanked the Duce for his understanding and support, persuading Ciano that the Nazis were "delighted with our line of conduct." On the day that the Germans invaded Austria, Mussolini responded in kind by arranging for the Gran Consiglio del Fascismo to endorse Italy's collaboration with German foreign policy.[5]

Second, however, the *Anschluss* wounded the Duce's pride. With his forces engaged in simultaneous quagmires in Abyssinia and Spain, Mussolini was both envious and resentful of his Axis partner's sudden and almost effortless success. Despite receiving an additional twenty-five battalions in December 1937 and January 1938, General Ugo Cavallero had been unable to gain control of the Ethiopian countryside. With Italian bombers employed off the coast of Spain, Italian forces in Abyssinia could not increase the scale of unrestricted poison gas attacks to counter the growing bands of guerrilla resisters, who were now supported by French intelligence advisers and a trickle of modern arms from France and the Soviet Union.[6] Even more frustrating for Mussolini than the state of affairs in East Africa was General Franco's recent refusal to turn the success of the Italian Corpo Truppe Volontarie (CTV) at the Battle of Teurel into a Nationalist offensive to end the civil war. Inspired by the *Anschluss* and determined to show Hitler and the democracies that Italy remained a power worthy of fear, Mussolini on 12 March instructed Air Force Undersecretary Giuseppe Valle to order Italian planes in the Balearics to begin terror bombing the inhabited sections of Barcelona. The Aeronautica obeyed this command without the consent or even the knowledge of Franco, who one week later pleaded for an end to the ruthless shelling that had killed almost one thousand civilians and wounded at least one thousand more. Reluctantly suspending the raids against Barcelona, Mussolini instead demanded that Italy's Majorca-based planes double the rate of their assaults on Republican ports and shipping.[7]

Finally, the *Anschluss* persuaded the Italians to reinvigorate their campaign to bolster Italy's strategic position in the Balkans. Ciano envisioned the expansion of Italian influence from Yugoslavia into Hungary, Romania, and Bulgaria. If Italy could establish a Balkan bloc under its leadership, there would be no risk that Germany would use Austria as a stepping-stone for expansion into southeastern Europe and eventually the eastern Mediterranean. Instead, the Italians hoped, such a Balkan bloc would demonstrate Italian strength, persuade Hitler to create Germany's *Lebensraum* in central Europe, specifically in Czechoslovakia and Poland, and lay the foundation for an equal Nazi-Fascist partnership. Following the *Anschluss*, Ciano reinvigorated his efforts to conclude a mutual defense pact with Yugoslavia. "At a time when there will soon be eighty million Germans in the heart of Europe, Rome's and Belgrade's friendship with Germany is a fatality; even though it is oppressive, it is real." The Duce and his foreign minister also decided that a "more complete [Italian] domination" of Albania would provide Italy with the necessary leverage to compel the Yugoslavs to sign an alliance with the Italians. Naval planning began in May 1938 for an immediate invasion of Albania, "even at the risk of setting fire to the European powder keg."[8] The Fascists had conceded central Europe to Germany but they were determined to become masters of the Mediterranean region, which in Italian minds included both Spain and the Balkans.

THE UNWILLINGNESS of some Frenchmen to embrace the Mediterranean policy of Daladier and Darlan dissipated with Hitler's annexation of Austria. As they had been two years before during the Rhineland crisis, the French were mired in domestic-political turmoil at the time of the *Anschluss.* The resignation of Premier Chautemps on the day that the Austrian crisis exploded precluded any resolute French response to Germany's latest affront to the continental status quo. Yet ironically it was a prolonged and bitter parliamentary debate in late February over the fate of Austria and Czechoslovakia that precipitated Chautemps's demise and France's pusillanimity. In the Chamber Delbos proved unable to withstand the onslaught from both the left and right. While Blum and his followers urged the administration to guarantee Austrian (and central European) sovereignty, Jean Montigny, Pierre-Etienne Flandin, and Louis Marin attacked the government for not pursuing a policy based on the abandonment of Eastern Europe, retrenchment behind the Maginot Line, and reconstitution of the Stresa front. Delbos weakly described Austrian independence as an "essential element of European equilibrium" but did not offer to defend Austria against German aggression. Crushed by the sudden resignation of Eden, Delbos told Bullitt days before the Chamber debate that "the entire policy he had attempted to carry out for the past two years had been destroyed. There was nothing for him to do but give up his shoes. He could not think of any constructive policy." Added to the government's failure to resolve the renewed labor unrest of late 1937 and avert another financial crisis and a weakening of the already unstable franc, France's inability to influence the accelerating pace of events in central Europe finally destroyed the Chautemps coalition on 10 March. The absence of a French government only augmented Hitler's desire to incorporate Austria immediately.[9]

For many on the political left and center in France, the *Anschluss* foreshadowed an inevitable war in the Mediterranean and emphasized the need for an alliance with Britain. Mussolini's refusal to support Austrian sovereignty without so much as a verbal protest indicated to President of the Chamber Edouard Herriot and Joseph Paul-Boncour, the new foreign minister who had served as the French permanent delegate to the League of Nations during the Ethiopian crisis, that "the entente between Germany and Italy has never been more serious." Colonel Maurice Gauché of the Deuxième Bureau, France's intelligence service, was convinced that Germany had agreed to compensate Italy in Egypt, Tunisia, and Spain in return for Italian capitulation on Austrian and probably Czechoslovak sovereignty. Terrified that the *Anschluss* would encourage the Italians to extend their intervention in Spain, the new Blum government reopened the Pyrenees frontier, allowing French and Russian arms to flow freely into Republican Spain.[10] Even the political Right in France conceded that reconstituting the Stresa front was no longer a reasonable expectation. The conservative *Revue Universelle* of 1 May argued that "the idea of separating Italy from Germany would be crazy."[11] Instead of hoping that Italy would ally with France against Germany, the Right now looked to Mussolini as the possible arbiter between the democracies and the Third Reich.

At the heart of French consternation following the *Anschluss* was the suddenly heightened prospect of a German move against Czechoslovakia. "Events seem inevitable," wrote Daladier. "Hitler, once again charged with audacity, could, and without hesitation, precipitate things and present Czechoslovakia and its allies with a dilemma: capitulation or war." Czechoslovakia was not only an ally that France was committed to defend but also held the key—namely, Russia—to the viability of an eastern front against a hostile Germany. Both France and Russia were allies of Czechoslovakia, but Russia was bound to defend the Czechs only if France did. Moreover, besides its famous armaments works at Skoda, Czechoslovakia possessed a formidable military garrison that the French estimated could withstand forty German divisions and protect the valuable oil fields of southeastern Europe.[12]

Yet the *Anschluss* had revealed that France was unprepared for even a limited war. Weeks before the Nazis marched into Vienna, French military and diplomatic leaders had accepted that France could not defend Austria's independence. In February Vuillemin informed Air Minister Guy La Chambre that "the situation is extremely grave. We do not know what the future holds but I am quite convinced that if a conflict erupts this year, the French air force would be crushed [*écraser*] in a few days." Daladier admitted in mid-March that all France alone could muster in the event of a war over Czechoslovakia was limited mobilization: "By the time we intervene, if we do, it is likely that the plight of Czechoslovakia will already be very critical."[13]

In addition to focusing on future events in Czechoslovakia, French military appreciations began reconsidering policy vis-à-vis Italy and the Mediterranean. Although a few strategists, such as General Louis Buisson, head of the army's strategic studies section, continued to argue that "we must recreate the Paris-Rome axis. . . . Whatever the price of an accord with Rome, it will never be too expensive," most were more circumspect about the value of an Italian alliance after the *Anschluss.* "Recent events confirm the solidarity, at least for the moment, of the Rome-Berlin Axis," opined Gamelin to the CPDN. "[Mussolini's] price for the *Anschluss* was without doubt the promise of Mediterranean mastery." Now pessimistic about achieving a constructive Franco-Italian friendship, Gamelin emphasized that "France, if it hopes to defend its metropolitan territory and its African empire efficiently, can dream of leading a successful war effort only *with alliances.*"[14]

Italy's quiescent reaction to events in Austria suggested to navy officials at the Rue Royale not only the presence of a durable Italian-German entente but also the possibility that Mussolini was now desperate to match his Axis partner's aggressive action. The bombing of Barcelona and the resumption of raids on Republican ports heightened these suspicions. The EMM anticipated that Italy, aware of its own economic and financial woes, would now employ the Italian air base in the Balearics to achieve a quick aero-naval success in the western Mediterranean—most likely at France's expense. Thus, it was Italy's growing presence in the Balearics that presented perhaps the greatest immediate threat to French security. In early March Admiral Bourragué, assistant chief of the naval staff, told the Quai d'Orsay that "we cannot subscribe to anything that permits, in any form whatsoever, the permanent establishment of Italian forces or influence in continental or island Spain (the Balearics), nor in any Spanish overseas possession."[15] French diplomatic reports reaffirmed the navy's apprehensions. Hoping to influence the course of Anglo-Italian negotiations, Paul-Boncour explained to the British that "the maintenance of this [Italian] base [in the Balearics], as well as those that exist south of the Pyrenees, will eventually constitute the most grave menace for our territory and for our Mediterranean communications."[16] French preoccupations after the *Anschluss* were not limited to Czechoslovakia and eastern Europe but also extended to Spain and the Mediterranean.

Despite its ominous warnings about the Mediterranean, the Marine Nationale was disinclined to languish in self-pity after the Nazis sealed the fate of Austria. Instead, Admiral Darlan and the EMM interpreted the *Anschluss,* and Daladier's admission that France could not militarily defend either Czechoslovakia or Spain from the Axis, as a call to arms. In late March he told the other French service chiefs that the Marine would soon be in a position to oppose an Italian landing on the northern coast of Tunisia and engage in a general battle there if necessary. The navy also was prepared to attack "with certain efficiency" Italy's Libyan supply and communication lines. Despite discouraging words from Gamelin and Vuillemin on the unpreparedness of their forces in the Mediterranean theater, Darlan arranged for joint aero-naval exercises to take place in the Mediterranean as soon as possible.[17] Genuine French planning for a Mediterranean war had begun.

The Marine also used the *Anschluss* to raise to a fever pitch its demands for an end to the "pause" in rearmament, particularly naval rearmament. The EMM argued that the 1938 armament budget did not address the expansion of the Italian navy that had occurred during 1937. The Regia Marina had just begun enjoying the fruits of Mussolini's 1936 naval construction program, which included the modernization of two World War I–generation battleships and a new fleet of submarines. The Italians had also received funding to lay the keels of two more first-line battleships, which would give Italy a decisive capital-ship advantage over France by July 1940. The EMM's Section d'Etudes Générales estimated that without a significant expansion of the current naval program, the Regia Marina's total fleet tonnage would surpass that of the Marine by the end of 1942. Moreover, France's navy had worldwide responsibilities that Italy's navy did not. "If the situation is not addressed," argued the EMM, "the superiority of the Italian navy [in the Mediterranean] in number and quality will become indisputable by 1939."[18]

FREE OF ALLIANCES or treaty obligations to the states of Eastern Europe and unwilling to accept that the dictatorships were bent on war against the democracies, the British acted less concerned than the French about the potential international repercussions of the *Anschluss.* Remarking on the very day that Nazi troops entered Austria that he was glad the Austrian "question was now out of the way," Chamberlain saw no need to reevaluate his European appeasement policy. Instead, the *Anschluss* "confirmed [the prime minister] in his opinion that the policy was the right one and he only regretted that it had not been adopted earlier." Appeasing Hitler, however, would now have to be achieved in a slightly more circuitous manner. Specifically, Italy was to be the primary short-term target of British appeasement, in the hope that a friendly Mussolini would mollify Hitler's long-term ambitions. As Chamberlain told his sister on the day after the *Anschluss,* "For the moment we must abandon conversations with Germany, we must show our determination not to be bullied by announcing some increase or acceleration in rearmament, and we must quietly and steadily pursue our conversations with Italy."[19]

The British service chiefs also interpreted the *Anschluss* as requiring Britain to address the Italian factor diplomatically rather than the German factor militarily. An attempt to reverse Germany's incorporation of Austria was not under consideration. Britain, according to the COS, could "do nothing to prevent the dog from getting the bone, and we have no means of making him give it up, except by killing him by the slow process of attrition and starvation." Most important, the service chiefs feared the strategic implications, particularly as it would affect the security of the Far Eastern empire, should Japan and Italy join Germany in a general war. Repeating a familiar admonition, the chiefs concluded, "Without overlooking the assistance we should hope to obtain from France and possibly other allies, we cannot foresee the time when our defence forces will be strong enough to safeguard our territory, trade and vital interests against Germany, Italy and Japan simultaneously." Although Chamberlain and Halifax used a draft of this report to justify—not as the basis for—their policies, it did persuade the Cabinet that British rearmament and a durable Mediterranean peace must now be pursued fervently.[20] Consequently, London did not officially or through diplomatic channels react to, much less condemn, Italy's deception of Britain over the *Anschluss.*

Chamberlain received almost unanimous support from both the Foreign Office and Parliament's foreign policy experts for continuing and even invigorating his Italian policy. Sir Alexander Cadogan, who had replaced Vansittart as permanent undersecretary at the FO in December 1937, began expressing strong positions after Eden's departure in February. Although Eden had selected Cadogan for his calm, dispassionate approach to policymaking, Cadogan's perspective on British foreign affairs more closely reflected Chamberlain's and Halifax's than Eden's. With a naturally grave face that was long in proportion to his height, Cadogan, like Halifax, had grown up in the English upper class and had studied history at Oxford. In April he echoed the prime minister's sense of relief over events in Austria, opining that "I can't work up much moral indignation until Hitler interferes with other nationalities."[21]

Many of Britain's most influential politicians, including Members of Parliament (MPs) Robert A. Butler, Stanley Bruce, Te Water, and Walter Dulantry, agreed that there was nothing Britain could have done to prevent the *Anschluss.* Butler, the parliamentary undersecretary for foreign affairs, spoke on behalf of this group when he explained that "it was the method even more than the act itself that was to be condemned." Discussions with Germany "at the moment" could not continue, but an understanding with Italy, "in the hope that she would exercise a moderating influence on Germany," was strongly encouraged.[22]

Such an analysis, linking the *Anschluss* to the need for talks with Italy, enjoyed support among British diplomats, who believed that events in Austria had surprised and agitated Mussolini. Perth suggested that the Italian government's "underlying resentment [with Hitler] is considerable" as a result of the *Anschluss* and the sudden presence of German troops on the Brenner Pass. Ambassador Eric Phipps in Paris reported that a well-connected "Italian friend" in Paris had confirmed Perth's analysis. Even Vansittart, now chief diplomatic adviser at the FO, told Labour Party MP Hugh Dalton that the Anglo-Italian conversations should seek to exploit Mussolini's rage over events in Austria and try to detach the two dictators from each other. Cadogan and Gladwyn Jebb, Halifax's private secretary, were so optimistic about the course of the Rome conversations that they both believed a new Stresa front was again possible. Only Orme Sargent, a skeptical, acerbic civil servant disillusioned by repeated British attempts to reach terms with Nazi Germany, speculated that the Italian reaction to the *Anschluss* would "inevitably cast a shadow of doubt and suspicion on the whole of the Anglo-Italian conversations." Sargent believed that Italy's acquiescence in the *Anschluss* meant that Britain should either capitulate in Hitler's building of a German world empire or oppose it resolutely through military cooperation with France, Belgium, Greece, Turkey, Poland, and Russia—unpalatable options for most British statesmen.[23]

The Anglo-Italian Easter Accords

It was Italy's failure to generate Yugoslav and Hungarian support for Italian foreign policy, not the *Anschluss,* that first led Mussolini and Ciano to react favorably to the renewed British efforts to reach an Anglo-Italian reconciliation in the Mediterranean. The Italians' intent was not to position themselves between the Germans and the British as a bulwark for continued peace in Europe but to improve Italian credibility in the Balkans, lull the British into complacency in the Mediterranean, and discourage the development of a firm Anglo-French entente.

The timely and independent, though unendorsed, diplomacy of Lady Chamberlain, the widow of the late Austen Chamberlain and sister-in-law to the current British prime minister, served as the catalyst for the Italian decision to begin negotiating with the British. Lady Chamberlain, who the Italians believed "wears a Fascist badge," spoke directly with both Ciano and Mussolini in January and February 1938, twice reading the Duce private letters she had received from her brother-in-law that bluntly expressed Chamberlain's determination to reach an accommodation with Italy in any way possible. Added to Lady Chamberlain's appeals were the official requests by Ambassador Perth for negotiations that would lead to a "total solution" of all outstanding Anglo-Italian questions.[24]

While Grandi's enthusiasm for a deal with the British strengthened Chamberlain's determination to negotiate with the Italians, Grandi's understanding of Fascist policy was uninformed or misinformed at best. As foreign minister in 1929–32, Grandi had argued that Italy should serve as the "determining weight" in the balance between the democracies and Germany. Yet Grandi's personal preference for the British and French and his well-known dislike of the Germans and outright antipathy for the Nazis influenced his diplomatic judgment. Thus, Ciano withheld from Grandi, among other things, details of the Duce's 6 November 1937 meeting with Ribbentrop: as late as mid-February 1938 Grandi was unaware that Italy had traded Austrian independence for Germany's acceptance of an Italian Mediterranean empire. The "secret channel" that Chamberlain believed he had to Rome was the joint product of the voluble and obsequious Grandi—who was determined to engineer an Anglo-Italian rapprochement—and Adrian Dingli, counselor to the Italian embassy. It in no way represented a genuine link to Mussolini's foreign policy.[25]

Lady Chamberlain and Perth revealed to Ciano and Mussolini the British prime minister's willingness to recognize Ethiopia, overlook the Spanish issue, endorse Italy's interests in the Middle East, and exclude all other Mediterranean powers from the discussions. This news persuaded the Italians that a treaty with Britain would weaken any future British or Anglo-French resistance to an Italian Mediterranean empire without jeopardizing the Rome-Berlin Axis. More than a week before official talks with the British began—and well before the *Anschluss*—Ciano directed his ambassador in Berlin to inform the Germans that any future Anglo-Italian treaty would be designed to improve Italy's drive toward Mediterranean hegemony by eliciting British recognition of Ethiopia and assuaging British fears about an aggressive Italian foreign policy; it would also further isolate France and benefit Germany. "An accord between us and the English will grant us more freedom on the continent and enable us to offer major support to the developments of Germany's continental policy." The foreign minister assured Bernardo Attolico, Italian ambassador to Germany, that the Mussolini-Ribbentrop understanding of 6 November 1937 remained the basis of Italian policy.[26]

The Germans welcomed Ciano's candid explanation. Through Attolico, Hitler responded, "Our friendship will not be broken. . . . we must stay united so as not to be eaten by the others." Soon thereafter Marshal Göring, speaking with Hitler's approval, explained to the Italian air attaché that no conflict existed between their two states. "Italy and Germany have analogous styles and doctrines, they have the same enemies, and they have admitted that they will not interfere with each other because, while Italy, being anchored in the Mediterranean, has her natural zone of influence in the Mediterranean, Germany's aims are oriented to the Northeast."[27] The Italian deception of Britain had begun.

It was the *Anschluss* that provided Britain with the final and most compelling motivation to sign the Easter Accords of 16 April 1938. First of all, an Anglo-Italian entente would improve Britain's desperate strategic dilemma by eliminating a potential enemy in the Mediterranean. Following the Easter Accords, the COS based any planning for a future war on certain Italian neutrality, and the CID approved only limited air defenses for Malta and Aden. Second, an arrangement with Italy would stem Germany's economic expansion into southeastern Europe. Supported by the British, the Italians would resist German economic penetration into the Balkans; without British support, the Italians would succumb to German pressure and align themselves definitively with the Nazis. Third and most important, a treaty with Italy would relieve the general state of tension existing in Europe. Expressing his approval of the Anglo-Italian accord, Butler explained that the "policy of HMG . . . is to enlarge the area of security wherever it may be possible not by alliances but by promoting such a measure of confidence and understanding as to remove the danger of alliances being formed against us."[28]

Italy's stakes for any agreement were high—the promise of British de jure recognition of Italy's conquest of Ethiopia and parity of Anglo-Italian interests in the Red Sea—and the Easter Accords were signed only five weeks after talks between Perth and Ciano began. In return, Italy consecrated the status quo in the Mediterranean and agreed to a "settlement of the Spanish question," an unspecified reduction of the Libyan garrison, and the opening of talks with the French aimed at a complementary Franco-Italian agreement. Mussolini's opposition to any direct reference to Palestine in the agreement and his stubborn refusal to associate the French government either directly or indirectly with the conversations presented obstacles that the British were inclined to overlook in the interest of reaching the accord.[29]

Some in the British government found disquieting both Italy's hostility to France and Britain's willingness to risk upsetting France by signing a bilateral pact with Italy. Duff Cooper, in particular, argued that strengthening Anglo-French relations remained the most effective deterrent to German aggression. "There is danger now of the success in Rome leading some people to think that friendship with France is a little less important than it was. If that happened then the success would be a disaster and Anthony [Eden] would be right." Such a perspective, however, was not widely shared. In a report to the Foreign Policy Committee (FPC) soon after conversations with Italy had begun, the foreign secretary suggested that the French, "unable to divest themselves of an ingrained distrust of the good faith of the Italian government," would likely be more responsible than the Italians for obstructing a resolution to the Spanish situation.[30] In early 1938 the British government was disinclined to consider seriously French concerns about affairs in the Mediterranean, much less any kind of Anglo-French entente.

Anglo-French Relations

The signing of the Easter Accords offered little comfort to the French, who interpreted the Italian refusal to address Palestine as a sign of Italy's determination to challenge France's position in Syria. Shortly after the Anglo-Italian agreement, a reliable French intelligence source revealed that the Fascists now believed a path had been cleared for Italy to acquire Savoy, Nice, Corsica, and Tunisia. "As a great Mediterranean and Moslem power," explained Daladier and his new foreign minister, Georges Bonnet, to the British, "France is closely interested in the Moslem world and therefore in the two Holy places of Islam." In any talks with Italy, France would insist that the Italians make similar engagements to France on French possessions in the Mediterranean and the Middle East.[31] With consensus in Paris moving away from an instinctive commitment to Eastern Europe, the heightened "imperial" element of French defense acquired as high, if not higher, a priority as concern for the future of Czechoslovakia. Daladier believed that a simultaneous consideration of these *two* issues, Czechoslovakia and the Mediterranean, would accelerate the development of an Anglo-French alliance.

In late April Chamberlain invited Daladier and Bonnet to Britain to discuss the deteriorating international situation, including Japan's recent creation of the "Reformed Government of the Republic of China" in Nanking. Having concluded their talks with Italy, the British now saw France as the next important actor in their general European appeasement. The absence of the socialists and Italophobes Blum and Paul-Boncour, whom the British considered a "positive danger to the peace of Europe," made the prospect of a Franco-Italian reconciliation not entirely improbable. Even a settlement of Germany's outstanding grievances was no longer out of the question. Chamberlain and Halifax hoped that talks in London would convince the French not to encourage Czechoslovak resistance and thus incite a European war.[32]

Before leaving for London, Gamelin and Darlan persuaded Daladier that it was essential for Britain and France to coordinate military resources and planning in anticipation of a future conflict against Germany *and* Italy. Recognizing that the British would likely be less enthusiastic about this prospect than the French, Gamelin emphasized that the French had the most to offer Britain in the Mediterranean: "The possibility of France carrying the initial effort against Italy, the eventual reduction by France of Spanish Morocco (in case of a hostile Spain) to assure the security of the southern shore of the Gibraltar Straits, the cooperation of our Levant forces in the protection of the Suez Canal—these would be the compensations to make the most of." Darlan insisted that an offensive or counteroffensive alignment in the Mediterranean required the cooperation of British and French air and naval forces.[33]

As a result, the French arrived in London determined to win British agreement for Anglo-French naval staff talks. Although the British Cabinet in February 1938 had authorized air and army staff conversations with France, the CID had insisted then and again in early April that the international situation did not require contacts between the two navies. The political implications of the ongoing Anglo-Italian conversations and the British 1937 commitment to send the main fleet to Singapore if war broke out in the Far East had precluded talks that in any way envisioned a war in the Mediterranean. Moreover, the British feared that news of Anglo-French naval conversations would reach the Germans and perhaps vitiate the Anglo-German naval agreement.[34]

In London, Chamberlain explained to Daladier that in an Anglo-French war against Germany, Britain's principal contribution would be in the air and at sea. Only two poorly equipped British divisions could be sent to the continent. Daladier presented an "impassioned" appeal for the British to recognize Hitler's drive for continental hegemony—a plea Cadogan described as "awful rubbish"—but quickly turned the topic of the conversation to the Mediterranean, where the French believed Italian hostility and collaboration with Germany could not be ruled out; therefore, detailed Anglo-French naval contacts were essential. Chamberlain explained to Daladier that he "thought it necessary to be very careful not to undo any good which had been achieved by these conversations with Italy by exciting Italian or German suspicions that we were now devising fresh military, naval or aerial combinations designed to injure those two powers." When Chamberlain argued that the Easter Accords eliminated the possibility of Italian cooperation with Germany, the French premier strongly objected. Daladier believed that Italy's most recent contributions to the Spanish war—including the terror bombing of Barcelona in March and the Italian offensive across Aragon in April—plus its ruthless poison gas campaign in Ethiopia, growing military presence in Libya, and refusal to condemn the *Anschluss* all justified a more detailed examination of strategic policies and possible military cooperation in all fields, especially between the two navies. Ultimately, after much wrangling, Daladier succeeded in persuading Chamberlain to authorize naval staff talks "in principle."[35]

Immediately following the Anglo-French ministerial conversations, the CID asked the COS to make arrangements and set boundaries for the upcoming naval staff talks with the French. The service chiefs turned to the Admiralty's planning division, which immediately noted that the object of these discussions would be "a political one, to meet the very strongly expressed wishes of the French." Concerned that the talks not result in a combined Anglo-French naval war plan, the Admiralty insisted that the exchange be at no higher than the attaché level. The scope of these discussions, asserted Planning Director Captain V. H. Danckwerts, should be rigidly limited to information concerning current naval dispositions and various technical details regarding communication and signal codes and port facilities. Most important, His Majesty's Government (HMG) should assume no new commitments: "A hard and fast line must eventually be drawn beyond which we cannot go without morally committing ourselves to act with France in war."[36] The COS included all the Admiralty's recommendations in the paper they submitted to the CID, adding that "Germany alone is to be assumed as the aggressor, and the contacts do not envisage the extension of war to other powers whether as potential enemies or potential allies." The Cabinet approved the service chiefs' report at the end of May, and the British naval attaché in Paris presented the guidelines to the Marine Nationale on 1 June.[37]

These rigid limitations made it starkly clear to the French that the British were not yet interested in planning for war as allies. Restricting consideration to a hypothetical war against only Germany—excluding the Italian factor—seemed not only strategically unrealistic but politically absurd. Gamelin reminded Daladier, however, that an all-encompassing Anglo-French alliance would not materialize easily or quickly. Recognizing that fighting a war without any British support would be catastrophic, and that low-level restricted staff talks were better than none, the French reluctantly accepted Britain's terms. The most incredulous was Darlan. Although the French naval chief was considerably less interested in formulating a detailed Anglo-French naval war plan than in reestablishing the extensive sharing of information that the two admiralties carried out in 1936 during the Mediterranean crisis, he and the EMM interpreted Britain's obstinacy on the subject of naval cooperation as a sign that British priorities in the Mediterranean had changed dramatically. The surrender of British dominance in the Red Sea as a result of the Easter Accords gave Italy a "strategic position of the first order" in the eastern Mediterranean, which menaced vital French communications to the Near and Far East. According to Darlan, the British had failed to recognize "the would-be assassin who tries to stab you in the back with his stiletto."[38]

Franco-Italian Relations

The conclusion of the Easter Accords encouraged the new French foreign minister, Georges Bonnet, to be optimistic about improving Franco-Italian relations. Bonnet was a highly educated politician who had been appointed by Daladier not because the two men had similar visions of Europe and foreign affairs but in order to maintain the centrist coalition in the Chamber. Although a small man with sharp features who was often chided for over-accommodating his young wealthy wife, Bonnet was widely respected for his acute intellect and extensive experience in French parliamentary politics. As a leader of the conservative Radicals, Bonnet generated support on the right because of his outspoken conviction that Czechoslovakia and

Poland were not worth jeopardizing French interests in war and that the key to European peace was a Franco-Italian rapprochement.[39] Bonnet's ideological perspective and his domestic-political constituency, as well as his conviction that France could not afford or withstand another war, influenced his conduct of French foreign policy.

Knowing that the British had expressed their desire for the Italians to conclude a similar, if not complementary, Mediterranean agreement with the French, Bonnet immediately instructed Blondel to meet with Ciano. The Italian foreign minister was congratulated on the successful outcome of the Anglo-Italian talks and assured that Ethiopia would appear high on the League's agenda the following month. In addition, the French government requested the opening of Franco-Italian negotiations to settle all outstanding issues. On 19 April Ciano informed Blondel that talks could begin, and that if France appointed a new ambassador to Rome and expressed its intent to recognize the Italian empire, an agreement was possible. The Fascists were willing to consider talks with France in the hope that the French would make significant colonial concessions to Italy, thus improving Italy's status as a great imperial power. In addition, the Reich in Austria had upset Italy by abolishing the special tariff for Trieste, ordering foreign residents to declare their foreign securities, organizing irredentist demonstrations, and publishing disparaging remarks about the Italian mountain population. In fact the Italian army took what Badoglio described as "very serious precautions" in the Alto Adige in April and drew up plans that considered the possibility of hostile German action along the Brenner. As Mussolini explained to his deputy, "The Germans will force me to swallow the most sour lemon of my life. I speak of the French lemon."[40] Again, these Italian steps reflected not a willingness to side with the Western powers against Germany but a determination to prove to Germany that Italy should be treated as an equal Axis partner.

Bonnet, who believed that the tide had turned strongly in favor of reconstituting the Stresa front but had been influenced by the skeptical Léger, directed Blondel to present Ciano with a twelve-point catalogue of desiderata for an accord with Italy. French support of a British resolution on Ethiopian recognition at Geneva would only follow an Italian declaration of noninterference in Spain, a new convention in Tunisia, a reduction of Italy's presence in Libya, a recognition of French interests in the Red Sea, and a variety of minor provisions regarding the status quo in the Mediterranean, Middle East, Suez Canal, and North Africa. This extensive list of French demands offended the Fascists and delayed any Italian response until after Ciano's visit to Albania and Hitler's visit to Italy in May. Mussolini refused to discuss the Spanish question with Paris and was particularly infuriated by

France's attempt to dilute the section of the Easter Accords that addressed the Red Sea region, which the Duce now regarded as an "Anglo-Italian *condominio.*" In fact Ciano believed that Italy's most important achievement in the pact was parity with Britain in Arabia. Buttressed by successful meetings with the Führer and excited about Ribbentrop's offer for a military assistance pact, Mussolini ordered Ciano to discontinue negotiations with the French by citing the porous border with Spain. Although disappointed, British officials agreed that "enormous quantities" of arms and munitions for Spain's government forces had streamed across the frontier during the spring of 1938, justifying Italy's refusal to make any pledges to France.[41]

But even the British could not predict the Italian wrath against France that would soon follow. In Genoa on 14 May, before Ciano had officially ended the Franco-Italian talks and two days after the League Council decided that members were free to recognize the Italian conquest of Ethiopia if they wished, Mussolini proclaimed that Italy and France were on "opposite sides of the barricade" in the Spanish affair—thus precluding any kind of amicable Franco-Italian relationship. Moreover, Mussolini extolled the *Anschluss,* reviled the democracies, declared the Stresa formula "dead and buried," and insisted that together the Fascist and National Socialist revolutions were "destined to set the tone for this century." Ciano described it as a "very strong, anti-French speech" during which the crowd hissed at every reference to France and "ironically" laughed about the Easter Accords. Soon after the Czech weekend crisis of 20–21 May, when he was "more exasperated than ever with France" on account of the renewed anti-Fascist tone of the French press and the latest estimate of Republican effectives crossing the Pyrenees frontier into Spain, the Duce ordered his party to create a "wave of Gallophobia to liberate the Italians of their last slavery: servitude toward Paris." Immediately, the Italian press throughout the peninsula embarked on an intense anti-French propaganda campaign.[42]

Nevertheless, the British and French diplomats in Rome refused to take Mussolini's pronouncements literally. Perth entirely discounted the Duce's rage, explaining it as the understandable consequence of France's support for the Spanish Republicans, anti-Axis comments in the French press, and an unenthusiastic public reception for Hitler during his visit to Italy. In British eyes, peaceful Anglo-Italian relations remained a prerequisite for securing the British Empire without depending on a French alliance. Speaking with Ciano only days after the Genoa tirade, Perth remained optimistic about Franco-Italian relations and implored the Duce in the future to speak highly of the Anglo-Italian accord.[43] Despite the particularly strong hostility Mussolini aimed at France, Bonnet directed both Blondel in Rome and French Ambassador Charles Corbin in London to continuing searching for an accord with Italy. In French eyes, Italy remained crucial for a dénouement of both the Spanish affair and the Czechoslovak crisis.[44]

But Ciano doused this French optimism on 2 June in Milan with a speech to the National Congress for the Study of Foreign Questions in which he commended Chamberlain, acclaimed the Easter Accords, and reaffirmed the strength of the Axis without ever mentioning France. The following day Ciano told Perth that Britain had to ratify the Anglo-Italian agreement without a complementary Franco-Italian treaty. François Charles-Roux, the French envoy to the Vatican, explained that Mussolini's French policy had changed dramatically during the month of May as a result of a burgeoning in the German-Italian entente, which now extended beyond the political to the economic, cultural, and military fields. Blondel finally recognized that negotiating with the Italians was now out of the question: the Italian game of "separating France from London . . . appears more clear than ever." Even an act of French goodwill, such as closing the Pyrenean border to military supplies or immediately recognizing Ethiopia, would not likely lead to a rapprochement with Italy.[45]

The change in the tone of Italian diplomacy again improved the standing of the Marine in the French government's policymaking circles. In particular, the threatening Italian presence in the Balearic Islands suddenly received more attention than it had earlier in the spring. The navy had emphasized at a meeting of the Conseil Supérieur de la Défense Nationale (CSDN) at the end of April that Italy's air base in the Balearics dangerously menaced French communications in the western Mediterranean. The stunning performance of Italian air power in Spain, combined with the weakness of French aircraft production and the formidable German air threat across the Rhine, suggested that in the event of war the Axis powers could gain immediate control of the air in the Mediterranean, jeopardizing troop transports from North Africa and trade communications with the Near and Far East. In light of Italy's possessions and capabilities, France was unprepared for a conflict in the Mediterranean. Not only was its navy's combustible liquid supply adequate for less than four months of war, but also many of France's most important Mediterranean ports and bases, such as Toulouse and Corsica, were virtually defenseless. These arguments impressed French army strategists, who agreed that the next war would occur simultaneously in central Europe, North Africa, and the Middle East. Given Italy's formidable naval power in the eastern Mediterranean and Britain's interests in the Far East, control of both sea and air communications in the western Mediterranean would prove essential to French survival.[46]

Suddenly, the French took a series of steps designed both to prepare for and to delay the clash with Italy. First of all, Daladier and his finance minister, Paul Marchandeau, persuaded the Chamber to pass the decree-law of 2 May, which contained a supplemental four-year shipbuilding program—

la tranche navale 1938 bis—that more than doubled the Marine's budget for the year. Specifically, the law accelerated the rate of construction and allocated funding for two additional first-line battleships, one cruiser, and an array of heavy destroyers and submarines—almost tripling the Marine's previous program. Second, Daladier in June and July ordered Corsica's weak antiair defenses improved and Beirut's port extended. What makes these naval and Mediterranean expenditures particularly significant is that they immediately preceded and succeeded another devaluation of the franc—Daladier attached the value of the franc to that of British sterling on 4 May—and the consequent reduction in France's gold reserves. To cover the additional rearmament expenditures and relieve the pressure placed on the Ministry of Finance, Daladier scrapped many recent social reforms and symbolically buried the parliamentary agenda of the Popular Front.[47]

In June the Daladier government finally sealed the frontier with Spain. Bonnet had been the principal proponent of closing the border since his arrival at the Quai d'Orsay in April. Although most French diplomats supported this position, Bonnet encountered stiff opposition from Blum and Herriot, who contended that France could no longer remain committed to the fallacy of nonintervention. Daladier, as he so often would during his tenure as premier, found himself in the middle of this largely ideological debate. Rather than taking Bonnet's side—the premier recognized that closing the frontier would not lead to a reconciliation with Italy—he based his decision on improving relations with Britain and postponing any clash with Italy until France was better prepared. But, bristling at the ceaseless stream of anti-French propaganda emanating from the Italian press, the premier also emphasized to Phipps that France would not hesitate to reopen the frontier if nonintervention did not take hold or if Britain succumbed to Italian pressure and ratified the Easter Accords without a Spanish armistice and evacuation of Italian troops from Spain.[48]

Yet while the young Daladier government acted more decisively to improve Mediterranean defenses and with less politicized and reflexive hyperbole directed against the Fascists than its predecessor, a deeply discouraging realization had begun to take root in Paris. At a time of escalating crisis over Czechoslovakia, many French decision-makers began to understand that Italy was successfully "driving a stake" in the Anglo-French friendship. Massigli, who as Léger's deputy had become the leader of a growing Quai faction that believed the Axis powers would relent only if confronted by a strong and extensive alliance, offered an analysis soon adopted by most at the foreign ministry:

> I am greatly worried about our relations with Italy . . . I persist in thinking (though I know our English friends do not share this opinion) that Mus-

solini's object is to separate France from Great Britain. In order to achieve this, he wishes to put the Anglo-Italian agreement into force while continuing to cold-shoulder and insult France. The effect upon Anglo-French relations if he succeeds will be deplorable.

Even Bonnet now pressured London to withhold implementation of the Anglo-Italian agreement until Italy concluded an arrangement with France. Not linking the Easter Accords to amicable Franco-Italian relations, warned the foreign minister, would upset French public opinion, damage Anglo-French relations and propel France closer to the Soviet Union. Although Halifax directed Perth to inform the Italians that the British viewed a Franco-Italian agreement as a "logical complement" to the Easter Accords, he indicated that the British did not regard even the resumption of Franco-Italian negotiations as a precondition for the eventual ratification of the Anglo-Italian agreement.[49]

Confident that their appeasement program for the Mediterranean could succeed with or without French participation, the British remained indifferent to the enduring, and even burgeoning, French anxiety vis-à-vis Italy and the Mediterranean region during the summer of 1938. British lack of concern about a possible Franco-Italian reconciliation reflects Britain's arrogance in the Mediterranean—a strange confidence that a Franco-Italian conflict would not embroil Britain. The British needed to hold this belief because they were determined to do nothing that would encourage the development of an Anglo-French alliance or place their Far Eastern empire in jeopardy. Yet the French perceived a direct connection between their talks with Italy, a general Mediterranean appeasement, and an eventual alliance with Britain. On the eve of the Czech crisis, this stark difference in perspective over Italy further strained Anglo-French relations.

Axis Relations

The tension that emerged in the Alto Adige shortly after the *Anschluss* represented a minor irritation to, rather than a fundamental rift in, the state of Italian-German relations. The Nazis soon relaxed the pressure placed on Italians in the region, and the Fascists agreed that this issue should not destroy the Axis. On 7 May at the Palazzo Venezia, Hitler reaffirmed the Nazi-Fascist friendship, pledged the inviolability of the Alpine frontier along the Brenner "for all time," and proposed a military alliance. Two days later in Florence, before the Führer boarded his train bound for Germany, Mussolini told Hitler, "No force will ever be able to separate us." Hitler interpreted Mussolini's enthusiasm as encouragement to advance Germany's plans against Czechoslovakia.[50]

Mussolini was particularly interested in Hitler's proposal for a military alliance. Italian intelligence from Tokyo and London had revealed that Japan had designed its navy for offensive purposes and that the Royal Navy had modified its shipbuilding plans in light of the Japanese program. Moreover, the course of the Anglo-American naval talks in January 1938 proved that the United States was extremely reluctant to intervene in the Far East. As a result, by early 1938 Mussolini envisioned an inevitable, isolated Anglo-Italian war in the Mediterranean, with France fettered on the continent by the Germans and Britain partially engaged in the Far East by the Japanese. General Pariani, who also anticipated an Italian clash with the West, suggested that Italy would have the greatest military advantage over Britain and France in the spring of 1939. A "lightning war," with simultaneous attacks on Egypt, Suez, southern France, and the Western fleets, would secure an Italian conquest of the Mediterranean.[51]

Following Hitler's visit to Italy, the Fascists sold aerial torpedoes to the Nazis and expressed officially to the Germans that Italy neither had any interest in the fate of Czechoslovakia nor would impede Germany's march through central Europe. Confident that the Duce had committed himself to the Axis, Hitler told his generals on 30 May that "it is my unalterable decision to smash Czechoslovakia by military action in the near future." A few days later, Hitler decided that Germany would invade Czechoslovakia on 1 October, motivating Germany's naval and military planners to begin thinking about closely coordinating German and Italian war strategies.[52]

Despite these developments, Mussolini heeded Ciano's advice and temporarily delayed the conclusion of an Italian-German alliance. Italy's desire for the recognition of Abyssinia and general military unpreparedness for war explain this decision; a determination to pursue the traditional Italian policy of "equidistance" does not. Ciano, who believed that Chamberlain had staked his whole political future on the Easter Accords, feared that the British prime minister would be driven from power if Italy signed a military agreement with Germany and without Chamberlain in control, the British government would never recognize Italy's claim over Ethiopia. Suspecting that the *Anschluss* had already weakened Chamberlain, the Fascists now assumed that Hitler's visit to Italy had damaged Chamberlain's Italian policy even further. Thus, at the end of May Mussolini directed his foreign minister to strengthen Chamberlain's domestic-political position by making a speech in Milan on 2 June that reaffirmed Italy's commitment to the Easter Accords.[53]

The Fascist leadership's realization that Italy's armed forces could not yet successfully fight a continental war, at a time when Germany's designs on Czechoslovakia were clear, also contributed to Italy's preference not to sign a military accord with Germany. The head of the army's operations and planning section wrote a forceful memorandum arguing that Italy was not a dominant continental power and should not expect ever to achieve continental hegemony. Because its strength lay in the Mediterranean, Italy should instead aspire to become an oceanic power. By exploiting its position in Albania, Libya, and the Dodecanese, Italy could invade Egypt, conquer Suez, and gain mastery over the Red Sea. Then, from Ethiopia, Italy could launch a formidable challenge to the powers of the Indian Ocean. But in an imminent European war, Ronco warned, Italy could only act defensively along its continental frontier; no attacks on France or even Yugoslavia could be contemplated.[54]

Unwittingly perhaps, this army analysis elevated the influence of the navy in Italy. If the consensus was that Italy should aim to achieve the status of an oceanic power rather than a continental one, then the heaviest responsibility for fulfilling this goal should fall to the Regia Marina. Yet the Italian navy was anything but enthusiastic about the prospect of an imminent war in the Mediterranean. A dearth of raw materials at Italy's naval yards had retarded construction and had delayed the entry-into-service date of most of Italy's new warships, often by as much as ten months. In February 1938 the navy reported that the battleships *Vittorio Veneto* and *Littorio,* the keels of which were laid in October 1934, would enter service in December 1939 and February 1940 rather than in May–June 1939 as originally planned. Three months later it was revealed that the extensive modernizations of the battleships *Doria* and *Duilio* would each be delayed by two months, preventing them from joining the fleet until 1940. And in the infancy of the 1938–39 program, two-thirds of the planned Spica class of torpedo boats were already many months behind schedule.[55] Besides these operational problems, Cavagnari had difficulty financing the naval programs that the Gran Consiglio had endorsed. After Felice Guarneri, the minister for exchange and currency, told the Defense Committee in February that "we are bankrupt," the Ministry of Finance explained to Cavagnari that it could not fund 25 percent of the navy's budget. The naval chief was compelled to seek financial help from the Istituto per la Ricostruzione Industriale (IRI), the publicly controlled holding company that operated significant portions of Italy's banking, steelmaking, shipbuilding, and communications industries.[56]

Perhaps most important, the naval staff faced a formidable and frightening strategic dilemma in the event of a European war: the prospect of Anglo-French naval collaboration. Early in 1938 it became clear to Carlo Margottini, Italy's naval attaché in Paris, that the French Marine had recognized the value of a significant British naval presence in the Mediterranean and had begun to cultivate a constructive working relationship with the Royal Navy. Hector C. Bywater, Britain's foremost expert on the Royal Navy, had, according to the Italian naval attaché in London, publicly recommended that Britain prepare for the likelihood of an Anglo-Italian clash in the Mediterranean. The presence of hostile and coordinated British and French naval forces in the Mediterranean would imperil the Regia Marina's "essential" responsibility, as Admiral Bruto Brivonesi described it, of "assuring in every eventuality the communication between the mother country and the empire."[57]

The alarm expressed in these reports from London and Paris increased following Hitler's visit to Italy, the subsequent Nazi admission to the Fascists that Germany would soon disregard the limits imposed by the Anglo-German naval agreement, and the Kriegsmarine's request in July for formal Italian-German naval staff talks.[58] But Italian naval staff officials still questioned the size and fighting efficiency of the German navy and feared implying the existence of coordinated planning for an Axis naval war against the democracies. New Italian naval intelligence in early July concluded—wrongly, as it turned out—that the French and the British had agreed to naval staff talks in order to prepare their navies for an aero-naval war in the Mediterranean. For Cavagnari and his fellow fearful and defensively minded admirals, the prospect of Italy's being dragged by the Germans into a war over Czechoslovakia, only then to be attacked in the Mediterranean by Europe's two most formidable naval powers operating collaboratively, was distasteful—to say the least. Afraid of both throwing fuel on the democracies' alleged fire and irritating Mussolini and the Germans, the Stato Maggiore della Marina (SMM) resisted German proposals for high-level naval conversations and instead invited two German naval officers to tour Italian ports and shipyards.[59]

The Czechoslovak Crisis

Although Mussolini heeded the advice of Ciano and Cavagnari not to pursue an alliance with Germany during the summer of 1938, the Duce had not abandoned his moral commitment to the Axis. In fact he drew closer to the Nazis in mid-1938 as a result of his growing hatred for the "vile, base, and insignificant" democracies. The French press, which claimed in June and July that the Italians had deserted the Germans by not agreeing to an alliance, turned Mussolini "more decisively and openly anti-French" than ever before. Britain's reluctance, because of the conflict in Spain, to ratify the Easter Accords persuaded Ciano at the beginning of July that "a crisis in our relations with London is almost inevitable." By the middle of the month Mussolini had told his foreign minister, "I will do anything to sever relations with France and England—nothing can come from there besides putrefaction [*pourriture*]."[60]

Italy's antipathy for the two Western European democracies had both ideological and geostrategic roots. The British and French moves in 1938 to strengthen their ties with Turkey particularly upset the Italians. Both Britain and France recognized that the *Anschluss* had given Hitler control of the financial and communications center of the Danube—Vienna—as well as Austria's economic stake in the Balkans. This development bred consternation among officials in London and Paris who had seen Germany's economic penetration into southeastern Europe expand deliberately over the preceding few years. Since 1934 the Germans, through a complex system of exchange controls, fixed pricing, and barter agreements, had created a Danubian zone dependent on Germany to sell its manufactured goods and to purchase its foodstuffs, oil, and other raw materials. By 1937 the economies of Romania, Bulgaria, Hungary, and Yugoslavia were to various extents tied to the German economy, accounting for 16 percent of Germany's foreign trade. By contrast, the Balkans at that time made up just 2 percent of British trade.[61]

In London, Lord Lloyd of Dolobran, chairman of the British Council, became the principal advocate for improving British relations with Turkey and challenging German economic preponderance in the Balkans. Despite Chamberlain's initial reluctance to approve Turkey's request for British credit of six million pounds for new warships, Lloyd and the British ambassador in Ankara, Sir Percy Loraine, continued to press the FO on the urgency of the situation in Turkey.[62]This intensive lobbying effort soon won an important endorsement from Halifax. In early May the foreign secretary advocated an arrangement with Turkey, citing not the tension in the Mediterranean but the expanding German influence in the Balkans:

> Beyond Turkey . . . lie the lands of the Middle East (Syria, Iraq, Palestine, Saudi Arabia, Egypt) through which run our sea or air communications with India. . . . If Turkey fell, however reluctantly, within the German orbit . . . German influence would spread freely through the Middle East. . . . It is therefore scarcely too much to say that Turkey has become not the main, but the only obstacle to the *Drang nach Osten*.[63]

Halifax favored Britain's redressing the balance of power in the Danube by extending British loans and credits to the Balkan states and purchasing products such as Greek tobacco and Romanian wheat and oil. He feared that otherwise, "Central and South-East Europe would tend to become to Germany what . . . the Dominions are to the United Kingdom," which would satisfy most of Germany's strategic raw material and foodstuff needs, strengthen its economy, clear the path for German continental hegemony, and enable Hitler to withstand economic warfare. Focused entirely on the German threat to the Balkans—and not the Italian threat in the Mediterranean—Chamberlain recognized the political imperative of an economic accord with Turkey. As a result, the Anglo-Turkish guarantee and armaments credit agreement was signed on 27 May, extending industrial and arms credits of sixteen million pounds to Turkey. Within a month, Chamberlain was confident that this arrangement had "practically put [the Turks] in our pockets," thwarting Hitler's attempt to assert Germany's dominance over southeastern Europe.[64]

The French signed agreements with Turkey six weeks later. In contrast to the British, the French identified Turkey as a strategically important power in the eastern Mediterranean that could improve French security vis-à-vis Italy. Although Germany's economic designs on Turkey were important considerations, the French attached great significance to Turkey's responsibilities in the eastern Mediterranean and to reports that Turkey's leaders generally disliked the Italian Fascists. The Turks' ability to close the Black Sea to all warships during peacetime—a privilege accorded Turkey by the Montreux conference of June 1936—was particularly significant for the French. General Charles Huntziger, commander of the French forces in the Levant, argued that a friendly Turkey could ensure the security of regional territories and the liberty of traffic through the Suez Canal and the Dardanelles. Moreover, Turkey could help France neutralize or destroy the Italian bases in the Dodecanese, sever Italian communications with Libya, or conduct offensive sorties against the Italian navy and peninsula. Whereas the British concluded only an economic arrangement with the Turks, the French signed both a friendship treaty and a secret military accord on 3–4 July. These two treaties extended and reinforced the accords of 1930 and 1937 and committed the two powers to maintaining the security of the eastern Mediterranean and specifically the territorial integrity of Alexandretta, a Syrian-controlled Mediterranean port near the Turkish border.[65]

The Italians interpreted these British and French forays into Turkey as predatory and a sign that Turkey had chosen to associate with the democracies rather than the Axis powers. Although the Italians had been supplying the Turks with war matériel since March 1938, Ciano turned down the Turkish ambassador's offer for an eastern Mediterranean pact in June. Instead, the Italian foreign minister ironically encouraged the Turks to make a coup de main on Alexandretta because France's position on the continent precluded her from any military reaction. The news of the Franco-Turkish treaty, which eliminated the possibility of any Turkish assault against France in the eastern Mediterranean, inspired the Italians to bolster their diplomatic position on the Danube by corrupting the integrity of the Little Entente and thus "further isolating Prague and France." To this end, the Duce directed his diplomats to work for a Budapest-Bucharest understanding. This goal required nimble diplomatic maneuvering on Italy's part. Cozying up to Budapest and Bucharest resulted in an invitation to attend a Romanian conference relating to the Danube and an offer to sign a military agreement with Hungary, both of which Italy had to refuse so that relations with Germany and Yugoslavia were not jeopardized. But Italy's persistence in the Balkans yielded favorable results in Bled, Slovenia, on 23 August, when Hungary and the states of the Little Entente signed an agreement that recognized Hungary's parity of arms and renounced the use of force among the four nations. Ciano and Mussolini exulted in this manifestation of France's weakness in central Europe and Italy's role in facilitating German revanchism: "The Bled meeting has marked a new phase in the crumbling of the Little Entente. Czechoslovakia is isolated. The system of French friendships is completely upset."[66]

The Italians also tried to take advantage of Britain's difficulties in the Middle East during the summer of 1938. When full-scale rebellion broke out in Palestine, Mussolini directed Pariani to double the size of the Libyan garrison's Italian-army force, from 17,000 to 34,000 men, by September. The Duce insisted that Italy have two army corps in Libya—one facing French Tunisia and the other, Egypt—before the Sudeten crisis erupted into general war. This order effectively repudiated the Anglo-Italian Easter Accords, in which the Italians had agreed to reduce the Libyan garrison by 50 percent at a rate of 1,000 men per week until it reached peacetime levels.[67] Stunned by the reversal of Italy's Libyan policy, Britain's Colonial Office pressed for Egyptian reinforcements on 7 September to offset the troops recently sent from Egypt to Palestine and those recently returned from Egypt to the British Isles. The abrupt expansion of the Libyan garrison to 67,000 Italian and Arab soldiers—an increase of almost 20,000 men in less than a month—persuaded the British to arrange for the formation in India of an infantry brigade, a mechanized regiment of artillery, and a field company of sappers and miners. Had it not been for the Munich agreement, these forces would have been transferred to Egypt in early October.[68]

Mussolini also demonstrated domestically his allegiance to the Rome-Berlin Axis. The publication of the Manifesto of Race in the Roman newspaper *Giornale d'Italia* on 14 July shocked most Italians and even many in the Fascist Party. The Manifesto declared that Italians—in contrast to Jews—were Aryans; marriage to or sexual intercourse with a Jew was considered a threat to the racial superiority of the Italian people. Under no direct pressure from Hitler to enact racial laws, the Duce designed the Manifesto to inspire Italians both at home and abroad. Most important, he hoped to reinvigorate the troubled pacification of Abyssinia by legislating the superiority of the Italian race. As he explained in Trieste, "The racial problem . . . is related to the conquest of the empire; history teaches us that empires are conquered with arms, but held with prestige. And for prestige we need a clear, stern racial conscience, which establishes not only differences but clear superiority." The Duce also wanted his countrymen to adopt a militaristic, domineering spirit that would enable them to triumph in a European war.

Fascinated by the success of National Socialism, Mussolini identified Italy's Jews as the means by which native Italians would "learn to be less sympathetic, to become hard, implacable, hateful. In other words: masters." Although many Jews had been active in the Fascist Party since the early 1920s, Mussolini in September announced, "The Jewish world was, for sixteen years, in spite of our policy, an irreconcilable enemy of Fascism."[69]

Thus, the Italians approached the Czechoslovak crisis and the Munich conference committed to the Axis foreign policy yet apprehensive about embarking on a European war. At the end of August, soon after a report that Germany's officers anticipated imminent action in Czechoslovakia, the Italians hurriedly sent the Nazis additional war supplies, including torpedoes, bombs and antitank mines. Even though the Germans refused to reveal their specific plans to the Italians, Mussolini had decided that Italy would join Germany against the democracies if the British intervened and turned the war into a generalized, ideological conflict. Italy intended to "march on the Axis line."[70]

Although this represented the approach to the crisis taken by the Palazzo Venezia, many of the Duce's subordinates did not fall into line. In particular, the Regia Marina was the least cooperative of Italy's three services, effectively restraining Mussolini's ability to intervene in the event of war. During the summer the navy was informed that if war should come, it would have to secure Italian communications in the Mediterranean and Red Sea—consistent with naval planning since 1936—and augment an army offensive against Egypt. Confident that the navy could not successfully perform both these tasks, Cavagnari announced at the end of August that many of Italy's newest available warships, including the light cruiser *Duca degli Abruzzi,* had failed their initial trials and had to be returned to dry dock for premature repairs. Shortly after Mussolini mobilized Italy's armed forces, Cavagnari revealed to the Italian service chiefs that the Regia Marina desperately lacked fuel, estimating that it only had enough crude oil to conduct war for six months. Finally, Italian naval intelligence reemphasized in September that the "tested" Royal Navy and the "agitated" French Marine were prepared to act immediately and collaboratively in the Mediterranean. Additional reports indicated that the English people were more prepared for war than ever before and that the French military believed France should fight Germany sooner rather than later.[71]

For those in Italy uneasy about an imminent war alongside Germany against the democracies, this cascade of information—all within a span of two weeks—verged on catastrophic. Yet the majority of Italian naval intelligence from London and Paris profoundly overestimated the degree of Anglo-French naval collaboration in the Mediterranean. There is little evidence, and even less probability, that the British and French conscientiously deceived the Italian naval attachés. Instead, Italian naval intelligence generally reported what the cautious Italian naval leadership wanted to hear, allowing the SMM to reach its preferred conclusion: an offensive naval strategy in the Mediterranean would have dire consequences for the Regia Marina.

Reflecting his determination to avoid war, Cavagnari on 30 August ordered two Italian instructional vessels temporarily docked in Kiel and Hamburg to leave German waters immediately and return to Italy by way of Plymouth, England. The symbolism of Cavagnari's ships hurriedly evacuating German ports and seeking shelter in British waters, all as the Sudeten crisis was reaching a boiling point, went well noticed in Rome and especially in Berlin, where officials had fully expected a reaction to events in Czechoslovakia "analogous" to Italy's response to the *Anschluss.* Although the Fascists at the foreign ministry and the Palazzo Venezia bristled at Cavagnari's action and successfully compelled the admiral to mobilize the fleet beginning 25 September, Ciano admitted the following day that the navy would have to sustain the "formidable" shock of an Anglo-French coalition at the outset of war and recommended that Italy's mobilization be reconfigured to achieve an "armed neutrality."[72] Clearly, the Regia Marina played a significant role in Mussolini's decision to accept Chamberlain's 28 September invitation to negotiate a settlement at Munich.

Perhaps no other issue has been so widely studied in interwar diplomatic history as the Anglo-French response to the crisis that led to the Munich agreement of September 1938, which gave Nazi Germany control of the Sudetenland in Czechoslovakia in return for Hitler's promise not to make war; however, the historiography has excluded from the Munich story the degree to which the Mediterranean figured into the settlement.

Throughout the summer British commanders in the Mediterranean, who believed that "our primary object should be to influence Italy to remain neutral," failed to persuade officials in London to increase the strength of both the Mediterranean fleet and the ground and air units in Egypt. London accepted the proposed suspension of British participation in the Nyon patrols—a policy change the British kept secret from France and Italy—but the navy was directed to keep its patrols "in being," depriving the Mediterranean fleet of most of its destroyers for security operations near Gibraltar, Malta, and Alexandria.[73] During the Czech crisis, Admiral Pound requested additional land and air defenses for Gibraltar, Malta, and Haifa as well as the transfer of capital ships from Gibraltar to Alexandria "to safeguard the [Suez] Canal and discourage intervention by Mediterranean and Far East powers." Officials in London sent the aircraft carrier *Glorious* and the majority of the Mediterranean fleet to Alexandria but demanded that *Repulse* return to home waters and that *Hood* and two destroyer flotillas operate from Gibraltar and the western basin. The British left only one fighter squadron at Malta and refused to improve either Gibraltar's or Haifa's defenses. After the Admiralty explained that Italy's uncertain attitude and Britain's dearth of adequate information about France's dispositions and naval plans justified these decisions, Pound asserted that the weak and scattered Mediterranean fleet could not defend the entire Mediterranean, much less deter Italy from intervening.[74]

Contemporaneous discussions in London about the level of naval rearmament contributed to the decision to deny the Mediterranean fleet reinforcements in mid-1938. Throughout the spring and summer Duff Cooper and Simon bitterly argued over whether Britain could afford to build a fleet large enough to defeat Germany and Japan at the same time.[75] At a Cabinet meeting in July, Inskip suggested that Britain either change its foreign policy to eliminate the possibility of a two-ocean war or instruct the Admiralty to build a smaller fleet "with more slender resources than those deemed adequate by the naval experts." Despite vehement opposition from Duff Cooper and Samuel Hoare, Inskip had the important support of both Chamberlain and Simon. The Cabinet decided that the standard of naval strength had to be tailored to fit the available financial resources.[76]

These financial constraints and the fact that many large warships were undergoing refits or modernizations and none from the 1937 program had yet entered service compelled officials in London to deprive the Mediterranean of adequate forces to deter Italian intervention in a general war over Czechoslovakia. Moreover, these officials recognized that Britain's inability to defend its interests in the Mediterranean made Italian neutrality an absolute prerequisite for a successful British war effort. Since the navy could not guarantee that Italy would abstain from a conflict, pressure was placed on the political wing of policy. Yet the British predisposition to pursue a peaceful reconciliation with Italy also reinforced their decision not to bolster the Mediterranean fleet to a level that could have adequately deterred Italian intervention. A strengthening of the Mediterranean fleet would have implied a British concern that the Italians could enter a war against the Allies, effectively imploding the rationale for pursuing a Mediterranean appeasement. To maintain the coherence of their foreign policy, the British could not seriously consider a Mediterranean naval reinforcement during the Czech crisis.

Despite the elevation of Italy's anti-French rhetoric in May and June, the Foreign Office retained its faith in a friendly Italy and now urged with more vigor that Britain ratify the Easter Accords, regardless of the state of affairs in Spain. Nichols, Ingram, and Perth agreed that "if HMG fail to bring the recently concluded agreement with Italy into force . . . the definite and final division of Europe into two opposing camps may become unavoidable," and in that circumstance a European war would quickly spread to the Mediterranean.[77]

The strength of these arguments increased during the Czech crisis, when war against Germany seemed likely. Fearful of facing the Italian-German coalition in war and convinced that Germany's lead in antiair defenses was gradually shrinking, General Hastings Ismay, secretary to the CID, recommended that Britain avoid confrontation at all costs in favor of fighting Germany in six to twelve months. In case Germany insisted on war now, Air Chief Marshall Sir Cyril Newall told Halifax, provoking Italy to join the fray against Britain should be avoided, and anything to persuade Italy to remain neutral should be pursued: "In the initial stages of war with Germany, it is of the highest importance that Italy should be kept out, so that we have time to develop our defensive position in the Middle East, having in mind possible future eventualities both in the Mediterranean and Far East."[78]

The foreign secretary was sympathetic to these points of view. Sir Noel Charles at the British embassy in Rome had assured Halifax in late August that Britain's ratification of the Easter Accords and economic support of Italy would guarantee Italian neutrality. Less than two weeks later, after a brief tour of northern Italy, Halifax adopted the same perspective: "The Italians are in a German mesh from which they dearly would like to extricate themselves, but are quite unable to do so without substantial help from Great Britain." In other words, both strategy-and policymakers in London desired either a peaceful settlement or at least an appeased Italy. The decision by Britain's "Inner Executive" for the Czech crisis—Chamberlain, Halifax, Hoare, and Simon—to invite Mussolini to broker a settlement at Munich seemingly accomplished both these aims.[79]

Largely in response to the mobilization of German, French, and Italian forces, Britain mobilized the Royal Navy on 27 September, two days before Chamberlain signed the Munich agreement. Although Pound later told Chatfield that "the mobilization went off extremely well and was a wonderful experience for everybody," the admiral's optimistic appraisal was no doubt a consequence of the Munich settlement itself.[80] The widely dispersed and weak Mediterranean fleet and the absence of any coordination with the Marine Nationale indicated that had war broken out in the Mediterranean as a result of the Sudeten crisis, Britain and France could have conducted operations against the Axis powers only in an ad hoc fashion.

In contrast to the British, the French approached the role of Italy and the Mediterranean in the Czech crisis with much consternation. In particular, decision-makers in France struggled with the hypothesis of an Axis war against France and Czechoslovakia. By the end of the summer the Czech crisis in France had evolved beyond a consideration about the future of the Sudetenland to encompass the distinct possibility of general war. Planning for that war—or how to avoid it—in many ways superseded all other French policy problems in August and September.

Bonnet, who had told the Czech minister in Paris that France would not go to war over the Sudetenland and who believed that France had to search for peace, attached great significance to Blondel's reports that Italian public opinion remained opposed to fighting alongside the Germans and would prevent Mussolini from intervening in such a war. Without Italy, Germany would not embark on a two-front war against France and Czechoslovakia. Adopting a view shared by Chamberlain, Bonnet argued that a successful appeasement of Italy would avert war.[81] Not everyone in French policy circles agreed with Bonnet. France's representative at the Vatican, Charles-Roux, conceded that public opinion in Italy disliked the Fascist government's treatment of France and its association with Germany but stressed that public opinion had little if any influence on the whims of the Fascist leadership. Germany and Italy, repeated Charles-Roux, were now definitively aligned with one another: "The evolution was rapid and very pronounced."[82]

Many influential Quai d'Orsay officials, such as Léger, Massigli, and Paul Comert, found Charles-Roux's analysis more compelling than Blondel's. A heated debate ensued at the foreign ministry on this issue and further enraged those opposed to Bonnet's foreign policy in general. As a result of their strong criticisms of French appeasement policy toward Germany *and* Italy, Comert resigned, and after Munich, Massigli was reassigned to Turkey as ambassador. Bonnet deemed Léger, an old friend of Daladier's who had documents hand-delivered to the premier twice daily, too politically powerful to dismiss. Lamenting the "return to power of the extreme Right elements" in France, Charles-Roux reported that the Fascists had "rejoiced" at the news of these changes at the Quai and suggested that the Italians now believed "Daladier's Cabinet was serving the interests of Italian Fascism."[83]

A similar though less contentious dispute also transpired among French strategists. Despite Daladier's order in June to reinforce Corsica in anticipation of a war in the Mediterranean, both air and army chiefs argued that a flurry of French activity on Corsica might provoke an otherwise unplanned Italian attack. French intelligence now believed that Germany would invade Czechoslovakia by the end of September, but no similar warnings had arrived from Italy. Moreover, France could not spare the antiaircraft guns necessary to secure Corsica. As Gamelin explained to the premier in late August, "I do not refuse to recognize that the island can eventually be used as a base for offensive aerial action against central Italy . . . [but] I consider it inopportune now to reinforce Corsica's antiair defenses by reducing those in the metropolis."[84] At the same time General Bührer, chief of the colonial general staff, demanded that the Marine assume additional responsibilities in the defense of France's eastern colonies. Darlan was agitated by Bührer's implication that the French army and air force had to defend against a German incursion and the navy's task was to secure imperial coastlines. What about the Marine's role in attacking Italy or, at the very least, defending France against an Italian attack in the Mediterranean or a German attack on French shipping in the Atlantic? Darlan refused categorically to redistribute any of his forces outside the western Mediterranean and the Atlantic.[85]

Increasingly, as the Sudeten controversy escalated, Darlan "found himself in a tunnel, following his own inclinations," as French naval historian Philippe Masson has written.[86] He became completely alienated from his army, air force, and colonial counterparts, who believed that France had no choice but to abandon Czechoslovakia and to make peace with Germany. Yet the naval chief neither languished in his isolation nor submitted to his colleagues' resignation. Instead, he took steps to prepare his own forces for what French naval intelligence believed was a likely, impending scenario: an Anglo-French war against Germany and Italy. Beginning on 1 September 1938, without any formal instruction from the government and as discreetly as possible, Darlan brought the Marine into a state of semimobilization. By 7 September half of the fleet was prepared to act immediately on Darlan's orders, while the other half remained on forty-eight–hours' notice. More than two weeks later, on 25 September, Daladier ordered the partial mobilization of France's armed forces.[87]

In the meantime, Darlan and his staff continued to press their case for an assertive Mediterranean war strategy. Conceding that "we must consider Germany as the master of the game against our interests," the admiral argued that France and Britain had to evaluate Germany's recent actions to determine the nature of any future conflict with Germany. Such an analysis revealed that German objectives were essentially strategic:

> Enclosed in the North Sea, the Reich needed a geographically well-placed ally to act against our empire and our maritime communications. Germany chose Italy, which cuts the Franco-British empires and maritime routes in two. Germany annexed Austria to communicate directly with Italy and the Mediterranean. Germany obtained the friendship of Franco to have at its disposal the northwest coast of Spain, the coast along the Gibraltar Straits, the Canary islands, and the Spanish territories in Mauritania. Germany concluded an ideological pact with Japan to inconvenience Britain and France eventually in the Far East and the Indian Ocean.

To defeat Britain and France, Darlan reasoned, Germany would have to destroy the British and French imperial systems, since "British and French salvation depends strictly on the cohesion of their empires and the security of their maritime routes." This German perspective indicated that the Mediterranean would become the central theater in an Axis war against Britain and France. Reiterating what he had pressed for the previous fall, Darlan explained that "our line of conduct is well sketched: we must first of all neutralize or destroy Italy (whose attitude is not currently in doubt) and Franco's Spain (absent certain guarantees that could be given to us), which constitute the two principal obstacles to Franco-British communications." Specifically, in the event of a general European war, Darlan called for an Anglo-French offensive against Spanish Morocco, the Balearics, Libya, and the Italian peninsula. "If we succeed in the operations and we close the Atlantic to Germany, we will breathe freely; Yugoslavia, Greece, Bulgaria, and Romania will march with us, as in 1918; Germany will succumb asphyxiated. If we do not succeed, we can only make peace, because our troops, particularly those in the Northeast, will be paralyzed." But all of this depended ultimately on an Anglo-French alliance, something that the British had scrupulously avoided. In fact it was not until 27 September, only hours before the Munich conference, that a definitive liaison between the British and French naval staffs was established.[88]

[3]

"The natural aspirations of the Italian people": October 1938–March 1939

Reactions to Munich

Daladier left Munich with the strong sense that he had been swindled. He referred to the British prime minister as that "desiccated stick," whose notion of appeasement he had never shared. The Anglo-French staff talks, for which Daladier had accepted the terms of the Munich agreement, were extremely limited in scope. He believed, on reflection, that the loss of an important ally in eastern Europe and the damage to France's eastern-front strategy were staggering concessions. Upon his return to France, Daladier—"eyes turned down, seemingly overwhelmed, prostrated"—was greeted by a throng of people cheering the premier for saving the peace. Speaking through clenched teeth, he commented, "These people are fools." Turning to his aides Léger and Jacques Raphaël-Leygues, he added, "Don't have any illusions. This is only a respite, and if we don't make use of it, we will all be shot."[1]

Also accompanying Daladier on 1 October in Bourget was Georges Bonnet, who reacted to the crowd's applause with a radiant smile, an energetic wave, and obvious pride. Perhaps no French statesman reveled in the Munich agreement as much as the foreign minister, with whom the desire in Paris to avoid war was identified most closely. Bonnet viewed the international landscape after Munich as tremendously conducive for achieving a French rapprochement with both Germany and Italy; France's political, military, and financial weakness left her no choice but to pursue accommodation with the dictator states. Fearing that the "next Munich" would lead to war, Bonnet sought to trade Germany the freedom to expand into Central and Eastern Europe with an agreement to respect the Franco-German frontier. In mid-October the foreign minister told Phipps that France "must no longer be exposed to the danger of being involved in war on behalf of Soviet Russia or Poland as a result of circumstances over which she has no control." Most who remained at the Quai d'Orsay after Munich shared this conviction. Léon Noël and Robert Coulondre, ambassadors to Poland and the Soviet Union respectively, each argued that France should reconsider her ties with Eastern Europe. Even Charles Rochat, a supporter of Léger and deputy director of the political and commercial affairs department at the Quai, recommended that France search for a method to limit her obligations in Eastern Europe.[2]

As much as European peace would rely on a Franco-German reconciliation, Bonnet knew it would also depend on a settlement of outstanding Franco-Italian differences. In contrast to the British, who envisioned Mussolini as a conduit to Hitler, the necessary intermediary step in the appeasement of Germany, the Quai approached Germany and Italy as two separate problems to be solved in similar ways. France had to accommodate Italy without sacrificing French security, either on the continent or in the empire. Although the French government had never ratified the Laval-Mussolini agreements of 1935, Bonnet believed that the issues discussed therein—along with those related to Ethiopia and Spain—held the key to repairing Franco-Italian relations. A Franco-Italian rapprochement would be attainable, according to the foreign minister, once the Spanish and Ethiopian affairs were resolved and after France consented to an Italian protectorate in Tunisia, Italian ownership of that part of the Djibouti–Addis Ababa railway that passed through Ethiopia, and an Italian representative on the Suez Canal board.

To ensure that this Italian policy garnered French diplomatic support, Bonnet transferred André François-Poncet from Berlin to Rome. Although not a career diplomat, François-Poncet had weathered eight tumultuous years in Germany. He was a top graduate of the Ecole Normale Supérieure who had married well, become an important player in the French steel industry, and moved laterally into the diplomatic corps. From Berlin, where he was thought to be Hitler's favorite foreign ambassador, he wrote lengthy dispatches about Nazi Germany's determination to redress its grievances as well as Hitler's high regard for Mussolini. The ambassador's conviction that France could and should reach a lasting modus vivendi with the Fascists persuaded Bonnet that François-Poncet would be the perfect French representative in Italy. France ended two years without official representation in Italy when François-Poncet assumed his new post on 7 November. Soon thereafter he presented his letters of accreditation to Vittorio Emanuele III and officially recognized the Italian monarch as emperor of Ethiopia.[3]

The new French ambassador arrived in Rome under inauspicious conditions. The Duce was not fond of him and before their first official meeting Mussolini told Ciano, "I will do everything to help him break his head. I do not like him." When Italy's Servizio Informazioni Militari (SIM) intercepted a private François-Poncet letter that described the Fascists as "servants who have become bosses," Mussolini's dislike turned to genuine hatred. After November 1938 the Duce refused to receive him and would not even acknowledge him at diplomatic receptions. Yet it was François-Poncet's nationality, rather than his opinions, that most influenced the Duce's antipathy. Raffaello Guariglia, the newly appointed ambassador to France, was instructed to approach affairs in Paris with a wait-and-see attitude. When Guariglia asked what the Duce considered Italy's mission in France to be, Ciano replied curtly, "Nothing." And when Guariglia assumed an assertive role in Franco-Italian relations during the winter of 1939, Mussolini arranged for his retirement.[4]

Nevertheless, the French ambassador in Rome remained optimistic about initiating an honest Franco-Italian dialogue that could facilitate regular consultation among Europe's four great powers. François-Poncet was particularly struck by the Fascists' resolve over Spain and lack of appreciation for France's recognition of Ethiopia. Expecting the Italians to raise all the issues outstanding since 1935, he was determined to work toward their resolution. But Ciano indicated that only a French renunciation of support for Republican Spain would clear the way for a Franco-Italian rapprochement. Even though the ambassador admitted that domestic politics would not allow France to abandon the Spanish Republic, he remained convinced that the Italian public opinion's distaste for Nazism and Mussolini's desire for increased liberty of maneuver vis-à-vis Hitler would eventually pave the way for a solution to the current Franco-Italian dilemma. By satisfying Italian colonial ambitions and affirming French strength and commitment to European peace, France could easily draw Mussolini out of Hitler's orbit. These French diplomats hoped to avoid war but also appreciated that, if war came, France could survive only with the help of alliances. A Franco-Italian reconciliation would improve the chances for an Anglo-French alliance and, most important, would make an alliance with the Soviet Union less imperative. An ideological preference for Italian Fascism over Soviet Communism, as well as a fear of war with Germany and a desire for a British alliance, motivated French conservatives to seek to improve relations with Italy. Ironically, François-Poncet and many others in Paris who shared Bonnet's political convictions did not recognize that the Spanish issue—for both ideological and geostrategic reasons—was a fundamental element of Fascist foreign policy. As Ciano confessed to his diary, "Those fools who have tried so hard to find fault with our intervention in Spain will one day perhaps understand that on the Ebro, at

Barcelona, and at Malaga were laid the foundations of the Roman Mediterranean empire."[5]

The policy and strategy reassessment that took place in London after Munich was more dramatic yet less unanimous than that which simultaneously occurred in Paris. Upon returning from Munich, Chamberlain told his Cabinet that his diplomacy had triumphed: he had orchestrated a meeting of representatives from the four major European powers that had resolved the Sudeten crisis. The prime minister wrote to Maurice Hankey, now retired from his position as Cabinet secretary but still an ardent Chamberlain supporter, that "we have at last laid the foundations of a stable peace" and confided to his sister, "We have avoided the greatest catastrophe." Despite the resignation of Duff Cooper and threats of departure from Oliver Stanley and Walter Crookshank, Chamberlain remained entirely confident in the correctness of his "making terms with dictators" policy, adding, "I see no one else who can do it."[6]

Chamberlain's policy of appeasement soon came under attack from many corners. Encouraged by a number of Conservative MPs, such as Winston Churchill, Harold Macmillan, and Brendan Bracken, who remained skeptical of Hitler's willingness to abide by international agreements, many members of the Cabinet urged the government to accelerate the pace of British rearmament. Chamberlain responded defiantly: appeasement derived from Britain's economic and financial frailty; since Britain could not afford massive rearmament, it must instead seek peaceful conflict resolution. Increasing British rearmament would not only incite an arms race, divide Europe into antagonistic blocs, and destroy the credibility of his appeasement policy but would also bankrupt Britain. Still, the prime minister agreed to consider what the services believed they needed "to repair the gaps." The navy asked the government to bolster its fleet of smaller vessels and to postpone the scrapping of the Royal Sovereign battleship class. The army wanted an adequately equipped field force for use on the continent and a fully equipped Territorial Volunteer Army. The Royal Air Force (RAF) demanded the immediate order of 1,850 fighters and 1,750 bombers. In response, the minister for the coordination of defense claimed that the proposals would "threaten that stability which is, after all, in our experience probably our strongest weapon of war." The chancellor of the exchequer opposed the building of heavy bombers, warning the newly formed Committee on Defence Programs and Their Acceleration that the "far reaching proposals now under consideration might have literally stupendous results on the financial stability of the country."[7]

Although the Foreign Office accepted the limited utility of "making terms with dictators," it shared the military's desire to accelerate British rearmament, believing that a stronger Britain could deter Germany from attacking

Western Europe. In effect, the FO proposed that Britain and Germany assume separate and nonconflicting spheres of influence over the European continent, with Britain protecting the West and Germany dominating the East—what one scholar has described as Britain's "Defence of the West" policy. The Munich settlement, according to Strang, had left Central and Eastern Europe "open to German political and economic domination." Laurence Collier of the FO's Central Department suggested that Britain entirely concede this region to the Germans. After Cadogan endorsed these policy prescriptions, Halifax at the beginning of November explained to Phipps that neither overt appeasement of nor resistance to Germany would prove productive: "It is one thing to allow German expansion in Central Europe, which to my mind is a normal and natural thing, but we must be able to resist German expansion in Western Europe or else our whole position is undermined."[8]

Despite this varied opposition, Chamberlain rejected any significant adjustment of his policy. The prime minister reluctantly accepted small increases in existing armament programs but refused to increase the scope of the programs themselves. He was even less accommodating about the FO's Realpolitik arguments, which he repudiated on principle—a principle that was closely related to Britain's increasingly threatened interests in the Far East. In late October the Japanese capture of both Canton and Hankow had given them exclusive authority over the eastern Yangtse. All the most important strategic outposts in China now belonged to Japan. On 3 November the Japanese proposed the creation of a "new order" in East Asia based on Japan's control of China and Manchukuo. If Britain ceded control of Eastern Europe to Germany, would it also allow Japan to exercise influence over the Far East? Would that mean the demise of the British Empire? This imperial argument garnered the prime minister support from a parliamentary majority, which gave him all the confidence he needed to pursue British "relations with the dictator powers, which will lead to a settlement in Europe and to a sense of stability."[9]

The first tangible expression of the renewed appeasement policy was the Cabinet's request of Parliament in late October to ratify the Easter Accords. The Foreign Office viewed this decision as compatible with its "Defence of the West" policy. Halifax believed that whereas Britain and France should secure their own "predominant positions" in Western Europe, Italy should be granted autonomy in the Mediterranean: "Although we do not expect to detach Italy from the Axis, we believe the agreement will increase Mussolini's freedom of maneuver and so make him less dependent on Hitler, and therefore freer to resume the classic Italian role of balancing between Germany and the western powers."[10]

Instead of defending the Mediterranean, the Foreign Office accepted Chamberlain's policy of relinquishing it to the goodwill of the Fascists. Thus, the FO's definition of the "West" *excluded* the Mediterranean. For all its differences with Chamberlain after Munich, the FO still believed that Mussolini could and should be appeased. Even though Chamberlain and the Foreign Office fundamentally misunderstood the Fascist regime's ideological and geostrategic priorities—partially as a result of their own conservative politics—the British needed to believe that a peaceful reconciliation with Mussolini was possible. Britain lacked the resources necessary to defend the British Isles, the Mediterranean, and the Far East. Confronting Italian expansion in the Mediterranean would have required close coordination—perhaps even an alliance—with France. Equally important, defending the Mediterranean would have implied that the stability of Britain's most important supply and communications route to the Far East was in jeopardy—an admission the British could not bear to make.

The Munich conference profoundly influenced Mussolini's foreign policy. As the "mediator" between the democracies and Germany, he found himself at the center of the world stage and, at least in his own mind, the ultimate arbiter of peace. Nothing pleased the Duce more than seeing his picture and name prominently displayed throughout the international press. According to Mussolini, Italy had finally attained the long-awaited recognition and prestige rightfully accorded a great power. But the more significant consequence of Munich was the effect it had on Mussolini's understanding of Europe's other great powers. The Duce believed that the democracies' pathetically weak reaction to Hitler's military threats manifested Germany's material and psychological superiority over Britain and France, and France's abandonment of one of its principal central European allies showed such pusillanimity that Mussolini expected the French soon to concede all of Eastern Europe to the Germans.[11]

Mussolini was not only envious of and impressed by Hitler's successful revanchism and revisionism but also frightened by it: the Italians had to join the German steamroller before it turned against Italy and, to prevent being marginalized by the Reich, Italy also had to expand its Mediterranean empire quickly. Less than a week after returning from Munich Mussolini convened a Gran Consiglio meeting to discuss the "Jewish problem" and its role in strengthening Nazi-Fascist solidarity. Claiming to have been an anti-Semite since the age of twenty-five, he accused the Jews of constituting what remained of the anti-Fascist opposition in Italy. Italo Balbo, governor general of Libya and former head of the Regia Aeronautica, Luigi Federzoni, president of the Senate, and General De Bono opposed Mussolini's proposal to place Italy's Jews under restrictions and prohibitions. Mussolini conceded that Italian racial purity and the existence of a Jewish peril were absurd notions but insisted that the anti-Semitic measures had important symbolic meaning: "The discriminatory measures do not matter. We need simply to raise the problem. Now anti-Semitism has been injected into the blood of the Italians. It will continue by itself to circulate and develop." Supported by every other member of the Consiglio, including Bottai, the discriminatory laws were approved. Public confirmation of the Consiglio's decision came on 10 November; in a series of decrees announced six days later the state now prohibited Jews from entering the professions and government service, marrying non-Jews, and employing non-Jews. On 21 November the Fascist Party expelled its Jewish members.[12]

Although Mussolini wanted to persuade his fellow dictator that Italy sympathized with the Reich ideologically, he and Ciano resisted Ribbentrop's frequent prodding in favor of a rigid Italian-German military alliance. Munich had persuaded the Nazi regime that war against the western democracies was inevitable and that alliances should be prepared accordingly. German war-gaming exercises in the fall of 1938 anticipated that Germany, Italy, and Japan would be allies in a coalition war against Britain and France. Having established particularly close political relations with Italy, Japan, and Spain, the Nazis were sanguine about a future war against Britain. In fact the German Seekriegsleitung argued in October 1938 that "Italy's active participation [would] improve the prospects of [German and Italian] oceanic cruiser warfare since the English sea routes in the Mediterranean [would] no longer be used, and ships [would] have to take the route round Africa." The naval staff even suggested to Germany's political leadership that Italy could eliminate British supremacy in the Mediterranean and destroy the British position in the Middle East and eventually in India.[13]

Italy's reluctance to sign an alliance with Germany did not reflect the Fascists' desire to keep open the possibility of an alliance with the West or a determination to remain Europe's peacemaker. Rather, the Fascists argued that a formal alliance with Germany was unnecessary because the totalitarian states were not at risk, and dangerous because it could be interpreted as a pact of aggression: "The alliance exists in practice. Why open the door to rumor with a pact whose only consequence would be to attract hatred against us as the provocateur?" The Italians wanted to extract as many colonial concessions as possible from the democracies, reserving war for those imperial goals that could not be acquired peacefully. This strategy would also provide additional time to improve Italy's military's preparedness for a general European war. Moreover, the Duce lamented that the Italian people would not yet respond enthusiastically to a military alliance with Germany.

Most Italians had been disgusted by the events of 9–10 November 1938, the anti-Jewish pogrom known as *Kristallnacht*. All over Germany, synagogues had been burnt or damaged, Jewish shops and offices looted, and windows smashed. Twenty thousand Jews had been arrested and incarcerated. Nevertheless, Mussolini privately expressed his approval of the Nazi *Kristallnacht* and advanced arrangements for an Italian-German cultural agreement that was signed on 23 November.[14]

Tension between Germany and Italy in the Danubian basin after Munich likely contributed to the Fascists' desire to postpone a formal alliance. In October Mussolini assumed the role of protector for the Hungarians, who at that time had designs on Slovakia, Ruthenia, and other areas in eastern Czechoslovakia that possessed significant Magyar populations. But the Germans, as a result of their recent Sudeten acquisition and future aspirations, supported the rump Czechoslovakian refusal to cede any territory to Hungary and opposed any sort of negotiated settlement of the matter. Nevertheless, Mussolini endorsed limited Hungarian claims on eastern Czechoslovakia because he and his foreign minister believed that a common Polish-Hungarian border—and perhaps eventually a Polish-Hungarian coalition—would retard Germany's march through Eastern Europe and allow Italy to strengthen its position in the Balkans. Finally, after almost a month of tense Italian-German conversations on the Czech-Hungarian problem, Ciano told Ribbentrop that the Czech-Magyar conflict should not divide Germany and Italy because it proved "the fact that all Franco-British influence in Danubian and Balkan Europe has collapsed forever." In Vienna on 3 November the Czech and Hungarian foreign ministers accepted Ciano's map, which allocated the southern strip of Ruthenia to Hungary. The Vienna conference prevented conflict from erupting but did not relieve the Ruthenian tension, which would not be resolved until the German acquisition of Bohemia and Moravia in March 1939.[15]

Military difficulties in both East Africa and Spain were additional Italian motives for delaying an alliance with Germany. Recognizing that the lingering affairs in Ethiopia and Spain were damaging Italy's ability to participate in a general European war, Mussolini believed that the conclusion of these two conflicts should precede an Axis military alliance. General Cavallero's army had swept through Ethiopia's Gojam province during the first half of 1938 and annihilated almost all of Abebe Aregai's 14,000 guerrillas. Their leader survived the onslaught, however, and many of Cavallero's exhausted and abused Ethiopian Askaris deserted to the guerrillas. Abebe Aregai's new band of rebels was also supplemented by anti-Fascist Italian veterans sent by the Comintern and the Deuxième Bureau, most of whom operated as intelligence agents, monitoring Italian radio traffic. But since much of that was not transmitted in code, the Ethiopian guerrillas in late 1938 steadily improved their performance against the Italians. Cavallero's final attempt to crush the Abebe Aregai insurgency in January–March 1939 failed dismally, compelling Mussolini and the Duke of Aosta to institute a pacification strategy based on political persuasion rather than military force.[16]

In Spain the July 1938 suspension of the Nationalist advance on Valencia to counter the surprise Republican attack across the Ebro had again disappointed the Fascist leadership. Finally, in November the Nationalists—supported by a strong contingent of CTV artillery and tanks as well as Italian aircraft—defeated the Republicans at the Ebro, giving Franco the opportunity to conquer Catalonia. At the end of January 1939 Italian-led Nationalist forces, under the command of Brigadier General Gastone Gambara, entered Barcelona. Two weeks later they reached the foothills of the Pyrenees. Mussolini now believed that the interminable Spanish conflict was nearing its end.[17]

Italian Claims on France

By mid-November Chamberlain was persuaded by a series of events—Germany's obstructionism over delineating the new Czech frontiers, Hitler's Saarbrücken speech in mid-October assailing peace, Joseph Goebbels's attack on British rearmament and the British press, the anti-Jewish pogroms of 9–10 November, and intelligence claiming that Hitler would soon target the British Empire—that the Munich agreement, alas, did not represent the triumph of peace in Europe. Both the FO and the COS now feared that France—weakened internationally by the collapse of its eastern alliance system and domestically by a crippling general strike that had virtually halted French rearmament—would not support Britain in a European war.[18]

Chamberlain decided that he had to reestablish French faith in his policy of appeasement—a policy that was now focused on Italy—and in a letter to his sister described his intention to visit Paris in late November:

> I felt it the right thing for many reasons—to give the French people an opportunity of passing out their pent up feelings of gratitude and affection, to strengthen Daladier and encourage him to do something at last to put his country's defenses in order and to pull his people into greater unity, to show France and Europe too that if we were more anxious to make friends with Germany and Italy we were not on that account going to forget our old allies, and finally to make it possible for me to go to Rome in January which is what I am trying to arrange.

Italy had become the centerpiece of Britain's policy because, in the wake of Munich and Germany's improved position in Eastern Europe, Italy could help secure Western Europe and could temper Germany's ambitions. Moreover, a peaceful Mediterranean was required to maintain the integrity of Britain's Far Eastern empire. Halifax explained to the FPC that Britain, even allied with France, could not—nor should it—prevent Germany from expanding into Eastern Europe. Though lamentable, this revanchism was acceptable because no British interests were at risk there. "We must, however, become as strong as possible and aim at securing the vital cord of the British Empire, namely, our communication through the Mediterranean by ensuring the friendship and goodwill of Portugal, Spain, Italy, Greece, Turkey, and Egypt, to which we could certainly add the Dominions and probably the United States."[19] For the sake of imperial stability and continuity, Britain had to pursue a general Mediterranean appeasement, and as the international situation had recently demonstrated, France would have to assume a positive role in the development of this British policy.

The French, besides asking for "greater support from Great Britain in the event of German attack on Great Britain or France," exhibited an intense anxiety over the lingering Spanish issue. Security for France was not limited to the western front and Germany; Italy and, by extension, Spain had become essential elements of French apprehensions after Munich. The premature British ratification of the Easter Accords, after Italy had repatriated fewer than half of its Spanish volunteers, infuriated the French. Suggesting in his talks with Chamberlain and Halifax that France and Britain propose a Spanish armistice, Daladier ranted that "the attitude of the Italian government in Spain is incomprehensible. If it has no desire to profit in Spain, why does it continue to intervene? Does it have an ulterior motive? Does it wish to ensure for itself an open port in the Balearics that would also permit it to intercept French communications with North Africa?" The British insisted that such a proposal would be useless without first reaching durable Anglo-Italian and Franco-Italian ententes. According to Chamberlain, "Spain has ceased to be a menace of Europe."[20]

Meanwhile, Mussolini decided that the time had arrived for Italy again to pursue his colonial ambitions in the Mediterranean. Not only had Ribbentrop and the Germans repeatedly assured Italy that they expected the Mediterranean soon to become a *mare italiano,* but the British had agreed to ratify the Easter Accords before the Spanish affair was completely "settled," without a reduction of Italy's Libyan garrison, and absent a complementary Franco-Italian agreement.[21] Naturally, then, the only great European power still standing in Italy's imperial path was France. The day after Perth announced Britain's intentions to ratify the Easter Accords, Mussolini and Ciano decided to claim Mediterranean concessions from the French, specifically at Djibouti, Tunisia, Corsica, and Suez, and to denounce the Franco-Italian agreement of 1935 in order to "synchronize our demands with the German colonial claims." At a meeting of the Gran Consiglio in late November, Mussolini repeated what he had told his foreign minister three weeks before:

> I announce to you the immediate goals of Fascist dynamism. As we have avenged Adowa, so we will avenge Valona. Albania will become Italian. . . . Then, for our security requirements in this Mediterranean that still confines us, we need Tunisia and Corsica. The frontier must be moved to the Var [River]. I do not aim for Savoy because it is outside the circle of the Alps. But I have my eye on Ticino, because Switzerland has lost its cohesive force and is destined one day, like so many small nations, to be demolished. All this is a program. I cannot fix the timetable. I merely indicate the directions of the march.[22]

Although De Bono, the highest-ranking general to join the Fascist movement before the 1922 March on Rome, concluded that "we can conduct a true imperial policy only in agreement with England," the Duce and his deputy thought otherwise. Mussolini told Ciano, "In Europe the Axis remains fundamental. In the Mediterranean we will collaborate with the English only as long as we can." This statement reaffirmed what the Duce had said in late October about the Anglo-Italian agreement: "I attribute no importance to [the Easter Accords] but it is desired by the still existing half-million of cowardly bourgeoisie upon whom I will unleash my third wave." On the morning of Mussolini's secret foreign policy speech to the Gran Consiglio, 30 November, Ciano spoke in the Chamber of "the natural aspirations of the Italian people" in the Mediterranean. Immediately, the deputies rose and shouted, "Tunis, Corsica, Nice, Savoy." Two weeks later, on 17 December, Ciano informed François-Poncet that Italy considered the 1935 Franco-Italian agreement "juridically, politically, and historically superseded."[23]

France reacted indignantly to Ciano's speech and Italy's denunciation of the Laval-Mussolini agreement. The Quai d'Orsay impressed upon both the British Foreign Office and the Italian Foreign Ministry that France had no intention of ceding any French territory to Italy. François-Poncet told Ciano that Italy had no legitimate claim beyond those stipulated in the 1935 accord. Even Bonnet made it clear to the British that France would refuse to participate in any conversation with Italy that addressed any issue beyond those of the 1935 agreement, recognizing that Italy "wants to makes its claims an international problem that would be settled to our detriment by a compromise that would either constrain us morally in our territories or risk our isolation." Corbin told the Foreign Office that Italy was attempting to drive a permanent wedge between Britain and France.[24]

Despite these French concerns, Chamberlain remained committed to his policy. On the same day that Ciano publicly demanded French concessions to Italy, the British prime minister told his Cabinet that "as the prospects for appeasement were not very bright in Berlin, it might be useful that [he and Halifax] should visit Rome." When Franco-Italian tensions subsequently escalated as a result of Ciano's claims, Chamberlain attempted to divorce Britain from this "Mediterranean conflict." He told the Commons that the British would not necessarily aid the French if Italy attacked France. A reconciliation with Italy was more important than an alliance with France for preserving the British Empire's integrity. Mussolini, Chamberlain explained to his sister, was now perhaps the only person who could mitigate Hitler's ambitions: "I feel that Rome at the moment is the end of the Axis on which it is easiest to make an impression. . . . An hour or two *tête-à-tête* with Musso[lini] might be extraordinarily valuable in making plans for talks with Germany."[25]

By contrast, France immediately demonstrated publicly its resolute opposition to Italian claims against France. During the first week of January Daladier visited Corsica, Tunis, and Algiers, where he declared that France would surrender "neither an acre of her territory nor any of her rights." At the same time France reinforced Djibouti and the eastern frontier of Tunisia. Upon his return to Paris Daladier told the Chamber that French security was incompatible with any sort of "renunciation" policy.[26] Less politically conservative and more fearful of the Fascist threat than the British, the French government refused to relinquish its Mediterranean empire and did not believe doing so would prevent—or necessarily improve France's chances in—a European war.

The British faced a disturbing situation. Not only was French rearmament languishing while German rearmament was flourishing, but the French were now mired in an intense and public dispute with that power the British most wanted to befriend. Although the FO officially recommended that Britain avoid interfering with the Franco-Italian conflict and continue pursuing Italian appeasement, Vansittart privately warned Halifax, "Your visit to Rome will be a risky proceeding, for at present we are being played with." Ambassador Perth lamented that even though "Signor Mussolini, and Signor Mussolini alone, determines the policy of Fascist Italy . . . Italian policy is based solely on self-interest, and the forces ranged with or against Italy are consequently a determining factor."[27]

This lack of unanimity about an appropriate British policy existed throughout Whitehall. Officials at the Treasury demonstrated a fervent desire "to dispel the atmosphere of suspicion and to develop one of collaboration on economic and financial questions [with the Italians] as soon as may be possible." Yet the COS insisted, in light of the increased risk of hostilities erupting in the Mediterranean, that Britain not accept any quid pro quo with Italy that would result in either abandoning Malta or promising not to fortify Cyprus.[28] Although all these various concerns raised the prime minister's anxiety level about his forthcoming trip to Rome, Chamberlain remained determined that this visit with Mussolini would establish a lasting Anglo-Italian entente and thus change the entire course of European affairs:

> I refuse to be discouraged by these controversies because I believe . . . that Musso[lini] is most anxious for Anglo-Italian friendship to develop. First, I take it, because he knows that the Italian people want it and loathe the Germans, second, because he wants our help economically to redress his trade balance and politically to find a way for him to escape from Spain and, thirdly, because he dislikes and fears the Germans and welcomes anything which will make him less dependent on them.[29]

As it turned out, Chamberlain's meetings with Mussolini were much less productive than the prime minister had hoped. Chamberlain spent most of the two sessions listening to the Duce explain Italy's commitment to the Axis, justify the scale of German rearmament, assail France and the Spanish Republic, ridicule the rumors of German plans to attack Poland and the Ukraine, and expostulate on the fate of European refugees. Instead of pledging to tame the Führer's ambitions, Mussolini refused to become part of a coalition that would guarantee Czechoslovakia's existing frontiers.[30]

Yet Chamberlain was anything but disheartened; he privately described his meeting with Mussolini as "a truly wonderful visit. . . . I am satisfied that the journey has definitely strengthened the chances of peace." Chamberlain reached this conclusion not because Mussolini promised anything—for the Duce guaranteed nothing—but because he believed he had made an important friend in Rome. Mussolini "confirmed that he liked me because I talked to him directly. As the day passed, it was evident that his liking increased." Two weeks later Chamberlain began "to feel at last that we are getting on top of the dictators. . . . They missed the bus last September and once you have done that in international affairs it is very difficult to reproduce the situation."[31]

The Italians' assessment of the value of their conversations with the British contrasted sharply with those of Chamberlain. Ciano confessed to his diary that "the matters which were discussed were not particularly important, and both parties betrayed their mental reservations. . . . Effective contact has not been made. How far apart we are from these people!" Following the first evening of talks Mussolini described his British visitors as "the tired sons of a long line of rich generations. They will lose their empire." After allowing German Ambassador Hans Georg von Mackensen to read the transcript of the meetings, Ciano telephoned Ribbentrop to say that "the visit was a farce [*una grande limonata*], totally innocuous." In fact it was Chamberlain's obsequious behavior in Rome that finally persuaded the skeptical Italian foreign minister that an alliance with Germany might indeed be both necessary and advantageous for Italy. "Having in our hands such an instrument," wrote Ciano, "we could obtain whatever we wish. The British do not want to fight."[32]

War Strategies Take Shape

After Italy denounced the Mussolini-Laval agreement in December, the Duce ordered the initiation of official military contacts with Germany. The service most reluctant to cooperate with the Germans was the navy, which had frequently eluded requests by Admiral Erich Raeder, commander-in-chief of the German fleet, to hold talks. Nevertheless, by the end of the month Cavagnari had authorized Admiral Giuseppe Raineri Biscia and Rear Admiral Raffaele De Courten to visit Berlin in January for meetings with Germany's naval staff. Although the conversations initially concerned only German acceptance of the London Naval Treaty's 40,000-ton limit for battleships and involved no exchange of views on war strategy, the naval relationship had been established. Within a month Italian naval intelligence had passed all its recent information on British ship movements and current dispositions to the Kriegsmarine.[33]

The talks with Germany motivated the SMM to protest further the Regia Marina's weakness. The delays in ship construction first reported in early 1938 had not been resolved. In fact the dates for Italy's four new or reconditioned battleships to come into service had now been pushed back until 1940 at the earliest. Until that time the navy's capital-ship strength would be far inferior to that of either France or Britain. The naval staff also lamented its relatively meager appropriation of Italy's military spending. Following the Sudeten crisis, Cavagnari persuaded Mussolini that the Regia Marina, if it were to play a role in an army offensive against Egypt, required a larger naval budget for new construction and the refitting of existing ships. The Gran Consiglio approved a supplemental appropriation that increased the existing 1938–39 budget by over 10 percent. Although this raised the navy's share of military expenditures for 1938–39 to 23 percent, the navy remained the service that the regime supported least. The air force accounted for 29 percent of military expenditures in 1938–39, and the army 45 percent.[34]

By the end of 1938, with an armed clash with France appearing more imminent every day and the army continuing to press its plans for a battle in North Africa, the Regia Marina had to reassess its role in the forthcoming conflict. Even though Mussolini coddled British diplomats and castigated French ones, most Italian strategists understood that Britain, not France, was Italy's principal rival in the Mediterranean. The chief of the naval staff, in particular, recognized that mastery of the Mediterranean ultimately required Italian control of the Suez Canal, the preeminent British possession in the eastern Mediterranean. A small, stout man with dark hair and eyes and thick eyebrows and mustache, Cavagnari was known for his acute intelligence, discretion, and quiet self-confidence. An autocrat who inspired awe and fear among Italy's sailors and respect among Italy's political and military elite, he derived considerable political power from his close friendship with Admiral Costanzo Ciano, Mussolini's principal naval adviser during the 1920s and father of Galeazzo. In contrast to most of his army and air force counterparts, he was not a monarchist with an aristocratic background. The son of a middle-class pharmacist in Genoa, Cavagnari was a card-carrying Fascist attracted to the regime's nationalist agenda of returning the Italian peninsula to its former greatness. Yet among Italy's military leadership, Cavagnari was the least mesmerized by the cult of the Duce. His loyalty was first and foremost to what he called the *Marina di Roma,* and he did not shrink from expressing his difference of opinions with Mussolini.[35]

In December Cavagnari's naval staff produced its most important prewar naval planning document, the DG 10/A2 memorandum, which indicated that the Italian fleet's primary strategic task was to secure the central Mediterranean. Specifically, the Regia Marina would maintain the communication line with North Africa—including the occupation of Malta—so that it could transport a fully equipped expeditionary force of 178,000 soldiers to Libya in eighty days. Thereafter, the navy would reinforce North Africa with 113,000 tons of supplies and 6,500 men each month. From Libya, the army would launch an attack on Egypt and Suez "to defeat the main enemy at a *vital point and open one of the doors* that close off Italy from free access to the oceans." In the event of belligerency, even though the Regia Marina would dedicate all its resources to the defense of this supply line, the number of days necessary to transport the corps to Africa would likely increase by sixty-five. All other offensive operations in the Mediterranean and Red Sea by the Regia Marina were strictly precluded by the presence of the French Marine Nationale and the size, proficiency, and experience of the Royal Navy.[36]

The army chief, Pariani, endorsed the navy's DG 10/A2 plan early in January 1939 but claimed that Italy was prepared to embark on this project almost immediately, rejecting the navy's recommendation for a "long period of time without active hostilities." In fact Pariani—who since early 1938 had been "convinced of the inevitability of [an Axis] war with the western powers . . . [a] war that will be won at Suez and Paris"—now demanded that the navy and air force adopt force structures and war plans that conformed with the army's predominant role in Italian offensive operations. In addition, the war ministry asked the government to expand its military expenditures in Libya by 64 percent "for the most urgent measures" to prepare the Libyan garrison for future offensive operations.[37]

In response, Italian naval intelligence—again reflecting Cavagnari's perspective—informed Badoglio, chief of the supreme general staff, that the army's plan to have the navy transport 178,000 men from Italy to Libya soon after the outbreak of hostilities was virtually impossible, especially if Malta remained in British hands. Britain had constructed over 600,000 tons (a gross exaggeration) of warships in 1938—200,000 more than any other power. Moreover, the intelligence outrageously claimed that the French navy now planned to launch an attack on Italy in the Mediterranean in coordination with a French invasion of Libya from Tunisia, perhaps as early as June. Meetings with German naval representatives had not assuaged these renewed Italian fears of an overwhelming and imminent Anglo-French assault on the Regia Marina. "It is considered axiomatic that our principal naval forces must, as long as possible, avoid battling with the nucleus of our principal adversaries; and it is considered risky to base our war plan on an operation that has immensely difficult maritime and terrestrial logistics."[38]

The SMM's study on the viability of sending an expeditionary force to North Africa inspired Badoglio to ask for an audience with the Duce and then call a rare meeting of the Italian service chiefs. In many ways, the navy's report expressed what the marshal wanted to hear. Born in Grazzano Monferrato and educated at the military academy in Turin, Badoglio had served in Ethiopia in 1896 and the Italo-Turkish war of 1911–12. Having commanded Italian forces at the victory of Vittorio Veneto and the defeat at Caporetto, he emerged from the Great War as one of Italy's most distinguished military figures. Although he served as governor of Libya in 1928–34 and commanded the forces that captured Addis Ababa in 1936, Badoglio was a reluctant supporter of Fascism. As a monarchist and renowned Francophile, he desperately hoped that Italy could avoid participating in any war against the democracies, especially one that aligned Italy with the dreaded Germans. However, as someone with "no scruples and . . . no political principles save opportunism," Badoglio had long valued his position of power within the regime more than his trepidation about its direction. [39]

In early 1939 Badoglio tried to moderate what he believed were irresponsibly aggressive views rampant within the army and air force. At the 26 January 1939 meeting with Pariani, Valle, and Cavagnari, Badoglio told his subordinates that Mussolini had no offensive intentions:

> First of all, the head of the government informed me that, in his demands against France, he does not at all intend to speak of Corsica, Nice, Savoy.

> These are initiatives taken privately, which are not part of the plan of action. In addition, he informed me that he does not intend to demand territorial concessions from France because he is convinced that she cannot make them: he would then be placed in a situation where he either would have to withdraw previous request (and that would not be dignified) or make war (and that is not his intention).

After quoting the Duce's directive that Italy establish a defensive alignment on the Libyan front, "leaving to France the responsibility of eventual action," the marshal then explained that the previously anticipated "action against Egypt no longer has any reason to exist." This radical change of strategy confounded and infuriated Pariani and Valle. Pariani asked how Badoglio planned to resolve the war against France: "On the defensive we risk finding ourselves trapped in a stalemate [*subire degli scacchi*]. We need to strike offensively somewhere." Valle agreed, asserting that Italy would be paralyzed if it did not attack the growing French air base on Corsica. "I am certain that in this defensive hypothesis, Corsica would be, every day and every hour, a springboard [*una pedana*] for the offensive against us."[40] Although Italian naval strategy required no adjustment in response to this new Badoglio directive, Cavagnari offered no support of Badoglio's position. Evidently, it mattered little to Cavagnari how the army and air force planned for war, as long as his ships were not compelled to place themselves needlessly at risk. He had lost his faith—if it ever existed—in the ability of Italy's services to coordinate their action. A profound pessimism had set in.

Information received by Cavagnari and the naval staff during the winter of 1939 only exacerbated this dire assessment of Italy and the international situation. Italian naval intelligence believed that if Italy did not send a substantial number of "highly trained soldiers" to the Aegean, the French would be in a position to gain control of that region in the event of war and deny the Regia Marina safe passage to the Dodecanese—bases that the navy required for any substantial operations in the eastern Mediterranean. It was assumed that Greek and Turkey were actively soliciting British and French friendship and that Turkey had agreed to place its troops on Greek islands should war break out.[41] Moreover, Italian naval intelligence reported in February and March that the French and British had begun planning for a joint offensive war in the Mediterranean. Among the many wild exaggerations, it was revealed that France planned to occupy Spanish Morocco and Minorca on the outbreak of war; that the Royal Navy planned to "neutralize" the German navy in the Atlantic while the French Marine attacked Italy's communication line to Libya; that the British and French navies intended to create a base of operations at Salonika at the beginning of any conflict; and that the British Admiralty had acquired a new "offensive spirit" that favored action against "the most yielding and perhaps the weakest seam in the defensive armor of potential enemies."[42] Finally, the SMM lamented that Italy's only potential ally—Germany—lacked both the strategic inclination and the naval strength to assist the Italian navy in a Mediterranean war against the democracies. In fact German naval officials preferred to hope for an extended period of peace rather than begin joint strategic planning with the Italians. Any strategy other than a defensive one, according to the SMM, was not only beyond the scope of the Regia Marina's capabilities but also a recipe for destruction.[43]

Although Badoglio correctly recognized that Mussolini's desire to attack the British had waned, the marshal clearly misinterpreted the Duce's intentions vis-à-vis France. In January Mussolini promised General Vittorio Ambrosio, the commander of the Second Army deployed along the frontier with Yugoslavia and a trusted military confidant, that Italy would soon "fight France." At the height of the battle for Barcelona, Ciano warned London and Berlin that Italy would declare war on France if French troops intervened in Spain. Responding to a series of insulting articles in the French press and intelligence that France planned to attack Italy in June, Mussolini declared that "these [French people] will be the first to fall. Certain offenses are punished with cannon and bombs." In early February Mussolini ordered the size of Italy's Libyan garrison doubled immediately in preparation for an attack on Tunisia. Badoglio's subsequent visit to Libya and conclusion that western Libya would not be prepared for defensive or counteroffensive, much less offensive, operations against Tunisia until the spring of 1940 failed to influence the Duce's determination to "wage war and defeat France, . . . destroying everything and leveling many [French] cities."[44] Despite Badoglio's wishes, Fascist animosity toward France had reached tremendous heights in early 1939.

Even before the Fascist regime made public its claims on France, the Bonnet/François-Poncet solution to the Italian and Mediterranean dilemma had encountered opposition among most officials in France's military and naval circles. Only General Vuillemin, the air force chief, favored the appeasement of Italy. Obsessed by the relative feebleness of the French air force, Vuillemin believed that France had to avoid war with Germany and Italy at all costs. General Bührer, the chief of the colonial army, and Admiral Darlan thought France should resist German and Italian expansion by focusing on strengthening the French Empire. But whereas Bührer wanted France to increase its presence in East Africa and Indochina, Darlan's concerns centered on the Mediterranean and North Africa.[45]

For the naval staff, the enactment of Italy's racial laws and Mussolini's refusal to condemn *Kristallnacht* demonstrated Italy's solidarity with Hitler, while the recent doubling in size of the Libyan garrison revealed Italy's expansionist ambitions in the Mediterranean. Throughout October and November Darlan and his Section d'Etudes reiterated that a German and Italian occupation of the Canary and Balearic Islands would menace the Strait of Gibraltar as well as the transport of French troops from North Africa to the European continent. Without the freedom of communications in the Mediterranean, France would be unable to fortify the western front, import oil from the East, and supply aid to its allies in Central Europe. Continuing to press its case for a Mediterranean offensive, the EMM in November—before the Fascists publicly demanded French concessions—informed its regional commanders that a war against Germany and Italy was now considerably more likely than one against only Germany. The Marine should plan on wartime troop transports from Casablanca and Dakar, by way of the Atlantic, since the Mediterranean would be an active war theater.[46]

Yet Darlan was unable to persuade Gamelin that France should adopt the Marine's proposed strategy. The problem was not that Gamelin after Munich had abandoned his support for an eastern front and embraced Bonnet's conciliation policy. In fact at the end of October Gamelin endorsed the position of General Louis Colson, the army chief of staff, who claimed that France had to construct a bloc from the Baltics to the Balkans which could resist pan-Germanism. But Gamelin also recognized that France could no longer rely on traditional continental communications with Eastern Europe. The Mediterranean had become a vital avenue to France's eastern allies and the only way for France to maintain its "ties with eastern Europe." Despite remaining hopeful that France could improve relations with Italy, Gamelin conceded that the likelihood of an attack on France and its imperial possessions by both Germany and Italy had increased since 1937. These circumstances required a "new orientation of our military policy" that included fortifying France's position in the Levant, improving relations with Turkey and Greece, creating bases in the eastern Mediterranean, mobilizing French industry, and ensuring a strict military accord with Britain—all so that France could successfully prosecute *une guerre de longue durée* against the Axis powers. Nevertheless, Gamelin continued to oppose, as he had in the past, any rash military offensive against Italy that would distract attention from France's principal enemy and greatest threat, Germany.[47]

As premier, Daladier had the difficult task of reconciling the various and, in this case, contradictory positions of his foreign minister and the military and naval chiefs. The premier also encountered widely varying opinions on foreign policy from domestic-political circles in France. Léon Blum and the

Socialist wing of the well-fractured Popular Front coalition demanded that France, by retaining and strengthening her European alliances, resist German and Italian expansion in Eastern Europe and the Mediterranean. Within Daladier's own Radical Party, Aimé Berthod allied with Bonnet and staunchly advocated a French retreat from Eastern Europe, an entente with Germany, and an arrangement with Italy that would allow France to safeguard her Mediterranean empire. And between these two extremes existed many complicated variations—most with significant numbers of adherents capable of influencing parliamentary decision-making.[48]

Although Daladier had definitively broken with the Popular Front—requesting decree powers; publishing decree laws that increased taxes, cut nondefense government spending, and reduced employers' overtime costs; and opposing the general strike that followed—he in no way adopted the right's foreign policy prescriptions. Daladier's difference with Berthod and Bonnet was about the Mediterranean. In late October he declared that "French security . . . is dependent on the freedom of communications between the mother country and its empire," and he remained convinced that Fascist Italy would strive to deny French liberty in the Mediterranean.[49]

These specific anxieties, which Daladier emphasized at the end of November when Chamberlain and Halifax visited Paris, were the product not only of his long-held personal inclinations but also of the warnings and recommendations of his trusted friend and confidant Louis Aubert, a historian and member of the French delegation to the League of Nations, who was intimately familiar with Italy's Ethiopian ambitions. Specifically, Aubert suggested a "policy of waiting," which consisted of maintaining France's eastern alliances yet concentrating French initiative on the Mediterranean. "It is in the Mediterranean," wrote Aubert, "where we must, as soon as possible, concentrate our diplomatic activity and where we must affirm our [military and naval] strength." Whereas a lack of strong independent allies in Eastern Europe, coupled with a powerful and determined Germany, compelled France to shun imminent confrontation on the continent, Italy's extensive and largely undefended metropolitan coastline, extraordinary dependence on certain seaborne trade (especially coal), and Libyan colony strategically located between Egypt and Tunisia all made Italy extremely vulnerable in the Mediterranean. "We must assert our force against the Axis and press hard against its weakest point, Italy." Moreover, Aubert asserted that it was in the Mediterranean where "British interests are entirely connected with ours." Operations there, in contrast to those in Eastern Europe, could draw Britain and France together and pry Germany and Italy apart. Finally, Aubert rejected the Bonnet/François-Poncet solution to the Italian problem: "It is not the moment to ask if, when, or where concessions can be made to Italy. Any concession would be incompatible with our security in the western Mediterranean."[50]

In addition to the theoretical arguments made by French diplomats and strategists, the state of the nation's armed forces also served as an essential consideration in the development of French foreign policy. In September 1938 Daladier had approved a rearmament budget for 1939 that was 34 percent less than the service chiefs had requested. Upon his return from Munich, Daladier expressed his intentions to focus less on the social programs of the Popular Front and more on building France's military strength. He appointed the conservative Paul Reynaud as finance minister, raised taxes, and sharply reduced all nondefense spending. These changes, and the matériel and manpower shortages the Czech crisis revealed, motivated the service chiefs to seek additional funding for rearmament.

But Reynaud and Robert Jacomet, the controller-general at the War Ministry, claimed that France could not afford any increase in spending on rearmament and suggested that the army and navy reduce their budgets to finance the cost of 1,000 American fighter aircraft. After proposing that the navy discontinue building its third 35,000–ton battleship, Reynaud added that France had to "ask the British to make a greater effort if they do not want to accept German hegemony on the continent." Darlan bristled at both these comments. France currently had only 220,000 tons of shipping in the Mediterranean, whereas Italy had 258,000 tons. Britain's Mediterranean fleet added another 230,000 tons, but Britain's Far Eastern commitments discounted the value to France of Britain's ships in the Mediterranean. "We cannot rely on the English fleet to assure our communications," wrote Darlan. "The crisis in September clearly proved that Britain would not only ask the French fleet for assistance in the Atlantic but leave to the French fleet security of the western Mediterranean." Although Darlan failed to win any additional funding for 1939, he retained the navy's original 1939 budget. Reynaud reluctantly consented to an increase of 500 million francs for the air force to purchase new planes. Because the decree laws of 2 November 1938 had not immediately offset the flight of capital caused by the Czech crisis, some rearmament would have to be postponed. In late November the finance minister told a Quai official that France simply could not pursue a full-scale buildup of land, sea, and air weapons.[51]

Germany's overwhelming superiority in the air and France's inability to redress the situation quickly reinforced Aubert's proposal for *une politique d'attente* on the continent: France was in no position to precipitate a conflict with the Nazis. For this reason, Daladier endorsed the accord that Bonnet signed with Ribbentrop on 6 December, which recognized the existing Franco-German border and promised mutual consultations on international issues of common concern. At the same time the premier's instinct to secure the Mediterranean and resist making any concessions to Fascist Italy—*une politique de fermeté*—was justified by the fact that the Italian air force was not as intimidating as the Luftwaffe and that the combined strength of the British and French naval forces dwarfed the Regia Marina. Thus, on 1 January 1939 Daladier reiterated his desire for Franco-British defensive cooperation against Germany on the continent and offensive or counteroffensive cooperation against Italy in the Mediterranean.[52]

Undoubtedly, Italy's anti-French propaganda campaign and the movement of Italy's Ethiopian troops to the border of French Somaliland in December contributed to this resolute declaration of French grand strategy. Yet these events did not engender Daladier's antipathy for Fascist Italy. The tenor of the premier's public response—his refusal to consider any concessions, his January visit to Tunis, Algiers, and Corsica, and the reinforcement of French troops in Djibouti and Tunisia—was a foregone conclusion. In fact Daladier's remarks about Italy and the Mediterranean at the 5 December CPDN meeting reflected exactly those that Aubert had made weeks before. Thus, the specific Italian claims on Tunis, Corsica, Nice, and Djibouti did not force a reassessment of France's Italian policies but facilitated a shift that most French statesmen and strategists had already seriously considered.[53]

Unfortunately, the premier did not define exactly what his proposed "offensive" strategy in the Mediterranean should entail, paving the way for a variety of interpretations by France's military planners. Exaggerated intelligence in early January that Italy would soon attack Djibouti absent a resolution of that particular demand brought the issue of Mediterranean strategy to the forefront. Bührer immediately requested a reinforcement of French air, land, and sea forces in French Somaliland, but both Darlan and Gamelin insisted that substantial forces could not be diverted to that distant theater. Yet their agreement ended there. Gamelin, who saw Djibouti as an important strategic asset for French possessions and resources in the Far East, thought that this "urgent question" compelled France to pursue *étroite collaboration* with Britain. In the meantime France should send two squadrons of fighters and two submarines to East Africa.[54] Darlan countered that France needed to strengthen its presence in the Levant rather than the Red Sea, since the majority of Italian reinforcements to Africa had been sent to Libya, not Ethiopia or Italian Somaliland. "The security of our empire cannot be built on a division a priori of our principal naval forces, but must be based on their concentration at an appropriate time and place according to the general situation. . . . any naval effort should favor those of our territories that are directly menaced." Although the naval chief believed that France and Britain had to cooperate to safeguard their empires and to defeat the Axis coalition in war, he opposed concluding an Anglo-

French naval war plan that would commit his forces to a rigid operational directive and likely subordinate him to the British first sea lord. Instead, Darlan suggested a naval arrangement that established common intentions and objectives, assigned spheres of action, and arranged for extensive sharing of information and intelligence.[55]

Asked at an 11 January meeting of the service chiefs how he planned to respond to an Italian attack on Djibouti, Darlan explained that the Marine was prepared to wreak havoc on Italian maritime communications to Libya and could swiftly and effectively bombard La Spezia, Naples, and Pantelleria. With help from the British, the Marine could also neutralize Italian bases in the Dodecanese. The naval chief proposed that this action occur simultaneously with air and ground assaults on Tripoli and Italy's northwestern frontier. There was almost unanimous resistance to Darlan's plans. Vuillemin thought that the bombing of Italian towns should happen only in response to Italian bombing of metropolitan France. General Auguste Noguès, the army's commander in North Africa, insisted that at least thirty-five days of preparation were needed after hostilities erupted before the army could carry out an attack on Tripoli. Gamelin, who believed that a simultaneous mobilization in North Africa and the Alps was impossible in light of the army's demands on the western front, suggested that France instead concentrate on passive forms of aggression against Italy, such as inciting domestic political unrest there and "asphyxiating" Italy in the Mediterranean by closing Suez and Gibraltar.[56]

The leaders of the French army and air force had played a very high card: Germany. The strength and menace of the German Wehrmacht precluded any weakening of French defenses in the Northeast. Moreover, the Nazis would likely exploit the opportunity provided by a French offensive against Italy to attack continental France earlier than they otherwise would. Although most politicians in Paris found such arguments quite compelling, Darlan refused to relent in the face of the French military's "tunnel vision" vis-à-vis Germany. He and the Section d'Études presented a series of impassioned memoranda attempting to show that a short-term offensive against Italy was consistent with, and in fact would contribute to, the long-term defeat of Germany. "The German *volonté* does not directly threaten any of our interests. The Italian *volonté,* on the other hand, threatens our patrimony and our essential interests. Above all we must conserve our empire; the rest is secondary. Therefore, with reservations that we cannot stand up to Italy in her claims, we must allow Germany freedom to act in the West."[57]

This serious strategic disagreement in France on a proper approach to the Mediterranean theater was undoubtedly a major contributing factor to the three-week delay in responding to Britain's 3 February proposal for an alliance and Chamberlain's first publicly issued guarantee to France three days later.

New intelligence about an increased threat to Tunisia only exacerbated the French debate. Reports arriving in February indicated that Italy had increased the size of its Libyan garrison from 66,000 soldiers at the beginning of January to approximately 85,000 less than two months later. More than seven thousand tons of war matériel had also been sent to Libya over the same period. In contrast, after reinforcements in late February, France still had only 42,000 men under arms in Tunisia, and Britain only 28,000 in Egypt. Italy also possessed a significant air force advantage in North Africa: there were 120 modern planes in Libya and another 150 in southern Italy and Sardinia; France and Britain each had fewer than fifty modern aircraft in the region. Although the Deuxième Bureau estimated that the Libyan garrison did not present a *danger immediat,* it concluded that "the only current menace is nevertheless in Libya."[58]

On the same day, 24 February, that the French finally accepted the British invitation for joint staff talks that envisaged a war against both Italy and Germany, Daladier called a meeting of the CPDN to hear the arguments for and against an offensive Mediterranean strategy. Bonnet, who was clearly marginalized in this debate, complained that contemplating any sort of hostile policy risked provoking an unnecessary war in the Mediterranean. Gamelin had downplayed the credibility of the Italian threat against Tunisia at a meeting of the service chiefs the week before but had admitted that Mussolini would likely strike in North Africa if Hitler goaded the Duce into action somewhere. Under the strain of the new intelligence, Gamelin reluctantly agreed to transfer troops discreetly from western to eastern Tunisia and to send two Senegalese battalions from East Africa to Oran as soon as possible. However, Gamelin repeated his preference for a defensive posture in Tunisia and, only in the event of war, an indirect attack on Italian trade and the Fascist regime. The premier found the military statistics from North Africa chilling and worthy of increased vigilance vis-à-vis Italy but not cause for a preemptive French strike against Italy. Therefore, Daladier compromised between the Darlan and Gamelin strategies, proposing that France take an offensive against Libya if Italy initiated operations against either Tunisia or Djibouti. Orders were given to reinforce Corsica with reserves from Morocco, coastal artillery, antiair defenses, and a submarine detachment. But no plans for attacking the Italian mainland were approved.[59]

The naval staff accepted this revision of its strategy the following week in a note that outlined, albeit vaguely, the Marine's endorsement of a limited allied Mediterranean offensive in the event of Italian operations versus any French territory: the Marine would defend French communications and troop transports across the Mediterranean; the Marine would carry out attacks on Italian bases in the eastern Mediterranean and the Red Sea; the Marine would sever enemy communications from Italy to Libya and Ethiopia; and—conditions permitting—the Marine would assist in attacking Italian territories in North Africa and the *outre-mer.* The naval staff acknowledged, in a great understatement, that successful completion of these tasks depended on British cooperation. Gamelin then formulated France's "general strategic concept for war," which was presented to the British before the staff talks began at the end of March:

> In a Franco-British conflict against Germany and Italy, it is *against Italy* that the first Franco-British offensive efforts must be made. We will cover ourselves on the German side, and we can envisage certain diversionary offensives to enhance the security of the eastern allied powers (Poland and Russia). We must therefore: isolate the Italian-German coalition by the constitution of a solid land front and by the interruption of maritime communications; if possible, take the offensive against Italy simultaneously in the Alps, Libya, and Italian eastern Africa.

With Daladier's approval of this general strategic concept on 9 March, a French war strategy acceptable to both Darlan and Gamelin had been formulated.[60] Even though this general strategic concept is notable for its lack of detail and clarity about how these "offensives" would be executed, it did represent a consensus among France's political and strategic decision-makers. It was a general framework document around which the French hoped to build comprehensive Allied war plans.

THE POST-MUNICH British foreign policy consensus on Italy and the Mediterranean did not extend to the country's strategic decision-making apparatus, which found itself in the midst of a contentious war-planning dispute. One of the most powerful voices in this debate was the Admiralty's. The new first sea lord and chief of the naval staff, Admiral Sir Roger Backhouse, was skeptical about the wisdom of current British foreign policy. Six feet, four inches tall, attractive and always impeccably dressed, Backhouse was a striking figure who exuded charm, poise, and intelligence. As commander of the Home Fleet during the Ethiopian crisis, Backhouse had grown increasingly confident that Mussolini and Hitler had colonial goals that could be achieved only through war against the Western democracies. Sharing the opinion of Britain's army officers in the Middle East, who "had such deep contempt for Italy and the Italians that they didn't seem to mind any odds," Backhouse thought that the democracies could easily and quickly defeat Italy and damage the Axis if they focused their initial efforts on the Mediterranean. Finally—and here the admiral preached heresy—Backhouse argued that Britain had overextended itself in the Far East. The Royal Navy could no longer provide adequate protection for all Britain's colonies and dominions, and the time had arrived to establish defense priorities. In a letter to Admiral Sir Percy Noble, commander of the China station, Backhouse denounced the Hong Kong Defence Scheme, which had been formulated before the naval chief's tenure at the Admiralty: "I fear myself that it would be a fearful shock to our prestige, and to our interests in general, if we had to let go in China, and I expect you will agree with this. On the other hand, we both must realize that there is a limit to what this country can do by itself." Expressing his opposition to sending a British fleet to the Far East and implying the need for Britain to seek alliances to help secure its empire, Backhouse concluded that "this little country of ours is expected to carry too large a share of the burden."[61]

Convinced that Britain needed a new worldwide naval strategy that placed emphasis on offensive rather than defensive action, and on the Mediterranean rather than the Far East, Backhouse looked outside the Admiralty for assistance in presenting such radical arguments to the establishment. The naval chief turned to Admiral Sir Ernle Drax, who as commander at Plymouth had been pressuring the Admiralty to draw up offensive war plans against Germany and Italy since the summer of 1937. Backhouse asked Drax to develop a coherent offensive strategy, "working quite independently of any Admiralty department or division except in so far as you wished to consult them." Drax accepted the post and appointed Vice Admiral Sir Gerald Dickens and Rear Admiral William Chalmers as principal members of his "OPC" staff.[62]

Drax's views of the appropriate British naval strategy were unconventional, to say the least. During the height of the Sudeten crisis, Drax and others in the Admiralty recognized that France and Britain had neglected any sort of planning—defensive or offensive—for the Mediterranean theater. Moreover, the lack of coordinated intelligence-gathering, fleet organization, and command and control assignments compelled the Admiralty to make hasty and uninformed decisions for the Mediterranean on short notice.[63] But where Drax strayed from the norm was his solution for ending this atmosphere of ad hoc decision-making. Drax firmly believed that Italy, in its inevitable war alongside Germany, would aim to garner Mediterranean hegemony at British expense, and "if we lose the Mediterranean, we will lose the war." In fact a hostile Italy represented a more immediate threat to the British empire than a bellicose Germany, which would move eastward before turning against the United Kingdom. Thus, Italy should be decisively "dealt with" before Germany. Since "Italy is an ideal country to attack by coastal bombardment," Drax recommended a combined Anglo-French air-, land-, and sea-based offensive against the Italian peninsula. He was not deterred by the prospect of collateral damage that would likely accompany large-scale bombing, for "modern war can be conducted most efficiently and successfully only by the wholesale slaughter of women and children."[64]

In mid-November, Admiral Dudley Pound, commander of the Mediterranean fleet, proposed a less radical offensive Mediterranean strategy than Drax's yet one still considered maverick by those at the FO who favored conciliation. The reserved, ambitious, and dogmatic Pound argued that protecting Egypt and the Suez Canal—the most important British assets along the shortest communications route to the Far East—should be a priority for British security, and the largest menace to these assets was Italy. In a war against the Axis powers, the Royal Navy and French Marine should assist the Anglo-French armies and air forces in conducting a two-front invasion of Libya from Egypt and Tunisia. Such a strategy would not only reflect positively on those eastern Mediterranean powers that might be contemplating throwing in their lot with the enemy and thus secure naval and trade communications through the Mediterranean, but might also eventually lead to the defeat of Italy, since its supply and reinforcement routes would be controlled by Britain and France. A defeated Italy would demoralize the German people and damage the Nazi war effort. The Admiralty dismissed Pound's suggestions not least because Britain's military leadership had concluded that its land and air forces in the Middle East were too weak to conduct any offensive action in North Africa. Drax repeatedly criticized the defense of Egypt and attacks on Libya as "valuable pin-pricks but hardly to be ranked as our primary offensive," and Backhouse remained committed to a strategy that would exploit Corsica, Malta, and Cyprus in a wartime assault on the Italian peninsula.[65]

What Backhouse, Drax, and Pound all agreed on, however, was the necessity of full-scale Anglo-French military discussions to consider the possibility of a hostile Italy and an active war theater in the Mediterranean. By November the COS and the CID also supported some extension of staff talks with the French but differed fundamentally with the Admiralty on the role that France should play in the Mediterranean. Although the first sea lord and his principal adviser hoped that the French would assist in a combined attack on the Italian mainland, the COS and the CID depended on France to offset Italy in the Mediterranean, should a hostile Japan compel the Mediterranean fleet to sail for Singapore.[66] This disagreement was irrelevant in the short term because Britain's political leaders in late 1938 ruled out further staff talks with the French, despite Daladier's specific pleas for joint naval cooperation and planning if not a comprehensive British commitment to France. Chamberlain, after all, had proclaimed publicly in December that Britain would not necessarily aid France if Italy attacked her. The British Empire would remain unaffected by events in the Mediterranean, and the Mediterranean would remain unaffected by the outbreak of a European conflict—or at least so was the thinking at 10 Downing Street.[67]

Despite the prime minister's persevering optimism, the COS continued to push for both accelerated rearmament and, now, a commitment to the continent. Lord Gort, chief of the imperial general staff, argued in December 1938—as he had since Munich—that the demise of Czechoslovakia increased the risk of a German invasion of Belgium and Holland, "certain interests in Western Europe which are vital to our existence," which would compel Britain to intervene on the continent. Although Air Marshal Newall and General Ismay rejected this assertion, Gort had the support of Backhouse, War Minister Leslie Hore-Belisha, and Navy Minister Lord Stanhope.[68] The army-navy alliance on the issue of improving relations with France became a powerful force in Whitehall, especially during the war scare of the winter of 1938–39. French intelligence in January 1939 reported that the Germans would soon seize the Netherlands and, from there, launch an air and submarine campaign against Britain. Even though the navy and the army doubted the accuracy of these reports, the rumors strengthened their position on Anglo-French staff talks. By the end of the month even Halifax, who like Chamberlain still believed that Britain should avoid participating in a Franco-Italian war, conceded that Britain must improve its military-industrial capacity so that it could begin preparing an expeditionary force for the continent. Not yet ready to make a formal commitment to the defense of France, Whitehall nevertheless appreciated the need to bolster France's confidence in British military strategy and to plan for the possibility of a German invasion of the Low Countries. On 26 January the FPC finally authorized joint staff talks with France on the hypothesis of a war against both Germany and Italy. At Britain's insistence, however, the potential hostility of Japan remained an unmentionable topic.[69]

On the same day as this historic meeting of the FPC, the Joint Planning Committee (JPC) coincidentally submitted to the COS the first draft of the "European Appreciation, 1939–40"—the most detailed British strategic review before war erupted in September. Its final version, submitted to the CID on 24 February, reflected the rising influence of the Admiralty and the new naval perspective on British war strategy. Referring to eventual operations in the Far East, the revised Appreciation radically qualified the promise given to the Dominions at the imperial conference of 1937 to send a fleet to Singapore in the event of a war with Japan: "The strength of that fleet must depend upon our resources and the state of the war in the European theatre." Moreover, instead of recommending naval attacks on Italian sea communications and bombardment of Italian bases in Libya in case of a hostile Italy—as the draft did—the final Appreciation emphasized that the primary British objective in this scenario should be to "exploit our naval superiority by attacking military objectives on shore, and [Italy's] seaborne trade, in order to lower her morale."[70]

It was Backhouse who demanded these two particular revisions. Not sending the fleet to the Far East and concentrating it at Gibraltar and Corsica for an overwhelming attack on the Italian mainland were two of the most often repeated strategic concepts in the series of OPC papers written in the winter of 1939. Drax and his associates argued that guaranteeing the supply lines to the Far East while Germany and Italy remained undefeated and in possession of British bases and lines of communication would be almost impossible. The prodigious size of the Japanese navy would require an extensive confrontation in the Far East; that same British force "can do far more toward winning the war by operating in the Mediterranean than it can by sitting at Singapore." Accepting Liddell Hart's description of Italy as the "soft spot" of the Axis, Drax argued that eliminating munitions factories and ports in Elba, La Spezia, Savona, Genoa, Sardinia, and Messina offered the best prospect for defeating Italy quickly. "The golden opportunity is in the first few weeks of war when [Britain and France] have a huge superiority in capital ships over Germany and Italy, when Japan is still wobbling on the fence, and the Italians have only two capital ships ready."[71]

Backhouse endorsed these proposals in his own evaluation of British strategy at the end of February. To defend against Germany's two battle cruisers and three pocket battleships, Britain had to retain six of its eleven active capital ships in home waters. The remaining five that could be sent to the Far East would be no match for Japan's fleet of ten capital ships; moreover, in order to retain the integrity of British imperial communications, at least three capital ships would be required in the Mediterranean to operate against Italy and its sea traffic. The Royal Navy was in a position to do little more in the Far East than safeguard British communications in the Indian Ocean; relieving Hong Kong or engaging the Japanese fleet was out of the question. Backhouse suggested that the current division of responsibility for Britain and France in the eastern and western Mediterranean, respectively, should be revised so that the two fleets could simultaneously attack the western and southern coasts of Italy at the outset of war. The French Marine should concentrate on the Genoa area, while the Italian coastal areas of the Tyrrhenian and the Ionian Seas should be the Royal Navy's obligation.[72]

Although the European Appreciation had vaguely accepted some of these "revolutionary" ideas, most of London's statesmen and diplomats did not endorse them in the spring of 1939. A heated discussion immediately erupted in the FO concerning whether or not to send a fleet to Singapore. Japan's steady subjugation of the Chinese since its military victories of October 1938 had raised fears about Britain's ability to secure the Far Eastern empire. Japan appeared eager to conquer not only the South China Sea but also the South Pacific. Sir John Nicholls of the Far Eastern Department argued that any imperial losses in these regions would be unrecoverable and thus would have tremendous psychological and economic repercussions on the Anglo-French position in Europe: "It is generally agreed that we must defend our possessions in the Far East against aggression at any cost and that we must be prepared, if necessary, to carry on a war there at the same time as we have a war on our hands in Europe, even if this means that the Mediterranean has to be temporarily abandoned."[73]

Those who were willing to sacrifice the British position in the Mediterranean if necessary were ironically also those who did not see an Italian threat in the Mediterranean worthy of a British fleet concentration. Ingram, Cadogan, and Halifax all agreed with the contention of the Southern Department's Sir Andrew Noble that despite recent Italian reinforcements in eastern Libya, "it cannot be said that we have yet any evidence that the Italians are planning a war in the immediate future against France or anyone else." Britain therefore should refrain from adding to its forces in Egypt or the Mediterranean.[74] The perceived absence of an Italian threat served the psychological function of reinforcing the predisposition of many in the British government not to oppose Italy militarily and instead to focus on securing the Far Eastern empire. To admit the existence of a genuine Italian threat would have considerably complicated Britain's defensive imperial strategy.

In a frantic attempt to adopt a coherent British policy before the start of staff talks with the French, Chatfield, the new minister for the coordination of defence, convened a special Strategical Appreciation Subcommittee (SAC) to resolve the controversy surrounding British strategic priorities in the Mediterranean and the Far East. Chatfield and Hore-Belisha argued that France and Britain could exercise economic pressure on Germany and Italy by controlling sea communications. This defensive strategy would enable Britain to send a fleet to the Far East for the "durable security" of the entire British Empire. The French Marine, with help from some light British forces, would offset any potential menace from the Italian Regia Marina. Backhouse and Stanhope asserted that a British display of naval strength at the outset of hostilities would improve British prestige and could be decisive on the attitude of important eastern Mediterranean countries and territories, such as Greece, Turkey, Palestine, and Egypt. A defeated Italy and a secure and friendly eastern Mediterranean would enable Britain, at that point, to release ships for duty in the Far East. The weakness of Italian defenses was such that only Hong Kong would be in jeopardy of falling into Japanese hands before British reinforcements arrived at Singapore—a loss that Britain could withstand. Lord Gort and Sir Kingsley Wood, the air minister, supported the policy that would aim initially "to knock out Italy." Nevertheless, Chatfield could not contemplate any British losses in the Far East: "If we were faced with such a war [against Germany, Italy, and Japan], it would be better to lose the eastern Empire by fighting than by default. In the first case, it would be an honourable defeat; in the second case, it would be a disgrace."[75] It was the starkly contrasting interpretations of the British Empire's relevance and the extent to which Britain should depend on alliances with other Western powers, rather than the efficacy of the proposed strategy itself, that served as the focus of this heated and unresolved debate.

To bolster his side in the imperial and strategic quarrel, Chatfield encouraged Captain Danckwerts of the Admiralty's planning staff to assess the Far Eastern naval situation in the event of a war with Germany, Italy, and Japan simultaneously. According to Danckwerts, Japan would likely intervene at a very early stage of the war and attempt as quickly as possible to seize territory and bases in the southwest Pacific, including Hong Kong, Indochina, Borneo, the Netherland East Indies, and New Guinea. With the United States reluctant to intervene, Japan would use these conquests as strategic stepping stones for launching offensive operations against Singapore, Australia, and New Zealand. "The longer Japan retains the initiative in the Far East, the greater will be the pressure that she will be able to bring to bear against our interests in that area . . . It is of paramount importance, therefore, that the naval reinforcements to be despatched to the East should be sent as soon as practicable after Japanese intervention." In the Mediterranean, Britain would depend on the strength of the French Marine to secure sea communications. Soon the JPC adopted this position, indicating that it "was anxious that the government not assume that to 'knock Italy out of the war at the outset' is a course of action which we consider to be feasible in the conditions with which we are now faced." Wallowing in confusion over Mediterranean and Far Eastern strategy, the COS admitted that there was no choice but to wait and learn where the French stood on the issue before attempting to reach any definitive British position.[76] They appreciated that, in any case, some sort of arrangement with the French in the Mediterranean was required.

Franco-Italian Relations before Prague

Ciano's Chamber speech at the end of November 1938 fundamentally challenged the Quai d'Orsay's views about Italy. Both Henri Hoppenot, director of the Quai's European Department, and Charles Rochat, adjunct director of political and commercial affairs at the Quai—among others— believed that Italy's calls for French concessions represented a new and particularly menacing step in Fascist foreign policy.[77] Although Léger's unforgiving opinion of Mussolini and Ciano gained support at the Quai, Bonnet and François-Poncet continued to preach moderation and patience with the Italians. Admittedly shocked by the audacity of Italy's demands and now even sympathetic to the view that Italian policy might be aimed at separating France and Britain, both the foreign minister and his ambassador in Rome remained confident that Italy eschewed armed conflict and pursued concessions through negotiation only because of her inferiority complex vis-à-vis Germany.[78]

The division of Spanish loyalist forces at the end of January 1939, making the Nationalists' victory increasingly likely, gave Bonnet and François-Poncet an opportunity to negotiate with the Italians. After Franco's capture of Barcelona, an Italian industrialist in France, Vicenzo Fagiuoli, who also served as an intelligence agent for the Italian Foreign Ministry, approached Paul Baudouin, director of the Banque d'Indochine; the two men had negotiated the sale to Italy of shares in the Djibouti–Addis Ababa railway following the Laval-Mussolini agreement of 1935. Fagiuoli told Baudouin that France had to make serious concessions to Italy before the two nations could achieve any genuine rapprochement. At the Quai, Baudouin offered to speak secretly with the Fascist leadership and ascertain its demands during his scheduled visit to Rome for a Franco-Italian consortium meeting. Bonnet thought this an excellent idea, and a skeptical Daladier reluctantly approved the mission. Through Fagiuoli, Mussolini and Ciano agreed to receive Baudouin in order to learn Daladier's private position on concessions to Italy, which publicly had been limited to the premier's forceful *Jamais*![79]

On 2 and 3 February Ciano and Baudouin discussed establishing a free zone in Djibouti, ceding to Italy the portion of the Djibouti-Addis Ababa railway in Abyssinian territory, supporting Italy's desire for several seats on the board of the Suez Canal Company, and granting Italians in Tunisia the right to retain their nationality. The Fascists agreed to continue negotiating, provided that Baudouin's mission remained a secret.[80] The fact that Ciano kept German Ambassador Mackensen well apprised of his talks with Baudouin reveals that the Italians had no intention of maintaining the mission's secrecy or negotiating with the French in good faith. After learning that the Frenchman Fernand de Brinon had mentioned to Ribbentrop on 6 February that a recent, clandestine French mission to Rome had laid the foundation for a Franco-Italian agreement, an infuriated Ciano arranged for the French journalist André Géraud (pseudonym Pertinax) to be informed of the French banker's visit to Rome. Géraud's exposé, the subsequent anger of French public opinion, and British complaint about French deception doomed the useless French initiative to failure. Under intense pressure from within the Radical Party not to succumb to Italian pressure, Daladier abruptly halted these diplomatic efforts on 9 February.[81]

The Baudouin initiative, despite the importance accorded it by Bonnet, had little effect on Fascist foreign policy. The order to double the size of the Libyan garrison was made two days after Baudouin left Rome. Even

François-Poncet asserted that Géraud's revelation had exacerbated Italy's anti-French press campaign.[82] Although Italian antipathy for France did not inspire the early February scheduling of an assault against Albania, the Baudouin visit failed to deter or even affect its planning. The Yugoslav cabinet crisis and the fall of Prime Minister Stoyadinovich, whom the Fascists had come to trust and admire, on 4 February motivated Ciano and Mussolini to attach a specific date—the first week of April—to the long-planned operations across the Adriatic. Ciano had proposed the occupation in October 1938, largely as a response to Germany's acquisition of the Sudetenland. Mussolini had ordered the reclamation of the Albanian Durrës plain and approved Ciano's plans to assassinate the king of Albania, but he had vacillated over the issue of occupation. A Danubian bloc under Italian auspices, with Yugoslavia and Hungary, had also become an important Italian objective after Munich, and the Duce worried that invading Yugoslavia's neighbor would drive the Serbs out of the Fascist camp. But once Stoyadinovich had been "liquidated" and a Croat agent informed Ciano that Prince Paul and his new prime minister, Bosko Cristich, were soliciting British and French friendship and support, the Fascists took immediate steps to bolster their military presence in the Balkans.[83]

Finally, the Baudouin mission accomplished nothing in the way of diminishing Mussolini's appetite for war with France. Confident that diplomatic means could solve the problems of Italians in Tunisia, the free port in Djibouti, the control of the Addis Ababa railway, and participation in the administration of the Suez Canal, the Duce had other claims against France, for "those territories which geographically, ethnically, and strategically belong to Italy, . . . that require measures of a very different nature to resolve." Mussolini believed that an isolated war against the detested French represented an ideal conflict for Fascist Italy, but he knew that it would not likely materialize. A war against France would soon expand into a war against Britain and France, not only as a result of their historical entente but also because Italian ambitions in the Mediterranean conflicted with British interests. Mussolini finally accepted this reality during the winter of 1939 when he began to discourage any effort to improve Anglo-Italian relations. At the end of February he recalled from London the "unfaithful" and "Anglicized" Dino Grandi and informed him that his mission would soon come to an end. At the same time Ciano instructed Attolico in Berlin to speak with the Egyptian ambassador there, a known Anglophobe, in an attempt "to weaken the ties between Egypt and London."[84]

The day after Baudouin left Rome, the Duce alluded to the inevitable war in the Mediterranean against the democracies in a document titled, "The March to the Oceans," which he included in the official record of a Gran Consiglio meeting. This paper asserted that maritime position determined a nation's independence: states that have free access to the oceans were independent; continental states and states lacking outlets to the high seas were dependent. Italy, with access to an inland sea but unable to communicate with the oceans without British and French acquiescence, represented a semidependent nation. Italy, according to the Duce, was imprisoned in the Mediterranean.

> The bars of this prison are Corsica, Tunisia, Malta, and Cyprus. The guards of this prison are Gibraltar and Suez. Corsica is a pistol pointed at the heart of Italy; Tunisia at Sicily. Malta and Cyprus constitute a threat to all our positions in the eastern and western Mediterranean. Greece, Turkey, and Egypt have been ready to form a chain with Great Britain and to complete the politico-military encirclement of Italy. Thus Greece, Turkey, and Egypt must be considered vital enemies of Italy and of its expansion . . .
>
> The aim of Italian policy, which cannot have, and does not have continental objectives of a European territorial nature except Albania, is first of all to break the bars of this prison . . . Once the bars are broken, Italian policy can have only one motto—to march to the oceans.

Whether Italy marched to the Atlantic or the Indian Ocean, she would face opposition from France and Britain. Thus, the fundamental importance of the Rome-Berlin Axis was "to have our backs protected on the continent" so that Italy could concentrate on prosecuting the war in the Mediterranean.[85]

Mussolini's specific "program" had evolved significantly over a period of nine weeks. In late November 1938 the Duce described his aims as Albania, Tunisia, Corsica, and a northern frontier that stretched to the Var—relatively modest aspirations that would give Italy certain control of the central Mediterranean and security on the continent. But now, in early February 1939, Fascism's international goals included not only all those already specified but also Malta, Cyprus, Gibraltar, and Suez; moreover, Greece, Turkey, and Egypt were described as "vital enemies" of the Fascist state. The ambition inherent in these new objectives was none other than Mediterranean hegemony, which would grant Italy access to the oceans and thus undeniable great-power status.

What accounts for the rapid extension of the Duce's foreign-policy "program"? At the turn of the year Mussolini decided to accept Ribbentrop's invitation to conclude a military alliance—an alliance that would allow Italy to expand its territorial and imperial goals. On New Year's day Mussolini urged Ciano to transform the anti-Comintern pact into a tripartite alliance because he "consider[ed] a clash with the western democracies increasingly inevitable and therefore he want[ed] to affect a military alignment in advance." Writing Ribbentrop the following day, Ciano admitted that "the tension between France and Italy has made the idea of the alliance with Germany much more popular in Italy and, for our purposes, this is a positive and concrete result." When the "phlegmatic slowness of Japan" delayed the signing of a tripartite pact, the Duce suggested a bilateral alliance instead. Although the Italians and Germans renewed and expanded their 1937 commercial agreement on 13 February, Mussolini insisted that the Axis powers take a genuinely "dynamic" step to counteract the accelerating pace of Anglo-French rearmament. An Italian-German alliance, according to Mussolini, "would be sufficient to meet an array of Anglo-French forces." By early March Hitler had expressed his commitment to "solidarity with Italy" and accepted Italy's invitation for formal staff talks; arrangements were put in motion to sign what would become known as the Pact of Steel. Mussolini immediately reversed his Hungarian policy of late 1938, refusing to respond to Budapest's cries for moral and material Italian support.[86] Hitler's path to a fully incorporated Czechoslovakia was now clear.

[4]

"Neither an acre of our territory nor a single one of our rights": March–August 1939

British and French Reactions to Prague

Germany's invasion of Bohemia and Moravia on 15 March 1939 occasioned a fundamental shift in some but not all aspects of British foreign policy. Although Britain had decided to ally with France and to expand the British Expeditionary Force (BEF) before the Prague coup, no commitment had been made regarding either the BEF's size or its destination. After Hitler's blatant repudiation of the Munich agreement, however, the British doubled the Territorial Army (TA) to twenty-six divisions, adopted conscription, and definitively promised to dispatch a field force to the continent if Germany attacked Western Europe. The British policy of appeasing Germany had run its course. Writing in his diary less than a week after Germany's annexation of independent Czechoslovakia, Cadogan concluded, "I'm afraid we have reached the cross-roads. I have always said that, as long as Hitler could pretend he was incorporating Germans in the Reich, we could pretend that he had a case. If he proceeded to gobble up other nationalities, that would be the time to call 'Halt!' That time has come."[1] The British now attempted to deter Germany from starting a European war by offering a guarantee of Polish independence on 31 March. Nevertheless, Chamberlain specifically avoided committing Britain to the defense of Poland's existing borders and he adamantly refused to seek close association with the Soviet Union in order to build a broad-based anti-Fascist coalition. War against Germany remained something the British government believed it could at least postpone.

Even though British continental policy adjusted after the Prague coup, British policy in the Mediterranean remained unchanged. In fact the growing likelihood of war against Germany reaffirmed Britain's determination to ensure a peaceful Mediterranean. British diplomats in Rome and Paris suggested that since the Fascists would perceive Prague as the "encirclement of Italy," an opportune time had arrived for France to search for an agreement with Italy. Although the British recognized that Bonnet and Léger held profoundly different views of the international situation, the FO believed that these two perspectives were not necessarily incompatible. Cadogan and Gladwyn Jebb argued that Britain should adopt Léger's policy of resistance to Germany and Bonnet's policy of accommodation to Italy. Not only did these policies match Britain's views of the international situation, but they also offered the British an opportunity both to strengthen Anglo-French relations and to ameliorate dissension within French policymaking circles. On 20 March Chamberlain wrote Mussolini with some desperation: "I earnestly hope that you may feel it possible, in any way that may be open to you, to take such action in these anxious days as may allay present tension and do something to restore the confidence that has been shattered." The following week Chamberlain told his sister, "I am hoping that something may be done in Rome to improve the situation."[2] For the British, Italy not only represented a fundamentally different beast from Germany but also held the key to the future peace of Europe.

An essential reason why the British tended to view the Fascists in a favorable light was the situation in the Far East. One week after Prague the British ambassador in Tokyo and former naval arms negotiator, Sir Robert Craigie, argued that the British must act immediately to keep Japan neutral in a future war. Craigie urged that the Royal Navy send a capital-ship squadron "at the earliest possible moment" to defend Singapore and British trade and communication routes with Australia and New Zealand. "Our policy of concentrating the whole battle fleet in home and Mediterranean waters has created here a false impression of British naval 'impotence' in Far Eastern waters, but there is still time to destroy this impression even on the assumption that no more than three capital ships could be spared for the purpose at present." Craigie offered diplomatic support to Captain Danckwerts's strategic assessment that "if Singapore falls to the Japanese, our Eastern Empire is at Japan's mercy." Despite Backhouse's claim that the loss of Egypt and Suez "would be most damaging to our prestige in Europe [and] for that matter all over the world," Chatfield reminded Chamberlain that in the six months it would take to defeat Italy, Japan could overwhelm Singapore. Only a resolute American commitment to counter Japanese aggression in the Far East could provide Britain with enough imperial security to support an offensive in the Mediterranean.[3]

The foreign policy leadership in London became discouraged by this lack of unanimity from the COS, especially the Admiralty, and disoriented by the passion of the arguments from both sides. Neither Halifax nor Cadogan, who later described the leaders of the Admiralty as "*all* half-wits," accepted or rejected the "Mediterranean-first" strategy espoused in the European Appreciation.[4] Chamberlain was so horrified at the thought of abandoning the Far East that he ordered Halifax to telegraph Ambassador Sir Ronald Lindsay in Washington to appeal to President Roosevelt for help in extricating Britain from this strategical dilemma. Chamberlain hoped that the United States would agree to send a fleet to Honolulu if Britain became involved in a war with Germany. A few days later U.S. Ambassador Joseph Kennedy reported that the U.S. fleet would return to the Pacific in mid-April, one month ahead of schedule. How the United States would act in the event of a European war, however, was not specifically disclosed.[5]

Despite these nebulous assurances from the Americans, Chamberlain refused to ally himself with the Mediterranean-first strategy. He promised J. A. Lyons, the Australian prime minister, that Britain and its navy would prevent any major operations against Singapore, Australia, New Zealand, or India. Although Chamberlain conceded that the size of the fleet "would necessarily be dependent on a) the moment when Japan entered the war and b) what losses if any our opponents or ourselves had previously sustained," he assured Lyons that the Mediterranean would not become a strategic problem for the British.[6] Nowhere in Chamberlain's official correspondence or personal writings does he show a vague interest in, much less a willingness to contemplate implementing, a strategy based on a Mediterranean fleet concentration and an attack on Italy at the outset of a general European war. Holding such a position would have been in direct contradiction to his continued stalwart belief in a temperate Italy desirous of maintaining her traditional balancing role between Germany and the Western powers. To have thought otherwise would have raised doubts about Britain's status as the world's premier imperial power: only a moderate and peaceful Italy would allow Britain any chance of sustaining its widely dispersed empire. At the end of March, with the COS confounded on Mediterranean strategy and the FO equivocal about Italy's intentions, the political leadership remained blindly committed to its policy of appeasing Mussolini and avoiding conflict in the Mediterranean.

THE NAZI annexation of Czechoslovakia also had significant repercussions in France. In contrast to the lingering British opinion that war could still be avoided, the French reaction to the Prague coup reflected a sober and resolute expectation of imminent war. Daladier told the Council of Ministers on 17 March that now "we have to prepare ourselves for war." The French demonstrated their support for the premier's position two days later when Parliament voted to grant Daladier decree powers until November to take all "measures necessary for the defense of the country." Besides weakening the domestic-political opposition to the Daladier government, these laws assigned priority to rearmament over the production of other goods and permitted the service ministries not to submit annual estimates to Parliament.[7]

A perceived change in the balance of power on the continent prodded the army and the air force, in particular, to respond immediately to this decree. The Deuxième Bureau on 16 March calculated that Germany's seizure of Bohemia and Moravia had increased Germany's comparative war strength by eighty divisions. Moreover, Germany now had direct access to a valuable Czech arms industry. The army staff estimated that Germany could mobilize 130 infantry divisions, with Italy capable of adding another sixty. In opposition, France could activate only eighty-five divisions and Britain had promised an expeditionary force of only two divisions.[8]

With the sudden shift in the balance of power in Eastern Europe, the French government discounted the fiscal concerns raised by Finance Minister Reynaud and endorsed a 50 percent increase in rearmament spending for the year. The French army received an additional 1,260 million francs and the navy a supplement of 1,596 million francs, but the largest appropriation went to the air force: an additional 8,797 million francs for a new rearmament program, "Plan V Reinforced." This plan called for France to build or acquire some 8,000 new aircraft, of which 3,094 would be first-line planes, by the end of 1940. The new credits effectively relegated the Marine to third among the French services; for the first time, Parliament allocated the air force a higher rate of expenditure than the navy. Darlan, who was infuriated by the sudden emphasis placed on the air force, argued that the naval supplement was not adequate to defend France against the rising Italian and German fleets:

> By acting this way we will only aggravate the weakness of our armaments, because aviation cannot substitute for the fleet in ensuring the liberty of our maritime communications; if these are severed, our planes will no longer have the fuel to fly. . . . It is curious to note that France, a world power that possesses a colonial empire whose cohesion can be maintained only by sea, is reluctant to maintain a entirely indispensable navy, while the countries that have almost no *outre mer* [Germany and Italy] are reinforcing their fleets in spite of grave difficulties. Without doubt they understand, in contrast to us landlubbers, that if we are deprived of free use of the sea, we will succumb.[9]

Although Darlan bristled at the navy's demotion, he either missed or ignored the most essential consideration for French rearmament in 1939: the extent of the British commitment. In 1939 the British Mediterranean fleet still existed and, united, the British and French navies were stronger than the combined Italian and German navies. In contrast, the British had promised to send only two ground divisions—the British aerial pledge was not fixed at all—to the continent in the event of war, leaving France at a profound disadvantage on the western front. French army and air force rearmament had to take priority over naval rearmament.

For these same reasons, the French after the Prague coup looked to Eastern and Southeastern Europe for additional resources that could help level the military balance against Germany in the forthcoming war. Poland, Romania, and Yugoslavia were immediately targeted, since the French had estimated that together they could field some 110 divisions. Although skeptical about France's ability to defend Poland against a German attack, the French followed the British lead in offering a guarantee to the Poles. On 23 March Germany agreed by treaty to provide Romania with technical advice and war matériel in return for Romanian oil and wheat. In response, eight days later France signed a bilateral commercial accord with Romania that mandated an increase in French import quotas for a variety of agricultural products and, most important, arranged for France to purchase 600,000 tons of Romanian oil by March 1940—a 20 percent increase over French purchases in 1938 and about 10 percent of Romania's total output. When the Deuxième Bureau reported on 5 April that the Germans aimed to establish complete control of Romanian wheat and oil, the French immediately began to search for ways to construct a "coalition" in Eastern Europe that would deny Germany access to the resources of that region.[10]

The renewed French interest in Eastern Europe after the German annexation of Bohemia and Moravia dealt a strong blow to Foreign Minister Bonnet's policy of retreat. Not only had Daladier and the service chiefs expressed an interest in improving France's ties to Eastern Europe but even Bonnet now recognized that German ambition was hegemonic and a Franco-German peace treaty improbable. Bonnet finally conceded that an eastern front, built around Poland and Romania, could play a critical role in French security. Rather than endorsing French guarantees to these two Eastern European states, however, the foreign minister suggested enlisting the help of the Russians. The Soviet Union could provide war matériel and raw materials to Poland and Romania if Germany moved farther eastward. The French guarantees would lack credibility, the foreign minister recognized, without a concomitant Russian agreement, since only the Soviets were in a position to provide direct support to the states of Eastern Europe. After the Prague coup, then, Bonnet adopted a policy that aimed to deter rather than bribe Germany from starting war. A virtual consensus existed for France's continental policy.[11]

Such was not the case with France's Italian and Mediterranean policy. Bonnet and François-Poncet interpreted Italy's surprised reaction to the Prague coup as a unique opportunity for France to wean Italy away from her dependence on the Axis. After a speech by Mussolini on 26 March, in which the Duce reaffirmed his commitment to the Axis and repeated Italy's claims on Tunis, Djibouti, and the Suez Canal, François-Poncet nevertheless concluded that the speech was "relatively moderate and prudent." Confident that the Italian people distrusted the Germans and would not accept an alliance with the Nazis, François-Poncet recommended that the French government ask Mussolini to outline a minimum program of French concessions. Coincidentally, Bonnet learned from an informant (code-named "Monsieur Nac" and likely a double agent) who had spoken with officials at the Italian embassy in Paris that Mussolini bristled at the "formidable extension of German influence and domination" into Central Europe and the Balkans and "sincerely desired" to resolve all outstanding Franco-Italian differences. The foreign minister then asked Baudouin to speak with Daladier about offering limited concessions to Italy.[12]

But the premier rejected the suggestions of Bonnet, François-Poncet, and Baudouin. "Unfortunately," wrote Daladier on the same day as Mussolini's speech, "simple negotiation has been displaced and complicated by a movement of opinion in Italy against France. . . . This anti-French attitude reflects the policy that the Italian government is following everywhere, especially Spain." The acquisition by French intelligence of a memorandum by Signor Gino Buti, a high-level diplomat at the Italian embassy in Paris, reaffirmed Daladier's conviction. Buti, who had just returned from Rome, where he had spoken with Ciano, indicated that only a "definitive and radical" arrangement could prevent a Franco-Italian war: Corsica, Dalmatia, Malta, and Tunisia had to be integrated into Italian national territory; the Mediterranean had to be recognized as a "vital Italian space"; Italy had to have free access to the oceans [and seas] through Suez, Gibraltar, and Istanbul; and Djibouti had to become an Italian protectorate. Anything less was unacceptable for the Fascists. Moreover, Buti wrote that Axis diplomacy aimed to "isolate France completely." Demonstrating the importance of this section of the document, Daladier underlined it and marked it with a dramatic "X" in the margin. After delivering a radio speech on 29 March that repeated his position regarding Italian demands—"we shall cede neither an acre of our territory nor a single one of our rights"—the French premier ordered Gamelin to take a certain number of "urgent military measures." "It is essential," Daladier told the head of the French armed forces, "to guarantee the government's entire liberty of action if it were suddenly the object of intimidation attempts, and to ensure the security of the metropolitan and colonial territory."[13] Concessions in the Mediterranean would have emasculated France internationally as well as elevated the great-power status of France's principal Mediterranean rival, Italy. As premier of France, Daladier could not consider taking such steps, which also would have had devastating domestic-political consequences. Persuading France's conservative politicians to go to war against a hostile Italy was preferable to explaining why France should relinquish her Mediterranean empire.

Italy's Invasion of Albania

Italy's reaction to the German acquisition of Bohemia and Moravia was considerably more stunned and indignant than to Germany's annexation of Austria the previous year. In contrast to their information before the *Anschluss,* Mussolini and Ciano were not forewarned of the Nazi move into Prague until the night before. Moreover, the extension of the Reich farther into the economic heartland of Central Europe tilted the Axis balance of power considerably toward Germany. Finally, the German seizure of Czechoslovakia effectively destroyed the Munich agreement, in which Mussolini and the Italian people took enormous personal pride. As Ciano wrote, "The Axis functions only in favor of one of its parts, which tends to have preponderant proportions, and it acts entirely on its own initiative, with little regard to us. . . . It is useless to deny that all this preoccupies and humiliates the Italian people." The foreign minister, who was outraged by Germany's duplicity, suggested to Mussolini that Italy reconsider signing an alliance with the Germans, insisting that Hitler "is disloyal and untrustworthy and we cannot carry on any policy with him." Without seeking Mussolini's approval, Ciano sent Fagiuoli back to Paris to ascertain from Baudouin if Daladier's position on concessions to Italy had changed since Prague. But the Duce remained committed to an Axis alliance. Conceding that Germany had now established unassailable hegemony on the European continent, Mussolini ordered a concentration of Italian forces on the Venetian border yet explained that he would not react in any way to the eventual German absorption of Hungary or Poland.[14]

Within Fascist circles in Rome, Ciano argued that the Prague coup demanded an Italian response that would "compensate" Italy for her commitment to the Axis during this crisis. Specifically, Ciano urged the Duce to invade Albania immediately. Mussolini differed with his foreign minister because he feared that the operation would damage the unity of Yugoslavia. Rumors had reached Rome that Vladimir Macek, a Croatian and the leader of the National Agrarian Party that opposed Serbian control in Belgrade, would exploit an Italian invasion of Albania to proclaim independence and place himself under German protection. While Mussolini could accept German domination of Central and Eastern Europe, he could not endure the extension of German influence into the Balkans. In fact Mussolini had wanted to sponsor a Croat insurrection that would eventually lead to a

Croat union with Italy. An Italian Albania and Croatia would set the stage for Italy's domination of the Balkan peninsula. Determined to create a self-sustaining Mediterranean empire that could coexist with, rather than depend on, the German continental empire, Mussolini privately declared that "no one will tolerate the sight of the swastika in the Adriatic."[15]

Two days after Germany's absorption of Bohemia and Moravia, Ciano communicated to Mackensen Italy's surprise about the annexation of the two provinces and concern about Nazi meddling in Croatia. Ciano explained that Germany's endorsement of the Mediterranean region as an Italian sphere of influence had been the basis of the Axis since November 1937. Any change in the status of Croatia in favor of Germany would elicit a fundamental reexamination of Italian policy and would likely break the Axis. On 20 March, after consulting with Berlin, Mackensen declared that "Germany is not interested in the fate of Croatia and recognizes the preeminence of Italian interests there. [Hitler] repeated that the Mediterranean is not, cannot, nor should it become a German sea." Ribbentrop then opened the door to Italy's attack on Albania by asserting in a letter to Ciano that Germany would support any Italian-directed modification of the Balkan status quo in the same way that Italy had accepted German moves in Czechoslovakia.

> You should understand the Führer has decided that for all Mediterranean questions, the policy of the Axis should be determined by Rome, and therefore Germany will never pursue a policy independent of Italy against any Mediterranean state. This decision by the Führer will always be an immutable law of our foreign policy. As the Duce was indifferent in Czechoslovakia, we are indifferent on the Croatian question and, therefore, we will act in this direction only in strict accord with Italian desires.[16]

Another German deal had been presented that Mussolini could not resist. Germany had endorsed the extension of Italy's Axis sphere beyond the Mediterranean and into the Balkans, only at the price of further German penetration into Central and Eastern Europe. Even Ciano was impressed by Hitler's post-Prague admission that Rome should dictate Axis foreign policy in the greater Mediterranean region. Welcoming Fagiuoli's news that the French negotiating position had not changed since Prague, the foreign minister rejected a proposal for Pierre Laval to visit Rome. Emboldened by Chamberlain's obsequious letter to Mussolini that described Italy's policy as "one of peace," the Duce hurriedly called a Gran Consiglio meeting on 21 March in which he fervently reaffirmed his policy of "uncompromising loyalty to the Axis," drew up Italy's first ultimatum to King Zog, and ordered an intensification of planning for the offensive against Albania. At a meeting of the Fascist Militia in Rome on 26 March, Mussolini not only repeated Italy's claims on Tunisia, Djibouti, and Suez but also reaffirmed his commitment to the Axis and his determination to build an Italian empire in the Mediterranean:

> The attempts to unhinge or ruin the Axis are puerile. The Axis is not only a relationship between two states: it is a meeting of two revolutions that exist in sharp antithesis to all the other conceptions of contemporary civilization. This is the strength of the Axis and these are the conditions of its duration . . .
>
> The Mediterranean geographically, historically, politically, and militarily is a vital space for Italy and, when we say the Mediterranean, we are naturally including the Adriatic Sea where the interests of Italy are preeminent but not intolerant of the Slavs.[17]

The fall of Madrid on 28 March, finally signaling Franco's victory over the Republican forces in Spain and representing, according to Ciano, "Fascism's greatest victory," accelerated the plans for an assault on Albania. Three days later Mussolini approved Cavagnari's plans for transporting men and matériel across the Adriatic and set the expedition's launch date for 7 April. At the same time Ciano issued Mussolini's ultimatum that demanded King Zog relinquish control of his state to Italy; he also notified Berlin and Budapest of Italy's intentions. The Italian troops who landed at Durazzo and Valona on Good Friday faced little opposition, enabling Italy to complete its Albanian annexation in only six days. Italy had taken Albania not only to match Germany's aggression but, in the words of Dino Grandi, to open "the ancient paths of the Roman conquests in the East to the Italy of Mussolini" and eventually to attain "our complete dominance of the eastern Mediterranean." Mussolini implemented a large-scale road-building program to improve both Italy's acquisition of important Albanian natural resources—especially copper, chromium, petroleum, and iron ore—and her overland access to Greece. Within 150 kilometers of Salonika, the Italians established a large army and air force garrison to secure the total dependence of the Balkan states on Fascist Italy.[18] Immediately, Greek intelligence informed the British and French that an imminent Italian attack on Corfu was anticipated, which would be followed by Italian action against Greece—plans that Italy in the spring of 1939 had indeed begun to formulate.[19]

British and French reactions to the Albanian coup and the Corfu threat were in stark contrast. Daladier, who had earlier in the month unsuccessfully requested an Anglo-French naval concentration in the Mediterranean, immediately ordered his service chiefs to take a "variety of indispensable precautionary measures," including the transfer of the entire Marine Nationale into or in immediate proximity of the Mediterranean. The premier explained that "it is in the Mediterranean where we must set to work, so that we are prepared to act with maximum force against Italy initially."[20] Two days later the French service chiefs received intelligence from a previously reliable source that on 20 April, Germany and Italy would launch simultaneous offensives stretching from Eastern Europe to the Middle East. Consequently, the French army and air force hurriedly finalized their plans for a Mediterranean war, and by 14 April the leadership of all three French services was prepared for operations against Italy. In the hope that France and Britain could respond to this news in a coordinated fashion, Daladier passed on this information to the British.[21]

Chamberlain's government had no intention of starting war over events in the Balkans. Even though Cadogan and many in the FO believed that Italy's attack on Albania proved Mussolini to be a "gangster" determined to revise the Mediterranean status quo, the permanent undersecretary admitted that "we can't *do* anything to stop it." Chamberlain only regretted that Mussolini sought international recognition from the act: "What I had hoped . . . was that Musso[lini] would so present his camp as to make it look like an agreed arrangement and thus raise as little as possible questions of European significance." Chamberlain refused to believe that Italy had any substantial Balkan ambitions—his entire imperial defense policy depended on a friendly Italy—and speculated that Italy's action in Albania represented an emerging crack in the Axis: "My own belief is that these alarms are started by Germans who hope to frighten us and others and at the same time frighten the Italians by saying similar stories about our intentions. One theory about the Albanian coup is that it is really intended to strengthen Musso[lini]'s hold on the Balkans against Germany." Chamberlain rejected Churchill's calls for Britain to seize Corfu and Minister Oliver Stanley's demand for Britain to renounce the Easter Accords.[22]

The political ramifications of the Albanian episode, however, compelled the British and the French to offer guarantees to Greece and to seek an alliance with Turkey. Greece and Turkey would become Britain's "barrier" in the eastern Mediterranean, analogous to Poland in Eastern Europe. Publicly, the guarantees were to demonstrate British determination to resist further Axis aggression in Eastern Europe and the eastern Mediterranean. In reality, the guarantee to Greece did not reflect a British willingness, or even readiness, to embark on a Mediterranean war. Halifax explained to the FPC that this guarantee was designed to reinforce the Easter Accords by rallying Greek advocacy to the principle of maintaining the Mediterranean status quo. Cadogan, who bristled at Mussolini's audacity, nevertheless admitted that Britain had to adopt a cautious policy that could not extend beyond guarantees: "We shall have quite enough abuse of 'Ice-creamers.' [The] difficulty is to steer between provocation and impression of impotence. If you are too bellicose, you provoke Dictators into doing something irrevocable. If you are too passive, you encourage them to think they can do anything."[23]

Reaffirming that Britain's new eastern Mediterranean policy reflected a symbolic rather than a military initiative, the COS recommended that Britain should offer the guarantee only if the Greeks were prepared to defend themselves. One week after Britain extended the guarantee to Greece, in fact, the Mediterranean fleet was ordered to leave Malta and concentrate at Alexandria, making British intervention in an Italian-Greece conflict even more difficult than it would have been before.[24] In contrast to the French forces, none of the British services took steps in April to prepare themselves for a war in the Mediterranean.

Britain and France also extended a guarantee to Romania, but in this case the French compelled the disinclined British to act. France insisted that support for Greece and Poland would leave Romania especially vulnerable to German revanchism in Eastern Europe. Halifax told his prime minister that Daladier, who had taken "rather too excited a view of the situation," needed some British reassurance. Despite Chamberlain's strong opposition, the Cabinet agreed to extend the Romanian guarantee. As the prime minister reluctantly conceded, the British "could not afford to differ from the French at this stage."[25]

Following the announcement of guarantees to Greece and Romania on 13 April, Britain pursued an alliance arrangement with Turkey. In early 1939 both Chamberlain and the joint planners had worried that a Turkish alliance would provoke a hostile Italy. Although these apprehensions dissipated after Italy's invasion of Albania, the British approached their negotiations with the Turks cautiously. Some at the Admiralty wanted to exploit Turkey's control of the Dardanelles to isolate Italy in the Mediterranean; others throughout Whitehall feared assuming additional obligations in the eastern Mediterranean. The Anglo-Turkish agreement of 12 May satisfied the latter group more than the former. It declared the two nations' intention to support each other "in the Mediterranean area" if war broke out there but it imposed no binding commitment on either state. Even though Turkey had refused to defend Greece from an Axis invasion, Chamberlain was enthusiastic about the treaty: "With the Turk's reply in the bag, I think we have gone a long way towards security in the Balkans."[26] The alliance proved unattainable, however, because Britain could not make the large economic and military contributions that Turkey demanded as a prerequisite, and Turkey would not make public its plans to close the Straits, isolate the Dodecanese, and place Turkish ports at British disposal in the event of a Mediterranean war. Ultimately, Turkey refused to sign a "public" alliance because Britain was unwilling to promise to defend the eastern Mediterranean and prepare jointly for a Mediterranean conflict.

France also endeavored to sign an alliance with Turkey, exhibiting more determination than the British in this effort and demonstrating a genuine anticipation of a war in the Mediterranean. The French began courting the Turks with the dispatch of René Massigli to Ankara in November 1938. Not long after he arrived in Ankara, Massigli suggested that France succumb to Turkey's demand to transfer Alexandretta from Syrian to Turkish control. The general staff soon reinforced Massigli's position, arguing that Turkish cooperation would not only strengthen an eastern front by reassuring other regional powers and aligning the formidable Turkish army on the Allied side but also provide a base from which the Allies could launch offensive operations in the Balkans. Although the Quai d'Orsay resisted this concession in early 1939, Bonnet reluctantly instructed Massigli in late April to initiate discussions with the Turks on this question. By the Franco-Turkish mutual defense treaty of 23 June, France transferred Alexandretta to Turkey and also agreed to provide Turkey with heavy artillery and antiaircraft guns, rifles, and grenades, and a credit of 160 million francs to purchase French matériel in the future. Franco-Turkish staff talks began the following month.[27]

The British decision to spur France into making colonial concessions to Italy provides additional evidence that Britain worked in April to prolong Mediterranean peace, not to prepare for a Mediterranean war. François-Poncet and Bonnet played an important part in the development of this British policy, pleading with the British to place high-level pressure on Daladier to settle Italian claims. Only by surrendering Djibouti, Suez, Tunisia, and the Addis Ababa railway to Italy, according to François-Poncet, would the French avoid "throwing Italy into a conflict on Germany's side." Bonnet believed that the alternative was a four-front war in which France would be wholly vanquished. Limited concessions would satisfy Italy's ambitions and reduce the likelihood of a general European war. At worst, the reduction in size of the French empire would usher in a new, more conservative French government. Recognizing that "the problem resides in Rome, but it is perhaps in Paris where it is most difficult to resolve," the two French diplomats independently and repeatedly told Perth and Phipps in late April and early May that "the time is now right" for France to begin negotiating in earnest with the Italians.[28]

In late April Halifax presented the Bonnet/François-Poncet case to the Cabinet: Britain should persuade France, he argued, that "reasonable" concessions to Italy were appropriate and "could not possibly be interpreted as proof of weakness." Chamberlain, who agreed that "the French were not doing their share in smoothing out their difficulties with the Italians," directed his foreign secretary and ambassador in Paris to "urge these and any other considerations that may occur to you on the French government and do your utmost to induce them to reestablish contact with the Italians." Daladier promptly rejected Phipps's appeal because he feared "a trap laid purposely by Italian gangsters to destroy the wonderful feelings of loyalty that now existed all over North Africa and even in Syria toward France."[29]

According to the British strategists who had contact with their French counterparts, France was still smarting from Britain's declared intention to defend the Far East rather than the eastern Mediterranean. Supported by an Admiralty paper in early May, which suggested that only a neutral Italy could assuage this intractable Anglo-French dispute, the prime minister remained confident that his Mediterranean appeasement policy was correct. As Chamberlain explained to his sister, "I gather that [Mussolini] has at last formulated his demands to the French and that they aren't too formidable. I have a feeling that if he is now handled judiciously it might be possible to give the Axis another twist and that this might be the best way of keeping Mr. Hitler quiet."[30] The British prime minister was still prepared to do almost anything to save the British Empire by averting war in Europe and the Mediterranean.

Anglo-French Staff Talks

Although Allied war planning related to dispatching the BEF to the continent was largely conceived by the British and accepted by the French, the same cannot be said of Allied planning for a Mediterranean war. The French arrived in London on 29 March for staff talks committed to a Mediterranean policy that had support at both political and military levels in Paris. In contrast, Britain began these negotiations without an established Mediterranean policy. As a result, the French set the agenda and profoundly influenced the development of Allied strategy in the Mediterranean.

The internal British discord on the Mediterranean was not apparent during the talks because the mavericks of British naval policy—principally Backhouse and Drax—did not participate. Backhouse fell ill with influenza in late March, and although he continued to run the Admiralty from his sickbed for a few weeks, his rapidly deteriorating health compelled him to relinquish his duties in early May. Without Backhouse there to keep him employed, Drax's tenure at the Admiralty expired at the end of March, and many were not disappointed to see the radical and irritable strategist go. Ironically, the head of the British delegation was Captain Danckwerts, the planning director who was opposed to the idea of an early Mediterranean offensive against Italy and had strong reservations about the Far Eastern defense implications of the European Appreciation.

One of the first subjects the British and the French discussed was the problem of a hostile Italy. The French had already submitted a somewhat vague proposal for early Allied operations against Italy in the event of general war.

The narrowness of the mountain belt between the Franco-Italian frontier and the Po Valley, the demands for French defense on the western front, and Italy's relative superiority in air power precluded an attack on continental Italy. Instead, the French envisaged an *Allied* offensive against Libya from both Tunisia and Egypt and a simultaneous attack on Italian sea communications in the central Mediterranean: "It could be rapidly launched and would require relatively few forces. It makes it possible for Italy to be attacked on her most vulnerable front. Success would have important repercussions, both in regard to control of the Mediterranean basin, and in regard to the subsequent attitude of Italy in the German-Italian alliance."[31]

The British delegation's response was to minimize the Italian threat and emphasize British weakness in North Africa. Without bases in the Indian and Atlantic oceans, Italy could not menace Allied trade diverted to shipping routes outside the Mediterranean. Italy's weak forces and vulnerable communications in Libya made an Italian attack on Egypt and Suez difficult, if not impossible. As Danckwerts' colleague Brigadier John Noble Kennedy explained to General Albert Lelong, head of the French delegation, "We must remember, too, that the enemy in this case [are] only the Italians." Since, given the poor state of Malta's antiair defenses, the Allies lacked a dependable base from which to launch offensive action against North Africa, the British suggested that the Allies initially aim to secure Allied sea communications and interrupt Italian lines with Tripoli and Benghazi. The French should concentrate the Marine in the western Mediterranean while the British operated a naval force in the eastern basin. Once its sea communications were secure, France alone would be in a position to take some offensive measures against Italy's western seaboard.[32]

The British explanation for proposing that France alone attack the Italian mainland—clarified in separate talks between Admirals Pound and Bourragué—hinged on the most controversial element of the first round of staff talks: Britain, admiting that it planned to dispatch a fleet of undecided size to the Far East if Japan entered the war on the Axis side, recognized that such a redeployment of naval forces could allow Italy to gain control of communications in the eastern Mediterranean. Though they were not surprised by Britain's Far Eastern priorities, Lelong and Bourragué pleaded that the Allies adopt a defensive strategy in the Far East, relying on the United States and the Soviet Union to contain Japan until Italy had been defeated. Danckwerts and Pound, however, stressed that Allied naval operations throughout the world depended on the Singapore base.[33] The importance of Singapore to French security seemed remote, but in the Britons' eyes the integrity of the vast British Empire was a prerequisite for successful Allied naval operations.

Nevertheless, the French did inspire a British reassessment of two essential considerations for joint Mediterranean planning. French concerns about

Britain's weak position in the Middle East resulted in a refortification of Egypt following the first round of joint staff talks. The SAC in early April approved a recommendation by the COS that the RAF immediately send one additional fighter and one additional bomber squadron to Egypt, increasing the number of British fighters there from forty-two to seventy-two and bombers from seventy-two to eighty-four. One month later the CID expanded the Middle Eastern command from one infantry brigade to a colonial division. And by July Britain had ordered one brigade of infantry with artillery and ancillary troops from Palestine and four battalions from India to bolster British troops in Egypt.[34]

At the same time, and again as a result of learning French views on the subject, the British began to abandon the Backhouse/Drax conception of an aero-naval bombardment of the northwestern coast of Italy and began to consider an attack directed against Libya. In early April Newall raised strong objections to Backhouse's theory that bombing the Italian peninsula could quickly knock Italy out of the war, especially if the French were reluctant to participate. Chatfield agreed that French intentions in the Mediterranean region significantly affected British planning there. The service chiefs then conceded that they were so intrigued by French planning for war in North Africa that they were willing to reconsider the idea: "We are not satisfied that the possibilities of offensive action against the Italians in Libya have been fully investigated. . . . We propose, therefore, to instruct the UK delegation to press the French delegation further on this point, particularly in view of the desirability of making joint plans for operations from Tunisia and Egypt." By July the British service chiefs had adopted in principle France's Mediterranean strategy, which aimed to make Italy's position in Libya and Ethiopia untenable, but explained that initially only France could carry out the plan.[35]

The British did *not* succumb to French pressure on the issue of defending the Far East. In fact during the month of April the British became increasingly resolute in their determination to support their eastern empire with a naval reinforcement. By the end of April Danckwerts explained to the French that "the fundamental idea underlying British Imperial defence [is] to maintain the security of the British isles on the one hand and Singapore on the other." Reaffirming that Britain would send a fleet to the South China Sea if hostilities erupted there, Danckwerts asked if France would be prepared to exercise control over the entire Mediterranean. A stunned Admiral Odend'hal could only respond that "it was better to give up temporarily the position in the Far East than to lose control of the eastern Mediterranean. . . . although the loss of Singapore would certainly be a severe blow, the loss of war in Europe would be infinitely more disastrous."[36] The official French reaction the following month proposed that the Allies "adopt provisionally in the Far East a defensive attitude." French naval forces were insufficient to prevent the reinforcement of Italian effectives in Libya or to control the shipping lanes in the Mediterranean. Thus, "a diminution of British naval forces in the eastern Mediterranean would allow Italy freedom of movement in that basin and would have considerable moral repercussions on the Balkans, Turkey, and the Arab world."[37]

French indignation about Britain's Far Eastern priority derived from the need to keep a balance of naval power in the Mediterranean. Britain and France had recently agreed that the Royal Navy would station as many as four of its modern 31,000-ton battleships at Malta and Alexandria. This British Mediterranean concentration meant that the Marine Nationale had to operate only two of its World War I–generation 22,500–ton battleships from Toulon and could establish a fleet of modern capital ships at Brest to protect the Atlantic shipping lanes from German raiders. But if the Royal Navy evacuated the eastern Mediterranean for the Far East, France alone would be left to contend with Italy's two 27,000–ton battleships—vessels that had already received new engines, new guns, new turrets, additional armor, new superstructures, and a host of smaller improvements. By July 1940 Italy would add two new 42,000–ton battleships and two additional reconditioned battleships to its Mediterranean presence. Even if France moved its entire Atlantic fleet into the Mediterranean, Italy would still maintain a 25 percent capital-ship advantage over France.[38]

Italy and the Pact of Steel

The British and French guarantees to Poland, Greece, and Romania further strained Anglo-Italian and especially Franco-Italian relations. Most Italian government officials believed that these guarantees, along with the progress of Anglo-Turkish and Anglo-Soviet negotiations and the adoption of British conscription on 1 May, amounted to an aggressive British policy of encirclement designed to stem any additional Axis expansion. The pretense of friendly Anglo-Italians relations could not be sustained any longer. Despite these guarantees, and reports that Britain had arranged to occupy the island of Crete in the event of war, Ciano admitted in mid-May that "the Duce is thinking more and more about jumping on [*saltare addosso*] Greece at the first opportunity." And even though Mussolini as recently as April had authorized the sale of military equipment to Turkey and had reassured Ankara that Rome had no designs on Turkey, the revelation in May of an Anglo-Turkish wartime military cooperation policy in the Mediterranean inspired Mussolini and his advisers to begin building an anti-Turkish Slavic bloc in the Balkans. Mussolini's contemptuous reception of Britain's new ambassador in Rome, Sir Percy Loraine, in late May finally persuaded Ciano that the "[Easter] pact is dead." Loraine's subsequent plea that "His Majesty's Government see no reason why the agreement should not be the keystone of Anglo-Italian relations for many years to come" was treated with contempt in Rome.[39]

Predictably, the Fascists' opinion of the French was worse than their view of the British. Even though François-Poncet in late April announced that France was prepared to resume discussions with Italy, Mussolini refused to sanction any formal talks with the French until a formal military agreement with Germany had been concluded. Daladier's speech of 12 May, in which the French premier reaffirmed his determination not to offer any concessions to Italy, motivated the Duce to demand an immediate halt to all conversations with the French ambassador. Particularly upsetting for Mussolini was the hostile tone of the French press both in Europe and abroad. For instance, the Italian consul in Tunis reported a dramatic rise in the level of anti-Italian violence by local Frenchmen and Arabs, generated by a French propaganda campaign "that claims in a deceptive and unbelievable way that the recent events in Albania demonstrate the menace of Fascism for the Islamic world." This French attempt to reverse Italy's four-year effort to build Muslim trust in Fascism deeply offended Mussolini. At the end of May the Duce explained that "he had no intention of relaxing the tension with France"; he was determined to annex Tunisia and Corsica. Two weeks later he told Ciano that once France was defeated in war, Italy would also acquire Algeria. As a sign of Fascist solidarity, Italy would offer Morocco to Spain on the condition that Italy retain free access to the Atlantic.[40]

Although Mussolini seemed to revel in the hardening of the democratic and totalitarian blocs in the wake of Prague and Albania, much of the Fascist leadership became uneasy about Germany's inclination to precipitate a general conflict. Before the end of April Hitler had renounced the Anglo-German naval agreement and abrogated the German-Polish nonaggression pact. The implications of these public remarks were corroborated by many private conversations: Göring spoke to Ciano about Poland in a manner reminiscent of the German's earlier remarks about independent Austria and Czechoslovakia; Admiral Canaris, head of the German *Abwehr,* told the SIM that "as soon as possible Germany will occupy the ancient territories of the Reich: Poland"; and Attolico warned that Berlin had planned "imminent German action against Poland."[41]

Besides Pariani and Valle, who had been impressed by their recent talks with General Wilhelm Keitel and General Erhard Milch respectively, and who had high expectations for the forthcoming Axis war, many military officials in Rome found the news from Berlin disturbing.[42] Cavagnari revealed that the Servizio Informazioni Segreto della Marina (SIS) could account for only 982 first-class Italian airplanes, far fewer than the air force's claim of more than 3,000. General Giacomo Carboni, the military attaché in

Paris, agreed that "the situation of our armaments is disastrous." Finally, at a Council of Ministers meeting at the end of April, the Duce recognized that the Italian military was entirely unprepared to participate in a general war, despite the boasting of the air and army chiefs; only the navy had evaluated its own strength honestly. An "entirely dissatisfied" Mussolini approved an acceleration in rearmament but assumed that the predicament could be rectified quickly. As Ciano commented, "The ammunition depots are devoid of ammunition. The artillery is out of date. Our antiaircraft and antitank weapons are completely lacking. There has been much bluffing in the military sphere, and even the Duce has been deceived—a tragic bluff."[43]

In May and June Cavagnari and Badoglio impressed upon Mussolini that Italy *alone* would confront Britain and France in the Mediterranean. Naval staff talks in April revealed that in any war with the Western powers the German navy would operate only in the Baltic and the North Sea. There were no plans for the Kriegsmarine to sail into the Atlantic, much less the Mediterranean. Cavagnari understood that the best Italy could hope for was a German offensive on the western front, which would preoccupy a substantial proportion of Allied ground, air, and even naval forces. A more likely scenario, however, was a German march into Eastern Europe, allowing the Allies to concentrate their efforts in the Mediterranean. The naval chief now believed that Anglo-French coordination in the Mediterranean was an established fact. Not only had the two nations each cautiously concentrated troops, aircraft, guns, and ammunition at Gibraltar following the Albanian invasion, but a recent Anglo-French naval demonstration in the western Mediterranean also represented, according to the Italian naval attaché in London, "palpable proof of the strict cooperation between the two navies."[44]

Air and ground operations also offered dismal prospects for Italy and additional motivations for seeking to postpone both a formal alliance with Germany and Italy's intervention in a general war. Cavagnari cited air force intelligence indicating that French bombers could attack metropolitan Italy, Italian maritime communications, Tripoli, and the Dodecanese with impunity. Badoglio reported that at least eighteen months of further defensive improvements were required before the Libyan garrison "would be able to reach a level of efficiency that guarantees we could not only face up to any sudden menace but impose our will on eventual adversaries." Libya's ground forces could not withstand either a British or French assault, much less a combined one, until the end of 1940 at the earliest.[45]

Ciano embarked on negotiations with Ribbentrop on 6 May in Milan with these concerns in mind. Lacking trust in Germany since Prague and having received countless assurances from François-Poncet, Perth, and Loraine that French colonial concessions were on the horizon, Ciano approached the negotiations with Ribbentrop skeptically and determined to persuade the Germans that war could not be contemplated in the near future. The German foreign minister, apparently aware of Ciano's unease, presented himself as "the standard-bearer of a policy of moderation and understanding." Ribbentrop indicated that the Axis had to achieve certain territorial objectives "within a few years" but implied that the pace of German dynamism had to slow down in accordance with current conditions: Germany, like Italy, needed a period of peace that "should not be less than four or five years." Ciano found these statements sincere and reassuring. That evening he telephoned the Duce, who ordered his foreign minister to make a public announcement of the forthcoming military alliance. In the Pact of Steel, which Ciano and Ribbentrop signed on 22 May in Berlin, the two foreign ministers affirmed that since their forces were still unprepared for the inevitable clash with the West, Germany and Italy both desired "a long period of peace—at least three years." And shortly before the signing ceremony, Hitler reassured Ciano that Italy would continue to direct Axis Mediterranean policy.[46]

The Duce was not forced to conclude an alliance with Germany out of fear. A downtrodden Mussolini, compelled to act in a way he did not desire, would not have decorated Ribbentrop with the Order of the Annunziata—making the bearer one of only twenty-four honorary cousins of the King of Italy—for the German foreign minister's role in negotiating the alliance. Nor did Mussolini see the pact as a restraining influence on Germany, as Ciano did, or as a response to the refusals by the French to make concessions or the British to provide aid. Instead, Mussolini viewed it as a powerful offensive military alliance directed against the democracies. It was a call not only to increase and improve Italian armaments and defense as rapidly as possible but also to strengthen Italian economic autarchy so that it could withstand the democracies' planned *guerra di usura* against the Fascist powers. Most important, the Pact of Steel represented for Mussolini a unity of ideological and geopolitical purpose between Germany and Italy, two totalitarian states that were determined to rearrange Europe's map and the world's balance of power. In Turin on 14 May Mussolini explained that the Axis, which "has been for many years a parallel act of two regimes and of two revolutions," would become "an inseparable union of two states and two peoples." Immediately after Ciano and Ribbentrop signed the pact, the Duce privately told his military chiefs that "the war between the plutocratic and egotistically conservative nations and the populous and poor nations is inevitable. On this premise, we need to prepare ourselves."[47]

Preparation, in this case, meant improving Italian armaments and autarchy and, specifically, planning to occupy the Balkans. On 26 May Mussolini and Ciano agreed to finance Macek's Croat movement with twenty million dinars via a Swiss bank in Zurich. In return, Macek promised to undertake a revolution against the Belgrade government within six months, to request Italian military intervention to restore order, and then to establish an independent Croat state in confederation with Rome. The Fascists envisioned "after some time" completely annexing Croatia. Control of both Croatia and Albania would establish Italy as the predominant power in the Balkans, which, the Duce believed, was a prerequisite for Italy's war in the Mediterranean. As Mussolini explained to his service chiefs,

> Immediately on the outbreak of war, we must seize the Balkans and the entire Danubian basin. We will not be content with declarations of neutrality; we will occupy these territories and exploit them for military, alimentary, and industrial supplies. This operation, which should be swift and carried out with extreme decisiveness, not only will knock out [*mettere fuori combattimento*] the "guarantees" for Greece, Romania, and Turkey but will provide us with security on our backside.[48]

Mussolini wanted the alliance with Germany and understood that it increased the likelihood of a war against the democracies—a war that offered him the opportunity to build a Mediterranean empire for Italy.

British and French Preparation for Peace in the Mediterranean

While the Anglo-French staff talks on the Mediterranean theater provided an opportunity for British strategy to coalesce around a single policy, they dislodged French unanimity on Mediterranean strategy and incited an atmosphere of desperation in Paris. No longer did the French service chiefs and statesmen work together to create a single, defensible French strategic position. Instead, as it increasingly appeared that the Nazis would go to war over Poland's refusal to restore the Baltic port of Danzing to German sovereignty, contradictory policy papers were dispatched to London in a frantic attempt to find a viable and energetic Allied Mediterranean strategy. This sudden deviation from the interservice coordination and cooperation that existed in early 1939 reflects the level of anxiety that consumed French officials during the summer of 1939.

The first divisive issue for the French was Italian neutrality. An important element of this debate was the effort by many Frenchmen to build a security system in Eastern Europe to defend those countries that France, despite her new obligations, could not protect. The "effective collaboration" of the Soviet Union, according to the Quai d'Orsay, was a critical element of this endeavor. French strategists, who had long resisted any sort of military arrangement with the Russians, also recognized that France required Soviet cooperation in Eastern Europe "to force Germany and Italy to fight on two fronts." With Italy now a presumed antagonist and France's land and sea routes to Eastern Europe effectively severed, the general staff admitted that only the Soviet Union could sustain France's eastern allies in a war against the Axis. "To the USSR," Gamelin explained to the British, "belongs the task of supplying an eastern front at least so long as our communications in the Mediterranean are not assured." Aubert endorsed the French search for a Russian alliance in late June, and in July Daladier directed his ambassador in Moscow "to make every effort" to secure an agreement with the Soviet Union.[49]

Yet the negotiations with the Russians were slow and inconclusive. With the Soviet Union uncommitted and Germany, Italy, and perhaps Japan and Spain as likely adversaries, the anticipated situation appeared dire. The four-front war that François-Poncet had postulated in April was looking increasingly likely. Thus, the British suggestion that Italy could be persuaded to remain neutral came, at least for the French army and air force, as welcome relief from a scenario that would have stretched resources far beyond capacity. Both Vuillemin and Gamelin admitted that a neutral Italy would allow French forces to concentrate on defending the German frontier and providing military assistance to Poland, Romania, Greece, and Turkey. Moreover, a neutral Italy meant a high probability of a neutral Spain also. The "situation would be less disadvantageous and the relation of forces less disproportionate if Italy were to remain neutral at the beginning of the conflict."[50]

Darlan's response to the question of Italian neutrality, though, was considerably more circumspect and reasoned than those of the army and air force. The naval chief admitted that Italian neutrality would be "precious" if Italy "openly disassociated herself from Germany." In that case, French maritime communications, the transport of troops from North Africa to the European continent, and the continued availability of supplies by way of the Suez Canal would be easy to secure. The Marine could concentrate almost exclusively on sinking German raiders and submarines in the Atlantic and intercepting Germany's seaborne trade. Darlan insisted, however, that all these advantages were predicated on unequivocal Italian neutrality, a position not likely to develop:

> Italy, in declaring neutrality, may hope to put our vigilance to sleep and induce us to denude the Mediterranean so that she might attack us suddenly under more favorable conditions. If there were any presumption that this was the Italian calculation, we would have to renounce completely any advantageous redeployment of forces, and then the benefit resulting from Italian neutrality would be more apparent than real.[51]

In other words, if Italy supported the German war effort without declaring belligerence, or if France and Britain had to keep their forces in the Mediterranean on the chance that Italy would eventually join the war, there was no value in Italian neutrality.[52]

Gamelin, who had not discussed Italian neutrality with France's ministers or even at a meeting of the French service chiefs, composed France's official position on the subject. He used Darlan's words of caution at the outset of his note but concluded with those of the army:

> It will always be a question, whether in the West or in the East, of organizing at the outset long and solid fronts facing Germany. . . . Italian neutrality would permit the provision of men and matériel for these fronts from the outset of a war and would facilitate the constitution of the large reserves which would have to be collected before undertaking a general offensive.[53]

In its entirety, the statement presented an ambiguous French opinion about Italian neutrality. But the British, especially those in the Admiralty, placed emphasis on its encouraging conclusion. Since the French recognized the benefit of Italian neutrality, they could be persuaded to adopt a conciliatory position toward Italy. Although the COS had authorized local commanders in North Africa, the Middle East, and the Red Sea region to discuss with their French counterparts operational directives for rendering untenable Italy's position in Libya, and eventually in Abyssinia, the Admiralty was simultaneously undermining the entire concept of a Mediterranean offensive.[54] In his last major dispatch from the Mediterranean before assuming his duty as the new first sea lord, Pound argued that the strength of Italian air power in the Mediterranean, and the corresponding inadequacy of British antiair defenses, precluded any offensive Allied action in North or East Africa. Pound insisted that even a sea-based offensive against Italy would have devastating consequences. The preponderance of Italian submarines and aircraft, the vulnerability of Malta, and the weakness of the French air force all indicated that the Royal Navy would "undoubtedly be subject to attrition to a much greater extent than the Italian [navy]."[55]

This defensive tendency in British strategic thinking had support in London's high political circles, where preparing for war and jeopardizing the empire were anathema to British policy. Although the Prague coup had compelled the British to adopt a policy of deterrence on the continent, Chamberlain remained unwilling to build a European coalition that could resist Germany in war. Fearful of dividing Europe into antagonistic blocs that would escalate international tension and drive the continent headlong into war, Chamberlain avoided making any commitment to the "distrustful" Russians. When the British Cabinet in late May finally decided to accept in principle Soviet proposals for an alliance, the "deeply suspicious" Chamberlain attached such onerous stipulations to the British negotiating position that such an alliance became extremely unlikely.[56]

One of the principal reasons that Chamberlain looked with disfavor on the idea was that he believed a Soviet alliance "would make any negotiation or discussion with the totalitarians difficult if not impossible." Despite Daladier's recent promise that France had no intention "to yield to [Italy's] campaign of violence and blackmail," the FO urged that Britain increase pressure on France to begin discussions with Italy immediately. At Chamberlain's request, Phipps was directed to reiterate Britain's desire for a Franco-Italian reconciliation, and Loraine was allowed to inform Ciano that Britain was "inducing the French to meet" Italy's claims.[57]

Another interservice conflict in France was generated in May by one more prescient intelligence report from Athens claiming that the Italians planned to launch operations from Italy's 90,000-man Albanian garrison into Macedonia and Greece, with Crete, Corfu, Salonika, and Thrace as their objectives. Combined with Italy's naval bases in the Dodecanese, the new strategic positions in the Adriatic and Aegean would establish indisputable Axis control of the Balkans and the Black Sea, and Italian preeminence in the eastern Mediterranean. The independence of France's new "ally," Turkey, would be directly jeopardized.[58]

The prospect of Britain's abandoning the eastern Mediterranean in favor of the Far East and Italy's achieving dominance in that region persuaded General Maxime Weygand, a tactless and outspoken nationalist and monarchist who had retired as army chief of staff in 1935 but retained an influential position within military, Catholic, and conservative political circles, to recommend an Allied expedition to Salonika—much as he had, ironically, during the First World War. An Allied foothold in the Balkans would discourage the Axis powers from moving against Greece and Turkey, provide a way station for Western supplies to Eastern Europe, and offer the Allies an outpost from which to launch operations against Germany and Italy. Like many of his military colleagues, Weygand viewed an eastern front as an essential aspect of any successful Allied strategy. "The eastern front here [in the Balkans] presents new possibilities, not only as a valuable line of defence, but as a potential field for taking the offensive, capable by a combination of land, sea, and air forces of giving us victory."[59]

Despite vehement opposition from the Marine Nationale, which argued that reliable security of the communication and supply line to Salonika could be assured only if Italy were definitively neutral, Gamelin attached great significance to the Salonika expedition idea: he agreed with Weygand that "the French flag should be at Salonika" to discourage Italy from contemplating action in the eastern Mediterranean. Surprisingly, Gamelin also believed that a proposal to send troops to the Levant, even if it lacked an endorsement from either the Marine or the French government, would generate a consensus for joint Anglo-French action in the Mediterranean. Having received approval only from the army staff, Gamelin suggested to Lord Gort, Chief of the Imperial General Staff (CIGS), that the Allies plan a mission to Salonika in the early stages of war.[60]

France's Salonika plan was quickly overshadowed by the outbreak of crisis in China. On 14 June Japanese soldiers and Chinese police under their direction blockaded the British concession of Tientsin, prohibiting any person from leaving and any goods except food from entering. The Tientsin crisis starkly exposed the vulnerability of not only Britain's position in the Far East but also her entire worldwide imperial system. Ambassador Craigie and the Far Eastern Department of the FO again demanded the immediate reinforcement of British naval forces at Singapore. At an FPC meeting on 19 June, Chatfield proposed dispatching seven capital ships to Singapore by mid-September. That evening Ambassador Kennedy telephoned to Halifax that the United States would not take any action beyond its current observation "with special interest" of the events in China. The COS then drafted a paper that accepted Chatfield's proposal and abandoned any intention to carry out an early Mediterranean offensive against Italy: "Britain could not, as hitherto contemplated, interrupt Italian communications with North Africa or undertake offensive naval action in that area. . . . Furthermore, we could not secure our own sea communications in the Mediterranean to Turkey, Greece, or the Black Sea."[61]

Although the CID ultimately decided to withdraw British forces from Tientsin, Britain reassured both the high command in Singapore and the Dominions that the Far Eastern commitment remained firm. Some in the government noted that Britain's response to Tientsin jeopardized both the Greek guarantee and the Turkish negotiations. Cadogan, in particular, believed that Britain had "bungled this thing [in Tientsin] sadly." But Chamberlain, who speculated that war would likely erupt in the Far East sooner than in Europe, remained fully confident that his policy was correct. Choosing weak deterrence for the Far East and naked conciliation for the Mediterranean, the prime minister asked the service chiefs to consider the strategic consequences of Italian neutrality.[62]

Italian Unpreparedness

Soon after signing the Pact of Steel, Ciano began to doubt the genuine viability of this new alliance. The foreign minister recognized that the pact was more popular in Germany than in Italy, admitting to himself that "the hatred for France has not yet been successful in engendering love for Germany." Even more disconcerting, however, was Ciano's growing understanding that Germany was not committed to the specific terms of the alliance. Cables from Guariglia in Paris and Attolico in Berlin throughout June and July indicated that the German-Polish tension had intensified rather than abated since late May. Ribbentrop made no attempt to disguise his open hostility to various proposals for a negotiated settlement of the Danzig issue. One week before Mussolini's scheduled meeting with Hitler on 4 August at the Brenner Pass, Ribbentrop declared Germany's disinclination to discuss her policy even with her new ally and then canceled the conference. Ciano's efforts to rein in Hitler's war machine had come to naught.[63]

Cavagnari was also skeptical about the value of this alliance. In early May the Italian naval chief accepted the German invitation for "conversations of a general character" and discussions about "purposes and principles of further collaboration." On the basis of this premise, the Italian naval staff expected to confer with the Germans on issues related to the availability of raw materials, the problems of maritime resupply, signal, and cipher communications, and information about other navies. Although the SMM conceded that an exchange of "general operational concepts" was "fundamental," it proposed that these strategic concerns be raised in the future, at a meeting that was not yet scheduled or even contemplated. In other words, Cavagnari traveled to Friedrichshaven in late June without any intention of coordinating Italian and German naval strategies.[64]

Much to Cavagnari's chagrin, however, naval strategy was one of the first principal subjects of the Friedrichshaven talks. Admiral Raeder opened the conversations, declaring that the Germans, once war began, would immediately engage the enemy in the Atlantic with both surface ships and submarines. The Germans hoped that the Italians would plan for operations in the western Mediterranean against France, taking advantage of Spain, the Balearics, and Sardinia to deny France the ability to transfer troops stationed in North Africa to the European continent. Raeder also recommended that Italy avoid embarking on any offensive against Egypt or Suez, since any Italian activity in the eastern Mediterranean would encourage France to attack Libya from Tunisia and Algeria. If, however, Italy could send a submarine force southward from Massawa or Assab into the Gulf of Aden and the Indian Ocean, the Axis powers could sever the Anglo-French trade routes and foil the Allies' economic war plans.

Citing his expectation for a simultaneous French attack on the Balearics and British attack on the Dodecanese, Cavagnari indicated that the Italian navy would have to remain on the defensive in order to secure communications between Sicily and Libya. The Regia Marina could neither begin offensive forays against the French nor weaken its underwater force in the central Mediterranean for the benefit of operations in the Red Sea and Indian Ocean. Cavagnari also forced the German naval chief to admit that all of Germany's largest, fastest, and most powerful warships would remain in the North Sea for the duration of the war against Britain and France. In view of the Kriegsmarine's anticipated absence from the Mediterranean, Cavagnari sought nonnaval assistance from Germany. But Raeder offered Cavagnari little strategic or operational comfort, enhancing the Italian naval chief's opposition to launching a war against the Western powers.[65]

In 1939 Cavagnari was preoccupied by the balance of naval power in the Mediterranean. His view of naval engagements was based on his understanding of the lessons of the First World War. He envisioned naval battles as predominantly large-scale traditional fleet conflicts, where the size and power of battleships would rule the day. Unfortunately, in 1939 Italy's battleship force had not yet come of age: all four of its 46,000-ton modern battleships were still under construction, and the first was not due to be completed until the spring of 1940. Two additional 30,000-ton battleships that were undergoing total reconversions were not expected to enter into service until the summer of 1940. Italy's battleship force in 1939, then, consisted of only two 29,100-ton but wholly rebuilt World War I–era battleships. By contrast, Britain and France had six modernized battleships, ranging from 28,500 to 35,500 tons, in the Mediterranean, with many larger and newer ones stationed in the Atlantic and prepared to reinforce their Mediterranean fleets if necessary. To Cavagnari, this battleship inequity between the Allies and Italy was a recipe for disaster.[66]

Cavagnari also feared Anglo-French naval cooperation. As independent potential foes in the Mediterranean, the Allies did not necessarily strike immediate alarm in the minds of the Regia Marina's admirals. But tightly allied, Cavagnari contended, the French and British fleets were an overt menace to the security of the Regia Marina and the Italian peninsula. As the commander of a fleet without an air arm or aircraft carriers, Cavagnari found the reports on extensive Anglo-French aeronautical collaboration in the Mediterranean particularly disheartening. Meanwhile, Admiral Canaris of the Kriegsmarine revealed in early July that the German military, especially the navy, was unprepared for the tasks it would face in a war against Britain and France. Italian naval intelligence was stunned, and the Regia Marina's chief was horrified. Even though the two navies had agreed not to pursue joint strategic planning, the Italians had assumed since Friedrichshaven that the Germans could confront at least some of the Allied naval forces in the event of war.[67]

Perhaps the most ominous report, however, came in late July from Margottini, who attributed Anglo-French optimism regarding the "imminent conflict" to "the grand strategy that the French and British have defined in a non-equivocal manner." Margottini explained that Britain and France planned "to resist Germany and concentrate in all fields (land, air, and sea; metropolis and North Africa) against Italy." Cavagnari concluded that this Anglo-French strategy had extended beyond the realm of theory into operational and tactical planning.[68]

In a 31 July analysis of Italian fleet exercises that had assumed an Anglo-French war against Italy with Turkey and Greece neutral, Cavagnari explained to Mussolini that the enemy's strategic alignment and the Regia Marina's error-ridden telegraphic communication system forbade any Italian offensive naval forays in the Mediterranean. Italian torpedoes, two recent tests had shown, were only 64 percent effective, and only 56 percent at night. As a result, the Regia Marina could do little more than provide protection to fast transport convoys between eastern Sicily and coastal Libya; passage by any other route or by any slow convoy would be "definitely very hazardous." Having already told the Ministry of Italian Africa that the navy could spare no surface vessels for operations off the coast of Somalia or in the Red Sea, Cavagnari now strongly recommended to the Duce that Italy not assume an offensive strategy or even posture in the Mediterranean:

> Between the two available systems—that with a scope which is primarily *offensive* and is parallel to the probable course of the enemy, and that with a scope which is primarily *exploratory* and is our normal course of action—it seems appropriate to choose *an intermediate system* . . . the offensive deployment runs the risk of everything going to nothing by a simple, even limited, change of course by the enemy.[69]

A report on 2 August from Mario Roatta, Italy's military attaché in Germany, that the Wehrmacht would have three divisions ready to invade Poland on 1 September, plus Ciano's own conviction that "we must avoid war," motivated the foreign minister to propose a visit to Germany in the hope of postponing war. Having just received Cavagnari's assessment of the recent naval exercises and Badoglio's frequent reminders of Libya's weakness, Mussolini agreed that Italy should work to delay the conflict.[70] In Berlin, Ribbentrop told Ciano that although war between Germany and Poland was now inevitable, he did not believe the conflict would expand into a general European war. France and Britain lacked the matériel to attack Germany or the Axis, and without taking the offensive the democracies could not defeat the totalitarian powers. Ribbentrop confidently predicted that the Soviet Union would not intervene and the United States would remain neutral. Nothing could be gained by further delay. The following day Hitler told Ciano that Germany would launch her attack at the end of August, and Poland would be liquidated by 15 October. If Britain and France chose to declare war, they would soon be defeated by the Axis powers' superior military resources.[71]

The results of these meetings persuaded Mussolini to reconsider his position on the forthcoming conflict. "Honor," the Duce told his foreign minister, compelled Italy to march with Germany if Britain and France declared war against Italy's Axis partner. But Mussolini continued to vacillate on an appropriate Italian reaction to general war, which he now knew was imminent. To preserve his freedom of maneuver, the Duce instructed Badoglio on 15 August to maintain "the strictest defensive" alignment without committing any act that would reveal Italy's position in the conflict. Should the Allies compel Italy into war, however, Mussolini directed the chief of his military to prepare for an immediate attack on Greece and, "after unleashing internal disorders in Yugoslavia," the seizure of Croatia. Badoglio warned that the Allies' principal effort against Italy would likely occur in North Africa, where Italy's Libyan colony lacked resources, matériel, and adequate defenses. Yet the Duce believed that a gain of territory in the Balkans would offset any short-term but recoverable losses in North Africa. Despite Badoglio's reservations, the Italian army before the end of August had revised its plans for offensive operations against Greece and Yugoslavia. Plans were also prepared for counteroffensive operations against Tunisia, Egypt, Djibouti, and British Somalia, and in the Aegean.[72]

But Ciano, who by late August was describing the Germans as "traitorous" and "treacherous and deceitful," and who had become convinced by Loraine and François-Poncet that Italy could achieve territorial revisions peacefully, refused to let Cavagnari's warnings go unheeded. The Italian foreign minister cabled Attolico and directed the ambassador to inform Ribbentrop that the Italian navy—the strongest of Italy's military services—was not ready for war. Ciano found additional support for Italian neutrality from Vittorio Emanuele III. The king, a cold, suspicious, and fearful man who had attended the late August maneuvers of the army of the Po, regarded the army's officers as unqualified, its equipment old and obsolete, and its overall preparedness "pathetic." Adding that Italian public opinion was decidedly anti-German, the monarch instructed Mussolini to take no "supreme decisions" without him.[73]

But perhaps the most persuasive argument against Italy's intervening in a European war was the nation's financial and economic condition. In June Felice Guarneri, minister of currency and exchange, had remonstrated that Italy by the end of the year under existing, peacetime circumstances would deplete her currency reserves by more than 500 million lire. National bankruptcy, according to Guarneri, could be avoided only if Italy "put a stop to her imperialistic policies." War or any other dramatic acceleration of Italian spending was financially impossible. Although the Duce discounted these concerns in June, the complaints in August by the Italian service chiefs of inadequate stocks of raw materials affirmed Guarneri's position. On 26 August Mussolini explained to Hitler that in order to sustain a war for one year Italy needed six million tons of coal, two million tons of steel, seven million tons of mineral oils, one million tons of timber, hundreds of thousands of tons of sodium nitrate, copper, iron, potassium salts, and rosin, and hundreds of antiaircraft batteries. Moreover, even if these resources and matériel were available on the open market, Italy could not afford them; Germany would have to provide them at no cost if Italy were to participate in any immediate war. Ultimately, it was the combined pressure from Ciano, Cavagnari, Badoglio, Guarneri, and the king that persuaded Mussolini, first, to urge the Führer to consider a negotiated settlement and, eventually, to choose not to intervene in the war against the Western powers.[74]

Hitler was shocked by Mussolini's refusal to intervene or provide military assistance to Germany. Joseph Goebbels, Hitler's propaganda minister, observed, "That's a serious blow for him." But Hitler's rage was directed at the Italian king, whom he had always despised, not at his friend, the Italian dictator. The Führer remained committed to the Axis and trusted that Italy would join the war after German successes on the battlefield. Indeed, the Duce had not in any way abandoned his ally: he not only endorsed the Soviet-German nonaggression pact, signifying that the Axis took precedence over his "anti-Bolshevik ideology," but also offered to support German industry and agriculture during the war—a proposal that Hitler immediately accepted. Mussolini explained to Hitler that regardless of Germany's action, "I have agreed to clarify the line of my action with you. Please consider my appeal as another demonstration of my unwavering solidarity."[75] The Duce's choice for Italian "nonbelligerence" was nothing more than a postponement of what Mussolini viewed as the inevitable: Italy's dynamic participation in a war of the totalitarian states against the decadent democracies.

British and French Intervention

In July and August officials in London buried Britain's offensive Mediterranean strategy and endorsed a preference for a neutral Italy—despite many voices of opposition. The Economic Pressure Subcommittee of the CID opined that Italian neutrality would complicate plans for an economic blockade of Germany, concluding that "the entry of Italy into the war on the side of Germany would be advantageous, rather than the reverse, to the Allies." General Sir Edmund Ironside, inspector general of British overseas forces, contended that a neutral Italy would benefit Germany by complicating Allied strategy. He urged the government to adopt an assertive Mediterranean strategy that would secure Egypt and the Suez Canal:

> We must attack—for we cannot win the war by defending ourselves—and we must attack where we can have the greatest effect. Italy is the Achilles heel of the Berlin-Rome Axis and we must concentrate on knocking her out. . . . Egypt, Palestine, and Turkey are the centre of the world and the centre of the British Empire. It is from here that we can prepare our offensive.

General Archibald Wavell, commander of British forces in the Middle East, also argued that winning control of the Mediterranean should be Britain's primary objective upon the outbreak of war. "The next war, as I see it, will be won or lost in the Mediterranean; and the longer it takes us to secure effective control of the Mediterranean, the harder will be the winning of the war." Admiral Andrew Cunningham, commander of the Mediterranean fleet, thought that "the surrender of the Italian Army in Libya coupled with attacks on the Italian coast in places where material damage can be done would certainly have a great moral effect and might well cause the Italians to lose heart." Raised in Dublin's middle class, Cunningham—who would become Britain's most decorated sailor in the Second World War—was a confident and forthright man with an implacable and resolute spirit. Cunningham told Pound, who had taken over as first sea lord from the dying Backhouse, that a Mediterranean offensive against Italy "appears to me to be the *only* plan before us and our Allies in the early stages." Even the *Daily Herald,* a Labour Party newspaper, declared that Italy's invasion of Albania required the government to act decisively in defense of Britain's exposed imperial interests. "From the days of Blake and Cromwell, the safety of our Mediterranean communications has been regarded as a paramount concern of British policy. It must always be so while Britain is a world Power."[76]

Yet some of the most influential policymaking voices in London disagreed with this Mediterranean-offensive perspective. On 12 July—one week after Chamberlain and Simon decided that Britain could not afford to build three capital ships annually[77]—the Joint Planning Committee asserted that a "knock-out blow" of Italy would take at least six months and would prove costly to the Royal Navy. Italy's large submarine force and numerous air bases in the Mediterranean would allow the Regia Marina and Regia Aeronautica to wreak havoc on British ships. The following week Pound declared that an offensive against Italy could succeed only if all three services, from both France and Britain, participated simultaneously. Even in this scenario, Pound warned that the Royal Navy would suffer capital-ship losses that could affect Britain's security in other theaters, especially the Far East:

> [I]f there is any doubt as to the attitude of Japan and the USA, we cannot, with our present strength, afford to risk the loss of these ships, as not only would this serious reduction in our capital ship strength afford every inducement to Japan to come in against us, but if she did so we should have insufficient ships to send to the Far East even if we abandoned the eastern Mediterranean.

Without much debate, the service chiefs in their meeting of 19 July agreed that an early defeat of Italy was impossible. In the event that Italy did declare war, the Allies should divert their shipping around the Cape, remain on the defensive, do nothing provocative, and concentrate on the economic strangulation of Italy by closing the entrances to the Mediterranean.[78] All initiative had been abdicated to the Axis.

These military arguments were combined with compelling political and diplomatic ones. Throughout June and July representatives from Australia and New Zealand demanded to know exact specifics about Britain's war plans for the Far East and the Mediterranean, and reminded the Admiralty of its repeated assurances after Munich that the naval guarantees would be honored. Australia's prime minister, Robert Menzies, even urged Chamberlain to demand that the French offer concessions to Mussolini. Neither this Dominion pressure nor the reluctance of the United States to act decisively in the Far East, however, caused a reappraisal of Britain's Mediterranean policy. Chamberlain and Halifax used these external factors to justify their enduring campaign for a Mediterranean appeasement, which was based on an ironic juxtaposition of arguments about the absence of a credible Italian threat and the extensive damage the Italian navy and military could inflict on British forces if there were a war in the Mediterranean. Without reference to the Dominions or the United States, the CID on 24 July concluded that "Italian neutrality, if it could be assured, would be decidedly preferable to her active hostility."[79] In other words, the British Empire stood its best chance of survival if the British could avoid conflict in the Mediterranean.

Chamberlain's determination not to get involved in a war in the Mediterranean and not to "give way" in the Far East had spurred a reconsideration of Britain's offensive Mediterranean strategy and an embrace of Italian neutrality as the solution to the Mediterranean dilemma. In mid-July Chamberlain reaffirmed his belief that Italy should remain the focus of the West's diplomatic energy: "As always I regard Rome as the weak end of the Axis and one should always be trying to bend it."[80] Bending, as Chamberlain tried to explain to Daladier, required that France—not Britain—offer colonial concessions to Italy. The thought of going to war against Italy, especially an early

Allied offensive, had been and remained entirely anathema to Chamberlain's personal convictions as well as to his foreign and imperial policy.

IT DID NOT take long for the French to determine where Britain stood on Mediterranean affairs. Chamberlain made a direct appeal to Daladier on 13 July for Franco-Italian reconciliation, "which has necessarily so important a bearing on the general situation." Although he appreciated France's difficulties with Italy, Chamberlain thought that "there might be considerable advantages in some further exploration of the position, and the information which comes to us from Italy suggests to my mind that the present would be an appropriate moment." On the same day Gamelin met with Gort, who revealed that the British opposed the French proposal for an Allied mission to Salonika and that Britain's stance on sending its Mediterranean forces to the Far East had become resolute since the Tientsin crisis. To offset British policy in the region, including Britain's "dangerously compromised" forces in Egypt, the French recognized they needed to strengthen their own forces in Syria. The French refused to open negotiations with Italy.[81]

Darlan's relentless campaign for Anglo-French action against Italy further exacerbated tensions in Paris concerning the Mediterranean. Without receiving authority from the French service chiefs or government, the Marine introduced revised but vague naval Mediterranean war plans to the Royal Navy. At an Anglo-French naval command conference at Malta in July, France's commander of the Mediterranean, Admiral Emmanuel Ollive, told Cunningham that France was now planning to bombard the western Italian coastline at the outset of war. Specifically, the French Marine would conduct operations against Genoa, Savona, and Palermo. Early in August Darlan informed Pound, "We remain convinced that naval success in the Mediterranean, as rapid as possible, is the surest way of striking the principal enemy: Germany." Darlan obviously hoped that, by agreeing to carry out the plans that he knew the British Admiralty, including Cunningham, had originally contemplated, France could procure consensus for a combined Mediterranean offensive strategy. Again in August Darlan told his colleagues, who were increasingly aware of his disenfranchisement, "It is in the Mediterranean, even the central Mediterranean, where we must act. All other theaters are secondary."[82]

Perhaps Darlan, who was frustrated at the lack of Anglo-French coordination for a joint Mediterranean policy, envisioned establishing Anglo-French naval solidarity on a Mediterranean strategy that could then be presented to the two governments as a fait accompli. Or perhaps Darlan, in the light of Gamelin's unendorsed declarations to Britain on Italian neutrality and a Salonika expedition, believed that the prevailing state of international affairs made such underhanded measures appropriate. Regardless, this sudden shift in French naval strategy, and the deceitful manner in which it was presented to the British, reflects the level of desperation that had consumed officials in Paris by the summer of 1939.

What is most surprising, though, is not only that Darlan and Gamelin were out of step with one another but that Daladier lacked the necessary courage, certainty, and leadership to garner unwavering foreign policy support from his subordinates. The French premier had rejected Chamberlain's 13 July plea to consider making concessions to Italy and looked skeptically on Britain's interest in a neutral Italy and opposition to an Allied Mediterranean offensive against Libya and Italian maritime communications. Citing French naval intelligence that claimed Italy would attack Yugoslavia and seek to occupy Salonika soon after the outset of war and opining that a neutral and sympathetic Italy would enable Germany to circumvent an Allied blockade, Daladier told Hore-Belisha in August that the Allies had to compel Italy to enter the war immediately: "This would give us a chance of an initial military success."[83]

Despite the renewed clarity of the premier's position on Mediterranean issues, the French army chief continued to pursue his own agenda and to undermine Daladier's. Gamelin, who was distraught that London had been unreceptive to his Salonika idea and who was increasingly concerned about the repercussions of the deteriorating Danzig crisis, informed the British over the summer that the Allied plan for a French assault against Tripoli at the outset of war was contingent on Spanish neutrality. He explained that if Spain went to war against the democracies alongside Germany and Italy, France would have to capture Spanish Morocco before moving against Libya; France therefore preferred a neutral Italy.[84] With Darlan's sudden interest in a naval bombardment of coastal Italy, Gamelin's preference for a neutral Italy and a mission to Salonika, and Daladier's support for an Allied ultimatum to Italy, the French presented themselves as internally confused and hopelessly discordant vis-à-vis Italy and the Mediterranean.

By contrast, the British were determined to pursue Italian neutrality. The viability of this British policy was bolstered by Loraine's report of 22 August that a "well-informed and reliable source" had learned that Italy "has no intention of being dragged into a general European war." General Ismay of the CID then sent an urgent appeal to the French, suggesting that a neutral Italy "would appreciably reduce our military commitments and our military risks" in North Africa, the Middle East, the Balkans, and the Mediterranean. The Allies should not initiate any action—even if Italy were technically neutral but overtly biased toward Germany—"which is likely to have the effect of bringing her in against us." Despite the acquisition by British intelligence of Regia Marina war instructions indicating that Italy was aligned definitively with Germany yet only could operate defensively in the central Mediterranean, Newall, Pound, and Chatfield suggested that the Allies offer a free zone at Djibouti and a seat on the Suez Canal Board "to ensure Italian neutrality." On 24 August the Admiralty authorized its fleets to increase their states of readiness but warned them to avoid movements that "cannot be disguised and might have political repercussions." Naval mobilization and the quiet assembly of the Mediterranean fleet at Alexandria were not ordered until 1 September.[85]

On the same day as Ismay's letter arrived in Paris, 23 August, Daladier called an emergency meeting of his closest diplomatic and security advisers to discuss the situation in light of the shocking Soviet-German nonaggression pact and the imminent German attack on Poland. While Bonnet argued for France to abandon the Poles and to search for a negotiated peace with Germany, the service chiefs believed that France had an obligation to fulfill the Polish guarantee. With British and French support, Poland would offer an "honorable resistance," preventing any German drive on the western front before 1940. Moreover, Gamelin and Darlan indicated that their services were prepared for war. Even Air Minister La Chambre, speaking on behalf of the absent Vuillemin, indicated that the balance of air power had improved since September 1938. In the Mediterranean, however, war could not be contemplated. Gamelin persuasively argued that a hostile Italy would significantly decrease the duration of Polish and Romanian resistance. With the possibility of a Franco-Soviet rapprochement now out of the question, a hostile Italy would eliminate the Mediterranean–Black Sea supply route to Eastern Europe and effectively bury any hope of establishing an eastern front. France would also have to weaken its position on the western front to provide adequate defenses in the Alps. Consensus was eventually reached, and Gamelin telephoned London the following day to say that France was "in entire agreement" with the views expressed in Ismay's letter.[86]

Nevertheless, France entered the war apprehensively. Vuillemin told his minister soon after the meeting of 23 August that the relative situation in the air remained dire for France and its allies. Britain and France had only "recovered in part" their deficiencies of September 1938. With many fewer bombers, fighters, and antiaircraft weapons, "the Allies and the principal friendly countries [are] still well dominated by those of the totalitarian states: Germany and Italy." The Deuxième Bureau, whose chief had seen a Soviet alliance as France's only salvation, also dreaded the current situation. Gauché told Colson on the day Germany invaded Poland that France had never before "entered a war in which the conditions were so unfavorable." Even Darlan, who mobilized the fleet on 27 August and who pressed the initial French war effort more energetically than any other French official, confessed to Admiral Jules Docteur his anxiety of the discord within the high command and the chaos caused by industrial mobilization. But perhaps the best example of this trepidation was Daladier's reluctance to sign the war directive on 3 September, the day that Britain and France declared war on Germany. Pressed by the navy to sign the declaration to be sent to France's regional commanders, Daladier told Darlan's emissary, Admiral Le Luc, to ask Gamelin instead. Gamelin, in turn, refused to initial the historic document. Finally, an hour and a half after the official opening of hostilities, Daladier reluctantly consented to sign the order. As Bullitt reported to Washington, France went to war with great consternation, not at all confident that Germany could be defeated yet cognizant that "the abandonment of Poland would mean that France and England would have to fight somewhat later in an even worse position and that they would lose their moral standing in the world."[87]

[5]

"Keep the Allies guessing": September 1939–January 1940

Italian Nonbelligerence

Nonbelligerence sat poorly with Mussolini. A great power, which he believed Italy had become, had a responsibility to uphold its alliance commitments and not shrink from the sacrifices of war. Although he understood that Italy was militarily and economically unprepared for war, the Duce in early September made it clear to his foreign minister that "he was not all happy" about his country's predicament. Ciano wrote that Mussolini hoped for an early peace because "the position of neutrality weighs heavily upon him." Other ministers reached similar conclusions. Giuseppe Bottai noted that nonbelligerence for Mussolini was "a failure, a betrayal." Felice Guarneri explained that Mussolini displayed the "mortified expression of one who was doing something popular against his will."[1]By contrast, Italian nonbelligerence quite satisfied Ciano. The foreign minister envisioned a "period of fat neutrality" so that Italy could "gather economic and military strength and intervene effectively at an opportune moment." Although he detested the idea of fighting alongside the "deceitful" Germans, neither did Ciano have any interest in the success of Britain and France, much less in joining the Allied cause. The "prudent policy" that he endorsed was "to fight like a lion to preserve peace for the Italian people."[2]

The repeated signs of Italian military unpreparedness assured the skeptical Mussolini that Ciano's approach to the war was the most appropriate for Italy. Carlo Favagrossa, minister of war production, reported to Mussolini in early September that Italy had only enough stocks of raw materials to fight for three months. General Carboni indicated that even if Italy had adequate supplies, its military would fare dreadfully in war because of its poor training, equipment, and command structure. Summarizing these themes for the Duce, De Bono described the state of the army as "materially and morally disastrous." Even Roberto Farinacci, a journalist, former head of the Fascist Party, and voice of the Fascist old guard who remained steadfastly committed to the Axis, admitted to Mussolini that Italian public opinion would continue to oppose intervention until the Duce could demonstrate that Italy possessed the forces necessary to embark on war.[3]

To this end, the Duce ordered Libya, Italy's most vulnerable point vis-à-vis the Allies, reinforced with 20,000 troops and a considerable amount of equipment. According to this plan, the Italian garrison in Libya would have a force of 151,300 men by the end of September. The Duce also spurred the armament industries to increase production to the extent that the shortages of raw materials, machine tools, and skilled labor would permit. Favagrossa was ordered to obtain from the service ministries estimates of the raw materials, armaments, and ammunition that each would need for one year of war. Preliminary estimates indicated that Italy could not consider intervention before mid-1940, and even then it would have supplies for only three months of war.[4]

The Duce was infuriated at his military's state of unpreparedness. In mid-September Italy only had ten first-line divisions. Thirty-five additional divisions were incompletely manned and ill-equipped, and Italy's two armored divisions were "armored only in name." Ciano told Mussolini that the official estimate of 2,300 combat-ready aircraft was "absurdly optimistic," and on 1 November it was revealed that the air force had only 600 modern aircraft that were not undergoing significant repairs. Amid these revelations, Farinacci and De Bono demanded that Mussolini sack Pariani and Valle. Soon after the British rejected Hitler's 6 October proposal to end the war with Poland divided between Germany and the Soviet Union, Mussolini replaced Valle with General Francesco Pricolo Pariani with Marshal Rodolfo Graziani as army chief of staff and General Ubaldo Soddu as army undersecretary. Badoglio and Cavagnari escaped the late October purge and, as a result, emerged considerably strengthened.[5]

When Badoglio first convened this new group of service chiefs, on 18 November, he announced that they would no longer consider "operations that do not correspond to reality." The marshal forbade his colleagues from speculating about foolhardy offensives, such as Pariani's plan to attack Egypt. Instead, they were to focus on building a "defensive system" in the colonies by improving their dismal stocks of food, ammunition, and fuel. Badoglio stressed that their principal responsibility was "the preparation of the armed forces without political discussions: whether we fight or not, whether we fight in the East or the West, is not our responsibility." Instead of struggling with Italian policy and strategy, which now belonged exclusively to Mussolini and Ciano, the service chiefs gratefully turned their attention to more traditional concerns, such as war preparation and interservice rivalries.[6]

Although the service chiefs had virtually abandoned war planning, Italy's leader was not prepared to assume that responsibility either. In the fall of 1939 the Duce struggled simply to define Italy's role in the war. On the one hand, Hitler had broken his Pact of Steel promise and gone to war more than two years before the Italians had anticipated. On the other hand, abstention from this war was out of the question. "The Italians," the Duce anguished, "after having heard my warlike propaganda for eighteen years, cannot understand how I can, now that Europe is in flames, become the herald of peace." Desperate not to remain on the sidelines long, Mussolini directed his foreign minister in early October to "throw kerosene on the flames" so that Britain, France, and Germany would fight bitterly, allowing Italy to enter the war eventually at equal strength. He then instructed Ciano to explain to Hitler that Italy intended to use the nonbelligerence period to prepare for intervention and to persuade the Italian people that Italy could fight a war successfully. Hitler was eager for the Italians to join the fray. Besides wanting to demonstrate Axis solidarity in the war, Hitler and Raeder believed that further German surface warfare against commercial vessels was contingent on Italian intervention, which would force Britain to deploy units from oceanic waters to the Mediterranean. Hitler told Ciano that Rome would continue to determine Axis policy in the Mediterranean and the Adriatic but warned that "Italy's absence from the struggle and the defeat of Germany would represent for Italy the end of her great imperial aspirations in the Mediterranean."[7]

Sensitive to German opinion of Italy, Mussolini endeavored to demonstrate that "Italy represents Germany's economic and moral reserve, and will be able to play a military role at a later time." Even Ciano believed that Italy had "to do everything possible for the Germans without rendering military solidarity." In mid-September Mussolini instructed Alberto Giannini, the director of commercial affairs at the Palazzo Chigi, to inform Germany's economic negotiator, Karl Clodius, that Italy would increase its exports to Germany of strategic raw materials and foodstuffs, such as bauxite, zinc, ore, nickel, copper, hemp, and a variety of agricultural goods. Approval was also given for Italian firms to sell the Germans armament components, such as machine parts, ball bearings, electric motors, screws, and Plexiglas. As a result, German imports from Italy in 1939–40 increased by more than 21 percent over 1938–39. In addition, the heads of SIM and SIS met with Admiral Canaris in Germany in mid-September and arranged to place German agents in France by way of Italy—providing the Germans with information about the organization of maritime traffic in the Mediterranean—and to allow the installation of German agents in Italian maritime centers and principal ports.[8]

The Italian and German intelligence officers also agreed that Italy could help the Germans evade the Allied blockade by transporting German goods on Italian merchant ships. Besides smuggling contraband that could be easily disguised—such as petroleum, iron, manganese, aluminum, phosphates, rubber, and fats—from neutral states to Germany, the Fascists would also support the purchase from abroad of finished products by independent Italian companies on behalf of the German government. After receipt the Italian firms would forward the material to Germany across the Brenner and through Switzerland. Finally, the Italians offered to facilitate German trade in any way possible. For example, three days after this meeting of intelligence officers, on 20 September, the director of exports of the German producer of Junkers aircraft asked if Italy would ship a "Ju 52" civilian aircraft to Brazil and return to Italy with German imports of Latin American agricultural goods. Although they had just rejected the Kriegsmarine's request to transfer German submarines to the Mediterranean, Cavagnari and Ciano consented to the Junkers shipment in early October. Soon thereafter Mussolini and Ciano separately promised Clodius that they would do everything possible "to ensure a maximum increase of Italian raw material deliveries to Germany and to have the Italian government expedite in all possible ways the transit of foreign ship cargoes through Italy to Germany."[9]

Yet relations between Italy and Germany in the autumn of 1939 were not free of tension. In fact the conflict over the South Tyrol/Alto Adige, in addition to the burgeoning Russo-German alliance, almost destroyed the Axis partnership. In negotiating the Pact of Steel, Hitler had implicitly agreed to remove the German-speaking population from the South Tyrol. For the Duce, such an event had been overdue since May 1938, when Hitler declared the inviolability of the Brenner frontier. Attolico and Heinrich Himmler, the chief of the Gestapo, had reached an understanding on the population transfer in June 1939, but war erupted before the two countries could sign a written agreement. The Germans finally did sign an implementation agreement on 21 October, but Mussolini soon decided that its 31 December deadline was too generous. Not only had the Nazis, under Russian pressure, removed more than 80,000 Germans from the Baltics within days of the Molotov-Ribbentrop agreement but the local National Socialist organizations had begun conducting a plebiscite in the South Tyrol and informing the German-speaking population that they could remain for as long as three years if they wished. On 21 November the Duce was so infuriated that he told Ciano the situation could lead to war with Germany. Besides protesting through diplomatic channels, Mussolini bolstered the Italian army's presence in the region and ordered the acceleration of fortification construction on the northern frontier. Eventually the Nazis relented and began slowly to relocate the German population out of the South Tyrol. Historian MacGregor Knox has persuasively argued that this struggle over Alto Adige and the sudden Italian activity along the Brenner were not signs of Italy's intention to join the Allies in war or even to abandon the Axis alliance but "an attempt by Mussolini to preserve Italian independence and bargaining power by rendering the country impervious to direct German threat."[10] It also demonstrated the Duce's wish to have the Italians' "backs protected on the continent" so that he could confidently turn his attention to realizing his Mediterranean and Balkan ambitions.

Mussolini's reluctance to become enraged over the possibility that the Russians and Germans would invade the Danubian basin following their conquest of Poland supports these arguments. Relying on Hitler's assurances of 1 October that Italian interests were predominant in the Balkans, Mussolini rejected Ciano's proposal to unite the Balkan countries in their opposition to intervention, believing that such an effort would lead Italy closer to neutrality. Instead, Ciano told Mackensen in mid-October that Mussolini had rejected the bloc project, remained faithful to the German alliance, was anxious to extend Italian influence throughout the greater Mediterranean, and was preparing for war "at a given moment." Referring to the inevitable Italian war against the West, Mussolini told Fascist leaders in Genoa at the end of September that "Centuries-old hegemonies are tottering. . . . We are prisoners in the Mediterranean—a large prison. Three entrances, but all well guarded and in the hands of enemies or adversaries."[11]

Britain, France, and Italian Nonbelligerence

Britain and France entered the war hopeful that time was on the Allies' side. Their initial war effort concentrated on a blockade that aimed to take advantage of their superior resources and control of the seas to tighten an economic noose around Germany's capacity to make war. At the same time, Allied rearmament would gradually eliminate Germany's military advantage. Although susceptible to Germany's short-term offensives, the Allies were confident that their economic-warfare strategy would enable them to defeat Germany in a long war. One of the bases of this strategy, however, was Italian neutrality. If Italy entered the war on Germany's side, many significant British and French interests in the Mediterranean would immediately be at risk. In contrast to German offensives in Eastern Europe, Italian aggression in the Mediterranean could not be disregarded. Military resources would have to be expended to stop the Fascists, further weakening the Allies' ability to defeat the Nazis. As a result, British and French policy in the Mediterranean reflected both the Allies' desire to entice the Italians to declare definitive neutrality (or even intervene against Germany) and the Allies' concern that their Mediterranean position remained vulnerable.

In Britain, Italy's ambiguous status in the war most affected the Admiralty. At the opening of hostilities the Mediterranean fleet based at Alexandria possessed by far the greatest British naval strength outside home waters. On 2 September First Sea Lord Pound suggested that British appeasement aim to establish Italy's neutrality on a firm basis so that he could redistribute the Mediterranean fleet and enhance Britain's resources on the Atlantic trade routes. By contrast, Andrew Cunningham, commander of the Mediterranean fleet, believed that Italy intended to "keep the Allies guessing" by taking whatever they would offer without ever declaring neutrality. Such a circumstance would prevent the Allies from employing all their Mediterranean forces against German raiders in the Atlantic, yet would entice the Allies to weaken the forces currently facing Italy. At the opportune moment, when Allied forces in the Mediterranean had weakened and Germany's dominance on the continent had been established, Italy would declare war on the Western powers.[12]

Cunningham found an ally of sorts in the new first lord of the Admiralty, Winston Churchill. On 7 September Churchill—whom Chamberlain had appointed to fortify the British war effort and stem Parliamentary criticisms of his policies—proposed that Britain send an unspecified number of capital ships to Gibraltar to intimidate Italy. The torrentially impatient Churchill hoped these ships would serve as an unspoken ultimatum to the Italians: either declare yourselves definitively neutral, or we will prepare for an imminent war against you. Churchill disdained the passive long-war strategy and believed that the Royal Navy's defeat of a hostile Italy would have important repercussions on the war against Germany. Although Pound objected to the first lord's dabbling in strategy, the naval chief's naturally quiet demeanor could not compete with Churchill's pervasive self-confidence and domineering style. Churchill presented his proposal to the War Cabinet on 18 September as if it had the full endorsement of the naval staff.[13]

Churchill's views of Italy and the Mediterranean, however, were not representative of the War Cabinet. Chamberlain had appointed the fiery backbencher, who had frequently and publicly criticized the prime minister's prewar foreign policy, principally to demonstrate both domestically and internationally that Britain was determined to prosecute the war against the Nazis. In fact both the Foreign Office and Chamberlain acted to quell Churchill's "reckless" proposals for the Mediterranean. Ambassador Loraine in Rome provided critical assistance in this effort. Tall, discreet, and well dressed, the shy but opinionated lifelong diplomat was a creature of the British establishment. Loraine, the son of a rear admiral in the Royal Navy, had grown up in London and attended Eton and Oxford before entering the foreign service. His prescient assurances throughout the summer of 1939 that Italy would remain outside a European war had considerably raised his credibility in Whitehall. After the war began, Loraine claimed that Dino Grandi, the former Italian ambassador in London and the current minister of justice and member of the Fascist Grand Council, had become his principal "source" in Rome. Loraine also contended that he was now "in collusion" with Ciano, who confided in him things that the Italian foreign minister did not discuss with Mussolini. In particular, Loraine believed, Ciano hoped that Italy would eventually, if treated with care in the interim, join the Allies in the war against Germany. Loraine even indicated in a private letter to Halifax, transported by British courier, that he alone was in a position to guide Italy through this transformation.[14] Loraine's ambition, arrogance, and condescending views of the Italians, as well as his conservative politics and supreme faith in the British imperial system, contributed to his enduring conviction that he could persuade the Fascists to join the Allied cause. Ironically, these personal traits and beliefs also made him easy for the Italians to deceive and manipulate.

Because Loraine reaffirmed the FO's preconceptions about Italian policy, the extent of his access only enhanced his credibility. Specifically, Loraine advised against either intimidating the Italians, which could drive them quickly into Germany's arms, or making them any offer, which Mussolini and Ciano could interpret as unwelcome "political bribery." Instead, basing his analysis primarily on the Italian public's revulsion for war, Loraine argued that Britain "should concentrate on rendering it politically possible and economically advantageous for Italy to remain neutral." Many of Britain's most influential cabinet ministers endorsed Loraine's recommendations. Although both Chatfield and Simon thought that Mussolini was an opportunist prepared to join whichever side seemed assured of victory, each was confident that the will of the Italian people not to go to war would dictate Mussolini's actions. Ever cognizant of his own domestic-political vulnerabilities, the prime minister in September continued to question Mussolini's ability to lead a reluctant Italian public into war. "I place my hope and indeed my confidence on the attitude of the Italian king, Church, and people. I do not believe that they will fight on behalf of Germany." Chamberlain even speculated that revolution would erupt in Italy before Mussolini could compel the Italian military to make war on Britain.[15] Despite the example set by Nazi Germany and more than fifteen years of Italian totalitarianism, many British statesmen assumed that democratic principles would restrain the Fascist dictator. With few solid arguments to defend their conviction that Italy would remain neutral, the British now clung to any possible rationale to support their opinions.

British policy toward Italy in September evolved directly from British assessments of Fascist Italy *before* the war—despite significant changes to the international landscape. According to Halifax, British policy "should be directed towards encouraging the Italians to turn to us, both by giving them an impression of our strength and, at the same time, demonstrating our willingness to treat them as friends and equals." Categorically rejecting Churchill's capital-ships-to-Gibraltar proposal, the Foreign Office stated that "anything that even looks like intimidation of Mussolini should be avoided." Citing the Libyan garrison's increase in size by over 20,000 men since the end of August, the War Office in mid-September asked for an end to the sharing of military information with Italy, "a declared ally of our enemy and with whom we may at any time find ourselves at war." But the FO again demurred on political grounds: "To discontinue this practice might arouse unjustified suspicions and this would be most unfortunate at a moment when it is of paramount importance to ensure that Italy shall not make common cause with Germany."[16] A war in the Mediterranean would drain Britain's defensive capabilities and upset her entire imperial security scheme; it had to be avoided. Moreover, there was unjustified anxiety that France would then expend some of its military resources in a Mediterranean war, making it easier for Germany to march on the West and directly threaten the British Isles.

THE FRENCH reacted to Italian nonbelligerence with more uneasiness than their allies across the Channel. Although France officially welcomed Italy's decision not to intervene, a debate soon raged within the country about the nature of Italy's position. Many Frenchmen, both in and out of the government, had distrusted the Fascists in Rome for years and believed that Mussolini's extralegal description for his "neither neutral nor belligerent" stance was a delaying tactic that would allow Italy to prepare for war against France without enduring the humility of neutrality. Some of these Frenchmen, most notably Georges Mandel, Count Carlo Sforza, and Schiff Giorgini, pressed for a preemptive French attack on Italy to eliminate it quickly from the war, to secure the Mediterranean, and to prevent the Italians from aiding the Germans. Yet many other Frenchmen, such as Anatole de Monzie and Bonnet, believed not only that Italian neutrality was precious to the French war effort but that France and Britain could and should buy it with territorial concessions. If necessary, even the sacrosanct French Mediterranean holdings of Corsica, Nice, and Savoy should be placed on the negotiating table.[17]

The renewed proposal to send an expedition to the Balkans in order to forestall a German or Russo-German assault on the Danube basin brought this debate over Italy to the level of high policy. For many, especially General Weygand, who assumed command of all French forces in the eastern Mediterranean in late August, an Allied occupation of Salonika offered a solution to the dilemma caused by the Nazi-Soviet pact, the rapid German successes in Poland, and the partition of Poland with the Soviet Union: instead of an eastern front, which was no longer militarily viable, the Allies could establish a southeastern front. In early September Gamelin, who believed that the Polish situation had become hopeless, suggested that a southeastern front could reverse the tide of the war by forcing the Germans to divide their armies. It could also provide a starting point for future military operations. Gamelin added that a resolute Allied stand in the Danube could "galvanize the Balkans," which would further restrict Germany's access to vital resources, notably Romanian oil, and preserve the integrity of Greece and Turkey and thus Allied control of the eastern Mediterranean. Successful Allied operations in that area might even draw the neutral Balkan states to the Allied side, increasing Allied forces by more than one hundred divisions.[18]

Despite the strategic appeal of a French expedition to Salonika, the naval staff opposed the idea and raised a series of logistical complications that effectively handcuffed all serious planning. Foremost among them was the transport of three full divisions—two from Syria and one made up of infantry from North Africa and cavalry from France—plus matériel and supplies to the Balkans (where Italy had known interests and ambitions) and through the eastern Mediterranean while Italy's status in the war remained in doubt. Darlan explained that such an operation would require 300,000 tons of shipping and forty-five days to complete; additional shipping would be required to maintain the resupply line. Either Britain would have to contribute commerce vessels, which it refused to do, or French naval forces would have to be transferred from their Atlantic trade-route duties. But the possibility of a hostile Italy made the proposal wholly unfeasible: France lacked adequate forces to provide the shipping *and* the protection for an operation that could be subjected to Italian offensive forays. Moreover, Germany stood to gain significantly by any weakened defense of the principal Allied shipping lanes in the Atlantic. Darlan opined that the navy could contemplate this expedition only if it were preceded by an air-sea-land assault against Italy and its colonies; nothing besides a defeated or definitively neutral Italy could make the Balkan plan viable. As Gamelin conceded in mid-September, "the constitution of a Balkan front remains entirely dependent on the attitude of Italy. . . . Regardless who considers our action in the eastern Mediterranean, the question always returns: What will Italy do?"[19]

Opinions in France on policy toward Italy differed widely. Preoccupied with deterring a German advance on the western front, Gamelin advocated a resolute appeasement of Italy. As early as the first week of war he asserted that "the action to conduct vis-à-vis Italy must take place principally on the diplomatic plane. Her neutrality would be infinitely precious to us." He told his colleagues on 7 September that he wished French diplomats would simply ask Mussolini, "What do you want?" To detach Italy from the Axis and facilitate an Allied occupation of Salonika, the French, according to

Gamelin on 12 September, should offer the Fascists significant compensation, such as the former German colonies in Africa and the constitution of a large state in the Danubian basin, under the control of the prince of the House of Savoy. Such concessions could be promised but not actually made until France had successfully prosecuted the war, yet they would satisfy Italy's colonial and continental ambitions. Moreover, Italy's acceptance of the proposal would place a formidable wedge between the two Axis powers. Gamelin confided to Marshal Henri Pétain that a *Grand Monsieur,* rather than the French ambassador in Rome, should present this bribe—sweetened with "a few billion francs"—directly to Mussolini. Once Italy accepted the French offers and declared her definitive neutrality, the Salonika expedition could proceed. In late September the Deuxième Bureau offered support to Gamelin's proposals by reporting that Italy, despite sending additional troops to Sardinia and Libya, "does not seem to believe that it will enter the war soon. The artistic treasures of Milan remain in place and no measure of precaution has been taken to protect them." The time had arrived, concluded the intelligence report, to search for an "exact formula for neutrality." Even Darlan, who had been hostile to the Italians since 1937, admitted in early October that since "the friendly neutrality of Italy is indispensable," France should offer colonial African concessions.[20]

The Quai d'Orsay did not share Gamelin's viewpoint. With the notable exception of the foreign minister, whom Daladier sacked and reappointed as justice minister in mid-September, most of the leading officials at the Foreign Ministry believed Italy would do nothing until circumstances compelled it to. In the meantime, it would build its arsenal and wait for an opportune moment to intervene against the Western powers—all without revealing its true intentions. Italy's refusal to declare belligerency *or* neutrality infuriated the Quai, especially Secretary General Alexis Léger, who thought that making Allied policy dependent on the opinion of the Italians was inherently debilitating, "since we have difficulty knowing what that opinion is anyway." Upon the outbreak of war, Léger had wanted to present the Fascists with an ultimatum to determine Italy's true status in the conflict; now he told Gamelin that Italy must be persuaded that France intended to fight until Hitler was defeated and that Italy's nonbelligerent status could not be sustained indefinitely. An Allied landing at Salonika could serve to clarify Italy's attitude: if the Fascists intended to side with Germany, Italy would oppose the Allied landing at Salonika and declare war against Britain and France, giving the Allies the opportunity to attack Italy with impunity as they had originally planned. If Italy perceived itself as a neutral but found the idea of declaring neutrality unacceptable, the Fascists would not interfere with Allied operations in southeastern Europe. Either way, the Italians would recognize the Allies' resolve to defeat Germany—a realization that could in and of itself, draw Italy to the Allied side. An expedition to the Balkans, according to Emile Charvériat, head of the political and commercial affairs directorate at the Quai, would "fix Italy in a position of suspense which [will] eventually facilitate a favorable evolution on her part."[21]

Between these two extremes—naked appeasement and reckless intimidation—fell the recommendations of François-Poncet. Conceding that Italian diplomacy continued "to play on two tables," the French ambassador in Rome argued that Italy was "evolving" toward a policy of "durable" neutrality. François-Poncet cited a number of factors to support this contention: the Fascist press no longer spoke of the advantages and necessities of the Axis; navigation services with the United States had been established; measures had been taken to ensure the safety of the nation's liquid combustibles; and the government had begun to seek to profit from the sale of matériel. The most important consideration, however, was "the affirmation, which becomes more clear every day, of Italian public sentiment for the maintenance of neutrality and against a war pursued alongside Germany." Because Italy's political milieu shared this particular sentiment, François-Poncet indicated that "for the first time, one has the impression that Mussolini is no longer the only ruler in Italy." Thus, the Allies should not attempt to disrupt such favorable progress with either concessions or provocations; all planning for operations in the Balkans should be suspended until Italy had "fully evolved." Bolstering his own arguments, François-Poncet reported that Ciano in mid-September had warned that forcing Italy to proclaim itself as either a "friend or enemy" of the Allies would be a "fatal mistake."[22]

Significant domestic-political influences affected Daladier's decision to adopt a compromise policy on Italy and the Balkans. Although the premier shared the views of Léon Blum and the center-left that the Nazi threat could be erased only by Germany's defeat in war, his government had become increasingly dependent on the center-right faction of the Radical Party, which had gained ascendancy within the party since Munich. Believing that Bonnet's pacifism weakened his government's determination to prosecute the war against Hitler and under pressure from the British to replace him, Daladier reshuffled his cabinet and asked for the foreign minister's resignation on 15 September. Yet the center-right rejected the premier's choice of Edouard Herriot as Bonnet's replacement. Herriot, it was feared, would hinder "correct relations" with Italy and Spain by shunning Realpolitik in favor of an ideological crusade against Fascism; any reasonable compromise with the dictators would be impossible. With few other choices, Daladier appointed Bonnet as justice minister and himself as foreign minister.[23]

Ever conscious of the domestic-political pressures within France and fearful of taking a controversial position, Daladier again steered a middle course in Italian and Balkan policy. With Italy, the premier endorsed the political approach suggested by François-Poncet and acceptable to Bonnet: "Press nothing. Offer nothing," he noted to himself on 12 September. One week later, at a meeting of his new cabinet, Daladier emphasized that France had to "keep the central door of the Mediterranean open." Conceding that Italy's position in the war was infuriatingly vague, the premier nevertheless explained that the Allies had to continue moving Italy closer to neutrality, "the preferable solution": "Although the word has not been officially pronounced, [Italian] neutrality seems to be *en bonne voie*."[24] At the same time Daladier endorsed the service chiefs' proposed Balkan strategy. In a meeting on 14 September with both staff officers and Quai officials, Daladier indicated that Russia's invasion of Poland as well as Germany's imminent defeat of Poland and likely attack on Romania compelled the French to establish a southeastern front. On 20 September the premier explained to his cabinet that a southeastern front was "indispensable to compel Germany to disperse its military forces and to make the blockade more effective." The following day the premier asked Weygand to establish a plan of operations for the eastern Mediterranean so that France "can gain a foothold in the Balkans as soon as possible." Aware of his seemingly contradictory Balkan and Italian policies, Daladier resolved to square the circle by discussing the issue with the British at the second interallied Supreme War Council (SWC) meeting in Brighton on 22 September. There he hoped to persuade the British to participate in both the Salonika operation and the cautious development of Italian neutrality.[25]

Allied Policy in the Balkans

Whereas the French intensely debated the concept of establishing a Balkan front, the British reached consensus on the question fairly quickly. Indeed, at the start of the war they already opposed the idea. On 7 September the Cabinet, with the support of both the COS and the FO, indicated that it "hoped that the French government would not authorize action in the Balkans such as discussed by British and French military authorities before the war." Soon after German troops invaded Poland, the Foreign Office and its diplomats began actively to prevent the extension of the war to the Balkan Peninsula. Staff talks with Greece were explicitly avoided so that British diplomats could demonstrate that neutrality was the only reasonable alternative for the Greeks. Similar appeals for continued neutrality were made to the Yugoslavs and the Romanians, although their two countries had no interest in intervening in the conflict. The underlying explanation for this concerted British effort directed toward the Balkans was a desire to preserve Italian neutrality and, perhaps, to persuade Italy to join the Allied side in war as it had done in 1915. When the Turks sought to expand a clause of the proposed Anglo-French-Turkish treaty to make it easier for Turkey to come into a war against Italy, the British definitively refused; the treaty was designed to attach Turkey to the Allied side, not to prepare Turkey for war against the Axis powers. As Halifax explained to Sir Hughe Knatchbull-Hugessen, the British ambassador in Ankara, "We still hope that by careful handling it may be possible to convert this [Italian] neutrality eventually into active cooperation on our side."[26]

One of the first British officials to draw this connection between Italy and the Balkans was Ambassador Loraine. Not only was he considered an expert on Italy, but his prior appointment had been in Ankara, where British military and diplomatic efforts in the eastern Mediterranean had been focused since before the war. As early as 5 September Loraine suggested to Halifax that Italy's neutrality was dependent on war not extending into the Balkans. Thus, Britain should sponsor a neutral Balkan bloc: "It would be a very grave error to give Germany the opportunity of attacking the South-East through the Balkans." Thereafter, the Foreign Office could not disentangle Allied policy toward the states of southeastern Europe from Allied policy toward Italy. If the Balkans became engulfed in war, it was presumed, the Italians would abandon nonbelligerence and intervene on Germany's side. According to this assessment, the Allies faced a stark choice: either a group of allied Balkan states and a hostile Italy, or a neutral Balkan bloc and a neutral but friendly Italy. The preference for the latter over the former was overwhelming. As Halifax wrote on 12 September, "A neutral and, *a fortiori*, a friendly Italy seems more valuable to us than the Balkans forced into belligerency. And the two are almost certainly incompatible."[27]

When Whitehall learned in mid-September that the Salonika idea had experienced a resurgence in Paris, the British services marshaled their resources to stymie the initiative. The COS immediately argued that Salonika was unsuitable as a base of offensive operations against German aggression in the Balkans: the hypothetical Allied line of advance northward into the Danubian basin passed through difficult and easily defensible country; communications into the interior were problematic; and the region was notoriously malarial and unhealthy. Though conceding that an expedition to Salonika would become strategically appropriate if Italy joined Germany in the war, both to defend Greece and Turkey and to strike against Italian possessions in the Dodecanese, the service chiefs explained that nevertheless "in this event it would be navally impracticable to establish a force there in the early stages and extremely difficult to establish it there later or keep it supplied. The provisions of the necessary shipping would raise serious problems. Moreover we should not have sufficient air forces available both for a Salonika force and for operations against the Dodecanese at the same time." Although the chiefs focused on the operational impediments to a Balkan front, they also returned to a fundamental strategic imperative for opposing the proposal. They expected Hitler to move into southeastern Europe before turning against the West: the conquest of Romania offered not only control of valuable oil fields but also access to the Bosphorus and the Aegean, both of which could alleviate the economic pressure placed on Germany by the Allied blockade. But they were also confident that a protracted Allied-German conflict in the Danube would compel Italy's intervention, and the prospect of having another enemy and another war theater in the Mediterranean truly frightened them. Such a situation would place British imperial interests in the Mediterranean or the Far East—or perhaps in both theaters—in stark jeopardy. In other words, Italian neutrality was more precious for the British than the integrity of southeastern Europe.[28]

One of the strongest opponents of the French Balkan proposal was General Ironside, who was appointed CIGS on 3 September. Ironside had a visceral reaction to the Salonika plan, recalling the follies of the Allies in that theater during the First World War. In that case, Ironside placed the blame on weak-willed British strategists who had succumbed to the emotional appeals of the French to conduct operations in the Balkans. Since evidently Weygand was again at the forefront of this French planning, Ironside campaigned vigorously in London against the French proposal. Fearing the prospect of ceding any command and control of Allied forces in the eastern Mediterranean, Ironside also warned his colleagues of Weygand's overriding ambitions for power and influence: "I put in this warning [about Weygand] because I foresee we may be led into a repetition of the unfortunate Salonika expedition of the late war." Moreover, the Germans would not easily overrun the Balkans: "My own view is that the more Hitler swallows in the way of Slavs and Balkan peoples, the more certain will be his eventual death from indigestion." Finally, as he admitted in his diary, "it seems to me that we want to have Italy neutral at the moment and nothing we do in the Balkans should irritate her into coming in against us."[29]

Perhaps the only influential statesman in London who appreciated the French perspective on the war, and specifically its southeastern theater, was Churchill. He speculated that Hitler had likely gained permission from the Russians to move next into Romania and toward the Black Sea, allowing the Germans to solve their problems of food and oil supply and thus to defeat the Allies' long-war strategy. For this reason, Churchill was "hopeful that we could get in Turkey" so that the Allies could provide aid to Romania, gain sea control of the Black Sea, and seal the three exits of the Mediterranean. Although the first lord's navy colleagues generally supported this viewpoint, Churchill's Mediterranean and Balkan–Black Sea ideas were not well received elsewhere in London. At a meeting of the War Cabinet on 21 September, Churchill expressed his desire "to see all the Balkan countries and Turkey also brought into the war. . . . We needed as many Allies in the Balkans as we could secure and it was not at all to our interest that the Balkans should be kept in a state of quiet, whilst France and ourselves were left to bear the full brunt of the German assault on the western front." Despite the first lord's conviction, and perhaps because of the similarity of his arguments to those of the French and his willingness to consider building a coalition of alliances, the Cabinet chose not even to discuss his ideas for the southeastern European theater; Churchill's opinions on the subject were excluded from the minutes of the meeting and placed in a confidential annex.[30]

In contrast, the War Cabinet found the prime minister's arguments on the Balkans quite compelling. Whereas the French believed that the Nazi-Soviet arrangement doomed the states of southeastern Europe, Chamberlain asserted that the fear of becoming involved in a war against the Soviet Union would prevent the Germans from invading the Danubian basin: "I cannot believe that [Russia] would think her interest served by a German victory, followed by a German domination of the Balkans." Allied operations in the Balkans, in other words, would incite rather than deter conflict there. Similar to his interest in preserving Italian neutrality, Chamberlain's assessment of the Balkan situation reflected his conviction that the British Empire's integrity depended on winning "a waiting war"—what Maurice Hankey called a "Fabian strategy"—which relied almost exclusively on the efficacy of blockade.[31]

In Late September at Brighton Chamberlain informed Daladier that as long as Italy remained neutral, the British would not consider a preemptive landing at Salonika or any preparations for such an operation. Instead, the British encouraged the French to work for the creation of a neutral Balkan federation under the direction of Turkey. Such a bloc of states theoretically would preclude the need for the Allies to defend the region from a German threat. According to Cadogan, Chamberlain "threw gentle showers of cold water on [the French proposal], and the French didn't seem entirely convinced by their own argument. It's moonshine to me." But by no means were the French entirely submissive. Daladier insisted, and Chamberlain reluctantly accepted, that the Allies at least consult with the Italians and the Turks about German ambitions in southeastern Europe and their potential reactions to an Allied expedition there.[32]

Yet for all intents and purposes the British had shelved the French Salonika idea. Without British participation, much less British support, the French could not conduct the expedition; French planners had hoped for the inclusion of British land and air forces and had depended on the use of British naval assistance, particularly shipping. On 28 September Gamelin, who had also grown increasingly confident that Hitler would launch an offensive against France rather than advance into the Balkans, canceled all reinforcements of Weygand's troops in Syria. Throughout the month of October Gamelin resolutely opposed all large-scale arms shipments to the states of southeastern Europe.[33] This development also served to solidify Italian and Mediterranean policy in London and Paris: the Allies were determined not to jeopardize Italian nonbelligerence by "offending Italian susceptibilities." The policy alternatives of provoking the Italians into war and bribing them into neutrality were both rejected. But the British and French still had fundamentally different conceptions of the Italians and thus divergent objectives for their Mediterranean policies. And these discrepancies continued to plague the Allies' overall conduct of the war.

Beginning in late September Loraine campaigned for Britain's sponsorship of a neutral Balkan federation that would include and thus would be headed by Italy; he believed that the resulting economic benefits would augment Italy's transformation from nonbelligerence to neutrality and eventually an alliance with the West. Mussolini "has left open the door to skip out of the Axis," the British ambassador repeated. Both the FO (which had already curtailed British propaganda in Italy at Loraine's request) and the War Cabinet agreed that the Fascists should be given a leadership role in a new Balkan federation.[34]

Notably, the War Cabinet had decided to act in opposition to the interests of its newest ally, Turkey. On 19 October Britain, France, and Turkey signed a mutual assistance treaty which required the signatories to lend all the aid and assistance in their power if they should become involved in a war in the Mediterranean region. During these negotiations Turkey's hostility to Italy was palpable. Believing that Italy's control of the Dodecanese directly threatened Turkish security, the Turks attempted and failed to expand a clause of the proposed treaty to make it easier for them to come into the war against Italy. They did not believe in Italian neutrality and feared that Italy would enter the war on Germany's side, invading the Balkans first, as soon as it had the military strength to do so. Not surprisingly, then, the Turks were vehemently opposed to the inclusion of Italy in any neutral Balkan bloc. Nevertheless, Chamberlain explained to his colleagues in the Cabinet in late October, Britain's newest ally would have to moderate its views to accommodate the Italians: "While . . . full justice should be done to Turkey for her attitude in this matter, it was necessary to avoid taking any action which might prejudice our chances of securing Italian cooperation in the plan for the establishment of a neutral Balkan bloc."[35]

The British sent France an aide-mémoire to this effect on 28 October. Admitting that the Italians had adopted a "position of equilibrium" between Germany and the Allies, the Quai d'Osay argued that it was doubtful that Italy would ever definitively abandon Germany and join the Allies in war. Thus, the Allies should continue their "policy of courtesy and reserve" toward Italy but should not grant it a predominant political voice in the Balkans, especially when Turkey and Greece opposed its participation. Only Turkey's leadership could guarantee that the bloc would not serve as an instrument of German penetration into the Balkans. Otherwise a Balkan bloc was unnecessary since the states of the region, including Bulgaria, had no intention of taking the initiative against the Allies. British and French interests in the Balkans, the Quai argued, were already well secured.[36]

This perspective derived from a variety of individuals associated with France's Italian and Mediterranean policy, demonstrating that the French had begun to coalesce on the subject. François-Poncet in Rome had reported throughout October that Mussolini's popularity and his admiration for Hitler had increased since the start of war. Consequently, although most in France hoped that Italy would remain neutral, few believed that Italy would ever join the Allies in war. Réne Massigli in Ankara, who was instrumental in developing the Anglo-French-Turkish accord, believed that the Allied position in the Balkans had to be centered on Turkey: Turkey had the strongest military in the Balkans, had control of the Dardanelles, could prove helpful in the event of an Allied expedition to the Balkans, and of those states was the most favorably inclined toward the Allies. Insisting that the Allies' priority should be supplying matériel to the Turks rather than catering to Italian aspirations in the Danube, Massigli also noted that the Fascist press in Italy spoke with great anticipation about becoming a leader in its "vital Balkan space." Such "Nazi language" alone should make the Allies wary about befriending the Italians. Both Henri Hoppenot, director of the Quai's European Department, and Maurice Dejean, chief of Daladier's diplomatic cabinet, agreed that the Allies could not concede the Balkans to Italy.[37]

On this subject, at least, the French were unanimous and their opposition to the British plan resolute. Britain had no choice, especially since the Italians had lost interest in the idea by the end of October, but to recommend in early November that the Allies abandon the project for a neutral Balkan bloc.[38] Although the principal reason that the initiative never materialized was that many of the Balkan states resisted it, there seems little doubt that contradictory British and French diplomacy revealed to the Balkans that the Allies had ulterior—and not common—motives for their interest in a neutral bloc.

Contraband Control in the Mediterranean

Control of contraband bound for Germany by way of the Mediterranean was an important aspect of the Allied blockade. With the exception of maintaining their own north-south convoy between Algiers and Marseilles, the French abdicated most of the Mediterranean to the British after the war began. The majority of the French Marine Nationale moved into the Atlantic to defend the principal trade routes from North and South America. Therefore, Britain's Ministry of Economic Warfare (MEW) largely established Allied blockade policy for the Mediterranean. Initially, contraband control was applied against all neutral flags that the MEW believed could be carrying cargo destined for Germany. Targeted vessels were brought to contraband control bases for inspection, and all suspicious cargo was confiscated. It was soon decided that the Italians had to be treated differently, however. On 6 September the British Admiralty ordered that Italian ships should be sent in for examination only if they were found to be openly carrying contraband consigned to Germany. Copies of ships' manifests were to be obtained whenever possible, but any Italian ship outward bound to Italian colonies was to be boarded only for identification purposes. Concerned that the French did not share these sensitivities, Francis Rodd of the MEW asked the Foreign Office to warn France "to show every leniency and consideration to Italian ships in the Mediterranean."[39]

As early as 18 September Britain suspected that many plots were already under way to defeat the blockade by way of the Mediterranean. These schemes were so extensive, the MEW estimated, that some 3.6 million tons of cargo, consigned to firms in Italy and Greece that were acting as forwarding agents, would travel through Trieste, Genoa, and a variety of Black Sea ports in the first year of the war. Therefore, Admiral A. H. Taylor, director of the Admiralty's economic warfare division, recommended that the Allies implement "full procedure" in the Mediterranean—meaning that all ships entering the Mediterranean at Gibraltar and Suez would be directed to Allied bases for inspection, and all goods destined for Germany would be confiscated. The Admiralty established full procedure on 25 September, but it failed to jeopardize Italy's role in defeating the blockade. First, full procedure could not interdict goods consigned to Italy, and without an Italian war trade agreement, Italy could import excessive amounts of resources and then export those surpluses to Germany. Second, the Allies lacked any contraband control bases in the Aegean, Ionian, and Adriatic Seas, allowing the transport of southeastern European supplies to Germany by way of Italian and Yugoslav ports without threat of Allied interception.[40]

The Allies understood the inherent weakness of their Mediterranean blockade, even under full procedure. In mid-September the British recognized that Italian imports of cotton, iron, and steel had increased significantly since the war had begun. Monthly Italian imports of oil, in particular, doubled in September. And most decision-makers in London knew that if the excess raw materials were not used to strengthen Italy's war machine, they would likely be shipped to Germany. Even guarantees by the Italian government, as experience in the First World War had proved, would not prevent intermediaries from acquiring some Italian imports and reshipping them to Germany.[41]

The War Cabinet's solution to this predicament, endorsed by the MEW, was to search for a trade agreement with the Italians whereby Britain would replace Germany as the principal supplier of Italy's coal, and Italy's imports would be rationed at their prewar levels to prevent the reexportation of goods to Germany. If Italy could not pay for British coal with hard currency, the Air Ministry agreed to purchase Italian bombers and resell them to the French government, and the Admiralty consented to buy unneeded Italian Isotta engines for torpedo boats, along with large amounts of hemp and mercury—which various British colonies could provide at a lower cost. A secret trade mission was sent to Rome in mid-September expressly to make these arrangements.[42]

On this score, the French were two steps ahead of their allies. Also interested in concluding a commercial agreement as a way to ensure Italian neutrality, Daladier had dispatched Hervé Alphand to Switzerland in early September. Although Alphand's mandate existed only in the economic realm, Bonnet emphasized to his negotiator the important underlying political nature of the mission. Consequently, in the protocol agreed to on 15 September and signed at the end of the month, France granted Italy a five-million-franc export credit and agreed to purchase from Italy 100,000 tons of sulfur, 25,000 tons of pumice stone, 500 tons of mercury, 1,500 railroad tank cars, and 10 tankers. But although the Italians agreed to the one-time sale to France of 600 aircraft engines and 500 trainers, they refused to enter into an extensive commercial arrangement for the sale of Italian war matériel. The Fascists also turned down France's offer to sell Italy 300 million lire of scrap iron on credit.[43]

Such agreements served primarily to improve Italy's balance of payments and to build its currency reserves, which in turn Mussolini used to bolster Italy's stocks of fuel and raw materials. While Italian imports from France dropped 35 percent in 1939 over the previous year, Italian exports to France remained unchanged; exports in 1940 jumped 20 percent, and imports fell another 18 percent. Aside from these economic ramifications, there were perhaps even more important political ones. The French had not only excluded any provisions to prevent the reexport of goods by Italy to Germany—a standard feature of any war trade agreement—but also accepted a deal that did not commit Italy to a Franco-Italian commercial relationship. In Mussolini's opinion, he had both enhanced Italy's ability to make war and maintained his commitment to the Axis.[44]

Historian Pierre Guillen has shown that throughout the phony war the French imported Isotta Fraschini airplane engines by way of the Gnome et Rhône firm in France, and munitions and petroleum products by way of a

Portuguese purchasing company, Aereo Portugesa, which served as a facilitator between independent Italian firms and Air France—at a total value of two billion francs. But this trade was not the consequence of the Franco-Italian commercial negotiations in September-October 1939. The Aereo Portugesa and Gnome et Rhône relationships dated back to 1937, and the individual firms involved arranged for most of this particular commerce before the war began. The Italian government, under pressure both to raise hard currency and to placate Italian industrialists, chose not to terminate these arms sales until May 1940.[45] In fact during this period there were also many other instances of direct sales of Italian matériel to French companies and even to the French government. Between October and December 1939 the Palazzo Chigi and the Ministero della Marina approved a handful of contracts negotiated independently between Italian and French firms. For instance, Barry, Rogliano et Galles of Marseilles purchased tanker engines from the Ansaldo company in Genoa; the Compagnie Française de l'Afrique Occidentale bought a colonial barge from the Navalameccanica company in Naples; and the French Ministry of Marine directly purchased diesel motors from Ansaldo and torpedoes from Fiume. Yet these cases do not represent the existence of a mutual Franco-Italian trading relationship. The Italian government did not arrange these sales and took no steps to reciprocate by purchasing French goods, as the French government had hoped.[46]

Unwilling to compromise on the basic tenet of a war trade agreement—no reexportation to Germany—the British had difficulty reaching a commercial arrangement with the Italians. Although the British offered to curtail their contraband control in the Mediterranean in exchange for an Italian promise to halt all trade with Germany, the Italians refused, considering any form of rationing a "sanction" and therefore unacceptable. After more than a month of negotiations that revealed little more than Italy's interest in selling agricultural products to Britain and Britain's willingness to sell coal to Italy, the British and the Italians on 27 October signed a commercial agreement that achieved basically nothing but the formal creation of an Anglo-Italian Joint Standing Committee. According to the treaty's protocol, this committee "shall consider what steps may be best taken to regulate commercial exchanges and communications by rail, sea, and air between the two countries and, in general, to lead to a closer collaboration between the two countries in the economic sphere."[47] In other words, the agreement set up a committee so that the two nations could continue to have commercial negotiations without having to admit that the talks so far had failed.

The difficulties in these Anglo-Italian negotiations disturbed Loraine especially because they came at a time when the British were also struggling to establish a neutral Balkan bloc that would include Italy. As a result, Loraine became increasingly sensitive to Ciano's complaints about the delays experienced by Italian ships at contraband control bases in the Mediterranean. Four passenger ships in particular had each been held ten days at Gibraltar before being allowed passage. Ironically, this circumstance arose because the British in early October decided to apply "special treatment" of Italian shipping for a period of two to three weeks in order not to prejudice the commercial negotiations in Rome. The Admiralty was notified that Italian vessels outward bound from the Mediterranean should not normally be examined at contraband control bases in the Mediterranean, and that Italian vessels entering the Mediterranean should be boarded only to establish identity and destination. In the event of suspicion of contraband, the Admiralty could seize or detain goods on Italian ships only with authority from both the MEW and the Contraband Committee in London. Consequently, although seizures of Italian cargo declined, delays at contraband control bases increased.[48] By the end of October Loraine was expressing serious concern about the general nature of contraband control in the Mediterranean and suggested that it be effectively discarded until an arrangement suitable to the Italians could be established: "I would most strongly urge that for some weeks yet the treatment of Italian ships should be lenient, even at the cost of contraband passing, pending the elaboration of a machine for cooperation."[49]

Despite mounting intelligence evidence in London and Paris that Italy had transported by sea hundreds of German citizens, had agreed to sell 42,000 tons of hemp to Germany, and regularly shipped liquid fuels to the Reich, Halifax endorsed Loraine's recommendation.[50] On 2 November the foreign secretary took steps to loosen contraband control in the Mediterranean further rather than to reestablish "full procedure," as the British had intended to do once the commercial negotiations had finished. Halifax explained to the MEW and the Contraband Committee that efficacy of the blockade could not take precedence over Italy's status in the war: "It is very important from the point of view of foreign policy that the inconvenience caused to Italy should be reduced to the indispensable minimum. . . . I am anxious that our contraband control should be exercised in such a manner as to give the Italians no ground for legitimate complaint." Shortly thereafter, on 13 November, the Admiralty sent orders to British contraband control bases in the Mediterranean that "for political reasons as well as in order to avoid unnecessary congestion delay and inconvenience . . . many of [Italy's] ships should be allowed to proceed at once." Halifax then directed the British embassy in Rome to inform the Fascists that they were receiving "specially favourable treatment in comparison to other neutral powers."[51]

The weakening of contraband control in the Mediterranean was accompanied by a reduction of the Allies' naval presence there in October and November. By 15 November virtually all the French navy had left the Mediterranean. The most powerful French force, the *force de raid,* was based at Brest under the command of Admiral Raoul Castex, who was charged with securing the Atlantic convoy and intercepting any German vessels that entered the Atlantic from the North Sea. Darlan consolidated his three western commands at Casablanca so that Admiral Jean de Laborde could direct the whole region from Oran to Dakar. The naval chief moved his command in the South from Toulon to Bizerte, where Admiral Esteva could remain in close contact with the British at Gibraltar. A tiny force of one cruiser and four sloops remained in Indochina, France's lowest defense priority.[52]

Britain's naval force in the Mediterranean also shrank. In late September most of that fleet's submarines were sent into the Atlantic, and all its modern eight-inch-gun cruisers were replaced by older six-inch-gun cruisers. At the end of the year the Mediterranean fleet was reduced to four small cruisers, one Australian flotilla leader, four Australian destroyers, and two submarines—leading an Admiralty staffer to comment, "Our strategy in the eastern Mediterranean is bound to be to a great extent paralysed until the attitude of Italy is clear beyond doubt one way or the other." In a note to Cunningham at the turn of the year, Pound apologized for "one withdrawal after another" but explained that they were dictated by the war and British policy: "We have not sufficient ships to go around and the only thing to do is concentrate on the danger spots . . . we have to move very cautiously in that area or we shall rub the Italians up the wrong way."[53]

Opposed to withdrawing from the Mediterranean without an Italian war trade agreement, Churchill in early October proposed that Britain ask Italy for a mutual withdrawal of troops from North Africa and a détente in the Mediterranean. The first lord hoped that the Italians, though resistant to any "rationing" of their imports, would have an interest in "preserving the immunity of the Mediterranean from war." Although Chatfield initially endorsed the idea, Churchill encountered stiff resistance from the COS, particularly the Admiralty. Tom Phillips, deputy chief of the naval staff, argued that "neutralising" the Mediterranean would be tantamount to abdicating Britain's strength as a sea power: "It is the continental countries, in no position to command the seas in war, that have always been in favour of such schemes." Planning Director Danckwerts added that Italy's attitude remained too ambiguous for Britain to ignore: "We cannot reduce the strength of our forces too much . . . in view of the difficulties and dangers inherent in reinforcing the Middle East in war time, should Italy unfortunately play us false."[54] In other words, Italy could not be trusted but working for Italian neutrality was the only policy the Allies could pursue in the Mediterranean. Moreover, it was essential for Britain to project itself as a great sea power, even though it lacked a navy that could defend its vast empire. The COS endorsed these inherent contradictions, arguing that a mutual withdrawal would benefit Italy considerably more than Britain: Italy would be able to move its forces rapidly back to Libya, whereas Britain could not do the same for Egypt. Less than a month after Churchill first proposed a détente in the Mediterranean, the War Cabinet suspended consideration of the idea.[55]

In France, Darlan also began to express consternation with the progress of the war. The naval chief argued that the French leadership had failed not only to prepare for war but also to conduct it in an assertive fashion. As he wrote in his journal in early October, "The Secretariat of National Defense plays its role marginally. The economic war and the maritime transports are not organized. I have the impression that [Gamelin] is a little too exclusively occupied with the Northeastern front and that he neglects or does not understand that his role in the Committee of National Defense is to organize for total war." Conceding that France had for twenty years prepared itself to fight a defensive war and could not immediately take the offensive against Germany, Darlan grew increasingly frustrated with the passive approach that the Allies had taken. He insisted that they could strengthen their "war of attrition" strategy by interdicting German imports *and* exports. This meant accelerating French shipbuilding, concentrating naval forces against Germany, and, necessarily, reducing the Allies' presence in the Mediterranean. Thus, "the friendly neutrality of Italy is indispensable," and concessions to Italy in North Africa, the Middle East, and the Balkans should be made to guarantee this neutrality. In an attempt to strengthen the blockade, the naval chief in November transferred the majority of his antiair defenses from the Mediterranean to the Atlantic and the North Sea. He also persuaded Daladier to begin reducing the French presence in the Alps and in Tunisia along the Libyan border to mitigate tensions with the Italians.[56]

Darlan pressed his concerns about Germany's exports on the British at the same time as the Allies realized that Germany was using the Italian port of Trieste extensively to import raw materials and resources from the Danube basin, and that the Allies were powerless to stop it without offending "Italian susceptibilities."[57] According to the French, the Allies could stem the majority of German's coal exports to Italy and thus solve the problems caused by the Allies' unwillingness to bribe Italy into a status of friendly neutrality, the Italians' refusal to accept any import rationing, and the Allies' inability to interdict German traffic in the Adriatic. The British provided 20 percent of Italy's monthly requirement of one million metric tons of imported coal. Germany and Poland supplied the remainder "in exchange for goods and favors received." But more than two-thirds of the German coal arrived by sea from Bremen and, after the outbreak of war, from neutral Rotterdam. If Britain could provide Italy with coal instead, the Germans would lose the advantage Italy had provided them; the blockade would be strengthened; and Italy would in due course move closer to the Allies and further from Germany. Less than a month after Halifax relaxed the blockade against Italy, the MEW in London and the War Cabinet agreed that German exports had to be stopped. The Enemy Exports Committee, the first Allied agency responsible for contraband control in the Mediterranean, was established and held its first meeting on 30 November.[58]

The Italians did not find the Allies' new approach to economic warfare particularly appealing. Throughout the autumn the Italian naval staff boasted that its frequent protests had initiated favorable changes in the nature of Allied contraband control in the Mediterranean. Cavagnari's refusal to allow Italian ships to stop at Port Said for inspections had been accepted by the British and, as a result, contraband control of Italian ships moving through the Suez Canal became voluntary. Aided by Admiral Raineri Biscia's negotiations with the British Admiralty throughout October, Ciano's appeals to the French and the British had successfully reduced the pressure placed on the Italians and curbed the number of Allied interceptions of Italian ships carrying goods destined for Germany. The naval staff reported that British confiscations of German contraband on Italian ships had dropped precipitously from 260,000 tons in September to less than 40,000 tons in October. In early November, Corso Pecori Giraldi, the Italian naval attaché in Berlin and the coordinator of Italian contraband trade with Germany, described the Allies' conduct in the war as "chivalrous," observing that "the control of neutral commercial ships has been conducted with a certain amount of generosity."[59]

Suddenly, the Allies had reversed course and jeopardized Italy's coal supply from Germany. On 24 November, after establishing an office for the coordination of economic warfare at the Palazzo Chigi, Ciano explained to the British and French ambassadors that the loss of 650,000 tons of coal per month would cripple Italian industry. The two diplomats agreed to intervene on Italy's behalf and seek a reconsideration of the Allied policy. Loraine went to Malta to speak with Cunningham about making the blockade "less irksome" to the Italians. By 6 December François-Poncet reported that the Allies had decided to postpone the interception of German coal specifically destined for Italy in the hope of reaching a commercial agreement with the Italians.[60]

Yet the conflict over German coal had just begun. In mid-December the British offered to supply Italy with 8.3 miliion tons of coal in 1940—70 percent of Italy's requirements. To enable Italy to pay for the coal, Britain would purchase twenty million pounds of goods from Italy, including hemp, sulfur, and—most important—large quantities of armaments and munitions. Halifax argued to the War Cabinet that this plan would maintain Italy's level of coal imports, sever an important German economic link to Italy, and allow Britain to acquire Italian armaments at no expense to Britain's hard currency reserves—all "without risking Italian opposition." Halifax then informed the MEW that he attached "the utmost importance for political reasons to the application of our control to ships of all nationalities, and particularly Italy, being as expeditious as compatible with the due exercise of the control so designed as to cause the minimum of irritation and inconvenience." The foreign secretary and his colleagues believed that British coal could purchase Italy's neutrality, or even an Anglo-Italian alliance, and tighten the blockade of Germany at the same time.[61] Despite the results of British and French commercial negotiations with Italy earlier in the fall, no one questioned whether or not Italy *would* agree to purchase anything from the British, much less sell them arms. Inadvertently, the British proposal set the stage for a rapid deterioration in Anglo-Italian relations and precipitated Italian intervention.

Despite their efforts at conciliation, the British had already angered the Duce. Throughout late November and December independent Italian shipping interests, who were dissatisfied with the Palazzo Chigi's handling of their earlier complaints, inundated the Palazzo Venezia with protests of British contraband control. At the same time Ribbentrop and Mackensen aroused Mussolini's ire by inquiring about "the constantly mounting . . . British encroachments on Italian commercial and shipping interests" in the Mediterranean. At the Gran Consiglio on 7 December Mussolini asserted that the measures taken by Britain in the Mediterranean directly affected the vital interests of Italy.[62]

Thus, when Ciano revealed that Britain wanted to replace Germany as Italy's supplier of coal, the Duce was infuriated and offended. Did the British not recognize that Italy remained an ally of the power Britain had declared war on? Were the British attempting the economic conquest of Italy? The Italians responded by threatening the British and French with imminent Italian intervention on the German side if the Allies severed Italy from its supply of German coal. As an alternative, the British offered an agreement that would include either Italian import quotas or the principle of enemy export control. Moreover, "as a demonstration of our goodwill," the British released all detained cargoes consigned to Italy on 28 December—what Halifax termed "exceptional measures . . . to reduce to the minimum the inconvenience, and consequent irritation, of Italian interests." But neither the relaxation of contraband control nor the latest British proposal mollified the Duce's hostility. On 18 January Mussolini told Renato Ricci, the minister of corporations and a member of Ciano's Economic Warfare Committee, that the commercial talks with the British should end: "I have the pleasure—I say *the pleasure*—to inform you that English coal can no longer arrive [in Italy]." Directing Ricci to substitute Italian lignite for the coal that was currently imported from Britain, Mussolini asserted that adjusting to life without British coal would "be a good lash of the whip for the Italians, so that they will more decisively follow the path of autarky."[63]

Desperately, Ciano and his committee tried to patch together a formula that would salvage an Anglo-Italian agreement. Guido Donegani, chief of the giant Montecatini Chemical Trust, prophesied that without either British or German coal, Italian industry "will suffer a sudden stoppage, with dire consequences for both production and society." Raffaelo Riccardi, the minister of currency and exchange, claimed that without the twenty million British pounds that the original agreement included, Italian purchasing power for raw materials, especially those of British origin, would decline precipitously. But once the British revealed that Italian arms sales to Britain were a sine qua non of any British coal shipments to Italy, all hope disappeared. Mussolini's commitment to the Axis forbade him to sell arms to the Allies, especially since Italy needed to prepare itself for intervention. "Governments, like individuals, must follow a line of morality and honor," he explained to Ciano. On 8 February Ciano informed Loraine that the Duce categorically refused to sell Britain matériel. As a result, the British decided to begin interdicting German coal exports to Italy on 1 March. Italy would be left to its own devices to recover the 650,000 tons per month in lost coal imports.[64] The Allied-Italian chasm no longer appeared reparable.

Diversion of Anglo-French Strategy from the Mediterranean

The question of whether or not to stop German coal exports to Italy was part and parcel of a larger debate about the proper war strategy the Allies should employ. The long-war strategy came under fire in late 1939. Again it was the French who most vigorously questioned the efficacy of the blockade and the appropriateness of postponing direct military engagement. Although the French could not persuade the British to endorse an Allied expedition to the Balkans, this unrelenting pressure for an active rather than a passive war strategy encouraged the British to support an Allied campaign in Scandinavia. The British opposed the French proposal to open a second front against Germany in the Balkans but eventually agreed that the Allies should search for a way to win the war rapidly. The stalemate in the Mediterranean over Italian nonbelligerence, as well as the increasingly menacing attitude of Italy, helped prod the Allies toward this shift in strategy from the Balkans to Scandinavia. In addition to believing that operations in the North Sea could defeat Germany quickly, the British suspected that a Scandinavian strategy would not upset the current Mediterranean situation and jeopardize Britain's imperial defense system. But since British and French conceptions of the Mediterranean remained conflicting, the two countries approached the situation in Scandinavia with different motivations—perhaps contributing to the Scandinavian debacle.

With the search for a neutral Balkan bloc under Turkish leadership at an impasse, the French in mid-November 1939 returned to the idea of arranging an Allied expedition to Salonika. The principal mover behind the resurgence of the Balkans as a theater for "decisive" operations against Germany was General Weygand, who passionately and cogently argued his case, spending as much time in Ankara, Alexandria, and Paris as with his own command in Syria. In fact Weygand soon gained the active support of not only Massigli and most of the French military attachés but also the local British commanders, Wavell and Cunningham. Asserting that the absence of Balkan solidarity invited a German or Russian incursion into the region, Weygand argued that the Allies had an obligation to "support and prolong the defensive efforts of our Balkan friends" and an opportunity to "put us in a position to impose on our adversaries a vast attritional front whose size as well as geographical and topographical aspects provide us with the means to undertake action that might be decisive." Aware of London's opposition to his plan, Weygand demanded only that the Allies prepare for an expedition to the Balkans by gathering the necessary shipping, holding staff talks with the Balkan states, sending arms to the Balkans, and assembling four or five divisions of land and air forces in Syria. If either the Germans or Russians moved into the Danubian basin, the Syrian force could respond by going immediately to Salonika, acting as the avant-garde of an eventual Allied force of fifteen divisions. Privately, he admitted that his Balkan strategy had been inspired by his fear of domestic Communism and his frustration with the formula "time is on our side," which had not improved the strategic situation but had only encouraged complacency. A long war "costs many lives, makes difficult the maintenance of morale, and encourages the Soviets' revolutionary projects [in France]." Thus, according to Weygand, "all loss of time not urgently justified is a crime."[65]

As they had in September, the French service chiefs again opposed the proposal for an expedition to Salonika. At a meeting of the chiefs on 27 November Darlan repeated his concerns about the demands placed on French shipping and added, "once again, it is necessary to certify that our action in the Balkans is subordinate to the attitude of Italy. If she is hostile, we will have to 'smack' [*taper*] her, and it will be difficult for us to withdraw the troops from France and North Africa." Gamelin agreed that the Allies had to resolve the Italian question before they could establish a Balkan front and end the "war of attrition" strategy; a war against the Italians would weaken, if not end, all operations in other theaters. "With Italy hostile," Gamelin told the service chiefs on 2 December, "we must admit that we will be unable to do great things."[66]

Despite the service chiefs' opposition, Léger and the Quai d'Orsay endorsed Weygand's Salonika plan. The political directorate argued that the Anglo-French treaty with Turkey and the failure to form a neutral Balkan bloc had changed the Balkan situation since the end of September. Massigli's relentless calls from Ankara, pressing for action in the Balkans as a way for the Allies to position themselves to uphold the bargain to the Turks, suggested that many of the logistical difficulties could be mitigated by landing at Thrace. Moreover, the Italians had shown that they had Balkan ambitions as well. As Massigli opined in January, "The Italian game is in concert with Berlin." Further Allied inaction in this region would invite the incursion of Germany, Russia, *and* Italy: "If we do not apply ourselves with the perseverance and will on which success depends, the temptation will be great in the spring for the Reich and the USSR to alter fundamentally the balance of power to their advantage and for Italy, with the opportunity for lucrative gains, to participate in their plot."[67]

With the political and military officials split on the Balkan issue, Daladier again turned to his trusted adviser, Louis Aubert. On 8 December Aubert argued that a German descent into the Danube was indeed possible, and that it could lead to Germany's domination of the Balkans, effectively destroying the efficacy of the Allied blockade; nor could the added contingencies of Russian and Italian intervention in the Balkans be ruled out. He concluded that the Allies should, at the very least, prepare to be able to intervene in the Balkan region in the spring. Daladier agreed that the treaty with Turkey permitted the Allies to contemplate the creation of a *dépôt de matériel* in the Middle East that could be sent to Thrace and would prove to the Balkan nations the Allies' determination to support their neutrality. The premier concluded, "We can no longer refuse to prepare on the diplomatic and military planes a common Anglo-French-Turkish plan of action in the Balkans." Discussing the situation with Weygand three weeks later, Daladier explained that he wanted action, "knowing that we can do nothing without taking risks." Yet again the premier resolved to raise the issue with the British in mid-December during the inter-Allied staff talks and at the next Supreme War Council.[68]

The British responded to the reports of France's renewed interest in establishing a Balkan front with exasperation. As he had three months before, General Ironside led the charge to dismantle the French proposal: although acknowledging that Weygand's determination to find a "decisive" theater for the war against Germany had much appeal, Ironside regretted that the Allies lacked the resources and unanimity to carry out Weygand's plans:

> It is the same old story. We are not ready and have not the material ready to support our small friends. . . . Until Italy has declared herself we cannot move troops. . . . The French seem to take a completely different attitude to

> us about Italy. We want to keep her friendly by every means in our power, because we do not want the trade in the Mediterranean stopped.

On 5 December the COS presented the War Cabinet with a review of the situation in the Middle East, concluding that they saw no reason to change their opinions on an Allied expedition to the Balkans. "Nothing that has happened since has caused us to alter our view that it is to our advantage to keep the war out of the Balkans as long as possible, and to avoid provoking Italian hostility." The French proposal to send matériel to Greece and Turkey was received in an equally negative tone. British resources in Egypt could not be weakened on account of the latent Italian threat in Libya; the redistribution of land and air forces from any other theater would weaken the expeditionary force to France. "It must be remembered," the chiefs asserted, "that our interests in the Middle East, important as they are, are not as important as the security of France and Britain, or of Singapore."[69]

Both the prime minister and the FO agreed with the service chiefs' position on the Balkans. Concerned with not upsetting "Italian susceptibilities," Halifax perceived a direct link between building an Anglo-Italian commercial relationship and preserving the British Empire through and after the war. In late November he explained to Loraine that "what we are willing to work for is the establishment of firm, friendly, and durable relations between the British and Italian kingdoms and empires, not merely during the present hostilities but also and indeed especially after their conclusion." The following month Loraine, who still believed that an Italian alliance with the West was possible, insisted that "a move in the Balkans by the Allies is not separable from the risk of embroiling ourselves with Italy." As he had in September, Chamberlain continued to doubt the French premise that Germany would soon embark on operations in the Danube: "I have seen no reason to change the belief that I have expressed all along, that Hitler will abstain from any action which would entail real fighting with heavy losses whether among his soldiers or civilians." Moreover, Chamberlain recognized that the outbreak of the Soviet-Finnish war on 30 November, and Italy's subsequent protest of Russian aggression, presented the Allies with a unique opportunity to draw the Italians decisively away from Germany. Nothing should be undertaken that would jeopardize this possibility. Thus, on 7 December the War Cabinet endorsed the COS's policy for the Balkans and Middle East without debate.[70]

At both the inter-Allied staff talks on 11 December and the SWC on 19 December, the British again vetoed any Allied action in the Balkans. Gamelin's admission at the outset of the former meeting that a landing at Thrace or Salonika would require not only Turkish or Greek cooperation respectively, but also Italian approval effectively undermined Weygand's plan. Because the Italian attitude was not yet "ripe," an operation to the Balkans under the current circumstances would risk opening another war theater in the Mediterranean. Despite this hostile audience, Weygand argued his case lucidly and vigorously, stressing that the Allied blockade in the Balkans was entirely ineffective and that only Allied preparation in the region could prevent a repeat of the disasters of the First World War. On the basis of his presentation, which even Ironside found "attractive," Weygand persuaded his British colleagues to support both arms shipments to and Allied staff talks with the Balkan states.[71]

Although Daladier attended the SWC the following week with his agenda weakened, the French premier hardly conceded the issue to his allies. Claiming that the Greeks and Yugoslavs already seemed willing to cooperate, Daladier insisted that the Allies open staff talks with these and other Balkan states specifically to prepare for an eventual "defensive" operation in the region. Only with preparation could the Allies fulfill their pledges to Romania and Turkey, and prevent German domination of the Danube. Chamberlain expressed his resolute opposition to the idea, citing the importance of not alienating Italy. As Sir Edward Bridges, secretary to the War Cabinet, who summarized the meeting, wrote, "The attitude of Italy is in fact an overriding consideration and it is essential to avoid offending her susceptibilities." Despite Daladier's surprising intransigence, it was clear that British assistance in this matter would not be forthcoming. France could not weaken her arsenal on the western front by sending matériel to the Balkans if the British would not at least strengthen the BEF. And without British naval help, Daladier understood that Darlan would refuse to transport the expedition through the eastern Mediterranean. For the time being, then, French diplomatic initiatives in Rome and the Balkans would have to suffice.[72]

Although both British and French planners continued to study the Balkan expedition plan for several months, December 1939 marked the height of its consideration. Politicians in London would not permit its execution as long as Italy remained outside the conflict. And with Italy's hostility rising, rather than falling, during the first months of 1940, the possibility of establishing a Balkan front continued to wane. Yet these strategic deliberations were not to no avail. Besides impressing upon the French Britain's paranoia about starting a war in the Mediterranean and upon the British France's determination to establish a southeastern front, the Balkan debate compelled planners on both sides of the English Channel to consider the efficacy of the blockade and the suitability of the long-war strategy. Suddenly the Allies, at the urging of the French, began searching for a feasible *plan de guerre*—one that would not only impose hardship on Germany but also offer a chance for the Allies to win the war quickly without jeopardizing their empires.[73]

In France, Darlan became the leading voice in the search for an alternative war strategy. Ever since the Allies had rejected his prewar plan for a Mediterranean offensive, the naval chief had become increasingly disenchanted with the manner in which the French (and the Allies) approached the war. In mid-December Darlan complained that "the country has the impression that there is no direction. It awaits a lightning war with massive bombardments and considerable losses. Seeing nothing happening, it must ask why we have bothered at all. We do not have a resolute and coherent policy." Questioning the Allies' passive strategy, the naval chief specifically focused his ire on the exclusive reliance on weak economic warfare: "The government decrees an intensive blockade of Germany and then strives not to apply it." At the end of December Darlan argued to Gamelin that the long-war economic strategy had to be abandoned. In a lengthy memorandum to Daladier three weeks later, the naval chief explained that if the Nazis did not embark on major military operations and their sources of supply in eastern Europe remained constant, Germany could "sustain a long war of siege," concluding that "our passivity will not facilitate our success."[74]

In late December the naval staff produced a report that incorporated many of Darlan's ideas. It argued that the blockade could hinder but not paralyze Germany's prosecution of the war; Germany had largely compensated for its lost commerce by new overland trade with neutrals in eastern and southeastern Europe. Only "strict rationing" of neutrals could make the blockade credible, yet experience had shown that rationing was not a viable alternative. Claiming that "time works against us," the naval staff asserted that the Allies would lose the war if they did not obtain a military victory by the fall of 1940. To obtain this success, the Marine suggested either the destruction of the Caucasus oil fields or the seizure of the Gallivare mines in northern Sweden. All the Soviet Union's oil, much of which was shipped to Germany, came from the Caucasus, and the Gallivare mines provided Germany with ten million tons of iron ore per year—40 percent of Germany's annual requirements. Either operation, according to the navy's Deuxième Bureau, "would have incalculable strategic consequences which could result in Germany's defeat."[75]

Although his staff preferred the Caucasus plan, Darlan in mid-January advocated the operation in Scandinavia. By cutting Soviet communications between Petsamo and Murmansk, the Allies could help the Finns recapture the port of Petsamo and stop German imports of Swedish iron ore. If the Germans responded to this development in the Allied blockade, the Allies could land an expeditionary force in Norway charged with traveling to Sweden and capturing the Gallivare mines. The important consequences of this essentially anti-German operation, Darlan explained to Gamelin and Daladier at the end of January, would be to provide aid to the Finns and "deliberately open hostilities with the Soviet Union"—a prospect that the politically conservative Darlan welcomed. Moreover, Darlan stressed an important, though admittedly secondary, motivation for this expedition: helping the Finns and challenging the Soviets "would definitely not displease Italy and Japan, and reaching a rapprochement with [Italy and Japan] would give us still more opportunities to shackle German supplies." With a neutral or friendly Italy, the Allies could even contemplate an eventual operation in the Balkans to open a southeastern front as well.[76]

Darlan received support for his Scandinavian ideas from almost all of France's principal decision-makers. Those who had been most enthusiastic for an Allied expedition to the Balkans were also the most optimistic about the prospects of gaining control of Sweden's iron mines. Agreeing that Allied intervention in Finland and Norway would precipitate an encounter that could have a variety of potentially beneficial repercussions, the CSDN in January opined that "whatever the inherent risks, the value of the stakes makes it worthwhile to embark on this action and to devote all our resources to it." Even Gamelin, who among the service chiefs was the most resistant to operations in Scandinavia, speculated that France could repair its relations with Italy by arranging for cooperative aid to Finland. After blockade officials expressed their interest in the occupation of the Gallivare mines, the political directorate at the Quai d'Orsay linked the plan to the Balkans and argued that success in Scandinavia would be "a strategic and moral coup decisive for the conduct of the war." One of the most fervent supporters was Daladier, who had been extremely disappointed by the defeat of the Balkan-expedition idea. The premier told Corbin that the proposed Scandinavian mission would provide help to the Finns, eliminate a principal source of German iron, and affect the nature of the war in other theaters: "The implications and eventual consequences of this decision extend far beyond its immediate practical results." On 13 January the premier instructed Darlan to prepare plans for Scandinavia. He later explained that he attached no political reservations to this intervention; even the prospect of a war with the Soviet Union should not deter the Allies.[77]

The Soviet attack on Finland and the Balkan debate with the French also inspired the British to consider sending an expedition to Scandinavia. On 16 December Churchill advised that the Allies lay a series of minefields in Norwegian territorial waters to force ships carrying iron ore to Germany into the open seas where they would be subject to Allied contraband control. If Germany could be cut off from all Swedish ore supplies by the end of 1940, "a blow will have been struck at [Germany's] war-making capacity equal to a first-class victory in the field or from the air, and without any serious sacrifice of life. It might, indeed, be immediately decisive." Having obtained the FO's endorsement, Churchill in late December became the most vigorous proponent of an Allied naval operation in Scandinavia, even at the risk of Soviet hostility. As he explained in a Christmas memorandum, "The supreme strategy is to carry the war into a theatre where we can bring superior forces to bear, and where a decision can be obtained which rules out all other theatres."[78]

Later that day the COS noted that once the ice melted the Germans would be able to import Swedish iron ore by way of Lulea in the Gulf of Bothnia. If the Allies sent an expedition through Narvik to occupy the Gallivare ore fields, however, Germany's supply would be permanently eliminated. The unexpectedly resolute and brave Finnish resistance to Soviet forces in late January, combined with the relentless French prodding for action and the deteriorating Anglo-Italian commercial negotiations, persuaded the British service chiefs to propose a six-division expedition to Narvik, Trondheim, and Namsos, supported by substantial air and naval commitments. The COS recommended that the Allies launch the mission before the end of March and "seize [the Swedish iron-ore mines] with both hands."[79]

Although the British became interested in a Scandinavian campaign primarily because of the immediate economic repercussions it could have on Germany, both the armed services and the diplomats appreciated that the Mediterranean situation and the sustainability of Britain's imperial defense strategy influenced the Scandinavian decision. When the Military Coordination Committee considered the idea on 20 December, a connection to the Mediterranean was immediately made. If this "vital import" to Germany could be interdicted, the Allies could "[ease] up on our control of other less important imports which Germany obtained, for example, from Italy." General Ironside claimed in January that "an expedition to Scandinavia would be the easiest way of stopping German aggression in the Balkans." Cadogan also recognized this link, advising against discussing the sensitive Balkan situation with the suspicious Italians now that operations in Scandinavia were contemplated. On 24 December the permanent undersecretary minuted, "Let us not annoy and/or alarm Musso[lini] until we have to," and the following day he noted in his diary, "Let's go easy on [the Balkans] till we know whether we are going to do anything, and whether we are going for Scandinavia. We can't do *both*!" Indeed, by 27 December the FO had decided to defer any approach to Italy about a potential Allied expedition to southeastern Europe "because the Scandinavian project was in the offing and it was clear the Allies would be unable to undertake commitments both in Scandinavia and in the Balkans." Even members of the War Cabinet recognized the broader implications of operations in northern Europe. At the end of December Lord Privy Seal Sir Samuel Hoare told Chamberlain that "I am more than ever convinced that Scandinavia both for its own importance and also for its influence on the other neutrals . . . is at the moment the key place in the war."[80]

Britain and France endorsed the Scandinavian strategy because it offered an opportunity to defeat Germany rapidly, but they also recognized that these operations—if not immediately successful—would affect Italy's role in the war. The French hoped that Scandinavia would help to establish Italy's durable neutrality and allow for an eventual Allied expedition to the Balkans. By contrast, the British looked to Scandinavia as a way to entice the Italians to the Allied side, to commit Italy to the defense of the Danube, and thus to eliminate the need for an Allied landing at Salonika or Thrace. Peace in the Mediterranean as well as the British Empire would be preserved. Again, this optimistic British perspective of Fascist Italy was a product of Ambassador Loraine's encouraging reports throughout January. The tone of Foreign Minister Ciano's recent speech to the Fascist Chamber and the exchange of visits between the king of Italy and the pope confirmed Loraine's opinion of 7 January "that Italian policy is preparing to veer toward us." Loraine had recently identified Ciano, Dino Grandi, and Italo Balbo as a group of influential Fascists—"three principal lieutenants of the Duce"—who had become increasingly disgusted with the Germans, were confident that Germany could not win the war, and were inclined toward a rapprochement with the Western powers. Evidence that Britain and France were hostile to Bolshevism and capable of defeating Germany "might very probably provide us with a cooperative link with Italy, of which the Duce would find it extremely awkward to disapprove." The Scandinavian campaign, which aimed both to strike at the heart of Germany's warmaking potential and to demonstrate the West's support for Finland in its war against the Soviet Union, would serve these purposes.[81]

At the inter-Allied staff talks in Paris at the end of January, the British service chiefs expressed their opposition to Darlan's plan to capture the port of Petsamo. Not only was the traffic between Petsamo and Murmansk insignificant, but also the port facilities at Petsamo could not accommodate an expeditionary corps. Even if arrangements could be made to improve the port, the distance between Petsamo and the Gallivare iron mines was too far for Allied troops to travel. Finally, taking Petsamo would offer little aid for the Finns. Explaining that his proposal was only a "study," Darlan accepted the British criticism without much debate. It appears that Darlan was entirely satisfied with the British alternative to land an expeditionary corps at Narvik and to lay mines off the Norwegian coast because that too would involve opening an active war theater in Scandinavia, striking a blow at Germany and the Soviet Union, and avoiding an Allied intervention in the Balkans. Daladier pressed for the British to assume command of the Narvik operation and insisted that the cooperation of Norway and Sweden not be a prerequisite. Chamberlain agreed to these two stipulations and indicated that he would send two British divisions to France the following day to prepare for this expedition, which would take place before 20 March.[82]

Many details were yet to be resolved, but the commitment to extending the war into northern Europe had been made. The rapid deterioration of Allied relations with Italy during February and March—and thus the sudden absence of a Balkan alternative—only intensified British and French resolve to act in Norway and Sweden. It is strange, however, that the increasing likelihood of a future war in the Mediterranean did not temper the Allies' desire for a conflict with Germany in Scandinavia. Yet the Allies—particularly the British—needed to believe that war in the Mediterranean could still be avoided. It was easier for the British to abandon the long-war strategy and open a Scandinavian campaign than to admit that the Mediterranean could soon become an active war theater. Such an admission would have been tantamount to abandoning Britain's entire imperial defense scheme.

[6]

"A drama that will remake the map of the continent": December 1939–June 1940

Mussolini's Decision for Intervention

Italian-German affairs remained fluid at the end of 1939. In addition to the enduring conflict over the German-speaking population in Alto Adige, events in Scandinavia and the Balkans threatened the stability of the Axis. Yet at the same time these events, especially when considered alongside the developing crisis over Italian coal imports, contributed to the maturation of Axis relations in early 1940 and the decision for Italian intervention. The Soviet invasion of Finland on 30 November stunned and infuriated the Italians. Spontaneous student demonstrations in support of Finland and hostile to Russia broke out throughout the country and lasted for more than a week. Ciano noted optimistically that "the people cry 'death to Russia' but think 'death to Germany.'" Although Mussolini had grown increasingly comfortable with the Soviets since August, largely as a result of their recognition of Ethiopia and Albania in November, even he condemned the Russian attack on the Finns. The Soviets' protest of the demonstrations and subsequent recall of their ambassador cemented Mussolini's reaction. He informed Mackensen in early December that Italy held the British and the French responsible for the greed of these Soviet "crooks" but reaffirmed that for Italian policy "Bolshevism remained enemy number one." Mussolini also encouraged Ciano to include direct attacks on the Russians in the foreign minister's speech of 16 December to the Camera dei Fasci e Corporazioni. When Finland asked the Italians to extend their moral support to the material realm, the Fascists agreed. In early January Mussolini approved the dispatch of Italian pursuit-plane pilots and air-artillery men to Finland.[1]

Although Mussolini and Ciano agreed on what policy Italy should follow with regard to Finland and the Balkans, they were motivated by different agendas. Ciano viewed the Soviet-Finnish war as an opportunity to foment anti-German sentiment in Italy and to ensure a durable Italian neutrality. After justifying Italy's choice for nonintervention to the Gran Consiglio on 7 December, the foreign minister laced his speech to the Chamber with "subtle anti-German poison" by focusing on Russia's aggression in Finland. As he wrote in his diary, reveling in the post-speech praises of Ambassador Loraine, "the first impression seemed uniquely anti-Bolshevik, while substantially it was anti-German." Ciano believed that his speech, which recounted Germany's premature precipitation of war and ridiculed its alliance with Russia, ensured that no Italian would ever march alongside the Germans: "Everyone now knows and understands that Germany has betrayed us twice."[2]

But Mussolini used the Russo-Finnish war as a means to reestablish the Axis relationship. At the Gran Consiglio he offered only an "intellectual acceptance" of Ciano's presentation on nonbelligerence. According to Bottai, who attended the meeting, Mussolini "still resists the cold analysis of Galeazzo." Shortly thereafter the Duce added to a draft of Ciano's Chamber speech a confirmation that the Pact of Steel remained in effect. Nevertheless, the speech was received poorly in many German circles. Ribbentrop, in particular, told Attolico that he was *furioso* about it. This cool reception motivated Mussolini's first letter to Hitler since the outbreak of war. In it the Duce emphasized that Italy was obligated to respond to the unprovoked Soviet attack against Finland. The tone of Ciano's speech, according to Mussolini, was explicitly anti-Bolshevik, not anti-German. The Duce pleaded with Hitler not to abandon the Anti-Comintern pact, which remained the essential ideological foundation of the Axis: "It is my definite duty to add that a further step in your relations with Moscow would have catastrophic repercussions in Italy, where the anti-Bolshevik unanimity, especially among the Fascist masses, is absolute, solid as rock, and indivisible." Concluding with a promise that Italy would remain Germany's political, economic, and military "reserve," Mussolini reaffirmed that the "attitude of Italy is within, not outside, the framework of the Pact of Alliance."[3]

The motivations of Ciano and Mussolini for Italy's policy in the Balkans also conflicted. In December François-Poncet informed the Italian foreign minister that the Allies were prepared to intervene in the Balkans to repel any German or Russian threat to that region. François-Poncet added an important caveat, to which Ciano attached great significance: the Allies would carry out this mission only if they had received prior agreement from Italy. Although he downplayed the German threat to the region and told François-Poncet that Italy would not associate with any anti-German move into the Balkans, Ciano implied that Italy would resist any Russian incursion and welcome Allied assistance. In fact Ciano had just extracted a promise from Hungary that it would not invade Transylvania in the event of a Russian attack on Bessarabia. The Italian foreign minister privately admitted that "what we are doing for Romania has the great advantage of placing us increasingly in the anti-German camp."[4]

By contrast, Mussolini endorsed the initiative to support Romania because of his renewed determination to occupy Croatia. The Duce believed that Bucharest in return would consent to Italy's assumption of a dominant position along the eastern coast of the Adriatic. With Italy in Yugoslavia, Romanian security against the Bolshevik menace would be enhanced. Whether or not Ciano briefed Mussolini in detail about François-Poncet's démarche of 24 December remains unknown. But what is not in doubt is that Mussolini had no intention of consenting to Allied intervention in the Balkans, much less joining the Allies in a war against the Soviet Union. In early December Mussolini indicated that he had no reservations about declaring war on France, if necessary, to claim Corsica and Tunisia. Meeting with Heinrich Himmler shortly before Christmas, Mussolini promised that "he would never allow the defeat of Germany to occur." Early in the new year the Duce informed his foreign minister that "unless Germany commits any irreparable errors, we will not renounce the alliance. Intervention with the French and British would confirm [the Allies'] military and colonial hegemony over Italy." When Ciano speculated in late January that he could persuade the Allies to endorse an Italian conquest of Croatia, Mussolini strongly disagreed. "One thing is certain," he explained to Ciano, "we shall never join [the Allies]."[5] Despite Mussolini's hatred for Bolshevism and Ciano's anger at the German betrayal of Italy, the Fascists never intended to march against their German allies. All Ciano could hope for was a durable neutrality, but Mussolini could not accept this humiliation and miss an opportunity to expand his empire by force.

During the first three months of the European war, Mussolini—intensely depressed about the indignity of nonbelligerence—accepted Ciano's perspective on Italy's necessary abstention from the war and allowed the foreign minister to control the levers of Italy's foreign affairs machinery. There was never an opportunity to draw Italy to the Allied side, and the first months of war presented the only slim chance the Allies ever had to bribe Italy into neutrality. Beginning in December and, ironically, at a time when Ciano's predominant influence appeared firmly established to the outside world, Mussolini reasserted himself in the making of Italian foreign policy. Preparation for war at Germany's side was the Duce's guiding principle. On 13 December Mussolini ordered Graziani to increase the army to a million trained men by the middle of 1940; the call-up began in February and was largely complete by May. By the new year Graziani and Farinacci—two men highly regarded by Mussolini—had both spoken in favor of war against the democracies. Emboldened by their enthusiasm, Mussolini on 11 January told Ciano that he anticipated intervention "during the second half of 1941."[6]

Reports that the Italian military would not be ready for war by late 1941 did not dissuade Mussolini. Despite the navy's stockpiling of increased oil imports from the United States and Mexico, Cavagnari argued that he would not have a full complement of artillery until 1943–44 at the earliest. Generals Badoglio, Soddu, and Favagrossa believed that the army, which currently had only ten fully equipped divisions, could not be adequately prepared until October 1942 at the earliest. At a meeting in January the army staff explained that its poor preparation was a direct consequence of inadequate raw materials. It estimated that the army's monthly allowance for iron was over 50 percent less than current production required; monthly copper supplies were less than 30 percent, tin less than 20 percent, and nickel less than 5 percent of current requirements. Only the air force thought its equipment could reach acceptable levels by the end of 1941. Mussolini found all these reports pessimistic, reflecting the Italian "race of sheep" that had not yet been transformed into a race of wolves. "When the vegetative instincts of a people predominate, only the use of force can save them." Speaking before the Fascist militia in early February, Mussolini concluded with the affirmation that the Italians would fight "that battle which will arrive soon."[7]

Two sets of meetings in late January and early February demonstrated the direction that Italian policy had now taken. In the Council of Ministers on 20 and 23 January Mussolini proclaimed that Britain and France, which had interests in direct conflict with Italy's, "can now no longer win the war." One recently intercepted British telegram and an intelligence report on France indicated that the Allies would not accept any modification of the Balkan status quo and had planned for an offensive against Libya. Thus, Mussolini claimed, Italy could not remain neutral indefinitely without having "to play in the B League of the European powers." Italy's status as a great imperial power depended on Italy's ability to fight and win a war. With his policy now clear, the Duce delved into war strategy. He intimated at conducting a "parallel war" in Croatia, allowing Italy to intervene without having to face Britain and France immediately. Taking solace in the Aeronautica's optimistic estimates and placing a priority on air power, the Duce anticipated "terrorizing" Italian "bombardments of France" and a decisive battle for control of the Mediterranean. Most important, Mussolini now insisted that Italy could intervene in late 1940. Over the course of two weeks, during which time many dismal military estimates had been produced, the Duce accelerated the timetable for war by one full year. While Ciano and Riccardi remained skeptical about Italy's prospects in the war, Mussolini's energetic presentation won the committed support of Paolo Thaon di Revel, the minister of finance, and Renato Ricci, the minister of corporations.[8]

At the annual meeting of the Supreme Defense Commission, the highest military-economic planning body in the Fascist state, on 8–14 February, Mussolini proved that he was bent on war regardless of his country's military and economic weaknesses. According to the Duce, Italy had to refocus her efforts on establishing genuine economic autarky. It was a question not of resources but of will. Mussolini asserted that Italy could extract ten million tons of coal and lignite a year in Istria, Sardinia, and Italy; steel production could double from two to four million tons per year; the aluminum industry could produce 70,000 tons per year instead of its current estimate of 40,000 tons; refineries could be built to produce aviation gasoline from Albanian oil; the new synthetic rubber plants that would begin operation in 1940 could provide at least a fifth of the country's annual requirement. Conceding that these developments could affect future military preparedness, the Duce highlighted Italy's favorable stockpiles of fuel as proof that intervention in the near future was not inconceivable. The navy, as a result of Cavagnari's foresight, would have 1,546,500 tons of crude oil available by June 1940—enough for eight to ten months of war. The army and air force would also have enough gasoline, diesel oils, and lubricating oils for at least six months of war by mid-1940. If Italy could time intervention well, most likely during the summer of 1940, it had the resources to fight a short decisive war. Despite its admittedly precarious position in strategic raw materials and, in particular, hard currency, Italy could not "remain absent from a drama that will remake the map of the continent."[9]

Part of Mussolini's misplaced confidence at the Supreme Defense Commission derived from his meeting with Prince Philip of Hesse, nephew of Kaiser Wilhelm II and a son-in-law of King Vittorio Emanuele III. Philip enthusiastically supported the Axis alliance, was closely connected with Pope Pius XII, and had frequently carried highly confidential messages between Hitler and Mussolini. On 8 February the prince confirmed that Germany would significantly increase coal exports to Italy once the freezing weather ended. Only three days after Loraine announced that the Allies would begin to intercept German coal exports to Italy—and despite opposition from Ciano, Riccardi, and Giannini—Mussolini declared that Italy would do everything in her power to satisfy German demands for hemp, copper, and matériel. Since January Italy had already sent Germany three planes, millions of lire worth of aeronautical equipment, 200,000 naval batteries, and 280,500 magnetic mines. After promising the Germans a substantial portion of the nickel from Italy's only nickel mine, the Duce now planned to send the Nazis 3,500 tons of copper, which would require the Fascists to extort copper from Italy's churches and citizens. Italy formally committed to fulfilling these German requests in return for Germany's promise on 22 February to ship at least 500,000 tons of coal per month to Italy by rail.[10]

The pending start of the Allied blockade of German coal exports only spurred Mussolini's enthusiasm for intervention. Despite the frequent attempts by Badoglio and Cavagnari to illustrate Italy's military and naval weaknesses, Mussolini at the end of February repeated his claims against France, citing Italy's need for "free access to the oceans." He also expressed to Ciano his "profound and honest conviction" that the Allies would lose the war. When U.S. Secretary of State Sumner Welles visited Rome in late February to promote neutrality and a peaceful resolution of the conflict, Mussolini "defended the German thesis with absolute intransigence" and then delivered the record of the conversation to the German ambassador. His demonstrations of goodwill toward the Nazis quickly paid dividends. On 10 March, after the seizure by the Royal Navy of thirteen Italian coal ships leaving Rotterdam and Antwerp, Ribbentrop went to Rome and presented the Duce with a letter from Hitler and a firm offer to deliver by rail one million tons of coal a month—effectively eliminating Italy's coal problem. Clodius and Giannini signed a secret protocol to this effect three days later. After Mussolini responded to the Führer, pledging to enter the war "at the appropriate moment" and to fight it "with Germany and parallel to Germany," arrangements were made for the two dictators to meet on the Brenner the following week.[11]

At the Brenner frontier on 18 March Hitler dominated the conversation, assuring Mussolini that France would be defeated in only a few months' time and that the Germans and the Italians were "indissolubly tied." Hitler was determined to prod Italian intervention, believing that it was a prerequisite for containing or defeating the British and initiating a German campaign against the Soviet Union. Although the two dictators did not discuss specific war strategies, Hitler understood that Italy could not fight a long war and that the Duce could not "do anything contrary to the interests of the Italian people." Mussolini assured Hitler that Italy, to defend its "honor and interests," would intervene on Germany's side but asked that Hitler delay Germany's attack on the Maginot Line until the summer, when Italy would have its newest battleships ready. Hitler ignored this appeal, responding that "a German victory would be an Italian victory, but the defeat of Germany would also imply the end of the Italian empire."[12] Arguments such as these, implying a direct connection between Italy's intervention in the war and her future imperial status, resonated in Mussolini's psyche and manipulated Fascist foreign policy.

After the Brenner meeting, Mussolini resolved to join the war as soon as possible and immediately following any German success in the West. As the Duce explained to his foreign minister, Italy's forces "will constitute the left wing, which will keep many enemy troops occupied without fighting, but will also be ready to enter into action at the appropriate moment." Recognizing that the Germans were prepared militarily to strike the West at any time, Ciano lamented that "the prospect of an imminent clash, in which [Mussolini] might remain an outsider, disturbs and . . . humiliates him."[13]

The Italian foreign minister soon accepted the inevitability of intervention. Aside from Mussolini's growing desire for a war that would establish the second Roman empire, Ciano was influenced by signs of British and French pusillanimity. After the French cabinet crisis of 19–20 March, the Italians received word that many in France wanted to send Pierre Laval to Rome to negotiate a Franco-Italian settlement. François-Poncet then offered to discuss with Ciano the cession of French Somaliland to Italy. On 21 March Cham berlain sent a message through Bastianini and Dingli that Britain maintained its continued attachment to a "policy of friendly relations with Italy." Mussolini and Ciano responded that they would agree to a compromise peace only if the British surrendered continental Europe to Germany and the Mediterranean region to Italy. These two attempts at naked conciliation revealed to Ciano that the democracies were no longer confident they could defeat Germany. Siding with the Germans could benefit Italy after all. Finally, the Regia Marina's interception of a British naval telegram, which claimed that Ciano did not support Mussolini's Axis policy and that the Duce had considered sacking his foreign minister, embarrassed and shocked Ciano into openly embracing the direction of Fascist foreign policy by early April.[14]

At the end of March Mussolini began to establish a specific course of action for Italian intervention. He produced a written directive for the eight most important leaders of the Fascist government, asserting, "Today a compromise is impossible." The Allies would continue to rely on a gradually tightening blockade while the Germans would continue the "phony war" and intensify air and naval operations. Germany would not launch a land offensive against the West until it was certain of a crushing victory. Once the Germans experienced success against the Allies' Maginot Line, the Italians could not postpone intervention any longer. Mussolini's memorandum continued:

> To believe that Italy can remain outside the conflict until its end is absurd and impossible. . . . the remaining hypothesis is a parallel war in which Germany's objectives would extend to include ours, which are summarized in the affirmation: liberty on the seas, access to the oceans. Italy will not truly be an independent nation until it possesses the bars of its Mediterranean prison—Corsica, Bizerta, Malta—and the walls of the same prison: Gibraltar and Suez. As a result of the problem of land frontiers, Italy can only become a true world power by resolving its maritime problem.

Alluding to a recent revision of the army's war plans, Mussolini stressed a defensive stance in the western Alps, Libya, and the Aegean; the occupation of Corsica; the "distrustful observation" of Yugoslavia from both the northeast and Albania; and offensives to guarantee Eritrea and against Gedaref, Kassala, and Djibouti. But the principal Italian effort would be taken by the navy, which would carry out "an offensive right down the line [*su tutta la linea*] in the Mediterranean and outside it." No specific naval objectives were given.[15]

Mussolini distributed the memorandum on 6 April following a meeting of the Council of Ministers in which he told his subordinates that he refused to let Italians "act as the democracies' whores, which would bring us into conflict with the Germans." Nor was remaining neutral a viable alternative, for that "would downgrade Italy as a great power for a century and as a Fascist Regime for eternity." Only intervention alongside the Nazis offered Italy an eventual "Mediterranean empire and access to the oceans." Either a stunning German success against the West or a tightening of the Allied blockade against Italy would compel Italy to declare war on Britain and France. Many of the ministers who had recently been extremely skeptical about joining the war, such as Ettore Muti, Renato Ricci, Thaon di Revel, and Raffaello Riccardi, now expressed themselves as committed interventionists. Grandi, Bottai, Badoglio, and Cavagnari stressed that Italy's financial condition and stocks of raw materials would allow it to conduct war for only three months; moreover, no supreme command with the Germans had been established. Mussolini ignored these appeals and ordered the service chiefs to produce studies for implementing his war strategy.[16]

Redefining Allied Strategic Policy

The news of Mussolini and Hitler traveling to the Brenner only two weeks after the extension of the blockade to Italy's seaborne coal shipments from Germany considerably heightened British apprehension about the Mediterranean. Writing on the day that the two dictators met, Orme Sargent challenged Loraine's perseveringly hopeful assessments of the Italian situation:

> I know the difficulty that Mussolini would have in carrying his country with him, but no one has denied that he could do it if he wanted to and if he were prepared to shut his eyes to what would be the ultimate effect on the Italian economy. . . . We cannot therefore safely exclude the possibility that against all reason he may put himself in a position from which he will not be able to draw back.[17]

The War Cabinet speculated that Hitler and Mussolini would arrange a deal whereby Italy would benefit at the expense of Yugoslavia, and Germany would benefit at the expense of Romania. Although Chamberlain remained skeptical of a German spring offensive, he now conceded that "Mussolini is an incalculable factor"—an admission that served as a devastating critique of his own imperial defense policy. On 18 March he asked Churchill whether the British could concentrate a fleet in the Mediterranean if the situation there suddenly deteriorated. In fact plans had already been made to send the battleship *Warspite* and its accompanying destroyers to the Mediterranean, and to establish a nine-division reserve force in the Middle East under one command that could operate in North Africa, the Balkans, or the Middle East. Foreshadowing a substantial change in the way the British government approached foreign affairs, British planners then told their French colleagues that "it is now necessary to redefine our broad strategic policy," which had not been reconsidered since April 1939.[18]

The week following Mussolini's return from the Brenner Sir Francis Osborne, the British ambassador to the Vatican, indicated that one of his informants had spoken to Filippo Anfuso, Ciano's deputy at the Palazzo Chigi, who revealed that Mussolini would embark on his own blitzkrieg in the Mediterranean by closing Suez and Gibraltar as soon as Hitler experienced any success in the West. Thereafter, Cadogan linked Mussolini to Hitler by describing them both as "double-crossing monkeys," while Halifax explained that "we in FO cannot guarantee that Italy will not at once join the Reich as a belligerent, should the Germans launch their *Blitzkrieg* and obtain what might be interpreted as an initial success." As a result of the altered international circumstances and the collapse of Chamberlain's policy, the FO no longer found Loraine's arguments credible.[19]

THE BRENNER meeting and Finland's surrender to the Soviet Union on 13 March compelled the Allies to reassess their war strategy. According to the British, the end of the Finnish-Soviet war eliminated the Allies' pretext that to infringe on Norwegian and Swedish neutrality would staunch the flow of iron ore to Germany. Instead of sending an expedition to Narvik and laying mines off the Norwegian coast, as had been planned, the British now proposed to mine the Rhine and bomb the Ruhr. But the French feared that these operations would incite the Germans to exact a devastating reprisal against France's industrial region in Alsace-Lorraine, including many vulnerable aircraft plants. French strategy was again at an impasse. The proposed operations in Scandinavia and Germany were unacceptable, and the unsettled situation in the Mediterranean made any operation against the Caucasus temporarily out of the question. It was this strategic stalemate that brought about a protracted foreign affairs debate in the Chamber on 19–20 March and led to Daladier's resignation as premier on 21 March.

Daladier's fall marked the zenith of dissatisfaction within French political circles about the conduct of the war. An overwhelming majority in the Chamber and Senate reproached Daladier for either getting France into war or not conducting it more energetically. His successor, Paul Reynaud, Daladier's finance minister, fell into the latter category. Reynaud and Daladier had long been political rivals. Less than five feet tall with high cheekbones, a sharp voice, and an almost expressionless face, Reynaud lacked the affable personal qualities that had served Daladier so well. A Parisian lawyer who lived luxuriously and resented Daladier's power, Reynaud missed no opportunity to assert that he was the man most qualified to lead France's war effort with renewed vigor and purpose. On 22 March he told the Chamber that he intended "to rouse, assemble, and direct French energy in order to fight and to win. . . . The stake in this war is an absolute one. Through victory we will save everything; in defeat we will lose everything." Reynaud had little leverage over party leaders, however, and could not receive a majority without support from Daladier's Radicals. Reynaud took over the foreign ministry, but he appointed Daladier as minister of defense and minister of war.[20]

One of the first stumbling blocs that the new premier had to address was the changing situation in the Mediterranean. A stack of intelligence assessments in March suggested that preserving Italian neutrality was no longer possible. According to the French military attaché in Rome, the interception of German coal to Italy had turned Italian public opinion against the Allies. The French consular representative in Fiume indicated that the Italian Silurficio Whitehead factory was in the process of building and shipping submarine torpedoes to Germany. Large amounts of Italian olive oil and cork were also being transported to Germany, while the Freiburg–Bâle–St. Gotthard railway line had begun delivering 100–120 wagons of coal to Italy every day. The mechanical and metallurgical sectors of Italian industry were now operating at levels they had never reached before. An Italian ship was scheduled to leave Buenos Aires at the end of March with aeronautical parts and equipment destined for Germany.[21]

Another report estimated that Italy's monthly petroleum imports from September 1939 through February 1940 had increased by 69 percent over 1937–38. Even though Italy consumed only 224,000 tons of petroleum a month, it was currently importing more than 365,000 tons every month. The account concluded that Italy was either supplying Germany with petroleum, stockpiling it in anticipation of war, or probably both. Captain Robert de Larosiere, the French naval attaché in Rome, reported a similar trend for fractionally distilled petroleum such as fuel oil, kerosene, gasoline, and paraffin: since September Italy had imported 2,166,000 tons of these liquid combustibles yet had consumed only 1,340,000 tons. After "declared" exports of 103,000 tons, Italy had amassed 723,000 tons of liquid combustibles in six months. Confident that Italy lacked adequate storage facilities for these products, de Larosiere in early March made "the presumption at the very least that petroleum products are passing from Germany to Italy" and urged the Allies to begin immediately controlling Italian petroleum imports "in an effective manner."[22]

Mussolini's meeting with Hitler at the Brenner Pass strengthened the credibility of this intelligence. In fact the premier's military cabinet asserted that in all likelihood the two dictators had made secret arrangements for Italy's imminent intervention. Both the general staff and the Quai d'Orsay agreed that economic warfare would never defeat the Germans, who had established dependable supply routes from and through Russia and Italy. An Allied victory was now entirely dependent on the opening of additional military fronts in Scandinavia, the Balkans, the Caucasus, or the Mediterranean. The Quai's European Department accepted that Mussolini would soon embark on war against the democracies, neither appeasement nor Italian public opinion could moderate the Duce's ambitions, methods of tightening contraband control against Italy should be contemplated, and the Allies should be "very vigilant with Italy" and include the Mediterranean in any future war planning. Even Gamelin understood that the Allies had to reformulate their Mediterranean strategy in the event of an Italian declaration of war. The Allies had to prepare "a very detailed plan of action" immediately.[23]

THE INTER-ALLIED staff talks of 23 March were less momentous than the French had hoped. Although the British service chiefs admitted that the overall strategic situation had deteriorated markedly, they remained somewhat hesitant about the prospect of opening new theaters of war. They feared that operations in Scandinavia and the Caucasus would incite the Soviet Union to intervene on Germany's side. Despite recognizing Mussolini's attachment to Hitler, the British avoided planning for a Mediterranean war; offensives could be contemplated against Libya and Abyssinia, but the Allies should remain on the defensive in the eastern Mediterranean. Since Italy did not yet represent a threat to Turkey, planning with the Turks should also be avoided. The British remained preoccupied with retaining the ability to defend the Far East, even though they acknowledged that Italy would likely not join the Allied cause or even remain neutral indefinitely. Reynaud told the British at the SWC on 28 March that the Allies should recognize this "new and perhaps decisive situation" and "forestall the initiatives of the enemy" by reversing policy. The Allies should immediately

> strike at the weakest points of [the enemy's] equilibrium without allowing him the leisure to consolidate; refuse him the protection of principles that he only invokes to shield his violations; use all the advantages that we can derive

> from the mastery of the sea and certain dominant geographical positions; and finally gather around us, by the strength and effectiveness of our action, the confidence and respect of states who extend [their allegiance] to the strongest.

Reynaud's appeals motivated the British to agree to establish new dates for the laying of mines in Norwegian territorial waters, to allow inter-Allied planning for the Baku project, and to consider a revision of Allied Mediterranean strategy.[24]

In fact French concerns about Italy and the need to act decisively provoked a dramatic shift in British policy and planning for the Mediterranean. At the end of March the British service chiefs "decided that a show of force was necessary to intimidate Italy," such as concentrating air, ground, and naval forces in the Middle East, the eastern Mediterranean, and the Red Sea. France, it was hoped, would concentrate its fleet in the western Mediterranean and strengthen its ground and air forces in the Alps and Tunisia. "It is essential that we should be in a position to go to war with Italy," wrote the COS, which also considered imposing stricter contraband control against German imports and exports to and from Italy. All these measures represented a significant "modification of policy since we have, so far, deliberately avoided offending Italian susceptibilities."[25] The Mediterranean appeasement had finally run its course and the imperial defense priority of the Far East had begun to be reconsidered. On 30 March Admiral Pound took steps to begin strengthening the Mediterranean fleet. Submarines and "slow-moving craft" were sent from China to the Mediterranean; the battleship *Warspite* and four destroyers left Scapa Flow for the Mediterranean; and Cunningham transferred his command from Malta to Alexandria.[26]

At the end of March the Foreign Office reversed the service chiefs' position that Allied planning with Turkey should be avoided. Cadogan identified Turkey as the "lynch-pin" of the eastern Mediterranean, asserting that "it would be risky to 'treat her rough.'" The FO instructed the Allied representatives at the Anglo-French-Turkish Aleppo conference to discuss the contingency of a hostile Italy. After months of ignoring Turkish appeals to plan for a war in the eastern Mediterranean against Italy, the Allies had finally consented. Moreover, on 4 April the War Cabinet directed the FO and the Ministry of Economic Warfare to form a committee under the leadership of R. A. Butler to reexamine the whole of Allied policy toward Italy, with particular reference to contraband control.[27]

The German Invasion of Norway and Denmark

Early in the morning on 9 April Mackensen presented the Duce with a letter from Hitler, revealing that the Germans had stormed into Denmark and

Norway overnight. Anticipating a German attack on the West and having heard a rumor of an impending German occupation of the Romanian oil fields, Ciano was nevertheless stunned by the German action: "The usual letter, in the usual style, to announce a stroke already carried out." Ciano warned the German ambassador that this act would elicit a "violent" reaction among the neutrals, especially the United States. But Mussolini was quite pleased with the news: "I approve Hitler's action wholeheartedly. It is a gesture that can have incalculable results, and it is the way to win wars. The democracies have been beaten by speed. I will order the press and the Italian people to applaud Germany's action without reservation." He later told Ciano that "his hands itch" with anticipation. Mussolini intended "to accelerate the tempo, taking advantage of the disorder that reigns in Europe."[28]

The weak reaction by the British and the French—"an offensive of speeches and articles that is absolutely useless for the purposes of war"—persuaded Ciano that Hitler's bold attack had indeed taken the Allies by surprise and could prove decisive. In particular, he was perplexed by Allied strategy. In Britain and France "everyone, or almost everyone, is convinced that Italy is preparing to go against them, but they will do nothing that might provoke or accelerate this Italian decision." Mussolini found this circumstance encouraging. On 11 April he wrote Hitler to explain that Fascist propaganda would begin disseminating interventionist rhetoric, the Italian fleet would be fully mobilized by the next day, and the preparations of Italy's other services would be rapidly improved. Laying the groundwork for his parallel war and ensuring that he could intervene on his own accord, Mussolini added that it was particularly important for the Axis not to drag the Balkans into war.[29]

Despite Mussolini's assurances to Hitler, Italy's service chiefs remained divided on how to prepare for war alongside the Germans. Badoglio generally accepted Mussolini's directive for a defensive posture in the Alps and in Libya, "distrustful observation" of Yugoslavia, and an offensive in East Africa and the Mediterranean, but he was determined to minimize the extent of any future Italian contacts with the "intrusive and arrogant Germans"; all discussions with the Germans were to be exclusively in "vague terms." Graziani, who wanted his staff to travel to Berlin to arrange a "concrete plan for Italian participation in the war," protested Badoglio's refusal to authorize Axis staff talks: "But we will not be able to do anything, even in the event of a French collapse and an insecure Yugoslavia behind our backs." Badoglio confidently assured his subordinate that an Anglo-French collapse would lead directly to a Yugoslav surrender. Italy could then "act exclusively with our own forces," preserving "our dignity," and preventing the Italians from having "to pay an extraordinary debt" to the Germans. Badoglio next convinced Mussolini that Italian prestige would not allow Italy's army "to act the part of second echelon troops" for the benefit of Germany.[30]

More important, perhaps, was the Italian service chiefs' reaction to the Duce's general strategic directive for the navy and the Mediterranean. Badoglio cautioned that the "offensive right down the line" did not mean that the Regia Marina should "throw itself headlong against the British and French fleets" but rather it should "attempt to dislocate and hinder, principally with submarines, the traffic of the adversaries." Soddu interpreted the directive as a "*guerre de course* in the Mediterranean, but without objectives." Pricolo observed that in the Mediterranean "we have too many illusions of an aero-naval offensive. The possibilities for this are slim indeed." Regardless of how the navy conducted this "offensive," Cavagnari explained that the its chances for success were now worse than they had been in September 1939: "Then the Franco-British forces were largely dislocated in the Atlantic. Today, with no additional German ships in operation, they have returned to the Mediterranean." He predicted that if Italy intervened, "one [enemy] fleet will place itself at Gibraltar and the other at Suez. We will asphyxiate inside the Mediterranean." Despite Mussolini's directive, the service chiefs concluded that Italy would have to remain on the defensive in the Alps, the Aegean, Libya, and even Italian East Africa.[31]

Following their meeting, Badoglio and Cavagnari expressed their serious reservations about the proposed Italian strategy directly to the Duce. Badoglio informed Mussolini that Italian intervention could have positive results only if the Germans had first "truly prostrated the enemy forces to such an extent that every audacity would be justified." Otherwise, all of Italy's war fronts, including East Africa and the Mediterranean, would have to assume a defensive character. On 14 April Cavagnari separately asked Mussolini for a "precise definition" of the "important strategic objectives" for the Mediterranean offensive. Cavagnari estimated that Allied defenses on Malta were so formidable that a successful amphibious assault against the island was unlikely. The enemy's "two huge fleets" prevented the Regia Marina from conducting offensive operations in either the eastern or western basins of the Mediterranean. In fact the Allies were in a position to inflict "immense" damage on the Italian fleet and could replace their own naval losses much more quickly than could Italy. "In the absence of the possibility of achieving important strategic objectives or the defeat of the opposing naval forces," Cavagnari argued, "entry into the war on our own initiative, with the prospect of remaining on the defensive even by sea, does not seem justified." Italy would arrive "at the peace negotiations not only without territorial bargaining counters, but also without a fleet and possibly without an air force." Cavagnari did not oppose war as such, but he stressed that waging it at this time would be a perilous gamble.[32]

The Allies were shocked by Germany's invasion of Denmark and Norway. The Allied mining of Norwegian territorial waters, which had only just begun, had to be abandoned, and plans for an Allied landing in Norway were hurriedly put into place. After having struggled to forge a strategy that could seize the initiative from Germany, the Allies were again compelled to react to German moves. The fast-changing situation in the Mediterranean inevitably affected the nature of that Allied reaction.

At a hastily convened SWC Reynaud demanded an "extremely rapid and powerful action" by the Allies in response to Germany's incursion into northern Europe. But little could happen instantly. The British and French troops that had been earmarked for action in Finland had already been dispersed and were not ready for immediate transport to Scandinavia. The best the Allies could do was plan for the landing of small numbers of French and British troops in southern and central Norway the following week. Upon learning that the British had already diverted the battleship *Warspite* back to home waters, Reynaud noted French intelligence that the Italian fleet had begun to mobilize and concentrate its forces at Taranto. It was assumed that the Italians were preparing to occupy Corfu as a prelude to a simultaneous assault on Greece and Yugoslavia. The French were now confident that Italy would soon join Germany in war, even if the Fascists did not directly attack the democracies. What measures could the Allies take to prepare for this eventuality? Churchill answered that a military response in the Mediterranean could be considered once the Scandinavian situation cleared: "It is evident that the current circumstances do not constitute a very favorable moment for dispatching important naval forces to the Mediterranean, but these circumstances cannot continue indefinitely." The SWC adjourned without making any arrangements to begin planning for a conflict in the Mediterranean.[33]

Yet three days earlier the British service chiefs had argued that "as far as can be foreseen at present," Italy "would be unlikely to throw in her lot with Germany." The chiefs also agreed that the Allies could not dust off and adopt the previous year's plan for a Mediterranean offensive. An attack on Libya would be considerably more difficult in the spring of 1940 than it would have been in the fall of 1939. The Italians had significantly augmented their defenses there, while the Allies had allowed their positions in Tunisia and Egypt to deteriorate. The Italian navy was for the moment the most intimidating military presence in the Mediterranean. Thus, Allied military policy in the Mediterranean and the Middle East in the event of Italian intervention, according to the COS, should remain "generally defensive," at least until the Allies "had developed their resources and were in a position to assume the offensive." Reports from Rome that Italy's financial, economic, and military condition could not support war confirmed the service chiefs' assertion that no Allied show of force in the Mediterranean was necessary.[34] Again, even at this late date, many strategists in Britain perceived it as their role principally to defend the British Isles and the Far Eastern empire. The odd combination of continuing to disbelieve that Fascist Italy would ever declare war on the Allies and continuing to overestimate the strength of the Italian navy reflected the service chiefs' motivated bias against preparing for war in the Mediterranean—a war that would require cooperation with France and jeopardize Britain's position in the Far East.

At the same time, however, Britain's Ministry of Economic Warfare began to question the efficacy of Allied policy in the Mediterranean, particularly the extremely porous blockade. Desmond Morton, the director of the MEW's intelligence division, urged Ismay and the COS to endorse a tightening of Allied contraband control methods in the Mediterranean: "A continuation of the present policy involves Italy making herself stronger as well as continuing to permit a leak of German trade through Italy. The longer this policy is pursued the more formidable an adversary Italy is likely to become." But this opinion was challenged by R. A. Butler, who argued for reopening trade negotiations with Italy and granting it far-reaching commercial privileges to ensure its continued neutrality. Most at the FO were inclined to agree with the MEW viewpoint.[35]

By 14 April, the day that Allied forces landed in Trondheim, consensus had been reached at the FO that Italy would take advantage of any Allied setback in Scandinavia to move against the Dalmatian coast and occupy the principal ports, with an aim toward transforming the Adriatic into an Italian lake. Halifax told the War Cabinet that it was now more likely than ever before that Italy would soon enter the war against the British, and that British acquiescence in an Italian conquest of Yugoslavia would have devastating political consequences in the Balkans, the Middle East, and elsewhere. Nevertheless, Chamberlain remained unconvinced that Italy would take such action: "While the situation had certainly deteriorated, it was not necessary to take all Signor Mussolini's threats literally. Threats of this kind formed part of the technique of dictators." All that Chamberlain would endorse was an aggressive propaganda campaign to persuade the Italians of Allied successes in Scandinavia.[36]

Meanwhile, the clamor in France for genuine Anglo-French Mediterranean planning was overwhelming. Although Admiral Odend'hal in London understood that the Scandinavian project had taken the highest priority, he was incredulous about the absence of Allied plans for the Mediterranean: "Italy's attitude is extremely unpleasant; that is the least we can say. Are we thinking of taking any precautions?" Ambassador Corbin answered this question negatively: "The temptation remains very great for the Italians to make a *coup de main,* to which they know that in the present circumstances a response on our part is not possible." In Paris, the Ministry of Blockade argued that Italy had strengthened its military and economic position significantly since September 1939, augmenting not only its armed forces but also its stockpiles of raw materials. The ministry estimated that

Italy could now conduct war for at least six months and by late 1940 would become "a real military power with whom we will have to deal."[37]

The Allies' Mediterranean predicament also frustrated Darlan, who had been the principal advocate for the "essential battle for iron" in Norway. The naval chief admitted that the "unsettling Italian attitude" prevented the Allies from concentrating exclusively on operations in Scandinavia. Because the British fleet was "practically absent from the Mediterranean," France's *force de raid* would have to remain at Brest—unable to participate in the clash with Germany. The Scandinavian situation could no longer be divorced from events in the Mediterranean. On 16 April, two days after the first Allied landings in Trondheim, the Comité de Guerre convened to consider how France would react to an Italian attack on Yugoslavia. The French reasoned that Mussolini would try to extend Italian territory into the Danubian basin at a time when he believed the Allies, preoccupied in Scandinavia, would not resort to war against Italy. Contending that such Allied acquiescence would discredit the Allies among all the Balkan states, including Turkey, the French believed that the Allies would have to respond decisively. Specifically, the French decided that the Allies should strengthen their naval forces in the eastern Mediterranean, discuss an Allied mission to Salonika with Turkey, Greece, Yugoslavia, and Romania, and prepare plans to occupy Crete. The French then appealed to the British for the creation of Allied plans that could be implemented immediately in the event of an Italian assault on the Dalmatian coastline.[38]

The British War Cabinet rejected these French recommendations. Chamberlain privately remarked that the French were trying to persuade the British to adopt "half-baked and impossible plans." In an interesting corollary to the French position, the British Admiralty explained that the campaign in the North Sea would deter Italy from embarking on aggression in the Mediterranean or the Adriatic. The director of foreign naval operations at the Admiralty wrote that "operations to establish Allied forces in Norway must take precedence over all other requirements . . . their success may well prevent any action by Italy which might involve us in war in the Mediterranean." The COS agreed, arguing that "we should concentrate only on the naval question of inducing the French to accept responsibility of the whole of the Mediterranean." Not only did operations in Scandinavia prevent the British from committing themselves to a conflict in the eastern Mediterranean, but also "the consequences of involving ourselves in war with Italy at the present juncture would unquestionably be more serious than anything we should lose by doing nothing to help the Yugoslavs."[39]

The French had a mixed reaction to Britain's proposal to abdicate the Mediterranean to France. Darlan welcomed the idea, immediately arranging for three Bretagne-class battleships to move from Oran to Bizerte and two Dunkerque-class battleships to leave the Atlantic for Oran. He also prepared to transfer the mobile naval antiaircraft batteries defending Paris to the eastern Mediterranean. Darlan then added details to his eastern Mediterranean war plan. After seizing Crete, the Marine Nationale would successively occupy Milos, Náxos, and Salamis. These Greek islands, used as naval bases, would facilitate the safe transport of Weygand's army from Syria to Salonika.[40] Although Gamelin endorsed Darlan's plan, others were less enthusiastic. Vuillemin indicated that the French air forces in the Levant, if compelled to operate alone, would not be ready for combat until 1 June. Odend'hal argued that a division of Allied forces would benefit the Axis because France would be solely responsible for upholding Britain's guarantees of Greece and Romania, as well as preserving the security of the Suez Canal and the integrity of the Turkish alliance. The neutrals would perceive this arrangement as the beginning of the end of the Anglo-French alliance. The Quai d'Orsay agreed with these arguments, advising the government to demand, at the very least, that the British join the French in making a joint demarche to the Balkan countries as a way of laying the groundwork for a future expedition to Salonika.[41]

Throughout the month of April Mussolini bristled at the enduring pessimism of his service chiefs. Even the king shared the chiefs' desire to remain outside the conflict until the Allies were on the verge of defeat. Two days after the German invasion of Denmark and Norway Mussolini lamented, "It is humiliating to remain with our hands folded while others write history. It matters little who wins. To make a people great they must be carried into combat, even if they have to be kicked in the ass [*a calci in culo*]. That is what I will do." He saved his most fulminous criticism for the navy, however: "If we do not seize this occasion to measure our navy against those of Britain and France, why should we have 600,000 tons of warships? Some coast guard cutters and some pleasure boats would be enough to take the *signorine* on excursions." The following week, while Ciano was in bed with influenza, Mussolini ordered Giovanni Ansaldo, Ciano's unofficial spokesman at the Palazzo Chigi, to deliver a radio address to the armed forces. Although the press did not report the speech, U.S. Ambassador William Phillips recognized it as the first public and authoritative statement that Italy's intervention was inevitable. Privately, Mussolini revealed that he anticipated an Italian declaration of war at the end of August. On 19 April he told the Hungarian military attaché, Lászlo Szabó, a long-standing confidante, that "in the West I will assume a defensive posture; on the seas I will attack; in the Balkans I will extend my *Lebensraum*."[42]

The Duce then received two important pieces of information that inspired him to take a more public stand than he had before. A Royal Navy telegram intercepted on 17 April indicated that the British believed Italy's intervention "improbable," and a letter from Hitler the following day described Germany's continued success in Norway despite the Allied landing there four days earlier. Furious that the Allies did not adequately fear Italian intervention and envious of Germany's recent successes, Mussolini on 21 April spoke before the representatives of the Fascist confederations in a tone that was "100 percent extremist and pro-Axis." In a palpable rage, Mussolini told his audience that despite appearances, Italy had ceased to exist as an independent nation. "For eight months," he shouted, "not one of our ships has escaped the often capricious controls of the British and French navies." Declaring that "we are prisoners in the Mediterranean," Mussolini explained, "It is useless for the Italians to concern themselves with eventual German hegemony on the continent because for eight months we have been subject to a maritime hegemony that attempts to deprive us of the materials that we are starved of." Using familiar rhetoric, Mussolini concluded that Italy's people would not enjoy true independence until they had "free open windows to the oceans." Emboldened by the enthusiastic response of his Palazzo Venezia audience, Mussolini visited the king the following day and proclaimed that "Italy is a de facto British colony, and there are some Italians who would like to see it become one de jure as well: a Malta multiplied a million times."[43]

While Ciano tried to assure the various British, French, American, and Balkan representatives in Rome that "Italy stands solidly behind Germany but until further notice does not intend to make its solidarity more complete," Mussolini's desire for war became increasingly implacable. On 24 April he received an official demarche from the French premier, who was frantically trying to avoid a war in the Mediterranean that would reduce France's ability to defend the western front against Germany. Reynaud expressed his conviction that France and Italy, despite their differing political ideologies, could thrive economically as peaceful neighbors. A Franco-Italian war should be avoided not only to maintain the European equilibrium but also to preserve "our glorious Mediterranean civilization." Ambassador Guariglia then asserted that among the French leadership there existed a genuine desire to dissociate France from Britain's anti-Italian sentiment and a willingness to grant Italy hegemony in the Mediterranean. Mussolini read Reynaud's letter with "satisfaction and contempt" and drafted a "cold, bitter, and contemptuous letter" in reply. Despite his attempts to moderate its tone, Ciano interpreted the final product as "proof of our provocative extremism." By the first week in May Guariglia reported that Mussolini's response had been a "cold shower" for the remaining pro-Italian Frenchmen, allowing the intransigent perspective of the Quai d'Orsay now to predominate in French policy.[44]

MUSSOLINI'S violent bombast also had an effect in London, especially because it came at a time when the situation in Scandinavia looked ominous. After one week of operations in Norway, the Allies had experienced success only at sea. Outnumbered, ill-equipped, and without air power, the Allied forces were routinely beaten by their German foes. Despite the British resolutions of the preceding week, Halifax was now convinced that Italy would soon enter the war against the Allies. As he explained to Charles in Rome, "Italy could not, and would not, tolerate a purely democratic Europe." The foreign secretary and Air Minister Sir Kingsley Wood argued that Britain had an obligation to respond immediately to any Italian action against Yugoslavia. On 20 April the War Cabinet agreed that the British should establish a "holding force" in the eastern Mediterranean. Steps were immediately taken to cancel the battleship *Malaya*'s return from the Mediterranean and to transfer two additional capital ships from home waters to Gibraltar. Moreover, the War Cabinet established a new subcommittee—the Committee on Coordination of Departmental Action (Italy)—to discuss the measures that would have to be put into operation on the outbreak of war with Italy.[45] Setbacks in Scandinavia, combined with French apprehensions about the Mediterranean, had compelled the British to reverse their Italian policy in a week's time.

The British service chiefs now had to consider the "genuine possibility" of war with Italy. Rear Admiral Tom Phillips, deputy chief of the naval staff, argued that in light of the enormous naval and air resources required in Norway, it was impossible to satisfy British requirements in Scandinavia and the Mediterranean at the same time. To prepare for Italian hostility in the Mediterranean, Phillips advised that the British abandon all efforts in southern and central Norway in favor of concentrating only on holding the northern port city of Narvik. Phillips recognized that such a decision would have unfortunate political repercussions but he explained that "by contrast with the Mediterranean, they were disadvantages which we could afford to accept, provided we took all possible steps to secure our position at Narvik." Finally acknowledging that Italy and the Mediterranean effectively controlled the conduct of the war against Germany in northern Europe, the COS on 22 April approved Phillips's recommendations and submitted his paper to the War Cabinet.[46]

Either Chamberlain had not received the COS report by the time he left London for the SWC or—in a desperate effort to save his policy and his government—he had rejected its conclusions. In Paris on 23 April, after Reynaud argued that the Allies should plan to respond to an Italian attack on Yugoslavia with an Allied mission to Salonika, Chamberlain countered that his information inclined him "to think that Signor Mussolini would continue to be as disagreeable as possible without actually going to war." Churchill then added that the state of the Allies' naval forces in the Mediterranean, unless significantly reinforced, precluded any offensive action. Despite Reynaud's protests and appeals for a naval reinforcement in the eastern Mediterranean, Chamberlain explained that "it would not be justifiable in present circumstances to move to the Mediterranean any naval forces which were expressly required for the Scandinavian campaign." The Allies should do nothing to precipitate hostilities with Italy.[47]

Upon his return from Paris, however, Chamberlain was placed under increasing pressure by the FO, the COS, and the MEW to discontinue the failing operations in Scandinavia and to prepare for conflict in the Mediterranean. A long report by Major General Ismay on 25 April precipitated the War Cabinet's decision the following day to evacuate southern and central Norway, to begin redeploying forces into the Mediterranean, and to divert maritime shipping around the Cape of Good Hope. On 30 April the government issued orders for a substantial air and army redistribution to the Mediterranean, the Middle East, and East Africa; "the manning of the defenses" at Alexandria, Haifa, Malta and Gibraltar; the transfer of the armored division in Egypt to the western desert; and the shift of *Warspite* to Alexandria. By 9 May the British had three battleships, one carrier, seven cruisers, eleven destroyers, and eleven submarines stationed in the eastern Mediterranean. Another battleship would arrive the next week, and three additional cruisers were based in the Red Sea. Not since August 1939 had the British had such a formidable military and naval force in the Mediterranean.[48]

These sudden British moves caused both frustration and acclamation in France. Reynaud and Gamelin, in particular, were incensed by Britain's unilateral evacuation from all of Norway but Narvik. The Frenchmen traveled to London as soon as they learned of this decision but could not dissuade the British.[49] By contrast, Darlan, who had recognized with chagrin the inherent difficulties of the Norway campaign, expressed enthusiasm for the British naval redistribution into the Mediterranean. Meeting with Admiral Pound the evening before the SWC, Darlan not only agreed to transfer the three French battleships at Oran and Bizerte to Alexandria but also indicated that the transfer to the Mediterranean of the majority of the French ships operating in Scandinavia as well as the entire *force de raid* had already begun. By the first week in May the entire French navy, with the exception of those few transport ships remaining off the coast of Norway and those few still in Indochina, was based in Mediterranean ports. The French army also reinforced its position in Tunisia and the Levant.[50]

Moreover, Darlan presented a detailed plan to Pound for a "vigorous offensive in the first hours of war" against Italy—something the British had only just begun to consider. Darlan suggested that the Allies close Gibraltar and Suez, cut Italian communications to Libya, occupy Crete and eventually Salonika, and finally deliver a crippling blow to Italy's industrial region by carrying out a naval bombardment from the Gulf of Genoa. Much as the British had been surprised in March 1939 by the French war plans for the Mediterranean, Pound was again unprepared to respond to Darlan's proposal. Although the British had already begun redeploying forces into the Mediterranean, they continued to oppose an expedition to Salonika. No Royal Navy vessel would operate within two hundred miles of an Italian air base; the Norway campaign had demonstrated the efficacy of air power against poorly defended ships at sea. Instead, the British suggested that Allied planes, operating from aerodromes in southern France, could attack northwestern Italy with impunity. Yet the lack of antiaircraft defenses in southeastern France discouraged the French from accepting this British alternative. Although the British informed France at the beginning of May that they did not intend to take an offensive against Italy if Mussolini attacked Yugoslavia, the British and the French had for the very first time initiated strategic discussions based on a potential war against Italy in the Mediterranean.[51]

The German Attack on the West

At 5:00 A.M. on 10 May the German ambassador presented the Duce with a letter from Hitler, announcing that the Wehrmacht had just invaded Belgium and Holland. As so many other times before, the Germans had been unwilling to trust the Italians with any details of the forthcoming attack against the West. Although Ciano again bristled at the Germans' treatment of their "ally," Mussolini "completely approved Hitler's action" and was certain "of the rapid success of the Nazi armies." In a letter to the Führer later that day, Mussolini declared that Italy would have two army groups ready facing France and Yugoslavia by the end of the month. He added that Italy's navy was now prepared for action. Ciano summoned the Croatian terrorist leader Ante Pavelic and directed him to prepare to "pass to the phase of execution." Any further delay of the "maturing Croatian situation" could cause "sympathies to orient toward Germany," raising the specter of a German presence in the Adriatic. In a show of the Fscists' new determination to achieve their Danubian aspirations, Mussolini recalled General Gastone Gambara, Italy's hero in the Spanish civil war, from Madrid and placed him in command of the forces that would invade Croatia in early June.[52]

The Italian general staff, as usual, was quick to counsel vigilance. Badoglio "fanatically defended" nonbelligerence, contending that it would take at least six months and six million German lives to pierce the Maginot Line. Soddu also urged the Duce to remain outside the war at least until the summer, believing that Italy should wait to see whether Britain and the United States—the principal threats to the Axis—would come to the defense of France. Graziani supported this position, explaining that the army could now mobilize less than fifty divisions at home and only twenty-four overseas, including indigenous troops. Italy's two armored divisions were "armored only in name." The army had only three groups of artillery (far less than it had during the First World War), only fifteen relatively modern antiaircraft batteries, and antitank weapons that were far inferior to the French army's. Graziani believed that this situation, combined with "grave deficiencies in raw materials" plus stocks of fuels and munitions that would not last longer than six months of war, meant that the army was unprepared even for an offensive against Yugoslavia. Air Marshal Balbo explained that Libya could not sustain a two-front war; the Italian garrison was outnumbered by a ratio of three to one by the British in Egypt and the French in Tunisia: "It is not only our enemies' numbers that preoccupy me, but also our armament. . . . our artillery, antitank weapons, and antiair weapons are all outdated. . . . we have fortifications that are so stripped of arms it is absurd." Until these deficiencies were overcome, Libya would be not an asset but an Italian liability in a "great European war." On 11 May Ciano noted that the general staff "has thrown timely cold water on our current military prospects."[53]

One of the most outspoken of Italy's military leaders was Cavagnari. The overt redistribution of Allied naval forces into the Mediterranean at the beginning of May terrified the Italian naval chief. During the first two weeks of May, Cavagnari presented the Duce with a series of intercepted British naval telegrams indicating that the Allies, once Italy intervened, planned to respond with "immediate action" in the Mediterranean. The Royal Navy eagerly anticipated this eventuality because, according to one British telegram, the Allies desired an enemy that they could "defeat heavily and swiftly." Specifically, the Allies would bombard northwestern Italy from the Gulf of Genoa and from air bases in southeastern France, attack Italy's bases in the Dodecanese, and sever Italy's communications with Libya. According to the SIS, Turkey and Greece had also begun preparing for a war in the eastern Mediterranean in collusion with the Allies and in opposition to the Italians. Cavagnari speculated that as soon as they had established naval preeminence in the Mediterranean, the Allies would sail into the Red Sea and attack Italy's position in Abyssinia. To make matters worse, Cavagnari had recently learned from his inspector general that the new battleships *Roma* and *Impero* would not be ready until December 1941 and August 1942 respectively, and the rebuilt battleships *Duilio* and *Doria* could not return to active service until September 1940 at the earliest. All these dates represented significant delays, further weakening the Regia Marina. This dire information reinforced Cavagnari's fear of a naval engagement with Britain and France and motivated him in late May to press Mussolini and Ciano to postpone intervention at least until the fall of 1940.[54]

Yet Mussolini hardly considered the leaders of the Italian military his principal advisers for establishing Italy's war policy. The Duce was struck by the Italian public's celebration of Hitler's victories; enthusiasm for a swift and profitable Italian war seemed suddenly to grow. Soon after Hitler launched his attack on the West, groups of students began marching through the streets of Rome shouting, "We want war." On 10 May Mussolini's daughter Edda told him that the country craved intervention; a continuation of neutrality would permanently dishonor Italy. When the Duce learned that the Pope had sent telegrams of support to the countries that Germany had invaded and that the king continued to favor permanent nonbelligerence—two Italian institutions Mussolini had grown to despise—his interventionist spirit rose again. On 13 May he received his first report from Hitler of Germany's numerous victories on the western front, inspiring the Duce to declare that the Allies "have lost the war. We Italians are already sufficiently dishonored. Any further delay is inconceivable. We have no time to lose. I will declare war within a month." Abandoning his plans for a parallel war in the Balkans, Mussolini now wanted the Italian navy and air force to attack France and Britain directly. The following day the Duce told Mackensen that "no longer is it a question of months: it is a question of weeks or maybe days."[55]

Cognizant of this change, Ciano reluctantly embraced intervention, provided that an Axis victory was clearly in sight. Ciano's Fascist ambitions and loyalty to the Duce outweighed his reluctance to ally with Germany in war. As he admitted to his diary, "Unfortunately, there is nothing that I can do to hold the Duce back. He has decided to act, and act he will. He believes in the German success and the rapidity of that success. Only a new development in military events can induce him to revise his decision, but for now things are going so badly for the Allies that one sees no hope." Even Dino Grandi, perhaps the most Anglophile of the Italian Fascists, confessed to Ciano on 20 May, "We should recognize that we were wrong about everything and prepare ourselves for the new times ahead." In fact the foreign minister even urged Mussolini to present the Germans with a list of Italian war aims: "If we must really throw ourselves head first into this adventure, then we should make a clear deal." Ciano proposed to meet with Ribbentrop after 1 June to give him a report that defined "how much should come to us at the end of the war."[56]

With Germany's offensive in the West succeeding and interventionist rhetoric in Italy escalating, the Allies began to contemplate genuine and imminent operations in the Mediterranean. The principal strategies they contemplated in the final month before war in the Mediterranean erupted were the two that had been proposed at the SWC in late April: an occupation of the Greek islands in the eastern Mediterranean and a bombing of northwestern Italy from southeastern France. As before, these Anglo-French strategic discussions were marked by considerably more discord than harmony, setting the stage for the Allies' initially weak prosecution of war against Italy.

The French called for a preventive occupation of Crete, arguing that the Allies lacked both the naval forces and the antiaircraft defenses to occupy and hold more than one large island in the Aegean. The island of Milos could become a strategic outpost for the Allies if Greek troops occupied it on the Allies' behalf. Darlan explained that even the French occupation of Crete—for which the troops, transports, and warships were available—could not be achieved without antiaircraft defenses provided by the British. Until the Italians were defeated, Allied naval operations in the Aegean would have to focus on neutralizing the Italian bases in the Dodecanese—a strategy that would also win a vote of confidence from the vitally important Turks. By preventively occupying Crete and dispatching additional antiaircraft defenses to the eastern Mediterranean, the Allies would be in a position to reduce Italy's position in the Aegean immediately after the Italians opened hostilities. According to Admiral Odend'hal, "If the Italians enter the war, we will want to begin with a spectacular display." Both Gamelin and Weygand had endorsed this plan for the eastern Mediterranean.[57]

The British service chiefs argued that the Allies could not embark on any mission to Crete until Italy had declared war on the democracies—an eventuality the British refused to regard as inevitable. Sending troops to Crete before the outbreak of war, even with the consent of Greece, would "almost certainly be regarded by Mussolini as the provocative action he is looking for." Even an Italian assault on Yugoslavia or Greece should not elicit such an Allied operation. British antiaircraft defenses—both guns and fighters—were inadequate in the eastern Mediterranean, and none elsewhere could be spared for that region. The War Cabinet agreed, deciding that the British should approach the Greeks and ask them to take steps to defend Crete against an Italian invasion. Local French and British commanders could plan for an eventual occupation of Crete, but the operation could not take place until the Allied command ordered it. Again the British had effectively vetoed an assertive French strategy for the eastern Mediterranean. Cadogan's diary entry for 16 May reveals the result of this British action: "meeting of committee . . . about what to do in Mediterranean if Italy comes into war. Not much!"[58] In the event of Italian intervention, the British hoped to fight a "phony war" in the Mediterranean, which would provide them with the best chance of preserving the Far Eastern empire.

The French refused to be so easily stymied, however. French interests in the Far East were far inferior to those in the Mediterranean, and France could not afford to fight a waiting war against Italy. Motivated by the capitulation of the Dutch army on 15 May, the French were determined to ensure that Turkey would intervene on the Allied side once Italy went to war, and confident that the reduction of the Dodecanese was an essential prerequisite to any other operation in the eastern Mediterranean. In Beirut on 20–21 May the French sought the cooperation of Turkish and British air forces—if not preemptively, then immediately after outbreak of war with Italy. The Turks agreed that the Allies had to launch an offensive in the Dodecanese but explained that they could not participate because Turkish air forces were required to counter attacks on Thrace or the Caucasus. In fact the Turks threatened to break their promises in the Anglo-French-Turkish military convention if the Allies did not provide the air forces necessary for an assault against the Dodecanese. With the spotlight turned on them, the British indicated that the air forces were unavailable because those few British aircraft in the region had to concentrate on securing the Allies' naval port at Alexandria.[59]

Despite Franco-Turkish pressure, then, the British did nothing to facilitate future Allied action in the eastern Mediterranean. In fact the British service chiefs in late May postponed the dispatch to the Middle East of 11,000 troops that the War Office had requested the preceding month, provoking the army to protest that Britain's presence in Egypt and Palestine was "well under establishment." According to the COS, an Allied seizure of Crete would be considered only if Italy attacked Greece or if the Allies "had proof that the Italians intended to go there themselves." No land or air support for Greece was anticipated in the meantime. The only approved British action in the theater was Cunningham's plan for the Mediterranean fleet, on the outbreak of war with Italy, to secure the eastern Mediterranean and Aegean and to cut Italy's line of communications to the Dodecanese. At Haifa in late May and early June the Allies misled the Turks by claiming that the occupation of Crete was already planned and agreeing that Rhodes should be taken as soon as possible after the outbreak of war with Italy. Privately, however, the British admitted to the French that Rhodes could be captured only weeks, if not months, after Turkey's intervention. Although the Turks had been reassured, the French left Haifa on 4 June with the understanding that no significant Allied action would occur in the eastern Mediterranean, other than gaining naval control of the region, unless Italy attacked Greece.[60]

At the same time the Allies also debated the British proposal to bombard the northwestern industrial region of Italy as soon as the Italians declared war on the democracies. At least partially to counter the French suggestion of preventive action in the Aegean, the British service chiefs suggested that the Allies, in the event of Italian intervention, attempt to destroy as much of Italy's industrial capacity as possible. The COS advocated a series of bombing sorties from air bases in southeastern France that would be directed principally against Milan, Genoa, and Turin. For specific targets, such as the alkali works at Rosignano, which was vital to many Italian war and civilian industries, the British suggested a combined air and naval bombardment. But the COS also insisted that "it would be more satisfactory for these operations to be a French responsibility." With Germany steadily moving westward, the likelihood of a German aerial assault against London grew every day. Thus, no British aircraft could be diverted from home defense. Since the Mediterranean fleet was now based at Alexandria, the naval responsibility also should be France's alone.[61] Underlying these British explanations was their continued unwillingness to cooperate closely with the French in the Mediterranean or to commit British forces that could otherwise be deployed for imperial defense.

The French did not embrace this British proposal. On account of their weak antiaircraft defenses in southeastern France, they indicated that they would consider such action only as a form of retaliation to the bombing of French towns by the Italian air force. Moreover, because the French would have to redistribute aircraft from the western front to the Alps region in order to conduct this operation, Vuillemin insisted that the RAF would have to replace these planes in northern France before the French air force could attack Italy. After recently sending four bomber groups and two fighter groups to the western front, France now had no bombers and only one fighter group in southeastern France. The French service chiefs also made this operation conditional on Britain's providing the necessary aerial defenses for the reduction of both the Dodecanese and the Balearics. Darlan offered to send the *force de raid* into the Gulf of Genoa to bombard the Italian factories along the coast but he insisted on British aerial protection. Given these parameters and their refusal to divert any of their own aircraft, the British in early June concluded that "it must be realised that with our available resources, nothing in the way of sustained operations against northern Italy can be undertaken at any rate for some time to come."[62] In essence, the French returned Britain's veto of the preventive occupation of Crete with an equally strong rejection of the strategy to bombard northwestern Italy. The Allies had failed to develop an assertive joint war plan that could mitigate or eliminate the effect of Italy's now widely anticipated intervention.

THESE INTRACTABLE and discordant talks on Allied strategy for the Mediterranean had triggered various desperate attempts by the democracies to persuade Italy to maintain its nonbelligerence. A simultaneous cabinet crisis in France and a change of government in Britain added to this confusion. Following the start of Britain's departure from Norway and immediately prior to the start of Germany's assault on the West, a protracted House of Commons debate on the conduct of the war compelled Chamberlain to resign and led King George VI to ask Churchill to form a new government on 10 May. Germany's breakthrough of the Maginot Line five days later and Hitler's subsequent report to Mussolini of his "greatest triumph" ensured that the coincidental pleas by Roosevelt and Churchill for Italy to forgo intervention were dismissed, according to Ciano," briefly and in a style needlessly harsh."[63]

But the main British effort to reconcile with Italy in the spring of 1940 was conducted in the economic sphere. At the end of April R. A. Butler recommended that the British strive to reopen trade negotiations with Italy by "painting on a broader canvas." Discussing the future of Europe "would indicate to the Italians that we were looking to a future in which we did not regard ourselves as the exclusively chosen race, but contemplated preserving the good things of the earth in company with the Italian people, who should have their proper share of them." On the basis of Butler's inherently arrogant and imperial arguments, the War Cabinet decided in early May—before Chamberlain's resignation—to loosen contraband control in the Mediterranean in the hope of reaching an agreement with the Italians. Ironically, just the week before, the government had sanctioned the strengthening of British forces in the Mediterranean and joint planning with the French in preparation for a war against Italy. Nevertheless, succumbing to demands by Ciano to abolish contraband control in the Mediterranean, the British by the middle of May had stopped intercepting all Italian ships and had released all merchandise in Italian ports. Halifax even offered, on the condition that Italy remain neutral, to settle Italian grievances in the Mediterranean at the peace table, where the Fascists could sit on an equal footing with the belligerents.[64]

These Anglo-Italian negotiations were suspended, however, immediately following the Belgium capitulation of 27 May. Ciano told Loraine that any additional economic initiatives were now useless because "we are on the brink of war." This development infuriated the Foreign Office, which had needed to believe that for the sake of their war effort and their empire, the Italians were negotiating in good faith. Cadogan documented in his diary a discussion at the FO of "what to do with the ice-cream vendors. Drown the brutes is what I should like to do." Belatedly, on 3 June, the War Cabinet directed the Admiralty to impose maximum restrictions on all contraband control in the Mediterranean. In addition, Italian shipping in colonial ports was ordered delayed on devious pretexts so that all Italian cargo could be seized in the event of war.[65]

The British were not alone in having seemingly contradictory strategic and diplomatic Italian policies during May 1940. The German assault into France in mid-May and the growing realization in Paris of an imminent defeat on the western front led to a concerted but desperate effort to keep Italy out of the war. François-Poncet proposed that France draw up such a long list of meaningful concessions that the Italians would have no choice but to begin negotiations. Charles-Roux persuaded Reynaud to try a different tactic, however, before abdicating France's entire position in the Mediterranean. On 25 May the French asked the British to persuade the Italians to mediate a Franco-German peace. Prime Minister Churchill found this suggestion repugnant and after a meeting of the War Cabinet that endorsed his position, told Reynaud on 28 May that the Allies should no longer attempt to conciliate the Italians but, instead, should prepare for Italian intervention.[66]

Nevertheless, frustrated at the failure to reach a common Allied strategy for the Mediterranean, the French leadership continued to search for a formula that would ensure Italy's continued neutrality. Defense Minister Daladier suggested that the French offer to rectify the Tunisian-Libyan frontier according to the 1935 treaty and to cede to Italy the Somali coast, the Addis Ababa railway, and the hinterland of Libya to the French Congo border. When Ciano ended Anglo-Italian economic negotiations, Reynaud immediately offered to hold a discussion with the Fascists on all Mediterranean questions that interested Italy. The French ambassador in Rome indicated that the French were willing to place both Tunisia and Algeria on the negotiating block. Some in the French cabinet were prepared to make very significant concessions to Italy, including their ally's position at Gibraltar.[67] Despite these new enticements, Ciano informed François-Poncet that he was "too late." Such offers would have been welcomed in 1938 but they were scorned in 1940. Ciano on 1 June rejected both this French demarche and the U.S. president's final appeal of 31 May.[68]

At the end of May Vittorio Emanuele III finally delegated command of the Italian armed forces to Mussolini. To celebrate this symbolic promotion and to bring his military leaders into line with his policy, Mussolini summoned Badoglio, Cavagnari, Pricolo, and Graziani to the Palazzo Venezia on 29 May—the day after Belgium's unconditional capitulation. As Ciano noted, Mussolini "had realized his true dream: to become the military *condottiero* of the nation at war." At the meeting the Duce declared that Italy could no longer avoid the war. Fighting on the Allied side was unthinkable. The Italians would join their ally, Germany, in the war by 5 June. "Further delay . . . will incur greater risks than . . . premature intervention." Mussolini confirmed that his directive of 31 March remained in effect. He offered no elucidation on his strategy but repeated his expectation that "we will remain on the defensive" on land and take an air and naval offensive in the Mediterranean. None of those in attendance questioned or sought clarification on either the Duce's strategy or his policy. The following day Mussolini gave Ciano a letter for

Hitler that announced Italy's intervention date as 5 June, unless the Führer desired to postpone it for a few days. According to the foreign minister's diary entry for 30 May, "The decision has been taken. The die is cast."[69]

Both Cavagnari and Badoglio, however, took immediate action to undermine the Duce's directive. After the meeting with Mussolini, Cavagnari sent a memorandum on the navy's "general concepts of action in the Mediterranean" to all of his regional commanders. The naval chief ordered his squadrons, upon intervention, to "maintain a defensive attitude in the West and the East, and an offensive/counteroffensive attitude in the central sector." Holding the channel of Sicily and preserving Italy's line of communications to Libya would remain the Regia Marina's principal responsibilities. No assault against Malta was contemplated, given that island's allegedly superior defenses. Despite the Duce's insistence on a general air and naval offensive in the Mediterranean as soon as Italy embarked on war, the naval chief concluded his fleet directive with this command: "Most important, avoid a decisive confrontation with the prevailing naval adversaries."[70] Either Cavagnari entirely misinterpreted Mussolini's conception of Italy's war effort or, more likely, the naval chief—fearful of the consequences of a naval battle against the British and French—had just blatantly disobeyed Mussolini's orders.

At a meeting of the service chiefs the following morning Cavagnari spoke neither of the navy's offensive plans nor its defensive intentions. Instead, he reminded his colleagues that three-quarters of Italy's submarines would be at sea at the outset of hostilities and that Italian merchant ships would be scuttled immediately prior to their capture. The other chiefs offered no queries about naval war strategy. The chiefs were principally concerned with the steps that Graziani had taken and would take to preserve the inviolability of the northern frontier. When Pricolo revealed that he had redeployed some of his forces in anticipation of an imminent strike against Yugoslavia, Badoglio immediately reproached the air force chief and demanded that the aircraft return to a defensive alignment. Pricolo then complained about the passivity of Italian strategy: "In conclusion our army is on the defensive. The navy has no definitive objectives. . . . The air force can and should take offensive action. It should, for example, take action against the bases on Corsica." Again Badoglio rejected this proposal, explaining that "this will happen later." Later that day, as if to reinforce his position at the morning meeting, Badoglio wrote his three subordinates that "until the armed forces are placed into a new disposition, your orders should be strictly defensive."[71] Mussolini had envisioned a bold Italian entry into the war, at least in the Mediterranean, but his service chiefs refused to put that strategy into effect.

Thereafter the final days of peace in Rome played out without much change. On 31 May Hitler asked that Mussolini postpone intervention until after Germany's forthcoming offensive against French airfields in the Northeast; he feared that the opening of a southeastern front could disperse the French air forces before the Luftwaffe destroyed them. Although he did not need Italy's participation in the war to defeat France, Hitler believed Italian intervention would threaten British interests in the Mediterranean, increase the likelihood that the British would sue for peace, and facilitate an eventual German attack on the Soviet Union. Acknowledging that the extra time would allow Balbo to complete military preparations in Libya, Mussolini told Hitler that Italy would open hostilities against the democracies on 11 June.[72]

But Badoglio and Cavagnari obviously had some limited influence on Mussolini in early June. Six days before intervention Mussolini informed Badoglio that instead of an air attack against France at the beginning, the Italian air force should concentrate on bombarding British ports in the Mediterranean. Italy would for the time being "remain an observer toward France." Badoglio then informed the service chiefs that Mussolini intended "to reserve the armed forces, and especially the army and the air force, for future events." In Badoglio's words, the Duce added that "I will invent nothing new: I will act as the Germans and the French, who faced each other for six months without doing anything." Badoglio explained that Mussolini agreed that Italy could take "action against the English forces in the Mediterranean" only after the "situation becomes more clear." Again Badoglio urged caution: "I recommend to you, my collaborators, that calm and serenity must distinguish the chiefs of staff. You should try to prevent chattering and shouting." In the rules of engagement that he dispersed on 7 June, Badoglio insisted that Italy embark on no offensive against France in the air or on land. Italian forces at sea were to attack British and French ships if they were encountered together, but French ships alone were to be spared. No air or naval objectives in the Mediterranean were identified. In short, no definitive plans for the war that Italy would begin to fight the following week were established. For those wondering how Italy would approach the war, Graziani offered this facetious but telling remark: "When the cannon sounds, everything will fall into place automatically."[73]

At 6:00 P.M. on 10 June, from the balcony of the Palazzo Venezia, overlooking a throng of Italians, Mussolini declared war on the democracies: "We take up arms to resolve, after the problem of our continental frontier is resolved, the problem of our maritime frontiers. We want to break the chains of territorial and military order that suffocate us in our own sea, because a people of 45 million cannot truly enjoy freedom if it does not have free access to the oceans." That evening, while preparing to leave the next morning for Pisa, where he would assume command of a group of Italian bombers, Ciano wrote in his diary, "I am sad, very sad. The adventure begins. May God help Italy."[74]

Epilogue

Mussolini went to war virtually alone. Despite all of the Duce's bluster and bombast, the Italian service chiefs had emasculated his strategic directive for war. As planned, the Italian army remained on the defensive in the Alps, Libya, the Aegean, and East Africa. The immediate but local setbacks that the Italian army suffered in both East Africa and Libya guaranteed that no land offensives would be undertaken for some time. The "offensive right down the line" that Cavagnari oversaw consisted of nothing more than the operation of Italian submarines and antisubmarine craft in and around Italy's port waters. These vessels were not directed to search out enemy ships but to engage them only if encountered. The Germans immediately expressed their irritation at the alarmingly defensive manner in which the Italian navy initially prosecuted the war. When some of the principal ships of Cavagnari's fleet finally did go to sea, their orders were to avoid rather than to seek enemy engagement. It was left to the air force to carry out Italy's only offensive foray immediately following intervention. But even this effort was not particularly effective or impressive. On the morning of 11 June the Italians conducted three air raids with ten aircraft against the island of Malta. According to the British, four of the planes were destroyed, little damage was done, and only twelve people were killed. During the month of June the Italians conducted an additional thirty-five strikes against Malta, but it was not until the end of the month that the British temporarily abandoned the island as a submarine base. Nevertheless, the SMM's 18 June study claiming that a landing on Malta would be exceedingly difficult precluded an Italian naval assault. Steadily improving antiaircraft defenses, therefore, allowed the British island to survive the Italian air barrage without capitulating.[75]

Although Mussolini had the power to send his country to war, Badoglio and especially Cavagnari had the determination and influence to ensure that the majority of Italy's armed forces would not fight it. The Duce's vision of a new Mediterranean empire could not outweigh Italy's insurmountable military, economic, and financial inferiority, paving the way for high-level military insubordination that the Fascist state at least initially accepted. What was important for Mussolini was to go to war politically on the Axis side. Nevertheless, it was this inherent contradiction between ambitions and capabilities, as well as genuine trepidation about the future among many in Italy's military leadership, that led to a series of catastrophic failures for Fascist Italy in its war of 1940–43.

The Allies went to war in the Mediterranean haphazardly. In some ways, there was much relief that Italy had finally acted definitively, allowing it to be treated as a genuine enemy. Cadogan confided to his diary that he was "rather glad. Now we can say what we think of these purulent dogs. . . . Hope we can give the Italians an early and hard knock." And indeed the Allies were in an advantageous position to do just that. Including the two Littorio battleships that were expected to join the Italian fleet in July, the Regia Marina had only six battleships, seven large cruisers, twelve small cruisers, and fifty destroyers. The Italians had no aircraft carriers and relied on shore-based aircraft to provide all their air support. By contrast, at the end of May the Allies had ten battleships, seven large cruisers, sixteen small cruisers, sixty-seven destroyers, and one aircraft carrier in the Mediterranean. Even though Italy possessed the two most modern battleships and a significant numerical advantage in submarines—108 to 58—the Allies enjoyed clear naval superiority in the Mediterranean. On land and in the air the Allies and the Italians were more evenly matched, although Allied intelligence well understood that the Regio Esercito and the Regia Aeronautica were not prepared for war. The Allies were also thoroughly cognizant of Italy's precarious financial and economic position.[76]

On 28 May, after the Belgium army had capitulated and Ciano had revealed that Italian intervention was a certainty, Churchill circulated a brief minute that he had written to the War Cabinet and the service chiefs. It was a strategic directive for British policy in the Mediterranean once Italy declared war:

> If France is still our ally after an Italian declaration of war, it would appear extremely desirable that the combined fleets, acting from opposite ends of the Mediterranean, should pursue an active offensive against Italy. It is important that at the outset collision should take place both with the Italian Navy and Air Force, in order that we can see what their quality really is, and whether it has changed at all since the last war.

Churchill repeated this strategic intention at the final meeting of the Supreme War Council before Italy intervened—a plan that all the British and French statesmen in attendance accepted as a well-established formula. Yet neither the British nor the French service chiefs, and surely not *both* the British and French chiefs, were prepared to embark on a Mediterranean offensive. On 29 May, after discussing the prime minister's instructions for the Mediterranean, the COS in London reached a "general agreement that while our forces in the Mediterranean would adopt a tactical offensive, we would have to remain on the defensive in the opening stages of war with Italy, owing to the Italian air superiority." On 4 June the chiefs disseminated to the British commanders in the Mediterranean and the Middle East their own perspective—not the prime minister's—on how the war should be fought. The British chiefs of staff had completely undermined the leader of the British government, and few people other than the service chiefs realized it. After describing the halfhearted Allied bombing of northwestern Italy that took place on 12 June as a "complete flop," Cadogan naively blamed its failure on French obstructionism and poor execution.[77]

There was less confusion and more resignation in Paris than in London. By the end of May, with the Germans steadily advancing toward Paris, the French had to rely on the British for the forthcoming war in the Mediterranean. It was understandably difficult for the French to contemplate a war against Germany *and* Italy when they were experiencing immense hardship fighting Germany alone. Both Daladier, now foreign minister, and General Weygand, who had replaced Gamelin as commander-in-chief of the French armed forces on 19 May, recognized that the Allies had no large-scale offensive operations planned to carry out against the Italians once Italy declared war. Events on the western front and the attitude of the British precluded the French from sending an expedition to Salonika, attacking Libya from Tunisia, or bombarding northwestern Italy or Tripoli. Selective military targets on the western coast of Italy could be bombed if Italian fighters were not too active in the area. Eventually, once the Turks intervened on the Allied side and with the aid of the Greeks, Crete and Milos could be occupied and Rhodes invaded. Upon encountering the Regia Marina at sea, British and French naval forces could selectively attack poorly defended Italian ships. Allied air and naval forces could, if necessary, prevent the Italians from reestablishing themselves in the Balearics. Finally, the Allies could foment unrest in Italian East Africa. But these were only possible *Allied* initiatives. For the moment, the Allied war against Italy would be based on closing the Mediterranean at Gibraltar and Suez and attempting to strangle Italy economically. Much as they had nine months earlier, the French were again preparing to conduct an Allied "phony war"—only this time it was to be fought against Italy.[78]

There were those in Britain and France who believed that the Allies' strategy for the forthcoming war in the Mediterranean was inadequate. Foremost among them were Cunningham and Darlan. Cunningham officially expressed his disagreement with London's directive that the Mediterranean fleet remain on the defensive when Italy intervened:

> At the commencement of hostilities I prefer to adopt the more limited object of controlling the Aegean and Eastern Mediterranean, which is not defen-

> sive since, to achieve it, the destruction of enemy naval forces in the Dodecanese and of any reinforcements sent to their assistance, as well as the ultimate liquidation of these islands, are necessary courses of action.

Cunningham also recommended that the Allies occupy Crete regardless of the political situation and that the fleet gradually move toward Italy to ensure that the Allies retained the initiative in the war: "When war is imminent, it is intended that a strong force including battleships should proceed to the westwards ready to counter Italian action on Malta or in other directions." Yet Cunningham admitted that without air cover, offensive operations in any part of the Mediterranean placed an unacceptable risk on his fleet. As it turned out, London denied Cunningham the aerial defenses he requested and thereby ensured that the limited offensives he envisioned would not be carried out.[79]

Darlan's opposition to Allied strategy in the Mediterranean was particularly virulent and counterproductive. The French naval chief laid all the blame for both France's inability to repulse the Germans and the Allies' passive strategy in the Mediterranean on the unstable French political system and the selfishness of the British people. It was the British, according to Darlan, who were responsible for granting Italy naval parity with France in 1922, disregarding Italian pirate submarine warfare in 1937, vetoing a Mediterranean offensive in 1939, postponing operations in Scandinavia, planning the BEF's evacuation of France before discussing it with the French, and refusing to embark on an eastern Mediterranean offensive either before or immediately after Italy intervened in June 1940. By the beginning of June, once it became evident that the Marine Nationale could not undertake a large-scale offensive in either the eastern Mediterranean or the Gulf of Genoa, the French naval chief began to contemplate making peace with Germany rather than continuing war with Britain.[80]

Conclusion: Vital Crossroads of the Second World War

Before 1935, British and French defense planning did not focus on Mediterranean security, seeing this vital crossroads as little more than an imperial transportation route and a staging ground for naval maneuvers and reviews. Despite Fascist foreign policy's revisionism in the 1920s and early 1930s, the British perceived Italy as a friendly power that favored the continuation of the status quo both on the continent and in the Mediterranean region. The French had been wary of Italy since 1919, and by 1926, Franco-Italian hostility had reached acute levels. But that conflict largely revolved around a struggle for influence in southeastern Europe and never threatened to erupt into direct confrontation. In fact, after the Fascist-Nazi breach caused by the failed Vienna *putsch* in mid-1934, France and Italy decided to lay aside their differences to form a common anti-German front.

Italy's invasion of Ethiopia in October 1935 threw British and French Mediterranean policy into disarray and compelled the two democracies, as well as Nazi Germany, to reconsider their views of Fascist Italy. What is often dismissed as "the Abyssinian diversion" actually started the chain of events that brought Italy into armed conflict with Britain and France in June 1940. Beginning in 1936 Germany and Italy developed the basis for a mutually advantageous partnership, which encouraged Italy to engage in proxy wars with France in Spain and East Africa. Yet the British government firmly believed that it could entice Mussolini away from ever-closer ties to Hitler. That diplomacy only created friction between London and Paris, while Fascist Italy took what it could from the British and continued to strengthen its ties to Nazi Germany.

At the center of this discord was Fascist Italy, whose attachment to Nazi Germany grew in 1936–38 from an appreciation of the strategic value of Germany as a continental ally to the recognition that Italy and Germany would soon be partners in an ideological battle against Britain and France. Hitler fostered Mussolini's expanding dependence on the Germans because the strategic and ideological basis for the Axis served the Führer's revanchist ambitions as well. With Hitler's encouragement, the Duce embarked on a policy that aimed to divide Britain and France so that he could broaden Italian power in the Mediterranean. As early as 1936 Mussolini identified Britain—and especially the politically influential Neville Chamberlain—as susceptible to deceitful Italian diplomacy, and France, governed by the leftist Popular Front, as the major obstacle to Italian aspirations in Spain, North Africa, and the Balkans. For that reason, the Italians began to antagonize the French even as they led the British to believe that Italy was interested in a peaceful Mediterranean.

By late 1937 Britain and France had adopted general foreign policies that were largely based on their dealings with the changing and now vital Mediterranean situation. Preoccupied by their vulnerable positions at home, in the Far East, and in the Mediterranean, the British sought to prevent the outbreak of war everywhere but especially in the Mediterranean—their third defense priority. Therefore, Britain's appeasement of Mussolini began well before and also outlasted its most infamous appeasement of Hitler. Indeed, the conciliatory policies that Chamberlain pursued in regard to Fascist Italy were the inspiration and model for his attempts to satisfy Nazi German aspirations in 1938–39. The French, who were less exposed in the Far East and more committed to Mediterranean security than the British, recognized the hostile intent of Fascist policy and began anticipating a war against Italy. The prospect of a conflict in the Mediterranean, as much as fear of a German attack on the western front, inspired the French to search for an Anglo-French entente. But even though the French modified their resistance to German revisionism in Eastern Europe to mollify the British, the adamant French view of Italy obstructed the formation of any definitive alliance with the British.

The demise of Austria, Czechoslovakia, and Albania, combined with the Easter Accords of 1938 and the Pact of Steel in 1939, exacerbated Anglo-French-Italian tension and enhanced the relevance of the Mediterranean crossroads to the rapidly changing European scene. Conspicuous Italian support for Nazi revisionism and the Italians' demands for substantial French concessions in the Mediterranean increased Germany's leverage over the democracies and further widened the Anglo-French gulf in regard to Mediterranean policy. Whereas the French had concluded by early 1939 that the Allies should resist all Italian claims and conduct a Mediterranean offensive against the weaker of the two Axis powers as soon as general European war began, the British fashioned the appeasement of Rome as the centerpiece of a policy that aimed to preserve European peace. Because the Allies could not agree on a Mediterranean strategy, neither could they devise an assertive response to further German aggression in Eastern Europe. The Allies' "phony war" strategy of economic warfare and blockade had its roots in the failure of the only viable military alternative: a Mediterranean offensive against a hostile Italy.

Despite Italy's decision not to intervene in September 1939, the vital Mediterranean crossroads continued to complicate matters for the Allies and improve fortunes for the Nazis. Again, it was Italy that created these Allied problems and Nazi opportunities. Through their diplomacy the Italians stated that they preferred neutrality but indicated that they would be forced into the war on the German side if Allied contraband control in the Mediterranean treated Italian shipping harshly. The Allies, who overestimated Italy's strength and feared its intervention in the war, granted it trading privileges not accorded to any other neutral, which in turn allowed the Fascists to import and reexport to Germany goods and raw materials essential for the Nazi war machine. As the Allies admitted in the spring of 1940, the Italian and Russian "pipelines" to Germany were permitting the Nazis to overcome the Allied blockade; the long-war economic strategy could not defeat Germany and thus would have to be replaced.

Yet even the decision to intercept German coal exports to Italy, followed by the recognition in March 1940 that Mussolini indeed intended to declare war on the democracies, did not unite British and French Mediterranean policy. Although both Britain and France conceded that the deteriorating Mediterranean situation had contributed to the Allies' decision to abandon the campaign in Scandinavia, they could not reach consensus on a Mediterranean strategy. As they had disagreed over building a neutral Balkan bloc and sending an expedition to Salonika in the fall of 1939—entirely because of differing interpretations of the nature of Italian neutrality—the British and French argued inconclusively in May 1940 over either attacking Italy's position in the eastern Mediterranean or bombing northwestern Italy once the Italians intervened. The Allies, in other words, entered the Second World War in the Mediterranean without any coordinated strategy that envisioned the defeat of their newest declared enemy, Italy. For lack of a better alternative on which they could agree, the Allies could only implement a "phony war" strategy against Italy in June 1940.

Fascist foreign policy had directly controlled developments in the Mediterranean in 1935–40 and critically affected the course of European affairs during those years. The starkly different responses of the British and French prevented them from comprehensively addressing either the Mediterranean or the general European situation. The Anglo-French conflict over strategy regarding Italy and the Mediterranean contributed to the formation of a confused alliance that could not respond in a decisive or coordinated fashion against either Axis power. The significance of the Mediterranean does not reduce the importance of the Anglo-German conflict on the continent for explaining the origins of the war, but it does reveal that international European politics in this period were a product of complex multinational relationships and that the imperial interests and ambitions of the European powers often eclipsed or shaped their continental policies. Hence, it demonstrates that in the beginning the Second World War was as much about the Mediterranean theater as the western front, and as much about the French and Italians as about the British and Germans.

THE PRIMARY antagonist in this story is Mussolini, who sought a far-reaching Mediterranean empire and built a political and military alliance with Nazi Germany in the hope of achieving it. After 1935, war against the democracies became an ever more fundamental aspect of Mussolini's formula for Italian greatness. In fact it became so essential to his imperial program that he drove his country into war despite Italian military and economic unpreparedness. Mussolini's foreign policy increasingly manipulated Italian military strategy as the late 1930s unfolded and war approached. Coherent strategic assessments that cautioned against Italian intervention were reluctantly accepted in 1939 but rejected in 1940 in favor of ill-founded convictions of anticipated military success. Both geostrategic necessity and ideological imperatives, the Duce believed, compelled Fascist Italy to intervene alongside Nazi Germany. Italian moral courage would outweigh Italian material weakness. It was a malevolent imperial agenda that the Fascist regime, having already assailed the traditions of Italian liberalism, embraced with little internal dissent.

Yet the Fascists can be admired for their carefully planned, consistent, and accomplished deception of the democracies. Mussolini, with the help of Foreign Minister Galeazzo Ciano, manipulated the British and the French masterfully: despite Italy's repeated assaults on the international status quo in the years before war erupted, Mussolini and Ciano garnered Western recognition of Italian Abyssinia, maintained Italian troops and matériel in Spain until Franco had defeated his opposition, and annexed Albania without causing an abrogation of the Anglo-Italian Easter Accords. Even after they concluded a military alliance with the Nazis and refused to condemn Germany's conquests of Austria and Czechoslovakia, the Italians retained the diplomatic initiative vis-à-vis the Allies. The Fascists resisted early intervention to give Italy an opportunity to enhance its economic and military strength so that Mussolini could join Germany in war whenever he wanted to. After the war began, the Fascists persuaded the democracies to loosen contraband control in the Mediterranean, allowing Italy to build its stocks of raw materials and to become a vitally important supplier of resources to Nazi Germany. And by refusing to abandon the Axis alliance with Germany, the Fascists prevented Allied forces from denuding the Mediterranean and thus facilitated Germany's successes on the continent.

Most important, the Fascist regime recognized British preoccupations in the Far East and French apprehensions about both continental and imperial security. The Fascist leadership also perceived Britain as a formidable power that Italy should not enrage prematurely, and France as a power dependent on Britain both on the seas against Italy and on the continent against Germany. France, not Britain, was vulnerable to a threatening diplomacy that demanded substantial imperial concessions in the Mediterranean. These Italian biases toward the British and French led to a Fascist foreign policy that encouraged British conciliation and French animosity simultaneously, causing the two democracies to reach contradictory interpretations of the Italian threat in the Mediterranean and paralyzing their attempt to respond to Nazi aggression.

Despite confusing messages from Rome, many of Britain's most important decision-makers continued to believe that the appeasement of Fascist Italy was the surest way to prevent conflict and preserve the sanctity of the Far Eastern empire. Foremost among them was Neville Chamberlain; until his government fell in May 1940, he remained determined to preserve peace in the Mediterranean at almost any cost. Chamberlain avoided confronting the Italians over the pirate submarine campaign, pursued the Easter Accords despite Italy's lack of protest over the German *Anschluss,* ignored the implications of the Italian race laws and the Pact of Steel, urged France to make colonial concessions to Italy, did not interpret Italy's Albanian invasion as an abrogation of the Mediterranean status quo, ensured that the Allies would not launch a Mediterranean offensive at the outset of war, and promoted lenient contraband control of Italian ships even after Italy had refused to buy British coal and Mussolini had met with Hitler at the Brenner Pass. Chamberlain's belittling and even racist views of the Italians contributed to his conviction that the Fascist regime was not capable of envisioning, much less realizing, a great Mediterranean empire that would jeopardize British interests in the region. With a few concessions in the Mediterranean, he believed, a satiated and grateful "Musso" would in turn help the British modify Hitler's bellicose ambitions.

The prime minister could not have implemented his conciliation policy alone, however. The chiefs of staff, and especially the Admiralty, rejected strategies that anticipated war and adopted those that would not provoke war—all in the name of preserving Britain's ability to defend the Far Eastern empire. Throughout this period the service chiefs both overestimated the strength and fighting ability of the Italian armed services and misperceived the intentions of the Fascist regime to intervene in the war. British intelligence failed to gather accurate information and allowed its analyses to be influenced by the cautious and imperial outlook of Britain's military leadership.

The incoherence of British strategic assessments in the Mediterranean resulted from the government's imperial defense policies, which forbade rational discussion and consideration of a naval and military strategy designed to eliminate the Italian threat in the Mediterranean. Even admitting that Italy was irrevocably committed to opposing them would have placed the British in a terrible psychological and political predicament, because they lacked the resources to oppose—alone—a hostile Italy, Germany, and Japan simultaneously. The formation of alliances, it was believed, could itself spark a war that would jeopardize the integrity of the British Empire. And if the British had to build alliance coalitions to confront these threats, how could they justify retaining such a vast empire? Ultimately, Britain's imperial status depended on a peaceful Mediterranean and a friendly Italy.

The Foreign Office too allowed its judgment of the vital Mediterranean situation to be influenced by Chamberlain's views. Most diplomats there shared the conviction that Italian goodwill could be bought and that Mussolini would be able to temper Hitler's aspirations. After September 1939, Ambassador Loraine in Rome even propagated the absurd notion that the Fascists could be drawn to the Allied side. Cadogan's frequent derogatory descriptions of the Italians as "ice-creamers," "monkeys," and "purulent dogs" underscores the British establishment's confidence that Italian moral inferiority would make Italy receptive to British conciliation. French appeals for Britain and France to prepare for war against Italy in the Mediterranean went disregarded largely because the British arrogantly perceived France as an ill-prepared and paranoid power in a desperate search for a British alliance. In fact throughout 1938–40 the British tried to remain aloof from Franco-Italian affairs, ignoring the potential consequences of a Franco-Italian conflict, encouraging French concessions to Italy, and demanding that France assume complete responsibility for Mediterranean security. Not until the Scandinavian campaign had almost failed and Italian intervention was imminent did British statesmen and strategists admit that the veil of ambiguity surrounding Italian aims had been lifted, paving the way for a policy that genuinely envisioned a British war in the Mediterranean.

In general, the French were less condescending and far more tough-minded than the British in regard to Italy's behavior. The French saw in Italy a true rival to France's Mediterranean preeminence and imperial stature, and they appreciated that Italy had the capacity to disrupt the Mediterranean status quo profoundly. Since the heart of the French empire was in and around the Mediterranean, not in French Indochina, Fascist foreign policy objectives in the Mediterranean directly threatened France's colonial possessions and great power status. The statesmen in Paris had fewer anti-Italian prejudices than their London counterparts and were more inclined to believe both that Mussolini's Mediterranean ambitions were insatiable and that his commitment to the Nazis would endure. The

French understood that Italy's annexation of Abyssinia and Albania in the face of international condemnation, Italy's active assistance in Franco's overthrow of Republican Spain, Italy's quiescent reaction to Germany's incorporation of Austria, the Sudetenland, and Bohemia-Moravia, and Italy's political and military agreements with Germany were all part of a program designed to establish Italian Mediterranean hegemony. The French also recognized that besides the strategic benefit to Italy of letting Germany fight Britain and France on the continent while Italy challenged them in the Mediterranean, Mussolini and Hitler were ideologically united in their hatred for the world's democracies.

Even though the French searched for every opportunity to commit British forces to the defense of France, the French did not temper their views on the Mediterranean to accommodate Britain's renowned preference for conciliation and "splendid isolation." They frequently impressed upon the British their convictions about the tenuous Mediterranean crossroads and their preference to deal harshly with the Fascists. In fact French fears about a rising Italian menace in 1937–40 served as catalysts for the various permutations of Anglo-French Mediterranean planning before and during the war. Allied strategy can no longer be interpreted as synonymous with British strategy. Indeed, had France wholly endorsed British policy in the Mediterranean, the Allied position vis-à-vis the Axis powers would not, arguably, have been nearly as confused as it was.

Yet French strategic assessments of Fascist Italy and the Mediterranean were not entirely unified and coherent. Preoccupied with the German threat, the Soviet menace, their East European allies, and the effort to establish an Anglo-French alliance, the French general staff shunned the idea of confronting Italy over the Spanish civil war and looked with disfavor on the plan for a Mediterranean offensive in 1939. Like the British, conservatives at the Quai d'Orsay also supported and encouraged a military strategy that avoided conflict with Fascist Italy. In the year after Munich Georges Bonnet and André François-Poncet argued that the Italians could be disentangled from the Germans and bribed into remaining outside any armed conflict. Motivated both by their fear of another war against Germany and their determination that France not ally with the Soviet Union, Bonnet and François-Poncet pressed hard for France to offer Italy colonial concessions.

Nonetheless, François Darlan and the naval staff persuaded Edouard Daladier that France's vital imperial interests in the Mediterranean were jeopardized by Fascist Italy and therefore France should prepare for a difficult war against Italy to preserve the French empire. These arguments motivated the premier in early 1939 to insist that the Allies coordinate their Mediterranean strategies. In this case, naval strategy and planning, though vague, indeed inspired French foreign policy and affected the conception of Allied policy. Yet the French found themselves at the mercy of the British because France lacked the military and economic strength to contemplate a war against Italy and Germany without British support. The inability of the British and French staffs during the spring of 1939 to reach an agreement on Allied strategy for the Mediterranean encouraged those in Paris who argued for a general Mediterranean appeasement and frustrated those who anticipated a war in the Mediterranean. These contradictions paralyzed French strategic policy. In the final months before war Daladier struggled between endorsing policies of assuaging or confronting Italy. After refusing any conciliation of Italy and supporting the concept of an early Mediterranean offensive in the event of a general European war, Daladier eventually succumbed to British pressure and acquiesced in a policy of Mediterranean appeasement.

Thereafter, throughout the "phony war," Allied relations in the Mediterranean followed a similar pattern: French suggestions and British decisions. Although they conceded most control of the blockade to Britain and the Royal Navy, the French remained more innovative on Mediterranean strategy than the British. It was the French who demanded a reconsideration of the Allies' "broad strategic policy" soon after Hitler and Mussolini met in March 1940. And it was the French who first recognized the strategic connection between the Scandinavian and Mediterranean theaters. By late May 1940, unfortunately, with the Germans steadily advancing on Paris, the French held even less sway over the Allies' Mediterranean policy than they had the year before.

The extension of the Second World War to the vital Mediterranean crossroads in the summer of 1940 was not caused simply by Italian opportunism. It was principally the result of an Anglo-French-Italian imperial conflict that had begun in earnest in 1935 and had yet to be resolved. The root of this conflict was Mussolini's stubborn determination to "march to the oceans"—an imperial Mediterranean policy that after 1936 generated German endorsement, French condemnation, British indifference, and Allied confusion as a result of differing imperial agendas. The Allies' reluctance to take decisive action against Fascist Italy during the first nine months of war shaped not only the manner in which the war initially unfolded but also subsequent events. The consequences of the Allies' Mediterranean policies in 1939–40 led to the early collapse of the French Republic in 1940 and placed the British in the desperate situation from which they barely escaped in 1940–1. And Britain's failure to appreciate the strategic and ideological relationship between Nazi Germany's continental revanchism and Fascist Italy's increasingly relentless obsession with creating a *mare nostrum* contributed to the collapse of Britain as a world power after the Second World War. This unfortunate circumstance was far more the fault of the British themselves, blinded by their own imperial consciousness and convictions, than the result of actions taken by either their allies or their enemies.

Notes

Chapter 1

1. PRO, CAB 21/413, Franco-Italian Agreements concluded at Rome on 7 January 1935, 22 January 1935; DBFP, 2/12, nos. 400 annex, 722, pp. 482–890; AUSA, 68, Collaborazione aerea Italo-Francese, 12–13 May 1935; Watt, "The Secret Laval-Mussolini Agreement"; Serra, "La questione italo-etiopica"; Minardi, "L'accordo militare segreto Badoglio-Gamelin"; Young, "Soldiers and Diplomats"; Nöel, *Les illusions de Stresa*, pp. 70–86.

2. Schreiber, "Italy and the Mediterranean in the Power-Political Calculations of German Naval Leaders, 1919–45," in Hattendorf, ed., *Naval Strategy and Policy in the Mediterranean*, p. 121; Schreiber, "Zur Kontinuität des Gross-und Weltmachtstrebens," pp. 147–71; Laval, *Laval parle*, p. 245; DDF, 1/11, nos. 109, 120, pp. 155–82; Salerno, "Multilateral Strategy and Diplomacy," pp. 45–64.

3. Marder, "The Royal Navy and the Ethiopian Crisis," pp. 1330–38; Quartararo, "Imperial Defence in the Mediterranean on the eve of the Ethiopian Crisis," pp. 190–91; Cohen, "British Strategy in the Middle East in the Wake of the Abyssinian Crisis," in Cohen and Kolinsky, *Britain and the Middle East*, pp. 21–40.

4. PRO, CAB 23/82, Cab. 42 (35), Cabinet meeting, 22 August 1935; PRO, CAB 16/136, DPR meeting, 23 August 1935; PRO, CAB 53/5, COS 149th meeting, 6 September 1935; Young, *In Command*, pp. 110–14; Adamthwaite, *France and the Coming*, pp. 32–6; Duroselle, *La Décadence*, pp. 147–57; Jordan, *The Popular Front*, pp. 33–103; Parker, "Great Britain, France and the Ethiopian Crisis," pp. 293–332.

5. DBFP, 2, xv, nos. 69, 81, 118, 305, 320, 374, pp. 81–477; Shorrock, *From Ally to Enemy*, pp. 143–58; Quartararo, *Roma tra Londra e Berlino*, pp. 246–58.

6. Mussolini, *Opera Omnia*, 12: 101; De Felice, *Mussolini il fascista*; De Felice, *Mussolini il Duce*; Knox, *Common Destiny*, pp. 59–71, 117–20; Moseley, *Mussolini's Shadow*.

7. ADAP, C, 4/2, nos. 337, 485, 486, 525, 579, pp. 697–1024; DDI, 8/3, no. 275; Robertson, "Hitler and Sanctions," pp. 418–21; Petersen, *Hitler-Mussolini*, pp. 468–71.

8. MAE, Eur 30–40, Italie, 303, Corbin to Flandin, 18 May 1936; SHM, 1BB2, 182, Mémento, 14 April 1936; SHM, 1BB2, 208, Durand-Viel to Piétri, 9 June 1936; SHM, 1BB2, 184, note au ministre, 6 July 1936; Thomas, *Britain, France, and Appeasement*, pp. 55–58; Shorrock, *From Ally to Enemy*, pp. 170–74, 181–86; Young, "French Military Intelligence and the Franco-Italian Alliance," pp. 143–68; Jordan, "Maurice Gamelin, Italy, and the Eastern Alliances," pp. 428–41.

9. Lord Avon, *Facing the Dictators*, p. 431; Dilks, *Chamberlain*; Parker, *Chamberlain*, pp. 3–11; Addison, *Road to 1945*, pp. 29–30; Colville, *Fringes of Power*, pp. 35–36; May, *Strange Victory*, pp. 170–72; Hardie, *The Abyssinian Crisis*, pp. 220–25.

10. NMM, Papers of 1st Baron, Admiral of the Fleet, Sir Alfred Ernle Montacute Chatfield, CHT 4/1, Chatfield to Backhouse, 27 March 1936; PRO, CAB 53/5, COS 178th meeting, 16 June 1936; PRO, CAB 23/84, Cab. 42(36), Cabinet meeting, 17 June 1936; Marder, "Royal Navy," p. 1354; *Dictionary of National Biography 1961–1970*, pp. 185–88.

11. DDF, 2, ii, no. 332, p. 501.

12. Moseley, *Mussolini's Shadow*, pp. 1–35.

13. Suvich, *Memorie*; Aloisi, *Journal*.

14. Aloisi, *Journal*, 1 April 1936, pp. 364–65; DDI, 8/4, nos. 208, 503, 514; Knox, "Il fascismo e la politica estera italiana," in Bosworth and Romano, *La politica estera italiana*, pp. 325–26; Petersen, *Hitler-Mussolini*, pp. 470–71; Wheatley, "Mussolini's Ideological Diplomacy," pp. 432–37; Robertson, "Hitler and Sanctions," p. 422.

15. Blum, *L'histoire jugera*, pp. 100–102; Jackson, *The Popular Front*, pp. 42–51; Serrano, *L'enjeu espagnol*, pp. 9–36; Dreifort, *Yvon Delbos*, pp. 38–156; Young, "French Military Intelligence and the Franco-Italian Alliance," pp. 148–63; Jordan, "Maurice Gamelin, Italy, and the Eastern Alliances," pp. 435–36.

16. Stone, "The European Great Powers and the Spanish Civil War," in Boyce and Robertson, *Paths to War*, pp. 212–17; Thomas, *Britain, France, and Appeasement*, pp. 89–108.

17. Guariglia, *Ricordi, 1922–46*, pp. 186–89; ASD, AG, UC, 9, 44/1, Accordo Balbo-Barrera, 31 March 1934.

18. ASD, AG, UC, 9, 44/4, Verbale della riunione tenuta a Palazzo Venezia, 6 December 1936; DDI, 8/4, no. 685, pp. 751–52; Ciano, *Diario*, 29 October 1937, pp. 50–51; Coverdale, *Italian Intervention*, pp. 74–84.

19. ADAP, C, 4/2, nos. 373, 414, pp. 752–809; ACS, MMG-AS, 17, Promemoria, 27 November 1935; PRO, FO 371/2041, R794/22, Drummond to Eden, 11 February 1936; PRO, FO 371/20018, E1293/19/31, Colonial Office memo, 6 March 1936; Brondi, *Un generale*, p. 49; Knox, "Il fascismo," pp. 324–25; Funke, *Sanktionen und Kanonen*, pp. 45–47; Quartararo, "Imperial Defence," p. 206; Robertson, "Hitler and Sanctions," p. 423.

20. ASD, AG, UC, 9, 44/2, Accordo Canaris-Roatta, 26 August 1936; DDI, 8/4, no. 819, pp. 892–96; Coverdale, *Italian Intervention*, pp. 85–103.

21. ASD, AG, UC, 9, 44/2, Colloquio Ciano-Neurath, 21 October 1936; ASD, AG, UC, 44/4, Verbale della riunione tenuta a Palazzo Venezia, 14 January 1937; ASD, AG, UC, 44/5, Communicazione Italiana–Tedesca al Generale Franco, 23 January 1937; Mussolini, *Opera Omnia*, 28: 67–71; Rovighi and Stefani, *La participazione italiana*, 1: 315–17; Ciano, *Diario*, 29 October 1937, p. 50.

22. Kershaw, *Hitler*, 2:24–25; Schreiber, "Italy and the Mediterranean," in Hattendorf, ed., *Naval Strategy and Policy in the Mediterranean*, pp. 122–23.

23. USE, H-6, 12, Ufficio Operazioni N. 8789, 2 November 1936; Ciano, *Diario*, 28 August 1937, 14 November 1937, pp. 29, 57; ASD, AG, US, 1/1, MMG, Collaborazione italo-germanica in Spagna, 4 December 1936; ASD, AG, US, 10/2, Verbale della riunione a Palazzo Venezia, 6 December 1936; Sullivan, "Fascist Italy's Military Involvement," pp. 704–5; Ferrari, "Dalla divisione ternaria alla binaria," p. 59; De Luna, *Badoglio*, pp. 164–66; Faldella, *L'Italia*, pp. 97–98.

24. PRO, CAB 24/262, CP 165 (36), Cabinet paper, 12 June 1936; PRO, CAB 24/263, CP 174 (36), Cabinet paper, 19 June 1936; PRO, CAB 24/264, CP 233(36), and CP 234(36), Cabinet papers, 31 August 1936; PRO, CAB 23/85, Cab. 56 (36), Cabinet meeting, 2 September 1936.

25. PRO, CAB 21/700, Review of Imperial Defence, 22 February 1937; PRO, CAB 23/87, Cab. 9 (37), Cabinet meeting, 24 February 1937.

26. USE, H-6, 12, Pariani memorandum, 9 February 1937 (original emphasis).

27. Perich, *Mussolini nei Balcani*, p. 22; Zamboni, *Mussolinis Expansionspolitik*; Ormos, "L'opinione del conte Stefano Bethlen sui rapporti italo-ungheresi," pp. 283–314; Tasso, *Italia e Croazia*, 1: 56–97; Cassels, *Mussolini's Early Diplomacy*, chps. 4 and 6.

28. Minute dated 25 March 1937 in Hoptner, *Yugoslavia in Crisis*, p. 83; Knox, *Mussolini Unleashed*, p. 36; Memorandum dated 11 December 1937 in Ciano, *L'Europa*, pp. 229–34; Ciano, *Diario*, 25 August 1937, 1 November 1937, 5, 29 December 1937, pp. 28–75.

29. DDF, 2/4, no. 395, pp. 686–7; SHAT, 2N 23, Procès-verbal du séance de la CPDN, 15 February 1937.

30. DDF, 2, v, nos. 152–54, pp. 244–47; MAE, PA-AP, Massigli, 93, Delbos to Corbin, 1 May 1937; SHAT, 2N 23, Procès-verbal du séance de la CPDN, 9 July 1937.

31. PRO, CAB 53/31, COS 590, Questions submitted by the Australian delegation, 31 May 1937; Roskill, *Naval Policy between the Wars*, 2: 347.

32. Dutton, *Eden*; Parker, *Chamberlain*, p. 94.

33. PRO, FO 371/21158, R 3453/1/22, Balfour to Nichols, 3 May 1937; PRO, FO 371/20710, C 3525/3/18, Sargent to Henderson, 13 May 1937; PRO, FO 371/20710, C 3683/3/18, Henderson to Sargent, 19 May 1937; PRO, FO 371/21175, R 3559/200/22, Phipps to Eden, 24 May 1937; BUL, Anthony Eden Papers, AP 13/1/58, Drummond to Vansittart, 2 July 1937; PRO, CAB 23/89, Cab. 30(37), 14 July 1937; BUL, AP 13/1/48/U, Vansittart to Eden, 26 July 1937; PRO, CAB 53/8, COS 214th meeting, 28 July 1937; PRO, CAB 16/182, DP(P) 5, 14 June 1937.

34. PRO, PREM 1/276, Hankey to Chamberlain, 19 July 1937; PRO, FO 954/13, Hankey to Eden, 23 July 1937; BUL, AP 13/1/48/R, Eden to Chamberlain, 24 July 1937; PRO, CAB 4/26, CID 1346–B, 28 July 1937; ASD, De Felice, Grandi, 47/112, Chamberlain to Mussolini, 27 July 1937; PRO, PREM 1/276, Mussolini to Chamberlain, 31 July 1937; DBFP, 2/19, nos. 15, 32, 40, 65, pp. 22–120.

35. ASD, AG, US, 10, Franco to Mussolini, 3 August 1937; ASD, AG, UC, 10, 46/1, Processo verbale della riunione a Palazzo Venezia, 5 August 1937; ASD, AG, US, 10, Conversazione fra Cavagnari e Moreno, 7 August 1937.

36. Bargoni, *L'impegno navale*, pp. 280–317; Giorgerini, *Da Matapan*, pp. 352–53; Frank, "Naval Operations," pp. 42–43; Sullivan, "Fascist Italy's Military Involvement," p. 716; Coverdale, *Italian Intervention*, pp. 306–16.

37. DDF, 2/6, nos. 326, 338, 345, 351, 364, pp. 573–647; Frank, "Naval Operations," p. 45.

38. Ciano, *L'Europa*, p. 210; Mussolini, *Opera Omnia*, 28: 239–42; DDF, 2/6, nos. 360, 365, 375, pp. 634–60; ASD, AG, UC, 84/2, Ciano to Mussolini, 2 October 1937.

39. Ciano, *L'Europa*, pp. 206–9; PRO, FO 371/21358, W 16254/23/41, No. 460, Ingram to Eden, 27 August 1937; PRO, PREM 1/276, Hankey to Chamberlain, 19 July 1937; PRO, FO 954/13, Halifax to Chamberlain, 4 August 1937, Chamberlain to Halifax, 7 August 1937, Meeting held in Secretary of State's room to deal with anticipated conversations with Italy, 10 August 1937, Chamberlain to Halifax, 15 August 1937; ASD, De Felice, Grandi, 50, 125/1, N 3599/2164, Crolla to Ciano, 23 August 1937; Ciano, *Diario*, 8 September 1937, p. 35.

40. PRO, FO 371/21357, W 15646/23/41, no. 1728/15, Pound to Admiralty, 15 August 1937; PRO, FO 371/21358, W 15802/23/41, Vansittart minute, 16 August 1937; PRO, FO 371/21357, W 15727/23/41, Notes of a meeting of Ministers, 17 August 1937; PRO, ADM 116/3917, M 05332/37, 23 August 1937; PRO, ADM 116/3917, M 04827/37, 6 September 1937.

41. BUL, AP 13/1/58/E, Eden to Halifax, 11 August 1937; PRO, FO 371/21179, R 5810/419/22, no. 492, Thomas to Eden, 25 August 1937; FRUS, 1937/1, Bullitt to Hull, 26 August 1937, pp. 117–19; PRO, FO 371/21358, W 16299/23/41, Eden memorandum, 30 August 1937; PRO, FO 371/21359, W 16584/23/41, Eden memorandum, 1 September 1937; PRO, FO 371/21358, W 16521/23/41, Eden memorandum, 2 September 1937; SHM, 1BB7, 40, Compte Rendu de Renseignements N 65, Nicolas-Barrelon to Gaudin de Villaine, 2 September 1937; PRO, ADM 116/3917, M 04827/37, Director of Naval Intelligence memorandum, 6 September 1937.

42. ASD, AG, US, 95, Franco note, 3 September 1937; ASD, De Felice, Grandi, 50, 125/1, N 3750/2245, Crolla to Ciano, 3 September 1937; Ciano, *Diario*, 4 September 1937, p. 33; Ciano, *L'Europa*, p. 209; PRO, FO 371/21404, W 16755/16618/41, no. 482(R), Ingram to Eden, 7 September 1937; Bargoni, *L'impegno navale*, pp. 317–42; Sullivan, "Fascist Italy's Military Involvement," p. 717.

43. PRO, FO 371/21358, W 16254/23/41, Ingram to Eden, 27 August 1937; PRO, FO 371/21359, W 16654/23/41, Sargent to Eden, 2 September 1937, W 16606/23/41, CP 208(37), 2 September 1937; PRO, ADM 116/3917, M 04776/37, Admiralty to C-in-C, Home, and C-in-C, Mediterranean, 2 September 1937.

44. SHM, 1BB2, 203, N 127 EMG 0, EMM to Campinchi, 7 September 1937; SHM, 1BB2, 110, N 821 EMG/3, Darlan note, 7 September 1937; SHM, 1BB2, 203, N 822 EMG/3, L'Appli-

cation des mesures internationales envisagées pour assurer la sécurité de la navigation en Méditerranée, 7 September 1937; Darlan to Ratyé, 21 September 1937 in *Lettres et notes de l'Amiral Darlan,* no. 27, p. 70; SHM, 1BB2, 204, Protection de la navigation commerciale et surveillance des eaux territoriales françaises en Méditerranée, EMM to Esteva, 20 October 1937; Sabatier de Lachadenede, *La marine française,* pp. 139–49.

45. PRO, ADM 116/3917, M 05077/37, no. 147/549/37, Bevan to Perth, 10 September 1937; Sabatier de Lachadenede, *La marine française,* pp. 133–81; Darlan, *Lettres et notes,* nos. 26, 27, pp. 68–70.

46. PRO, ADM 116/3917, M 04776/37, Admiralty to C-in-C, Home, and C-in-C, Mediterranean, 2 September 1937; PRO, FO 371/21404, W 16802/16618/41, CP 211(37), 6 September 1937; PRO, CAB 23/88, Cab. 34(37), Cabinet meeting, 8 September 1937.

47. MAE, PA-AP, Massigli, 99, Massigli to Léger, 13 September 1397; MAE, P-40, Léger, 12, Corbin to Léger, 17 September 1937; SHM, 1BB2, 204/1, Les Minutes de la conférence de Nyon, 10–11 September 1937; SHM, 1BB2, 204/1, L'Accord de Nyon, 13 September 1937; USMM, 3309, Ciano to Eden and Delbos, 17 September 1937; PRO, FO 371/21406, W 17645/16618/41, no. 540(R), Ingram to Eden, 19 September 1937; Ciano, *Diario,* 13, 21 September 1937, pp. 36, 39.

48. Ciano, *Diario,* 19 September 1937, p. 38; ASD, AG, UC, 53/2, Ciano to Grandi, 18 September 1937; PRO, FO 371/21168, R 6763/69/22, Perth to Eden, 8 October 1937; Pedriali, *Guerra di Spagna,* pp. 70–92, 327–44; Preston, *Franco,* pp. 208–93; Frank, "Naval Operations," p. 46; Sullivan, "Fascist Italy's Military Involvement," p. 722.

49. Bottai, *Diario,* 4 September 1937, 31 October 1937, pp. 119–20; Ciano, *Diario,* 29 September 1937, 27, 29 October 1937, 20 November 1937, 31 January 1938, pp. 40–91.

50. Kershaw, *Hitler,* 2:47–50; Wright and Stafford, "Hitler, Britain, and the Hoßbach Memorandum," pp. 82–95.

51. ASD, AG, UC, 53/1, Ciano to Mussolini, 20 October 1937; ASD, AG, UC, 84/2, Ciano to Mussolini, 22 October 1937; ACS, SPD-CR, 32/15, Proposta per il 170a riunione del Gran Consiglio del Fascismo, Mussolini, 11 December 1937; Mussolini, *Opera Omnia,* 29: 32–34; Ciano, *L'Europa,* pp. 212–25; Ciano, *Diario,* 27 August 1937, 7 October 1937, 1, 22, 28 November 1937, 1, 11, 27 December 1937, pp. 29–74.

52. Ciano, *Diario,* 14 September 1937, 2 November 1937, 1, 12, 19 December 1937, 3 February 1938, pp. 37–93; Arisi Rota, *La diplomazia,* pp. 136–40.

53. USMM, 2688, 5, N 1876 R.P.: Progetti operativi, Piani di Operazioni, Cavagnari to Badoglio, 18 November 1937; USE, I-4, 2/1, Verbale della seduta presieduta da S.E. il Capo di Stato Maggiore Generale, 2 December 1937; USE, H-6, 14, P.R. 12: Direttive generali, Pariani, 1 January 1938; USE, H-6, 14/2, P.R. 12: Teatro d'operazioni del Mediterraneo, Ufficio operazioni II, MMG, 1 January 1938; USE, H-6, 14/4, P.R. 12: Teatro d'operazioni dell'Africa settentrionale, Ufficio operazioni II, MMG, 1 January 1938.

54. Crouy-Chanel, *Léger;* Leeds, *These Rule France,* p. 342; May, *Strange Victory,* pp. 146–47.

55. PRO, FO 371/21175, R 6460/200/22, Phipps to Eden, 29 September 1937; PRO, FO 954/8, Phipps to Eden, 30 September 1937; CAC, PHPP 1/19, Phipps to Eden, 10 October 1937; PRO, FO 371/21162, R 7531/1/22, Phipps to Eden, 1 November 1937, Vansittart minute, 6 November 1937; PRO, FO 371/20736, C 8234/270/18, Anglo-French conversations in London, 29–30 November 1937.

56. DDF, 2/6, no. 465, pp. 814–17; DDF, 2/7, nos. 54, 61, 88, 138, pp. 102–231.

57. PRO, FO 371/20736, C 8234/270/18, Anglo-French conversations in London, 29–30 November 1937; DDF, 2/7, no. 287, pp. 518–45; MAE, Eur 30–40, Italie, 272, N 83, Cosme to Delbos, 28 December 1937; SHM, 1BB2, 185, 17/3, No. 2 EMG. 2: Compte-Rendu de Renseignements, 6 January 1938; MAE, Eur 30–40, Italie, 272, Crémieux to Massigli, 8 January 1938.

58. DDF, 2/7, no. 287, pp. 518–45; PRO, FO 371/20736, C 8234/270/18, Anglo-French conversations in London, 29–30 November 1937; Dreifort, *Yvon Delbos,* pp. 95–150.

59. Decoux, *Adieu Marine,* pp. 337–38; Coutau-Bégarie and Huan, *Darlan,* pp. 23–34, 116–19; Hood, *Royal Republicans,* pp. 156–57.

60. SHM, 1BB2, 208/12, Darlan note, 12 November 1937; SHAT, 2N 24, Campinchi to Daladier, 24 November 1937; SHM, 1BB2, 208/11, Darlan note, November 1937; SHAT, 2N 24, Campinchi to Daladier, 24 November 1937; Salerno, "The French Navy and the Appeasement of Italy," pp. 73–80.

61. FRUS, 1937 3:153, Léger to Hull, 13 July 1937; Dreifort, *Myopic Grandeur,* pp. 105–94.

62. SHAT, 1K, 224, 9, Gamelin note, Projets pour la séance prochaine, 9 November 1937; SHAT, 2N, 24, Gamelin to Daladier, Réponse aux questions concernant la situation en Méditerranée, 28 November 1937; SHAT, 2N, 24, Procès-verbal du séance de la CPDN, 8 December 1937; DDF, 2/7, no. 325, pp. 633–44.

63. Le Goyet, *Mystère Gamelin,* pp. 227–28; Alexander, *Republic in Danger;* Gamelin, *Servir,* 2:445; Jordan, *Popular Front,* p. 53; May, *Strange Victory,* pp. 127–33.

64. Gamelin, *Servir,* 2: 89–92; Alexander, *Republic in Danger,* pp. 97–99; Réau, *Daladier,* pp. 15–174; Simon, *J'accuse,* p. 150; May, *Strange Victory,* pp. 113–17; Parker, *Chamberlain,* p. 142.

65. SHAT, 2N 24, Procès-verbal du séance de la CPDN, 8 December 1937; DDF, 2/7, no. 325, pp. 633–44; SHAT, 2N 24, Daladier memorandum, 22 December 1937; SHAA, 2B 104, N 2720/3–OS/EMAA, 27 December 1937; Young, "French Military Intelligence," p. 150.

66. SHAA, 2B 104, N 2658/3–OS/EMAA: Plan de Renseignements, Deuxième Bureau to Vuillemin, 15 December 1937; SHAA, 2B 104, N 2720/3–OS/EMAA: Instruction personelle et secréte destinée aux généraux commandants d'armée aérienne, 27 December 1937; Young, "French Military Intelligence," p. 150.

67. NMM, CHT 4/1, Chatfield to Backhouse, 8 October 1937; PRO, CAB 23/89, Cab. 37(37)5, Cabinet meeting, 13 October 1937.

68. PRO, FO 371/21162, R 7531/1/22, Phipps to Eden, 1 November 1937, Vansittart minute, 6 November 1937; PRO, PREM 1/210, Eden to Chamberlain, 3 November 1937; PRO, CAB 21/588, Hankey to Inskip, 2 November 1937; PRO, CAB 21/588, Hankey to Vansittart, 3 November 1937 (original emphasis).

69. PRO, FO 371/20961, F 11201/9/10, Lindsay to Eden, 17 December 1937; BUL, AP 13/1/60/E, Eden to Duff Cooper, 17 December 1937.

70. NMM, CHT 4/10, Pound to Chatfield, 22 December 1937, Chatfield to Pound, 30 December 1937, Pound to Chatfield, 7 February 1938, Chatfield to Inskip, 25 January 1938; PRO, CAB 53/36, COS 680, 4 February 1938; PRO, FO 371/22106, F 407/84/10, Lindsay to Cadogan, Cadogan, Chatfield, and Chamberlain minutes, 10 January 1938; BUL, AP 13/1/49/V, Chamberlain to Eden, 7 January 1938; PRO, FO 954/13, Cadogan to Eden, 12 January 1938.

71. PRO, CAB 53/37, COS 691, 21 February 1938; Gibbs, *Grand Strategy,* 1: 419–20.

72. PRO, PREM 1/276, Eden to Chamberlain, 1 January 1938; BUL, AP 13/1/49/Y, Eden to Chamberlain, 9 January 1938; PRO, FO 371/22418, R 343/43/22, no. 24, Phipps to Eden, 12 January 1938; PRO, FO 371/22403, R 1194/23/22, Information suggesting the possibility of aggressive action by Italy against Britain in the spring of 1938, 20 January 1938; PRO, WO 190/596, Conversation with Delbos in Geneva, 28 January 1938; PRO, FO 371/21593, C 608/36/17, no. 62, Phipps to Eden, 28 January 1938.

73. PRO, FO 371/22418, R343/43/22, Strang minute, 13 January 1938; PRO, CAB 21/579, Combined Plan for the Defence of Egypt, 18 January 1938; PRO, CAB 53/36, COS 686, 14 February 1938; PRO, CAB 53/37, COS 691, 21 February 1938; PRO, CAB 21/580, Hore-Belisha to Inskip, 24 February 1938, no. 115, Halifax to Lampson, 7 March 1938; NMM, CHT 4/8, Chatfield to Little, 11 November 1937; BUL, AP 13/1/49/Z, Chamberlain to Eden, 13 January 1938.

74. PRO, ADM 167/100, Admiralty Board minutes, 3 February 1938; PRO, CAB 24/274, CP 24(38), 8 February 1938; Gibbs, *Grand Strategy,* 1:292–93.

75. PRO, PREM 1/276, Eden to Chamberlain, 31 January 1938; PRO, CAB 23/92, Cab. 5(38), Cabinet meeting, 16 February 1938; PRO, CAB 24/275, CP 42(38), Duff Cooper memorandum, 18 February 1938; PRO, CAB 23/92, Cab. 9(38), Cabinet meeting, 23 February 1938.

Chapter 2

1. PRO, FO 371/22311, R 1414/137/3, Perth to Eden, 16 February 1938; PRO, FO 371/22403, R 1615/23/22, no. 74, Perth to Eden, 17 February 1938, R 1610/23/22, no. 236, Halifax to Perth, 21 February 1938; PRO, CAB 21/579, Vansittart to Eden, 16 February 1938; PRO, PREM 1/276, Eden to Chamberlain, 17 February 1938.

2. May, *Strange Victory,* p. 177; Roberts, *Holy Fox*; Parker, *Chamberlain,* p. 142; Réau, *Daladier,* p. 222; PRO, CAB 23/92, Cab. 11(38), Cabinet meeting, 9 March 1938.

3. ASD, AG, UC, 3/2, minutes of meeting held at Palazzo Venezia, 6 November 1937; Ciano, *Diario,* 6, 24 November 1937, pp. 54, 61.

4. Ciano, *Diario,* 13, 16 February 1938, 11 March 1938, pp. 98–111; ASD, AG, UC, 4, 2, Ciano to Grandi, 18 February 1938; ASD, AG, GM, 26, Ciano to Mussolini, 12 March 1938; PRO, FO 371/22314, R 2369/137/3, no. 74, Phipps to Halifax, 11 March 1938; PRO, FO 371/22315, R 2434/137/3, no. 138, Perth to Halifax, 12 March 1938, R 2484/137/3, no. 143, Perth to Halifax, 13 March 1938.

5. ASD, AG, UC, 87/2, Hitler to Mussolini, 11 March 1938; Ciano, *Diario,* 12 March 1938, p. 111–12; ACS, SPD-CR, 32, 16, Gran Consiglio del Fascismo, 12 March 1938.

6. Ciano, *Diario,* 8 January 1938, pp. 85–86; Sullivan, "The Italian-Ethiopian War, October 1935–November 1941: Causes, Conduct, and Consequences," in Ion and Errington, *Great Powers and Little Wars,* pp. 189–91.

7. Ciano, *Diario,* 24, 29 January 1938, 26 February 1938, 1, 4, 20 March 1938, pp. 89–115; ASD, AG, UC, 46/3, Mussolini to Franco, 2 February 1938, Franco to Mussolini, 16 February 1938; Pedriali, *Guerra di Spagna,* pp. 351–60; Sullivan, "Fascist Italy's Military Involvement," p. 723; Preston, *Franco,* p. 302; Coverdale, *Italian Intervention,* pp. 347–54.

8. Ciano, *Diario,* 13, 15, 26 March 1938, 7, 30 April 1938, 19 May 1938, pp. 112–38; USMM, 2728, 1, Ufficio di Stato Maggiore note, Rapporto di fine primo periodo addestrativo della Regia Marina, 31 May 1938.

9. Journal Officiel de la République française, DPAN, 25–26 February 1938; FRUS, 1938/1, Bullitt to Hull, 21 February 1938, pp. 24–27; DGFP, D/1, nos. 133, 346, pp. 233, 569–70; Dreifort, *Yvon Delbos,* pp. 184–90.

10. SHAT, 2N, 25, Procès-verbal du séance de la CPDN, 15 March 1938; CAC, PHPP 1/20, Phipps to Halifax, 26 March 1938; PRO, FO 371/22338, R 3035/162/12, no. 205, Fraser to Phipps, 16 March 1938.

11. Quoted in Micaud, *The French Right,* pp. 156–58.

12. AN, Daladier Papers, 496AP, 8, Dr5, Daladier note, Situation de la Tchecoslovaquie, April 1938.

13. SHAT, 2N, 227, 3, N 29 EMG-SE, Bertrand to Daladier, 14 February 1938; SHM, 1BB2, 185, 17/1, N 216 EMG-SE, Section d'Études Générales note, 1 March 1938; SHAA, 2B, 104, N 0990 3/EMA, Gamelin note, Memo sur la Conduite de la Guerre sur Terre, 7 March 1938; Gamelin, *Servir,* 2: 315, 3: 11; SHAA, Z, 12949, 1, Vuillemin to La Chambre, 15 January 1938; SHAT, 2N, 25, Procès-verbal du séance de la CPDN, 15 March 1938; SHAT 5N, 579, 6, Section de Défense Nationale, La question tchécoslovaque, 15 March 1938.

14. SHAT, 5N, 579, 3, Buisson note, L'alliance France-Italie, 13 March 1938; MAE, P-40, Daladier, 1, N 1,777/S, Gamelin to Daladier, 16 March 1938; MAE, P-40, Daladier, 1, Gamelin note N 1082, 14 March 1938 (original emphasis).

15. SHM, 1BB2, 94, 2e Bureau Bulletin d'Études N 51, Le Potentiel de guerre de l'Italie, 1 March 1938; MAE, Eur 30–40, Italie, 281, N 34 EMG-SE, Bourrague to Charveriat, 3 March 1938.

16. MAE, Eur 30–40, 272, N 133, Blondel to Paul-Boncour, 20 March 1938; MAE, Eur 30–40, 272, Corbin to Paul-Boncour, 21 March 1938; MAE, Eur 30–40, Italie, 272, N 949–53, Paul-Boncour to Corbin, 22 March 1938.

17. SHAT, 2N, 225, 1DN3, réunion des Chefs d'EMG, 17 March 1938; SHM, 1BB2, 130, N 305 EMG.3, Darlan to C-in-Cs, 26 March 1938.

18. SHM, 1BB2, 208, 12/13, Darlan note, Composition et puissance de la flotte, 4 Decem-

ber 1937; SHM, 1BB2, 220, 3/4, Situation actuelle, 1 January 1938; SHM, 1BB2, 208, 11, Darlan note, 7 January 1938; SHM, 1BB2, 210, 1, Bertrand note, 5 February 1938; SHM, 1BB2, 220, 1/2, Comparison des tonnages en service, 15 Febuary 1938.

19. PRO, CAB 23/92, Cab. 12(38), Cabinet meeting, 12 March 1938; PRO, CAB 27/623, FP(36) 25th meeting, 15 March 1938; BUL, NC 18/1/1041, Neville to Hilda, 13 March 1938.

20. PRO, CAB 53/36, COS 697, 16 March 1938; PRO, CAB 53/37, COS 698 (Revise), 28 March 1938; PRO, CAB 27/623, FP(36) 27th meeting, 21 March 1938; PRO, CAB23/93, Cab. 15(38), Cabinet meeting, 22 March 1938.

21. PRO, FO 800/269, Cadogan to Henderson, 22 April 1938; *Dictionary of National Biography 1961–1970*, pp. 164–66.

22. TCL, RA Butler Papers, F79/4, minutes of a meeting, 13 March 1938.

23. PRO, FO 371/22315, R 2493/137/3, No. 147, Perth to Halifax, 13 March 1938; PRO, FO 371/22418, R 2988/43/22, No. 179, Phipps to Halifax, 20 March 1938; PRO, PREM 1/276, Vansittart note, 19 February 1938; Cadogan, *Diaries*, pp. 62–66; PRO, FO 371/22315, R 2434/137/3, No. 138, Sargent minute, 14 March 1938.

24. Ciano, *Diario*, 22 December 1937, 1 January 1938, 1, 13 February 1938, pp. 71–98; ASD, AP-GB, 24/2, Ciano to Mussolini, 3 January 1938.

25. ASD, AG, UC, 89/1, N. 1023/466, Grandi to Ciano, 19 February 1938; Ciano, *Diario*, 7, 9, 15 February 1938, pp. 95–99; Nello, *Un fedele disubbidiente*, pp. 22–195; Sullivan, "From Little Brother to Senior Partner," in Alexander, *Knowing Your Friends*, pp. 86–87.

26. ASD, AG, UC, 46/2, Attolico to Ciano, 11 January 1938; ASD, AG, UC, 4/1, Ciano to Attolico, 8 February 1938; ASD, AP-GB, 25/1, N 168R/40, Ciano to Attolico, 22 February 1938, Ciano to Mussolini, 22 February 1938; ASD, AG, UC, 4/2, Ciano to Attolico, 17 March 1938; Ciano, *Diario*, 3 January 1938, 16, 17 February 1938, pp. 82–100.

27. ASD, AG, UC, 4/2, Attolico to Ciano, 4 March 1938; ASD, AG, UC, 84/2, Ciano to Mussolini, 8 March 1938; ASD, AG, GM, 26, Ciano to Mussolini, 12 March 1938; ACS, MAG-1938, 69, Germania, N 2015/S, Presentazione al Maresciallo Göring, Liotta to Valle, 6 April 1938.

28. PRO, FO 371/22618, W 8006/11/41, Admiralty note, 21 May 1938; PRO, CAB 2/7, CID 326th meeting, 2 June 1938; PRO, CAB 2/7, CID 331st meeting, 27 July 1938; PRO, FO 371/22425, R 3634/194/22, no. 112, Hoare to Halifax, 25 March 1938; TCL, RAB, F79/33–34, Butler note, May 1938.

29. PRO, CAB 21/562, no. 14/6/9: Anglo-Italian conversations, Perth to Halifax, 26 April 1938.

30. CAC, PHPP, 3, 2, Duff Cooper to Phipps, 20 April 1938; PRO, CAB 27/627, FP(36)55, Halifax memorandum: Anglo-Italian Conversations, 11 March 1938.

31. MAE, Eur 30–40, Italie, 308, N 939, Corbin to Paul-Boncour, 7 April 1938; SHAT, 2N, 227, 3, Les Conversations franco-britanniques, 29 April 1938; PRO, AIR 9/78, C 3687/G, Visit of French Ministers to London, 29 April 1938; DDF, 2/9, no. 258, pp. 561–88; DBFP, 3/1, no. 164, pp. 198–234.

32. Cadogan, *Diaries*, pp. 71–74.

33. SHAT, 2N, 227, 2, N. 237/DN.3, Gamelin note, 4 April 1938; MAE, P-40, Daladier, 1, N. 286/DN.3, Gamelin note, 24 April 1938; SHM, 1BB2, 210, 5, N. 405/EMG.3, Darlan note, 21 April 1938; SHAT, 2N, 224, 1, N. 250/DN.3, Accords d'États-Majors, Daladier to Paul-Boncour, 8 April 1938, N. 89, Accords d'États-Majors, Bonnet to Daladier, 25 April 1938.

34. PRO, CAB 2/7, CID 309th meeting, 10 February 1938, CID 310th meeting, 17 February 1938, CID 319th meeting, 11 April 1938.

35. PRO, CAB 24/276, CP 109(38), Halifax note, 3 May 1938; Cadogan, *Diaries*, 29 April 1938, p. 73; Reussner, *Les Conversations franco-britanniques*, pp. 195–202.

36. PRO, ADM 116/3379, PD 06792/38, Danckwerts memo, 6 May 1938, PD 06888/38, Danckwerts memo, 17 June 1938.

37. PRO, CAB 53/38, COS 727, 20 May 1938; PRO, CAB 23/93, Cab. 26(38), Cabinet meeting, 25 May 1938; PRO, ADM 116/3379, PD 06849/38, Danckwerts to Holland, 1 June 1938.

38. SHM, 1BB7, 42, N 65/P, La Position britannique en Méditerranée Orientale, du Tour to EMM, 26 May 1938; SHAT, 2N, 227, 2, N 93 EMG-SE, Darlan to Gamelin, 30 May 1938; PRO, ADM 116/3379, N 3/38, Holland to Phipps, 10 June 1938.

39. Bois, *Truth on the Tragedy*, p. 61; Boothe, *Europe in the Spring*, pp. 102–3; May, *Strange Victory*, p. 160.

40. DDF, 2/9, no. 183, pp. 378–79; ACS, MMG-AS, 68, 12, N 3698, Badoglio to Cavagnari, 27 April 1938; USE, H-6, 13, D/2, Ufficio Operazioni I, Sezione 2/a note, Il problema operativo alla frontiera nord in seguito all'Anschluss, 25 April 1938; Ciano, *Diario*, 16–24 April 1938, pp. 126–30.

41. Noël, *Illusions de Stresa*, pp. 123–24; PRO, FO 371/22426, R 4132/240/22, Phipps to Halifax, 21 April 1938; ASD, AG, UC, 61, De Peppo to Ciano, 29 April 1938; ASD, AG, UC, 61, Blondel to Ciano, 3 May 1938; Ciano, *Diario*, 10 April 1938, 5, 12, 17, 20 May 1938, pp. 124–39; PRO, FO 371/22426, R 4781/240/22, Perth to Halifax, 12 May 1938, minutes by Roberts, Nichols, and Cadogan.

42. Mussolini, *Opera Omnia*, 29: 99–102; Ciano, *Diario*, 14, 19, 30 May 1938, 3 June 1938, pp. 136–46.

43. PRO, FO 371/22438, R 4893/899/22, no. 457, Perth to Halifax, 17 May 1938, R 4947/899/22, no. 461, Perth to Halifax, 18 May 1938; ASD, AG, UC, 84/2, Ciano to Mussolini, 18 May 1938; ASD, AG, UC, 89/2, Ciano to Mussolini, 21 May 1938; ASD, AP-GB, 24/2, Ciano to Mussolini, 22 May 1938.

44. MAE, Eur 30–40, Italie, 319, Bonnet to Corbin, 19 May 1938, Bonnet to Corbin, 24 May 1938; MAE, Eur 30–40, Italie, 338, N. 242, Blondel to Bonnet, 30 May 1938; DDF, 2/9, nos. 351, 369, 373, pp. 746–87.

45. Ciano, *Diario*, 30 May 1938, 2 June 1938, pp. 143, 145; ASD, AG, UC, 84/2, Ciano to Mussolini, 3 June 1938; MAE, Eur 30–40, Italie, 319, Blondel to Bonnet, 2 June 1938; PRO, FO 371/22426, R5293/240/22, Phipps to Halifax, 3 June 1938; MAE, Eur 30–40, Italie, 273, N 335, Charles-Roux to Bonnet, 13 July 1938; MAE, Eur 30–40, Italie, 308, N 263, Blondel to Bonnet, 10 June 1938; MAE, PA-AP, Massigli, 92, Blondel to Massigli, 5 July 1938.

46. SHAT, 2N, 224, 1, N 287/DN.3, CSDN note, L'Importance stratégique de l'Espagne, 24 April 1938; AN, 74AP, 17, Stocks de Guerre de Combustibles Liquides, 4 April 1938; AN, 496AP, 34, Dr5, Darlan note, La Situation actuelle de la flotte française, 25 April 1938; SHAT, 2N, 273, 4, Centres des Hautes Études, Étude de stratégie combinée, 25 April 1938.

47. SHAT, 5N, 583, 2, N 160/DN, Daladier to Gamelin, 11 June 1938, Défense de la Corse, Darlan to Gamelin, 12 July 1938; SHAT, 5N, 583, 4, N 551/DN.3, Daladier to Campinchi, 15 July 1938; Frankenstein, *Le Prix du réarmement*, pp. 169, 187–90, 303–13.

48. CAC, PHPP 1/20, Phipps to Halifax, 30 June 1938, Phipps to Halifax, 1 July 1938, Phipps to Halifax, 16 July 1938.

49. MAE, P-40, Cabinet Bonnet, 9, Massigli note, La France et la Grande-Bretagne à l'égard de l'Italie, 5 June 1938; MAE, Eur 30–40, Italie, 319, Bonnet to Corbin, 20 June 1938; PRO, FO 371/22427, R 5392/240/22, Halifax to Perth and Phipps, 14 June 1938; PRO, CAB 23/94, Cab. 29(38), Cabinet meeting, 22 June 1938; MAE, Eur 30–40, Italie, 319, N 1647–53, Corbin to Bonnet, 7 July 1938; Girault, "The Impact of the Economic Situation on the Foreign Policy of France," in Mommsen and Kettenacker, *The Fascist Challenge*, pp. 209–26.

50. Ciano, *Diario*, 5, 9 May 1938, pp. 133–34; Domarus, *Hitler*, 1: 860–1; Kershaw, *Hitler*, 2:99.

51. ASD, AP-GB, 31, 2, Giorgis to SIS, 18 February 1938; ASD, RD-L, 1031, N 212, Flessibilità del programma di riarmo britannico, Calderara to SIM, 15 March 1938; ASD, AP-GB, 31, 2, N. 1542/698, Crolla to Ciano, 18 March 1938; ACS, MMG-AS, 64, Inghilterra, N. 3483, Ciano to SIS, 14 April 1938; ACS, MMG-AS, 60, Inghilterra, N. 272, Conversazioni navali fra l'Inghilterra e gli Stati Uniti, Brivonesi to MMG, 1 February 1938; Ciano, *Diario*, 1, 12, 25 December 1937, 3, 9, 14 February 1938, pp. 64–98.

52. ACS, MMG-AS, 221, Riunione presso il Duce, 20 May 1938; Ciano, *Diario*, 26 May 1938, pp. 141–42; ADAP, D/2, nos. 151, 221, pp. 209–85; Casali and Cattaruzza, *Sotto i mari*, pp. 191–97; Schreiber, *Revisionismus und Weltmachtstreben*, pp. 136–39.

53. Ciano, *Diario*, 8, 17, 19 March 1938, 5, 20, 24 May 1938, pp. 110–41.

54. USE, H-6, 12, N 21/89, Situazione strategica italiana, Ronco to MGG, 21 June 1938.

55. USMM, 2703, 3, Dir. Gen. Armi and Armamenti Navali to Cavagnari, 15 February 1938; USMM, 2695, 5, Situazione delle Unità in costruzione ed allestimento, Falangola to Cavagnari, 16 February 1938, 10 May 1938.

56. Ciano, *Diario*, 6 February 1938, p. 95; USMM, 2703, 3, B 4087, Finanziamento del programma navale 1938, Cavagnari to Thaon di Revel, 1 April 1938.

57. USMM, 3272, 1, N 45 G.5/6, Margottini to MMG, 19 January 1938; ACS, MAG-1938, 68, Inghilterra, N 600449, Ciano to SIS, SIM, and SIA, 25 January 1938; ASD, AP-F, 38, 2, Guariglia to Ciano, 5 February 1938; USMM, 2746, 2, Brivonesi note, 20 March 1938.

58. ACS, MMG-AS, 60, Germania, N 905, Pecori-Giraldi to MMG, 20 July 1938; Ciano, *Diario*, 27 June 1938, p. 152; Schreiber, *Revisionismus und Weltmachtstreben*, pp. 136–39.

59. USMM, 3276, 6, N 871, Margottini to MMG, 4 July 1938; USMM, 2712, 3, B 11620, Oliva to MMG, 13 August 1938.

60. Ciano, *Diario*, 24 June 1938, 1, 5, 17 July 1938, pp. 152–59.

61. PRO, FO 371/21702, C 3594/541/18, Industrial Intelligence Centre report, 25 March 1938; Basch, *The Danube Basin*; Pratt, *East of Malta*, pp. 138–39.

62. PRO, FO 1011/192, Lloyd to Loraine, 14 April 1938; PRO, FO 1011/193, Loraine to Nicolson, 25 August 1938.

63. PRO, CAB 24/276, CP 112(38), 7 May 1938; PRO, CAB 23/93, Cab. 23(38), Cabinet meeting, 11 May 1938.

64. PRO, CAB 27/623, FP(36) 26th meeting, 18 March 1938; PRO, CAB 24/277, CP 127(38), 24 May 1938; BUL, NC 18/1/1054, Neville to Ida, 28 May 1938; PRO, CAB 27/623, FP(36) 30th meeting, 1 June 1938; BUL, NC 18/1/1056, Neville to Ida, 18 June 1938.

65. SHM, 1BB2, 185, 17/3, N 2/EMG.2, Compte-Rendu de Renseignements, 6 January 1938, Huntziger note, Note relative aux accords militaires à établir avec la Turquie, 19 February 1938, N 179, Lahalle to EMM, 15 July 1938.

66. ACS, MMG-AS, 66, Turchia, Materiale navale alla Turchia, 28 March 1938; ASD, RD-L, 1059, 6, N 4074/1761, Rapporti politico economici fra la Gran Bretagna e gli stati Danubian e Balcanici, Crolla to Ciano, 5 August 1938; ASD, RD-L, 1059, 6, N 7492/4241, Attività economica Francia-Gran Bretagna nel Bacino danubiano, Prunas to Ciano, 17 August 1938; Ciano, *Diario*, 23, 24 June 1938, 17, 18 July 1938, 24 August 1938, pp. 151–68.

67. USE, H-9, 2, 3, N 1002, Promemoria, Pariani to Mussolini, 14 July 1938; Ciano, *Diario*, 27 March 1938, p. 118; PRO, CAB 21/560, no. 668, Halifax to Phipps, 2 April 1938.

68. PRO, CAB 21/595, Note of a conference held at the Colonial Office, 7 September 1938; PRO, CAB 21/580, CID paper no. 1444–B, 13 July 1938; PRO, CAB 2/7, CID 329th meeting, 19 July 1938; PRO, CAB 21/580, no. 478, Halifax to Lampson, 30 September 1938.

69. Mussolini, *Opera Omnia*, 29: 144–47; Ciano, *Diario*, 10, 30 July 1938, 8 August 1938, 18 September 1938, pp. 156–80.

70. ACS, MMG-AS, 64, Germani, Materiale della guerra alla Germania, 25 August 1938; ASD, AG, UC, 5, Ciano to Attolico, 30 August 1938; Ciano, *Diario*, 19 August 1938, 2, 8, 17 September 1938, pp. 166–79.

71. ACS, MMG-AS, 189, 17, Cavagnari to Mussolini, 26 August 1938; ACS, MMG-AS, 70, 8/B, B 13933, Cavagnari to Valle, 28 September 1938; USMM, 2760, 1/3, N 635 G.I/I, Margottini to MMG, 21 September 1938; ASD, RD-L, 103, Brivonesi to Grandi, 30 September 1938; ASD, De Felice, Grandi, 54/142, N 4672, Grandi to Ciano, 10 September 1938; USMM, 2760, 1/3, N 757, Prasca to SIM, 20 September 1938.

72. ASD, AP-I, 55, N 6281/1852, Attolico to Ciano, 1 September 1938; USE, H-9, 2, 2, N 1430, Marras to MGG, 27 August 1938; Ciano, *Diario*, 30 August 1938, 26–28 September 1938, pp. 170–86.

73. PRO, FO 371/22617, W 6078/11/41, no. 1543/10, Pound to Admiralty, 10 May 1938, W 6078/11/41, no. 1414/11, C-in-C Home to Pound, 11 May 1938, W 6303/11/41, Cox to Mounsey, 16 May 1938; PRO, ADM 199/853, no. 1230/26, Admiralty to Pound, 26 May 1938, no. 1235/26, Admiralty to Pound, 26 May 1938, no. 0123/27, Pound to Admiralty, 27 May 1938, no. 2130/2, Admiralty to Pound, 2 June 1938; PRO, FO 371/22618, W 8006/11/41, M 02959/38, Seal to Mounsey, 21 May 1938, W 8392/11/41, Carter to Roberts, 24 May 1938, W 9051/11/41, M 02959/38, Jarrett to Roberts, 20 June 1938, Cadogan minutes 27, 28 June 1938.

74. PRO, ADM 1/9543, no. 1848, Pound to Admiralty, 23 August 1938, no. 1450, Admiralty to Pound, 27 August 1938; PRO, ADM 199/853, no. 2203/31, Pound to Admiralty, 31 August 1938, no. 1652/31, Admiralty to Pound, 31 August 1938, no. 0048/1, Pound to Ad-

miralty, 1 September 1938, no. 1848/31, Pound to Admiralty, 1 September 1938, no. 1950/14, Admiralty to Pound, 14 September 1938, no. 1114.19, Pound to Admiralty, 19 September 1938, no. 1345/19, Admiralty to Pound, 19 September 1938, no. 1816/20, Pound to Admiralty, 20 September 1938.

75. PRO, CAB 24/276, CP 92(38), 8 April 1938, CP 104(38), 28 April 1938; PRO, PREM 1/346, Hopkins minute, 28 April 1938; PRO, T 172/2111, Simon to Duff Cooper, 9 May 1938; PRO, ADM 167/101, Duff Cooper to Simon, 27 May 1938; PRO, PREM 1/346, Simon to Chamberlain, 24 June 1938.

76. PRO, CAB 24/278, CP 170(38), 12 July 1938; PRO, CAB 23/94, Cab. 33(38), Cabinet meeting, 20 July 1938, Cab. 35(38), Cabinet meeting, July 1938; PRO, T 172/2111, Simon to Duff Cooper, 26 July 1938.

77. PRO, FO 371/22427, R 5565/240/22, no. 580 (123/95/38), Perth to Halifax, 11 June 1938; PRO, FO 371/22438, R 5876/899/22, Ingram note, 4 July 1938; PRO, FO 371/22413, R 6557/23/22, Nichols minute, 26 July 1938.

78. PRO, CAB 21/544, Ismay memorandum, 20 September 1938; PRO, FO 371/22438, R 7762/899/22, Newall to Halifax, 23 September 1938.

79. PRO, FO 371/22438, R7253/899/22, no. 785, Charles to Halifax, 24 August 1938; PRO, FO 800/318, Halifax memorandum, 5 September 1938; BOD, MS. Simon 10, fols. 1–23, 29 September 1938.

80. PRO, ADM 205/3, Pound to Chatfield, 11 October 1938.

81. DDF, 2/10, nos. 238, 500, pp. 437–38, 877–80; MAE, Eur 30–40, Italie, 273, N 1336, Blondel to Bonnet, 17 August 1938; MAE, Eur 30–40, Italie, 308, N 386, Blondel to Bonnet, 19 August 1938.

82. MAE, PA-AP, Massigli, 93, Charles-Roux to Massigli, 14 August 1938; MAE, P40, Cabinet Bonnet, 9, Charles-Roux to Massigli, 20 August 1938.

83. Massigli, *La Turquie,* pp. 17–21; De Monzie, *Ci-devant,* p. 54; Réau, *Daladier,* p. 151; Crouy-Chanel, *Léger,* pp. 118–9, 149; May, *Strange Victory,* p. 151; MAE, P40, Cabinet Bonnet, 9, Charles-Roux to Bonnet, 26 August 1938.

84. SHAT, 5N, 583, 2, N 1524 30S/EMAA, Plan d'équipment de la Corse, Vuillemin to Gamelin, 21 July 1938, N 623/DN.3, Plan d'équipment de la Corse, Gamelin to Daladier, 24 August 1938; DDF, 2/10, no. 458, pp. 819–21.

85. SHM, 1BB2, 182, N 625/DN.3, Plan d'ensemble de défense des colonies, Gamelin to Darlan, 24 August 1938, N 124 EMG-SE, Plan d'ensemble de défense des colonies, Darlan to Gamelin, 1 September 1938; SHAT, 5N, 579, 1bis, N 833/DN.3, Réunion des Chef d'EMG, 28 September 1938.

86. Masson, *La Marine française,* p. 24.

87. SHM, 1BB2, 84, EMG2/R, N 574/EMG 2–R, Un renseignement sur l'attitude éventuelle de l'Italie en cas de conflit, De Villaine to Gamelin, 12 September 1938, N 880/EMG 2–R, Note de Renseignement: État d'esprit en Italie et la mentalité de Mussolini, Glotin to De Villaine, 14 September 1938; SHM, 1BB2, 172, N 43 EMG-SE, La crise de septembre 1938, 31 March 1939; Coutau-Bégarie and Huan, *Darlan,* p. 153.

88. SHM, 1BB2, 208, 14, Darlan note, Note au sujet de la politique française de défense nationale, 26 September 1938; MAE, Eur 30–40, Gran Bretagna, 259, N 2369–71, Corbin to Bonnet, 14 September 1938.

Chapter 3

1. Raphaël-Leygues, *Chronique,* pp. 118–19; Bullitt, *For the President,* 6 February 1939, p. 310; Réau, *Daladier,* p. 285; Crouy-Chanel, *Léger,* p. 235; Young, *In Command,* p. 215; May, *Strange Victory,* p. 168. Jean-Paul Sartre's version of Daladier's reaction to the Bourget crowds claims that Daladier commented not "These people are fools" but "These assholes [*cons*]!" See his *Les Chemins,* 2: 1132–3.

2. PRO, FO 371/21612, C 12161/1050/17, no. 675, Phipps to Halifax, 12 October 1938;

DDF, 2/12, nos. 164, 197, 216, pp. 275–378.

3. Bérard, *Un Ambassadeur,* 1: pp. 106, 392; Massigli, *La Turquie,* pp. 17–9; De Monzie, *Ci-devant,* pp. 53–55; Davignon, *Souvenirs,* p. 13; May, *Strange Victory,* p. 151; Shorrock, *From Ally to Enemy,* pp. 237–41.

4. Ciano, *Diario,* 5, 8, 29 November 1938, 13 January, 1939 3 March 1939, pp. 208–60; Guariglia, *Ricordi,* p. 357.

5. ASD, AG, GM, 27, 1, Ciano to Mussolini, 9 November 1938; ASD, AP-F, 33, 2, Ciano to Mussolini, 2 December 1938; Ciano, *Diario,* 9, 29 November, 1938 2 December 1938, 22 February 1939, pp. 210–55; Ciano, *L'Europa,* pp. 380–87; DDF, 2/12, nos. 288, 318, 330, 379, 433, 434, pp. 509–846.

6. PRO, CAB 23/95, Cab. 47(38), Cabinet meeting, 30 September 1938; CAC, HNKY, 4, 30, Chamberlain to Hankey, 2 October 1938; BUL, NC 18/1/1072, Neville to Hilda, 15 October 1938, NC 18/1/1075, Neville to Hilda, 6 November 1938.

7. PRO, CAB 23/95, Cab. 48(38), Cabinet meeting, 3 October 1938; PRO, CAB 24/279, CP 234(38), 21 October 1938; PRO, CAB 27/648, D(38), Committee on Defence Programs and Their Acceleration second meeting, 28 October 1938; PRO, CAB 27/648, D(38), Committee on Defence Programs and their Acceleration third meeting, 31 October 1938; PRO, CAB 24/280, CP 247(38), 3 November 1938.

8. PRO, FO 371/21659, C 14471/42/18, Strang memoranda, 24 November 1938, Collier memorandum, 29 October 1938, Cadogan to Halifax, 15 October 1938; PRO, FO 800/311, Halifax to Phipps, 1 November 1938. Imlay, "How to Win a War," chap. 4, has shown that the FO endorsed a "Defence of the West" policy.

9. PRO, CAB 23/96, Cab. 51(38), Cabinet meeting, 31 October 1938, Cab. 53(38), Cabinet meeting, 7 November 1938.

10. PRO, CAB 23/96, Cab. 50(38), Cabinet meeting, 26 October 1938; PRO, FO 800/311, Halifax to Phipps, 1 November 1938. Parliament ratified the Easter Accords on 1 November, and they came into effect on 16 November.

11. Ciano, *Diario,* 27–30 September 1938, pp. 185–89; ASD, AG, UC, 89, 2, N 6895, Attolico to Ciano, 4 October 1938.

12. ACS, SPD-CR, 32, 16, Gran Consiglio del Fascismo, Dichiarazione sulla Razza, 26 October 1938; Ciano, *Diario,* 6 October 1938, p. 193; Bottai, *Diario,* 6–8 October 1938, pp. 136–37; *Le leggi e i decreti reali,* 1938, p. 1261; Anfuso, *Dal Palazzo Venezia,* pp. 84–86.

13. Salewski, *Die deutsche Seekriegsleitung,* 3:28–63; Schreiber, "Die Rolle Frankreichs im strategischen und operativen," pp. 208–12; Schreiber, *Revisionismus und Weltmachtstreben,* pp. 139–43; quote in Schreiber, "Italy and the Mediterranean," in Hattendorf, ed., *Naval Strategy and Policy in the Mediterranean,* p. 123.

14. ASD, AG, UC, 53, 1, meeting at Palazzo Vecchia attended by Mussolini, Ciano, and Ribbentrop, 28 October 1938; Ciano, *Diario,* 28–29 October 1938, 12, 23 November 1938, pp. 203–15; Ciano, *L'Europa,* pp. 373–78.

15. Ciano, *Diario,* 3 October–3 November 1938, pp. 191–207 (quotes 15, 28 October, pp. 197, 203); ASD, AG, GM, 27, 1, Ciano to Mussolini, 23 October 1938.

16. Sullivan, "The Italian-Ethiopian War," pp. 191–92; Del Boca, *Gli italiani,* 3: pp. 307–37; Sbacchi, *Ethiopia under Mussolini,* pp. 55–70; Cavallero, *Il dramma,* pp. 62–8.

17. Rovighi and Stefani, *La partecipazione italiana,* pp. 185–401; Sullivan, "Fascist Italy's Military Involvement," p. 710.

18. BUL, NC 18/1/1076, Neville to Ida, 13 November 1938; PRO, FO 371/21658, C12816/42/18, Ogilvie-Forbes to Halifax, 21 October 1938; PRO, FO 371/21783, C11616/11169/18, Vansittart note, 11 October 1938; PRO, CAB 27/624, FP(36) 32d meeting, 14 November 1938; PRO, FO 371/21600, C14025/55/17, Phipps to Halifax, 16 November 1938; PRO, FO 371/21592, C12637/55/17, Sargent minute, 16 November 1938.

19. BUL, NC 18/1/1075, Neville to Hilda, 6 November 1938; PRO, CAB 27/624, FP(36) 33d meeting, 21 November 1938.

20. MAE, P-40, Cabinet Bonnet, 9, Séance entre Bonnet, Daladier, Chamberlain et Halifax à Paris, 24 November 1938; AN, 496AP, 11, Dr3, sdrb, Conversations Franco-Britanniques, 24 November 1938; PRO, FO 371/21592, C14652/13/17, Visit of British Ministers to Paris, 26

November 1938; DBFP, 3/3, no. 325, pp. 285–311; DDF, 2/12; no. 418, p. 821; BUL, NC 18/1/1071, Neville to Ida, 9 October 1938.

21. ASD, AG, UC, 53, 1, meeting at Palazzo Vecchia attended by Mussolini, Ciano, and Ribbentrop, 28 October 1938; ASD, AG, UC, 6, 1, N 7895/2365, Attolico to Ciano, 15 November 1938; Ciano, *Diario*, 6 October 1938, 7 November 1938, pp. 193, 209.

22. ASD, AG, UC, 85, 1, N 9161, Ciano to Grandi, 14 November 1938; ACS, De Bono diary, notebook 43, 2 December 1938; Ciano, *Diario*, 5, 8, 30 November 1938, 2 December 1938, pp. 208–20.

23. ACS, De Bono diary, notebook 43, 30 November 1938; MAE, P-40, Rochat, 23, Ciano to François-Poncet, 17 December 1938; ASD, AP-F, 33, 2, Ciano to François-Poncet, 17 December 1938; Ciano, *Diario*, 24 October 1938, 16, 26, 30 November 1938, 17 December 1938, pp. 200–225.

24. MAE, P-40, Daladier, 2, N 3688–99, Bonnet to Corbin, 27 December 1938; MAE, P-40, Hoppenot, 4, Bonnet to Corbin, 1 January 1939; PRO, FO 371/23791, R 153/7/22, Ingram to Phipps, 5 January 1939.

25. PRO, CAB 23/96, Cab. 57(38), Cabinet meeting, 30 November 1938; BUL, NC 18/1/1075, Neville to Hilda, 6 November 1938.

26. AN, 496AP, 12, Dr2, sdrb, N 1145–51, François-Poncet to Ciano, 25 December 1938; SHM, 1BB2, 207, 1, N 1119 EMG3, Darlan to Chef de la 4ème region, 26 November 1938; SHM, 1BB2, 186, 1, N 20/DN.3, Gamelin to Daladier, 7 January 1939; Daladier, *Défense du pays*, 7 January 1939, pp. 128–32; PRO, FO 371/23791, R 223/7/22, Phipps to Halifax, 8 January 1939; DPAN, 26 January 1939.

27. PRO, FO 371/23791, R 192/7/22, Ingram minute, 4 January 1939; CAC, Vansittart, 2/38, Vansittart to Halifax, 13 December 1938, R 71/7/22, Perth to Halifax, 31 December 1938; PRO, FO 371/23796, R 9/9/22, Perth to Halifax, 27 December 1938.

28. PRO, T 188/157, Leith-Ross to Perth, 22 November 1938, Leith-Ross to Perth, 5 December 1938; PRO, CAB 53/10, COS 265th meeting, 21 December 1938; PRO, CAB 53/43, COS 814, 23 December 1938.

29. BUL, NC 18/1/1081, Neville to Ida, 8 January 1939.

30. ASD, AG, UC, 61, Ciano to Mussolini, 11 January 1939, Ciano to Mussolini, 12 January 1939; Ciano, *L'Europa*, pp. 395–404; PRO, FO 371/23784, R 434/1/22, CP 8(39), 19 January 1939.

31. BUL, NC 18/1/1082, Neville to Hilda, 15 January 1939, NC 18/1/1084, Neville to Hilda, 5 February 1939, NC 18/1/1085, Neville to Ida, 12 February 1939.

32. Ciano, *Diario*, 11, 12 January 1939, pp. 238–39.

33. USMM, 3273, 3, N 1474, Giraldi to MMG, 22 November 1938; ACS, MMG-AS, 73, Germania, N 1590, Giraldi to MMG, 16 December 1938; USMM, 3249, 5, Oliva note, Conversazioni navali italo-tedesche, 12 January 1939; ACS, MMG-AS, 73, Germania, N 1800, Movimenti navi Britanniche, Oliva to MMG, 5 February 1939.

34. USMM, 2386, 9, N 303/U.T., Oliva to Instituto centrale di statistica, 1 March 1939; *Il bilancio dello Stato*, pp. 257, 407; Minniti, "Il problema degli armamenti," pp. 42–45; Fioravanzo, *La marina italiana*, 21/1: 302–32.

35. *Dizionario Biografico degli Italiani*, 22: 564–70; ACS, MMG-AS, 180, Iscrizione al PNF, Cavagnari to Starace, October 1935.

36. DG 10/A2 cited in Gabriele, *Operazione C3*, pp. 221–26 (original emphasis).

37. Ciano, *Diario*, 14 February 1938, p. 98; USE, H-9, 3, Potenziamento militare della Libia, MGG to Mussolini, 1 January 1939.

38. ACS, MMG-AS, 72, Inghilterra, N 135, Costruzioni navalie nel 1938, Brivonesi to SIS, 11 January 1939; USMM, 3249, 5, Oliva note, Conversazioni navali italo-tedesche, 12 January 1939; ASD, RD-F, 288, 4, N 343/155, Manovre navali francesi nell'Atlantico, Guariglia to Ciano, 14 January 1939; Ciano, *Diario*, 14 January 1939, p. 240; ASD, RD-F, 288, 4, N 31, Manovre navali francesi nell'Atlantico, Margottini to SIS, 16 January 1939; USE, I-4, 6, 3, Gandin to Badoglio, 20 January 1939.

39. Pieri and Rochat, *Badoglio;* Sullivan, "From Little Brother to Senior Partner," pp. 97–103.

40. USE, *Verbali delle riunioni,* 1: 1–8.

41. ACS, MMG-AS, 118, 17, N 23249, Personale fanalista dell'Egeo, SMM to SIS, 14 October 1938, N B16107, Segnalamenti delle isole italiani dell'Egeo, Cavagnari to Ciano, 17 November 1938; USMM, 3279, 15, N 600385/C, Rapporti militari turco-greco, MdAE to SIM, SIS, SIA, 21 January 1939; ACS, MMG-AS, 118, 17, N B710, Segnalamenti delle isole italiani dell'Egeo, Cavagnari to Ciano, 21 January 1939.

42. ACS, MMG-AS, 73, Francia, N 54, Margottini to SIS, 25 January 1939; USMM, 3276, 6, Bollettino segreto verde N 1052, SIM to SIS, 17 February 1939; ASD, RD-F, 288, 4, N 601010, MdAE to SIM, SIS and SIA, 22 February 1939; ASD, RD-L, 1077, 3, MdAE to SIM, SIS, and SIA, 14 March 1939.

43. USMM, 3266, 2, Situazione delle flotte inglese e tedesca, 4 February 1939; ACS, MMG-AS, 73, Germania, N 358, Conversazione avuta con S. E. Raeder, Pecori-Giraldi to MMG, 23 February 1939.

44. NARA, T821, 145, 000211–12, Ambrosio minute, undated (accompanying correspondence indicates that Ambrosio spoke to Mussolini on 27 January 1939); USE, I-4, 6, 13, N 4212, Preparazione bellica Libia occidentale, Badoglio to Mussolini, 2 March 1939; Ciano, *Diario,* 5, 11, 15 January 1939, 5, 19 February 1939, pp. 235–54.

45. SHAA, 2B, 104, N 141 EMGAA/s, Vuillemin to Gamelin, 25 October 1938; SHAT, 5N, 579, 17, N 74/s, Bührer to Gamelin, 19 October 1938.

46. SHM, 1BB2, 182, 1/A, N 145 EMG-SE, Défense des Colonies, Darlan to Gamelin, 14 October 1938; SHM, 1BB2, 210, 5, N 146 EMG-SE, Darlan to Gamelin, 17 October 1938; SHM, 1BB2, 208, 12, Section d'Études note: Des conditions de la guerre dans la situation internationale présente, 12 November 1938; SHM, 1BB2, 115, N 1120 EMG.3, Darlan to Commanders-in-Chief, 26 November 1938; SHM, 1BB2, 128, N 1122 EMG.3/OP and N 1123 EMG.3/OP, Darlan to Commanders-in-Chief, 26 November 1938.

47. SHAT, 2N, 224, 1, N 853/DN.3, Gamelin note, Note sur la situation actuelle, 12 October 1938; SHAT, 5N, 579, 1, Colson note, Note sur la situation actuelle, 26 October 1938; SHAT, 2N, 224, 1, N 935/DN.3, Gamelin to Daladier, 26 October 1938.

48. Imlay, "How to Win a War," chap. 3; Greene, *Crisis and Decline,* pp. 225–51; Ageron, *France coloniale ou parti colonial?* pp. 250–67.

49. Parti républicain radical et radical-socialiste, *35e Congrès du Parti républicain radical et radical-socialiste,* 1938, pp. 368–89.

50. MAE, P-40, Daladier, 2, Aubert note, Politique extérieure de la France après Munich, 21 October 1938, Aubert note, Politique extérieure de la France, 16 November 1938.

51. SHAT, 5N, 579, 1, Gamelin note, Note sur les programmes dans le domaine terrrestre, 26 October 1938; SHM, 1BB2, 208, 1, N 151 EMG-SE, Darlan to Gamelin, 4 November 1938; SHAT, 2N, 25, 3, Réunion avec M. Jacomet, 25 November 1938; SHAT, 2N, 25, 3, Procès-vebal de la séance du CPDN, 5 December 1938; SHM, 1BB2, 208, 13, Darlan note, 3 December 1938; AN, 74AP, 17, Conversation Hoppenot avec M. Paul Reynaud, 30 November 1938.

52. MAE, P-40, Daladier, 3, Daladier note, Aide à demander la Grande-Bretagne dans le cas où nous aurions à faire face à une coalition germano-italienne, 1 January 1939.

53. SHAT, 2N, 25, 3, Procès-verbal du séance de la CPDN, 5 December 1938.

54. SHM, 1BB2, 182, 1/A 14, N 12 EM/Col., Bührer to Gamelin, 10 January 1939; SHM, 1BB2, 186, 1, N 20/DN.3, Gamelin to Daladier, 7 January 1939; SHM, 1BB2, 182, 1/A 14, N 70 DN.3, Gamelin to Darlan, 18 January 1939; MAE, P-40, Hoppenot, 3, N 71/DN.3, Gamelin to Daladier, 18 January 1939; SHAT, 5N, 583, 5, N 142/DN.3, Défense de la côte des Somalis, Gamelin to Daladier, 27 January 1939.

55. SHAT, 2N, 227, 3, N 1265 EMG.3, Darlan to Gamelin, 29 December 1938; SHM, 1BB2, 185, 18, Section d'Etudes note: Les états du Levant sous mandat, 1 January 1939; SHM, 1BB2, 182, 1/A 14, N 32 EMG.3, Défense de la côte française des Somalis, Darlan to Gamelin, 11 January 1939, N 14 EMG-SE, Défense des colonies, Darlan to Gamelin, 25 January 1939.

56. SHAT, 2N, 225, 1DN3, Réunion des Chefs d'EMG, 11 January 1939.

57. SHM, 1BB2, 94, Bulletin d'études no. 56, Lahalle note, Les théâfatres des opérations de la méditerranée orientale, December 1938; SHM, 1BB2, 208, Section d'Etudes note: L'An-

gleterre et la France peuvent-elles soutenir un conflit contre l'Allemagne et l'Italie? 24 January 1939.

58. AN, 496AP, 12, Dr2, sdrb, EMA-2ème bureau, Note sur les effectifs en Libye et en Tunisie, 16 February 1939; SHAT, 5N, 579, 3, Note sur la situation des forces italiennes en Libye et sur celle des forces franco-britanniques en Tunisie et en Egypte, 22 February 1939; SHAT, 7N, 2524, SAE, 2ème Bureau note, Italie, 27 February 1939.

59. SHAT, 5N, 579, 1bis, N 338/DN.3, Réunion des Chefs d'EMG, 17 February 1939, N 0655, Gamelin to Noguès, 18 February 1939; SHAT, 5N, 579, 3, Analyse du procès-verbal de la réunion des Chefs d'EMG, 27 February 1939; SHAT, 2N, 25, 3, Procès-verbal du séance de la CPDN, 24 February 1939; SHM, 1BB2, 208, Note manuscrite, 26 February 1939; SHAT, 2N, 224, 1, N 457/DN.3, Daladier note, Note sur les questions espagnoles, 11 March 1939; SHM, TTA, 13, N 279 EMG-3, Défense de la Corse, Darlan to Daladier, 9 March 1939, N 299 EMG-3, Défense de la Corse, Darlan to Ollive, 11 March 1939.

60. SHAT, 2N, 228, 1, État-Major Général de la Marine, Note sur la collaboration Franco-Britannique, 2 March 1939; SHAT, 5N, 579, 2, N 424/DN.3, Gamelin to Daladier, 6 March 1939 (original emphasis); SHAT, 5N, 579, 2, N 225/DN, 9 March 1939.

61. *Dictionary of National Biography 1931–1940,* pp. 26–27; PRO, ADM 205/3, Backhouse to Pound, 11 October 1938, Backhouse to Noble, 14 November 1938, Backhouse to Stanhope, 24 March 1939; Manuscript Diaries of the late Field Marshal Lord Ironside (Copyright-The Lord Ironside), 7 October 1938.

62. OPC presumably stood for "Offensive Planning Committee." CAC, Drax, 2, 10, Backhouse to Drax, 15 October 1938; PRO, ADM 205/3, Backhouse to Drax, 18 October 1938.

63. Cunningham, *Sailor's Odyssey,* p. 195.

64. CAC, Drax, 2, 8, Possible Offensive Action, 14 September 1938, Notes on War Plans, 21 October 1938.

65. PRO, ADM 116/3900, M 07145/38, Strategical Aspect of the Situation in the Mediterranean, Pound to Admiralty, 14 November 1938; PRO, FO 371/21592, C 14653/13/17, Bridges to Cadogan, 25 November 1938; PRO, CAB 53/10, COS 265th meeting, 21 December 1938; CAC, Drax, 2, 19, Mediterranean Strategy, 25 January 1939; CAC, Drax, 2, 11, Major Problems for CNS and other COS, 7 February 1939.

66. PRO, CAB 53/10, COS 261st meeting, 10 November 1938; PRO, FO 371/21592, C 14287/13/17, COS 795, 18 November 1938, C 14613/13/17, COS 799, 21 November 1938, C 14653/13/17, Bridges to Cadogan, 25 November 1938.

67. PRO, CAB 23/96, Cab. 56(38), Cabinet meeting, 22 November 1938; PRO, FO 371/21593, C 15682/13/17, 12 December 1938; AN, 496AP, 11, Dr3, sdrb, Conversations franco-britanniques, 22–24 November 1938; MAE, P-40, Cabinet Bonnet, 9, Seance entre Bonnet, Daladier, Chamberlain, et Halifax, 24 November 1938; PRO, FO 371/21592, C 14652/13/17, Visit of British Ministers to Paris, 26 November 1938.

68. PRO, CAB 21/510, The role of the army in light of the Czechoslovakia crisis, October 1938; PRO, AIR 8/235, The situation of the bomber force in relation to the principle of parity, 2 November 1938; PRO, CAB 53/42, COS 799, 21 November 1938; PRO, CAB 3/8, Hore-Belisha note, CID 1498–B, 13 December 1938; PRO, CAB 53/43, COS 811, 19 December 1938; PRO, CAB 53/10, COS 256th meeting, 21 December 1938; PRO, CAB 53/43, COS 825, 16 January 1939.

69. PRO, ADM 205/3, Backhouse to Meyrick, 9 January 1939; PRO, CAB 53/44, COS 830, 25 January 1939; PRO, CAB 23/97, Cab. 3(39), Cabinet meeting, 1 February 1939; PRO, CAB 24/282, CP 23(39), 27 January 1939; PRO, CAB 27/624, FP(36) 36th meeting, 26 January 1939.

70. PRO, CAB 53/44, Draft European Appreciation, 1939–40, 26 January 1939; PRO, CAB 53/45, COS 843, 20 February 1939.

71. CAC, Drax, 2, 19, Notes on Foreign Office Letter of 12 January, 20 January 1939, Drax to Pound, 24 January 1939, Mediterranean Strategy, 25 January 1939; CAC, Drax, 2, 11, Major Strategy, 1 February 1939; CAC, Drax, 2, 9, OPC 10, 3 March 1939; CAC, Drax, 2, 11, Mediterranean and East Indies Forces, 12 March 1939; PRO, ADM 1/9897, M 02268/39, OPC 13, 16 March 1939.

72. PRO, CAB 16/209, SAC 4, 28 February 1939; PRO, ADM 1/9900, PD 07516/39, Backhouse to Cunningham and Danckwerts, 2 March 1939.

73. PRO, FO 371/23981, W 3784/108/50, Nicholls minute, 1 March 1939, Strang minute, 2 March 1939, Fitzmaurice minute, 8 March 1939, Howe minute, 8 March 1939, W 4683/108/50, Vansittart minute, 16 March 1939.

74. PRO, FO 371/23544, F 1338/471/61, Fitzmaurice memo, 27 January 1939; PRO, FO 371/23816, R 1213/399/22, Noble minute, 20 February 1939; PRO, FO 371/23793, R 1379/7/22, Noble, Ingram, Cadogan, and Halifax minutes, 22 February 1939.

75. PRO, CAB 16/209, SAC 1st meeting, 1 March 1939, SAC 2d meeting, 13 March 1939.

76. PRO, ADM 1/9897, M02969/39, Naval Situation in the Far East in the Event of War with Germany, Italy, and Japan simultaneously, 22 March 1939; PRO, CAB 55/15, JP 382, 27 March 1939; PRO, CAB 53/10, COS 284th meeting, 27 March 1939.

77. AN, 496AP, 11, Dr2, sdra, Hoppenot note, Revendications italiennes, 5 December 1938; MAE, P-40, Rochat, 23, Visées italiennes sur la Tunisia, Rochat to Bonnet, 9 December 1938.

78. MAE, Eur 30–40, Italie, 309, N 3565–77, François-Poncet to Bonnet, 3 December 1938, N 566, François-Poncet to Bonnet, 3 December 1938; MAE, P-40, Daladier, 2, N 3688–99, Bonnet to Corbin, 27 December 1938.

79. Baudouin, "Un voyage à Rome," pp. 69–74; Ciano, *Diario*, 28 January 1939, p. 244; MAE, P-40, Cabinet Bonnet, 9, Bonnet note, Note concernant le voyage de Baudouin à Rome, 28 February 1939; Bonnet, *Fin d'une Europe*, 2: 69.

80. MAE, P-40, Cabinet Bonnet, 9, Baudouin to Bonnet, 3 February 1939; Ciano, *Diario*, 2 and 3 February 1939, pp. 246–47; Bonnet, *Le Quai d'Orsay*, pp. 249–50.

81. Ciano, *Diario*, 6 February 1939, pp. 248–49; Noël, *Illusions de Stresa*, pp. 139–40; Baudouin, "Un voyage à Rome," p. 80; PRO, FO 371/23793, R 1243/7/22, Perth to Halifax, 21 February 1939.

82. Ciano, *Diario*, 5 February 1939, p. 248; AN, 496AP, 12, Dr2, sdrd, N 593, François-Poncet to Bonnet, 16 February 1939.

83. Ciano, *Diario*, 13, 16, 19, 22, 27 October 1938, 14, 24 November 1938, 3, 6, 19–20 December 1938, 8, 15, 17 January 1939, 6, 7 February 1939, 9 March 1939, pp. 195–262.

84. Ciano, *L'Europa*, p. 393; Ciano, *Diario*, 19, 23 February 1939, pp. 254–56.

85. NARA, T586, 405, 000039–46, Mussolini, Relazione per il Gran Consiglio, 5 February 1939; Ciano, *Diario*, 4 February 1939, p. 248.

86. ASD, AG, UC, 85, 1, Ciano to Ribbentrop, 2 January 1939; Ciano, *Diario*, 1 January 1939, 8, 13 February 1939, 5, 8, 10, 11, 13 March 1939, pp. 233–63; Ciano, *L'Europa*, pp. 392–94.

Chapter 4

1. Cadogan *Diaries*, 20, 28 March 1939, pp. 161–64.

2. PRO, FO 371/23794, R 2012/7/22, Perth to Halifax, 20 March 1939; FO 371/23784, R 1852/1/22, Campbell to Halifax, 20 March 1939; FO 371/23794, R 2163/7/22, Phipps to Halifax, 30 March 1939; FO 1011/205, Phipps to Loraine, 6 April 1939; FO 371/23794, R 1939/7/22, Jebb to Cadogan, 21 March 1939, Cadogan minute, 22 March 1939; FO 371/22967, C 3858/15/18, Chamberlain to Mussolini, 20 March 1939; BUL, NC 18/1/1091, Neville to Ida, 26 March 1939.

3. PRO, FO 371/23560, F 2885/456/23, Craigie to Halifax, 23 March 1939; PRO, ADM 1/9909, M 02397/39, Danckwerts minute, 22 March 1939, Cunningham minute, 23 March 1939, Backhouse minute, 24 March 1939; PRO, FO 371/23982, W 5721/108/50, Memorandum on Seapower, Churchill to Halifax, Chamberlain, and Chatfield, 25 March 1939; NMM, CHT 6/4, Chatfield to Chamberlain, 29 March 1939.

4. Cadogan *Diaries*, 22 April 1939, p. 176 (original emphasis); PRO, FO 371/23981, W 4831/108/50, Nichols minute, 15 March 1939, Cadogan and Halifax minutes 16 March 1939.

5. PRO, FO 371/22967, C 3859/15/18, Notes of a meeting of ministers held at 10 Downing Street, 19 March 1939; PRO, FO 371/23560, F 2879/456/23, Halifax to Lindsay, 19 March 1939; PRO, FO 371/23560, F 2942/456/23, Lindsay to Halifax, 24 March 1939, F

2963/456/23, Halifax to Lindsay, 24 March 1939; FRUS, 1939/1, Kennedy to Hull, 22 March 1939, p. 88; LC, Leahy Diary, 2/229, 11–14 April 1939.

6. PRO, PREM 1/309, Chamberlain to Lyons, 20 March 1939.

7. Zay, *Carnets secrets,* 17 March 1939, p. 46; Béguec, "L'Evolution de la politique gouvernementale et les problèmes institutionnels," in Rémond and Bourdin, *Édouard Daladier,* pp. 55–74; Jacomet, *L'Armement,* p. 213; Frankenstein, *Le Prix du réarmement,* pp. 209–17.

8. AN, 496AP, 11, Dr4, sdrb, Note sur la situation crée par la disparition de la Tchécoslovaquie, 2ème Bureau to Daladier, 16 March 1939; SHAT, 7N, 2293, 10, Gamelin to Daladier, 17 March 1939; SHAT, 1N, 43, 4, Gamelin to Daladier, N I509/s, 18 March 1939; MAE, P40, Charveriat, 2, N 251, Didelet to Gamelin, 16 March 1939.

9. AN, 74AP, 17, Reynaud to Daladier, 24 March 1939; AN, 496AP, 11, Dr4, sdrd, Reynaud to Daladier, 24 March 1939; SHM, 1BB2, 220, 4, Les Constructions navales, 21 March 1939; SHM, 1BB2, 222, 5, Crédits supplémentaires en 1939, 28 March 1939; SHM, 1BB2, 222, 5/5, Décret-lois, 28 March 1939; SHM, 1BB2, 220, 3/4, Tranche de Remplacement 1940, 3 April 1939; SHAA, 1B, 5, 2/2, Procès-Verbal pour la réunion du Conseil Superieur de l'Air, 28 March 1939; SHAA, Z, 12934, 2, Tableau des Avions du Plan V modifié, 28 March 1939; SHM, 1BB2, 220, 3/4, Darlan note, Nécessité d'une nouvelle tranche, 4 April 1939; Frankenstein, *Le prix du réarmement,* pp. 209–13, 309.

10. Kaiser, *Economic Diplomacy,* p. 286; Jackson, "France and the Guarantee to Romania, April 1939," pp. 242–72; Imlay, "How to Win a War," chap. 5.

11. AN, 496AP, 13, Dr2, Bonnet to Coulondre, 5 April 1939; MAE, P40, Cabinet Bonnet, 16, La réponse de l'URSS aux propositions faites par M. Georges Bonnet à M. Souritz, April 1939.

12. MAE, Eur 30–40, 274, N 2074, François-Poncet to Bonnet, 19 March 1939; MAE, P40, Cabinet Bonnet, 9, Note de Monsieur Nac, Informateur, 29 March 1939; AN, 462AP, 23, Bonnet to François-Poncet, 30 March 1939; MAE, P-40, Cabinet Bonnet, 9, Bonnet note, 1 April 1939; DDF, 2/15, nos. 162, 166, 175, 193, pp. 224–71.

13. MAE, P-40, Daladier, 3, Inconvenients de negociations avec l'Italie, 26 March 1939; AN, 496AP, 12, Dr3, sdra, N 3513/42, Buti to le Marquis Capranica del Grillo, 27 March 1939; DDF, 2/15, no. 165, p. 293; Daladier, *Défense du pays,* pp. 171–75; SHAT, 5N, 579, 1, N 3.196, Daladier to Gamelin, 29 March 1939.

14. Ciano, *Diario,* 14–19 March 1939, pp. 264–69; NARA, T586, 25, 000043–44, Mussolini to Ciano, 16 March 1939.

15. HL, Phillips Diary, 55M-69, 19, 17 March 1939; Ciano, *Diario,* 15–17, 20 March 1939, p. 264–67; ASD, AG, UC, 90, 2, N 4753/23 P.R., Ciano to Jacomoni, 24 March 1939.

16. ASD, AG, UC, 85, 1, Ciano to Mussolini, 17 March 1939, Ciano to Mussolini, 20 March 1939, Ribbentrop to Ciano, 20 March 1939; Ciano, *Diario,* 17, 20, 21 March 1939, pp. 267–70; Ciano, *L'Europa,* pp. 418–22.

17. ASD, AG, UC, 85, 1, Ciano to Ribbentrop, 24 March 1939; PRO, FO 371/22967, C3858/15/18, Chamberlain to Mussolini, 20 March 1939; ASD, AG, UC, 53, 2, Mussolini to Chamberlain, 31 March 1939; ACS, SPD-CR, 32, 17, 184a riunione del Gran Consiglio del Fascismo, 21 March 1939; Ciano, *Diario,* 20, 21, 23, 26 March 1939, pp. 269–71; Mussolini, *Opera Omnia,* 29: 249–53.

18. USMM, 2764, 8, N 8891: Direttive per le spedizione in Albania, 1 April 1939; ASD, AG, UC, 90, 2, Mussolini to Jacomoni, 5 April 1939, N 5527 P.R., Jacomoni to Ciano, 6 April 1939; Ciano, *Diario,* 28 March–7 April 1939, pp. 273–81; NARA, T586, 449, 026903–07, Grandi to Mussolini, 7 April 1939.

19. DBFP, 3/5, nos. 97 and 101, pp. 145–47; DDF, 2/15, no. 332, pp. 537–38; PRO, CAB 53/11, COS 288th meeting, 9 April 1939; Ciano, *Diario,* 12 May 1939, pp. 296–97.

20. AN, 496AP, 11, Dr5, sdra, Procès-verbal des décisions prises au cours de la conférence tendue au Ministers de la Guerre, 9 April 1939; CAC, PHPP, 1, 22, Phipps to Halifax, 1 April 1939.

21. The same intelligence source had accurately predicted that German forces would enter Prague at 9:00 A.M. on 15 March 1939. SHAT, 2N, 225, CSDN, Réunion des Chefs d'EMG, 11 April 1939; SHAA, 2B, 104, N 932 3–OS/EMAA, Instruction particulière sur l'exécution des opérations aériennes initiales contre l'Italie, 14 April 1939; SHAT, 2N, 224, 1, N

707/DN.3, Gamelin to Daladier, 14 April 1939; SHAA, 2B, 104, N 1246 3–OS/EMAA, Vuillemin to Campinchi, 11 May 1939; PRO, FO 371/23740, R 2527/661/67, Phipps to Halifax, no. 156, 9 April 1939.

22. Cadogan *Diaries*, 7 April 1939, p. 170 (original emphasis); BUL, NC 18/1/1093, Neville to Ida, 9 April 1939; PRO, CAB 23/98, Cab. 19(39), Cabinet meeting, 10 April 1939.

23. PRO, CAB 23/98, Cab. 19(39), Cabinet meeting, 10 April 1939; PRO, CAB 27/624, 42d meeting, 11 April 1939; Cadogan, *Diaries*, 8–9, 22 April 1939, pp. 170–76.

24. PRO, CAB53/47, COS 873(JP): 1 April 1939; PRO, CAB 23/98, Cab. 20(39), Cabinet meeting, 13 April 1939.

25. PRO, CAB 23/98, Cab. 19(39), Cabinet meeting, 10 April 1939, Cab. 20(39), Cabinet meeting, 13 April 1939; BUL, NC 18/1/1094, Neville to Hilda, 15 April 1939; Cadogan, *Diaries*, 12–13 April 1939, p. 173.

26. PRO, CAB 55/15, COS 873, 1 April 1939; PRO, CAB 27/624, FPC 41st meeting, 10 April 1939; PRO, CAB 16/209, FO annex to SAC 6th meeting, 17 April 1939; PRO, CAB 27/624, FPC 43d meeting, 19 April 1939; BUL, NC 18/1/1099, Neville to Hilda, 14 May 1938; PRO, CAB 16/219, AD2, Loans and credits to other governments, 20 June 1939, AD28, Relative strategic importance of countries requiring arms from the United Kingdom, 5 July 1939.

27. Massigli, *La Turquie*, pp. 198–221; MAE, PA-AP, Massigli, 99, Lagarde to Massigli, 12 April 1939; SHM, 2BB7, L5, N 66, Lahalle to Marine, 27 April 1939; SHAT, 2N, 235, 5, EMA note, Note concernant une collaboration éventuelle avec la Turquie, 10 May 1939; SHAT, 5N, 579, 1, DF25, Note sur une éventuelle collaboration militaire avec la Turquie, 23 May 1939; SHAT, 5N, 579, 1bis, N 1335/DN.3, Réunion des Chefs d'EMG du 16 June 1939, Jamet to Daladier, 26 June 1939; SHAT, 7N, 2524, SAE, Suggestions pouvant être retenues pour l'établissement d'un accord militaire avec les Turcs, 7 July 1939; SHAT, 5N, 579, 11/11, EMA note, Propositions relatives à une cession symbolique à la Turquie, 21 July 1939; AN, 496AP, 11, Dr8, sdrb, Bonnet to Massigli, 8 August 1939.

28. AN, 496AP, 12, Dr3, sdrc, N 1559–60, François-Poncet to Bonnet, 15 April 1939; AN, 462AP, 23, François-Poncet to Bonnet, 19 April 1939, Bonnet to François-Poncet, 23 April 1939, François-Poncet to Bonnet, 27 April 1939; MAE, P-40, Cabinet Bonnet, 9, Bonnet note, 2 May 1939; AN, 462AP, 23, François-Poncet to Bonnet, 11 May 1939; DBFP, 3/5, nos. 194, 214, 226, 228, pp. 222–52.

29. PRO, CAB 23/98, Cab. 21(39), Cabinet meeting, 19 April 1939; PRO, FO 371/23794, R 3077/7/22, Halifax to Phipps, 20 April 1939; MAE, P-40, Léger, 12, Corbin to Léger, 9 May 1939; PRO, FO 371/23795, R 3166/7/22, Phipps to Halifax, 22 April 1939.

30. SHAT, 2N, 229, 1, Danckwerts to Lelong, 2 May 1939; PRO, ADM 116/3863, M00710/39, Section XVII of Naval War Memorandum (Eastern), Admiralty Plans Division, 5 May 1939; BUL, NC 18/1/1096, Neville to Hilda, 29 April 1939.

31. SHM, 1BB2, 183, 1, DF3: Aperçu Général d'une Action Offensive contre l'Italie, 31 March 1939; English translation appears in PRO, CAB 29/160, AFC(J)23.

32. PRO, AIR 9/104, AFC(J)5th Minutes, 31 March 1939.

33. PRO, CAB 29/160, AFC(J)15, 30 March 1939; SHM, TTA, 5, EMG/o, Resumé de la séance du 31 Mars 1939 après-midi à l'Amirauté, 31 March 1939; SHM, TTA, 5, EMG/o, Compte-rendu des conversations d'État-Major, Bourrague to Darlan, 4 April 1939; SHM, 1BB2, 183, 1, N. 56/S, Lelong to Gamelin, 5 April 1939.

34. PRO, CAB 53/46, COS 858, 8 March 1939; PRO, CAB 16/209, SAC 11, 3 April 1939, SAC 4th meeting, 6 April 1939; PRO, CAB 2/8, CID 355th meeting, 2 May 1939; PRO, CAB 2/9, CID 364th meeting, 6 July 1939; PRO, CAB 21/582, Newall to Gort, 31 July 1939.

35. PRO, CAB 16/209, SAC 4th meeting, 6 April 1939, SAC 17, 13 April 1939; PRO, CAB 53/11, COS 290th meeting, 19 April 1939; PRO, CAB 53/11, COS 309th meeting, 19 July 1939.

36. SHM, TTA, 5, EMG/o, N CL 8, Odend'hal to Daladier, 8 May 1939, Odend'hal to Daladier, 29 April 1939; PRO, AIR 9/104, AFC(J)11th Minutes, 25 April 1939.

37. SHM, TTA, 5, EMG/o, N CL 8, Odend'hal to Daladier, 8 May 1939; SHM, TTA, 5, EMG/o, Odend'hal to Daladier, 29 April 1939; PRO, AIR 9/104, AFC(J)11th Minutes, 25 April 1939; SHM, 1BB2, 183, 2, DF16: Note de la délégation française sur les conséquences d'une intervention Japonaise, 12 May 1939.

38. SHM, 1BB2, 220, 1/2, Comparison des tonnages en service, 15 February 1938; SHM, 1BB2, 220, 3/4, Balance des forces navales normalement stationnées en Méditerranéen, 15 February 1939.

39. ASD, AP-GB, 32, 1, N 2194/981, Provvedimenti di ordine militare adottati dalla Gran Bretagna, Grandi to Ciano, 2 May 1939; USMM, 3279, 17, N 214422/C, Concessione di Crete all'Inghilterra come base militare, Ciano to MMG, 13 May 1939; ACS, MMG-AS, 78, Turchia, Oliva to MMG, 14 April 1939; USMM, 3279, 15, Bollettino segreto verde N. 1113: Turchia, SIM to MMG, 3 May 1939; ASD, AP-GB, 35, 1, Loraine to Ciano, 8 June 1939; Ciano, *Diario,* 1, 3, 12, 18, 27–28 May 1939, 8 June 1939, pp. 292–308.

40. ASD, AP-I, 63, 2, N 09033/2191, Aspetti della situazione politica, Silimbani to Ciano, 18 April 1939; Ciano, *Diario,* 25–26, 30 April 1939, 10, 12, 31 May 1939, 14 June 1939, pp. 288–310; ASD, AP-F, 40, 1, N 4075/1801, Guaraglia to Ciano, 16 June 1939.

41. Ciano, *Diario,* 16, 20, 28 April 1939, pp. 285–90; USE, H-9, 3, 3, Germania e l'eventualità di operazioni contro la Polonia, MGG to Mussolini, 6 May 1939; ACS, MAG-1939, 81, Germania, N 2159/S, Situazione aeronautica tedesca, Liotta to MAG and SIA, 9 May 1939, Ilardi to MAG, 6 June 1939.

42. ASD, AG, UC, 4, 4, Marras promemoria, 5 April 1939; Montanari, *L'esercito italiano,* pp. 387–402; Toscano, "Le conversazioni militari italo-tedesche," pp. 344–65; Ceva, "Altre notizie sulle conversazioni militari italo-tedesche," pp. 151–82.

43. Ciano, *Diario,* 29 April 1939, 2 May 1939, pp. 290–92.

44. USMM, 2741, 9/1, Rapporto di missione a Berlino, Salza to Cavagnari, 24 April 1939; USMM, 3276, 8, N 777, Cooperazione navale franco-britannico e considerazioni sulla Gibilterra, Brivonesi to MMG and SIS, 20 May 1939.

45. ACS, MAG-1939, 81, Germania, Ilardi to MAG, 6 June 1939; USE, I-4, 6, 13, N 4494, Preparazione bellica Libia occidentale, Badoglio to Mussolini, 13 June 1939; USE, H-9, 6, 13, Promemoria sulla preparazione bellica della Libia occidentale, MGG to Mussolini, 16 June 1939.

46. ASD, AG, UC, 85, 1, Ciano to Mussolini, 7 May 1939; Ciano, *Diario,* 6–7, 21–23 May 1939, pp. 294–300; Ciano, *L'Europa,* pp. 428–34.

47. Mussolini, *Opera Omnia,* 29: 272–75; Ciano, *Diario,* 14, 17 May 1939, pp. 297–98; USE, H-9, 3, Memoria del Duce, Mussolini to Cavagnari, Valle, and Pariani, 27 May 1939.

48. USE, H-9, 3, Memoria del Duce, Mussolini to Cavagnari, Valle, and Pariani, 27 May 1939; Ciano, *Diario,* 24, 26–28 May 1939, pp. 300–303; Fioravanzo, *La marina italiana,* 21/1: 348–50.

49. AN, 496AP, 11, Dr5, sdre, untitled note, 5 May 1939; AN, 496AP, 13, Dr3, Extraits des notes personelles du Ministre des Affaires Etrangères, 26 May 1939; SHAT, 2N, 225, N 1001/DN3, Gamelin to Daladier, 15 May 1939; SHAT, 7N, 3439, 3, Conversations militaires franco-britanniques, 3 July 1939; MAE, P-40, Daladier, 3, Aubert note, Economique-politique-stratégie, 23 June 1939; AN, 496AP, 11, Dr6, sdrc, Daladier note, Pour l'entretien avec Doumenc, 29 July 1939.

50. SHAT, 2N, 229, 1, Note sur les conséquences possibles d'une attitude initiale de neutralité de la part de l'Italie, 9 May 1939; SHAT, 2N, 229, 1, N 937–DN.3, Gamelin to Darlan, N 938–DN.3, Gamelin to Vuillemin, 10 May 1939, N 1268 3.OS/EMAA, Vuillemin to Gamelin, 15 May 1939.

51. SHM, TTA, 14, Mai, N. 620 EMG-3, Darlan to Gamelin, 17 May 1939.

52. A similar argument appears in Murray, "The Role of Italy in British Strategy," pp. 43–49.

53. SHAT, 2N, 228, 3, DF23: Note sur les conséquences de la neutralité eventuelle de l'Italie, 20 May 1939.

54. PRO, CAB 53/11, COS 290th meeting, 19 April 1939; PRO, AIR 9/117, Notes on discussion with French General Staff at Rabat, 6 May 1939; SHAA, 2B, 107, IIIB, N 339/SA, Nogues to Gamelin and Daladier, 7 May 1939; PRO, ADM 1/9898, M05713/39, Report on the Anglo-French staff conference at Aden, 3 June 1939; SHM, TTA, 16, N 2–EM.Col, Compte-rendu de la conférence tendue à Aden, 22 June 1939.

55. PRO, ADM 116/3900, M04978/39, Pound to Stanhope, 10 May 1939.

56. BUL, NC 18/1/1096, Neville to Hilda, 29 April 1939, NC 18/1/1100, Neville to Ida, 21 May 1939; PRO, PREM 1/409, Soviet Objections to Anglo-French proposals of May 26th, Chamberlain minute, 6 June 1939; Imlay, "How to Win a War," chap. 6.

57. PRO, CAB 27/624, FPC 48th meeting, 19 May 1939; TCL, RAB, G10, 26–31, Butler note, 1 June 1939; MAE, P-40, Rochat, 18, Notes prises au cours de l'entretien franco-britannique entre Daladier, Bonnet, et Halifax, 20 May 1939; PRO, FO 371/23795, R 4278/7/22, 22 May 1939, R 4436/7/22, Loraine to Halifax, minutes by Noble, Cadogan, and Halifax, 23 May 1939; BUL, NC 18/1/1102, Neville to Ida, 10 June 1939; PRO, FO 1011/204, R 4308/399/22, Sargent to Loraine, 3 June 1939; DBFP, 3/5, nos. 570, 593, 638, 650, pp. 611–703.

58. SHM, 1BB2, 184, Balkans, Lahalle to Gaudin de Villaine, 19 May 1939.

59. MAE, PA-AP, Massigli, 104, Rapport du Général Weygand sur sa mission à Ankara, 20 May 1939; SHAT, 2N, 225, 1DN3, N 2242, Léger to Gamelin and Daladier, 25 May 1939; SHAT, 2N, 225, N 433/DN3, 3 June 1939; Weygand, "How France is Defended," pp. 473–77.

60. SHM, 1BB2, 210, 5, N 88 EMG-SE: Note sur l'intérêt d'une occupation préventive de Salonique, 2 June 1939; SHAT, 2N, 225, 1DN3, Réunion des Chefs d'EMG, 3 June 1939; SHAT, 5N, 579, 9, N 1141/DN.3, Gamelin to Daladier, 5 June 1939; SHAT, 2N, 229, 2, Indications données par le Général Gamelin au cours des conversations franco-britanniques, 13 July 1939; SHAT 2N, 235, 6, Gamelin to Daladier, 17 June 1939.

61. LC, Leahy Diary, 2/262, 12–14 June 1939; PRO, CAB 16/183A, COS 928, 18 June 1939; PRO, CAB 53/11, COS 303d meeting, 19 June 1939; PRO, CAB 27/625, FPC 52d meeting, 19 June 1939; Cadogan, *Diaries*, 16 June 1939, p. 188; PRO, CAB 53/11, COS 304th meeting, 20 June 1939; PRO, CAB 16/183A, COS 931, 24 June 1939.

62. PRO, CAB 2/8, CID 360th meeting, 22 June 1939; PRO, CAB 2/9, CID 362d meeting, 26 June 1939; PRO, ADM 205/1, 14/31/72, Record of a meeting in the Prime Minister's room at the House of Commons, 28 June 1939; Cadogan, *Diaries*, 20 June 1939, p. 189.

63. Ciano, *Diario*, 24 May 1939, 20 July 1939, 14 August 1939, pp. 300–328; ASD, AP-F, 40/1, N 4075/1801, Guariglia to Ciano, 16 June 1939; ASD, AG, UC, 8/1, N 4630/1391, Attolico to Ciano, 23 June 1939, N 4704/1419, Attolico to Ciano, 26 June 1939, N 5006, Attolico to Ciano, 7 July 1939, N 5657, Attolico to Ciano, 28 July 1938.

64. USMM, 2741, 9/1, Cavagnari to Raeder, 3 May 1939, N 751, Prossime conversazioni navali, Pecardi Giraldi to MMG, 9 May 1939, Raeder to Cavagnari, 17 May 1939, N G.1322, Löwisch to MMG, 27 May 1939, Schema di risposta alla letter dell'addetto navale germanico, 1 June 1939, B 7983, Scambio di comunicazioni con l'addetto navale tedesca à Roma relative alla materia da trattare nell'incontro di Friedrichshaven, Cavagnari to Ciano, 14 June 1939.

65. USMM, 2741, N 1011, Conversazioni navali del 20–21 giugno, Pecori Giraldi to MMG, 23 June 1939; ADAP, D/6, Appendix I, nos. 12–14, pp. 943–9; Schreiber, *Revisionismus und Weltmachtstreben*, pp. 163–81.

66. Cavagnari, "La Marina nella viglia e nel primo periodo della guerra," pp. 370–86; Fraccaroli, *Italian Warships*; Sadkovich, *The Italian Navy*, p. 32; Mallett, *The Italian Navy*, pp. 130–59; Giorgerini, *Da Matapan*.

67. ACS, MAG-1939, 80/Inghilterra, N 580A: Notiziario dell'addetto aeronautico à Londra, 4 July 1939; ASD, AP-GB, 32/1, N 3366/1509, Crolla to Ciano, 18 July 1939; ASD, AG, UC, 8/1, N 1/3335, Lais to Cavagnari, 22 July 1939; USMM, 2767, 1, N 5RP/AC, Cavagnari to Pecori Giraldi, 1 July 1939; USMM, 2741, 9/1, N 1093, Pecori Giraldi to MMG, SIS, 7 July 1939.

68. ACS, MMG-AS, 73/Francia, N 474, Margottini to Guariglia, 28 July 1939; USMM, 2767, 1, N 5RP/AC, Cavagnari to Pecori Giraldi, 1 July 1939.

69. USE, I-4, 5/1, Promemoria, Gandin to Badoglio, 12 July 1939; USMM, 2767, 1, Salza to Cavagnari, 9 July 1939; USMM, 2767, 1, Salza to Cavagnari, 26 July 1939; USMM, 2765, 11, B 8633, Piani operativi, Cavagnari to Teruzzi, 5 July 1939; USMM, 2767, 1, Osservazioni sulla manovra EN 17, Cavagnari to Mussolini, 31 July 1939 (original emphasis).

70. ASD, AG, UC, 8/1, N 22.22/A-4, Roatta to Attolico, 2 August 1939; Ciano, *Diario*, 6, 9, 10 August 1939, pp. 325–26.

71. ASD, AG, UC, 85/2, Colloquio col Ministro degli Esteri del Reich à Salisburgo, Ciano to Mussolini, 11 August 1939, Primo colloquio col Führer à Berchtesgaden, 12 August 1939,

Secondo colloquio col Führer à Berchtesgaden, 13 August 1939; Ciano, *Diario,* 11–13 August 1939, pp. 326–28; Ciano, *L'Europa,* pp. 449–59.

72. Ciano, *Diario,* 13 August 1939, pp. 327–28; USE, I-4, 6/13, N 4625, Badoglio to Valle, Cavagnari, and Pariani, 17 August 1939; ACS, AFI, Job 1, frames 000233–36, Badoglio to Mussolini, 22 August 1939, Mussolini to Badoglio, 23 August 1939; USE, I-4, 7/6, N 808779, Teruzzi to Badoglio, 24 August 1939; USE, H-6, 15/EJ, Memoria relativa piano operativo EJ, Ufficio Operazioni I/ Sezione 3 to Commando del Corpo di Stato Maggiore, 24 August 1939; USE, I-4, 7/5, N 4691, Badoglio to Valle, Cavagnari and Pariani, 29 August 1939.

73. ASD, AG, UC, 9/1, Note sulla conversazione con Ribbentrop, Attolico to Ciano, 18 August 1939; ASD, AP-GB, 33/2, Loraine to Ciano, 26 August 1939; Ciano, *Diario,* 24, 27 August 1939, pp. 333–36.

74. ASD, AG, UC, 87/2, Mussolini to Hitler, 26 August 1939; Ciano, *Diario,* 2 June 1939, 26, 27 August 1939, pp. 305–36; DDI, 8/13, Appendice I, pp. 400–401.

75. Kershaw, *Hitler,* 2:213–17; ASD, AG, UC, 87/2, Mussolini to Hitler, 25 August 1939, Hitler to Mussolini, 27 August 1939; ASD, AG, UC, 10/1, Mussolini to Hitler, 29 August 1939; Ciano, *Diario,* 29 August 1939, p. 337.

76. Manuscript diaries of the late Field Marshal Lord Ironside (Copyright—The Lord Ironside), 1939/3, 16 July 1939, permission to quote from 1939/2, 18 June 1939; PRO, CAB 47/6, ATB 176, Plan for Economic War against Germany, 18 July 1939 WO 201/2119, Notes for BGS, Middle East Command, Wavell to Gort, 3 August 1939; BL, Cunningham Papers, 52560, Cunningham to Pound, 24 July 1939; "A Vital Interest," in *Daily Herald,* 11 April 1939, p. 8.

77. PRO, ADM 167/103, Board Minute 3646, 15 June 1939; PRO, ADM 167/104, Additional Needs of the Navy, Stanhope to the CID, June 1939, PRO, CAB 2/9, CID 364th meeting, 6 July 1939; PRO, CAB 24/287, CP 118, 18 May 1939, CP 149, 3 July 1939.

78. PRO, CAB 53/51, COS 942(JP), 12 July 1939; PRO, CAB 53/52, COS 946, 18 July 1939; PRO, CAB 53/11, COS 309th meeting, 19 July 1939; PRO, CAB 16/183A, DP(P)65 Revise, 24 July 1939.

79. PRO, CAB 2/9, Annex to CID 362d meeting, 26 June 1939; PRO, PREM 1/324, Menzies to Chamberlain, 15 June 1939; Ironside Manuscript Diaries, 1939/2, 10 July 1939; PRO, FO 371/22975, C 10103/15/18, Record of meeting between Halifax and High Commissioners, 11 July 1939; PRO, FO 1011/66, Loraine to Halifax, 21 July 1939; PRO, CAB 2/9, CID 368th meeting, 24 July 1939; Murray, "The Role of Italy in British Strategy," pp. 43–49; Pratt, *East of Malta,* pp. 190–97.

80. Cadogan, *Diaries,* 15 August 1939, p. 195; BUL, NC 18/1/1107, Neville to Hilda, 15 July 1939; AN, 496AP, 12, Dr4, Chamberlain to Daladier, 13 July 1939.

81. AN, 496AP, 12, Dr4, Chamberlain to Daladier, 13 July 1939; SHAT, 2N, 229, 2, Indications données par le Général Gamelin au cours des conversations franco-britanniques, 13 July 1939; SHAT, 5N, 579, 1bis, Réunion des Chefs d'EMG, 17 July 1939.

82. BL, Cunningham Papers, Cunningham to Pound, 26 July 1939; PRO, ADM 1/9905, M08874/39, Report of Anglo-French conversations at Malta, Appendix II, 2 August 1939; SHM, 1BB2, 208, 14, Comment se deroulera la guerra maritime? 3 August 1939; SHM, TTA, 9, 1939/Plymouth, Mémento de la conférence de Plymouth, 8 August 1939; SHM, 1BB2, 182, 1, Résumé de la conférence entre Darlan et Pound, 8 August 1939; Reussner, *Les Conversations,* pp. 287–89.

83. PRO, PREM 1/329, Daladier to Chamberlain, 24 July 1939; CAC, Hore-Belisha papers, 5, 64, Notes of conversations with General Gamelin and M. Daladier in Paris, 21 August 1939.

84. PRO, AIR 9/117, Notes on discussion with French General Staff at Rabat, 6 May 1939; SHAA, 2B, 107, IIIB, N 339/SA, Nogues to Gamelin and Daladier, 7 May 1939; PRO, CAB 53/11, COS 309th meeting, 19 July 1939; PRO, WO 106/2028, Brantes to Cornwall-Jones, 2 August 1939.

85. PRO, CAB 21/565, 14/6/26, Halifax to Campbell, 22 August 1939; PRO, FO 1011/66, Loraine to Halifax, 22 August 1939; PRO, CAB 21/565, 14/6/26, Ismay to Jamet, 23 August 1939, Ismay minute, 24 August 1939; PRO, ADM 223/488, Translation of secret Italian handbook dated 25 June 1939, Godfrey to Danckwerts, Phillips and Pound, 30 August 1939; PRO,

CAB 55/11, COS 312th meeting, 24 August 1939; PRO, CAB 29/160, AFC(J)104, 30 August 1939; PRO, ADM 199/339, M015906/39, no. 1115/30, Admiralty to CinCs, 30 August 1939.

86. SHAT, 5N, 579, 1, Réunion des Ministères de la Guerre, 23 August 1939; AN, 496AP, 15, Dr6, sdrb, Note du Ministre des Affaires Etrangères, 23 August 1939; MAE, PA-AP, Hoppenot, 7, Journal de Bonnet, 26 August 1939.

87. SHAA, 2B, 104, N 167 EMGAA/S, Vuillemin to La Chambre, 26 August 1939; Gauché, *Le Deuxième Bureau,* pp. 103–4; Docteur, *La Grande Enigme,* p. 55; Auphan, *L'Honneur,* pp. 238–40; FDRL, PSF, 19, France, no. 1543, Bullitt to Welles, 22 August 1939.

Chapter 5

1. Ciano, *Diario,* 2, 24 September 1939, p. 341–51; Bottai, *Vent'anni,* pp. 135–36; Guarneri, *Battaglie economiche,* 2: p. 499; Knox, *Mussolini Unleashed,* p. 44.

2. Ciano, *Diario,* 4, 5, 9, 30 September 1939, pp. 342–54.

3. Ciano, *Diario,* 4, 5, 10 September 1939, pp. 342–45; ACS, SPD-CR, 44, 39/E, Farinacci to Mussolini, 13 September 1939; Guarneri, *Battaglie economiche,* 2: p. 434.

4. USE, I-4, 7/6, Forza della Libia, MAI to MGG, 16 September 1939; USM, *In Africa settentrionale,* pp. 60–61; Knox, *Mussolini Unleashed,* p. 55; ACS, AFI, 53, 026394–406, Preperazione militare italiano, 13 September 1939; ACS, MAG, 1939, 30, 3, N 1849, Favagrossa to Pariani, Cavagnari, Valle, 24 September 1939.

5. ACS, SPD-CR, 44, 39/E, Farinacci to Mussolini, 13 September 1939; Ciano, *Diario,* 10, 15, 18, 24 September 1939, 1–2, 16, 27, 31 October 1939, pp. 345–63; Pricolo, *La Regia Aeronautica,* pp. 125–31; Knox, *Mussolini Unleashed,* pp. 56–57.

6. NARA, T586, 405, 000073–97, Verbale della seduta dei Capi di Stato Maggiore, 18 November 1939; USMM, 2765, 11, B 13874, Badoglio to Cavagnari, 12 October 1939; Giorgerini, *Da Matapan,* p. 414; Santoni, "The Italian Submarine Campaign," in Howarth and Law, *The Battle of the Atlantic,* p. 323.

7. Ciano, *Diario,* 1–2, 4, 7, 9 October 1939, pp. 355–57; Schreiber, *Germany and the Second World War,* 3:8–98; Schreiber, *Revisionismus und Weltmachtstreben,* pp. 202–48; ASD, AG, UC, 85/2, Colloquio col Führer, Ciano to Mussolini, 1 October 1939; Ciano, *L'Europa verso la catastrofe,* p. 472.

8. Halder, *Kriegstagebuch,* 1: 3; Guarneri, *Battaglie economiche,* 2: 447–49; Ciano, *Diario,* 12, 14 September 1939, 18, 25 October 1939, pp. 346–62; ADAP, D/8, no. 149, p. 121; ACS, MMG-AS, 84/Germania, N 1/3729, Lais to Cavagnari, 17 September 1939; USE, H-9, 4/1, Promemoria, Tripiccione to Pariani, 17 September 1939.

9. ACS, MMG-AS, 84, Germania, B 11659, Cavagnari to Ciano, 20 September 1939; Ciano, *Diario,* 27 September 1939, p. 353; ACS, MAG, 1940, 184, 9/V/7, N 1217, Trasporto di forniture tedesche all'estero su navi italiane, Liotta to Ilardi, 20 September 1939, N 74471, Ilardi to Anfuso, 29 September 1939, N 234793, Anfuso to Ilardi, 9 October 1939, N 79050, Ilardi to Liotta, 11 October 1939; ADAP, D/8, nos. 231, 277, pp. 198–250.

10. Ciano, *Diario,* 12 September 1939, 11 October 1939, 9, 11, 26 November 1939, pp. 346–68; NARA, T586, 405, 000039–46, Relazione per il Gran Consiglio, Mussolini, 5 February 1939; De Felice, *Il problema,* pp. 102–7; Knox, *Mussolini Unleashed,* pp. 59–61.

11. Ciano, *Diario,* 15, 16, 19–20, 28 September 1939, 1–2, 12 October 1939, pp. 347–59; ASD, AG, UC, 62, Guariglia to Ciano, 29 September 1939, 85/2, Colloquio col Führer, Ciano to Mussolini, 1 October 1939; ASD, AP-I, 61/3, N 557R/210, Blocco difensivo balcanico, Ciano to Talamo, 30 September 1939, N 5113R, Blocco dei neutri, Ghigi to Ciano, 3 October 1939; Ciano, *L'Europa,* pp. 466–77; ADAP, D/8, nos. 96, 266, pp. 77–240; Mussolini, *Opera Omnia,* 29: 315–17; Knox, *Mussolini Unleashed,* pp. 50–52; Marzari, "Projects for an Italian-led Balkan Bloc," pp. 767–88.

12. Roskill, *The War at Sea,* 1: 48, 584; PRO, CAB 79/1, COS(39) 1st meeting, 2 September 1939; BL, Cunningham Papers, 52558, Cunningham to Doodles, 10 September 1939.

13. PRO, FO 371/23787, R 7251/1/22, Kirkpatrick minute, 7 September 1939; CKS, Stanhope Papers, U1590, C658, Pound to Stanhope, 24 September 1939; PRO, ADM 205/2, Report of the First Lord of the Admiralty to the War Cabinet, 18 September 1939.

14. PRO, FO 1011/204, Loraine to Cadogan, 13 October 1939; PRO, FO 1011/66, Loraine to Halifax, 13 September 1939; *Dictionary of National Biography 1961–1970*, pp. 676–77.

15. PRO, FO 371/23820, no. 897, Loraine to Halifax, 17 September 1939; NMM, CHT 6/2, Chatfield to Lothian, 26 September 1939; BOD, Simon diary, 11, 19 October 1939; BUL, NC 18/1/1121, Neville to Hilda, 17 September 1939, NC 18/1/1123, Neville to Hilda, 1 October 1939.

16. PRO, FO 371/23820, R 7686/399/22, no. 658, Halifax to Loraine, 19 September 1939; PRO, FO 371/ 23787, R 7251/1/22, Cadogan minute, 8 September 1939, R 7722/1/22, War Office to Foreign Office, 17 September 1939, Nichols to War Office, 19 September 1939, R 7766/1/22, Foreign Office memorandum, 19 September 1939.

17. MAE, P-40, Cabinet Bonnet, 9, Bonnet note, 5 September 1939; Shorrock, *From Ally to Enemy*, pp. 272–73; Réau, "La Conduite de la guerre et les prémices de la défaite," pp. 91–114.

18. SHAT, 1K, 130, 1, 2/1, Voyage de Général Weygand à Ankara—rapport, 12 September 1939; AN, 496AP, 16, Dr1, sdra, Gamelin to Daladier, Etude sur la situation politique et militaire préparée en vue de la reunion du Comite de Guerre, 7 September 1939; SHAT, 2N, 26, 1, Procès-verbal de la réunion du Comité de Guerre, 8 September 1939; SHAT, 1K, 224, 9/14, Gamelin MS notes, 9 September 1939; SHAT, 27N, 5, 1, Gamelin note, N 7/i, Note sur l'intérêt essentiel d'un théâtre d'opérations de l'Orient Med, 12 September 1939.

19. SHAT, 2N, 24, 2, N 56–FMF.3, Darlan to Gamelin, 9 September 1939, N 54/3.EMDN, Gamelin to Daladier, 10 September 1939; SHAT, 27N, 9, 3, N 66 FMF-3, Darlan to Gamelin, 11 September 1939, N 86 FMF-3, Darlan to Gamelin, 14 September 1939; SHAT, 2N, 231, 1, N 174 FMF-3, Darlan to Gamelin, 28 September 1939; SHAT, 27N, 5, 1, N 14/i, Projet de Note sur le probleme des Balkans, Gamelin note, 19 September 1939.

20. SHM, 1BB2, 210, 1, Gamelin note, Note concernant la conduite générale de la guerre, 8 September 1939; AN, 496AP, 16, Dr1, sdra, Procès-verbal de la réunion du Comité de Guerre Restreint, 8 September 1939; SHAT, 27N, 5, 1, Réunion des Commandants en Chef du 7 September, 8 September 1939; SHAT, 1K, 224, 9/14, Gamelin MS notes, 11 September 1939; SHAT, 27N, 5, 1, Gamelin note, N 8/i: Note sur l'attitude Italienne, 12 September 1939; SHAT, 27N, 62, 1, Deuxième Bureau note, Compte-rendu sur l'attitude Italienne, 14 September 1939; SHAT, 2N, 224, 2, Conseil Superieur de la Defense Nationale note, Note sur la situation actuelle, 28 September 1939; SHM, 1BB2, 208, 11, Darlan note, 11 October 1939.

21. MAE, P-40, Rochat, 12, Léger note, 8 September 1939; SHAT, 1K, 224, 9/14, Gamelin MS notes, 7 September 1939; MAE, P-40, Daladier, 4, Direction politique note, Constitution d'un Front d'Orient, 20 September 1939.

22. MAE, Eur 30–40, Italie, 275, N 3821–23, François-Poncet to Daladier, 20 September 1939; AN, 496AP, 18, Dr3, sdra, N 3965, François-Poncet to Daladier, 15 September 1939; MAE, P-40, Daladier, 4, N 3750–60, François-Poncet to Daladier, 16 September 1939.

23. CAC, PHPP 2/1, Cadogan to Phipps, 6 September 1939; Rossi-Landi, *Hommes Politique*, pp. 27–32; Réau, *Daladier*, pp. 368–72; Imlay, "How to Win a War," chap. 7.

24. MAE, P-40, Daladier, 4, MS notes, 12 September 1939; SHAT, 2N, 224, 2, N 1085/DN, Daladier to Gamelin, 14 September 1939; MAE, PA-AP, Dejean, 2, Note pour le Conseil des Ministres, 19 September 1939; SHAT, 27, 9, 1, N 15/i, Considerations developpées au course de la réunion dans le Cabinet du Daladier, 19 September 1939; MAE, P-40, Cabinet Bonnet, 9, Conversation avec M. Nac, 2 September 1939; MAE, Eur 30–40, Italie, 256, N 386, Bonnet to Marine, 7 September 1939.

25. SHAT, 27N, 5, 1, N 11/i, Réunion des Commandants en Chef, 15 September 1939; SHAT, 27, 9, 1, N 15/i, Considerations developpées au course de la réunion dans le Cabinet du Daladier, 19 September 1939; SHAT, 1K, 224, 9/14, Gamelin MS notes, 19 September 1939; MAE, PA-AP, Dejean, 2, Note pour le conseil des ministres, 19 September 1939; MAE, P-40, Daladier, 4, Note pour le Conseil des Ministres, 20 September 1939, Daladier note, Note sur la situation actuelle, 21 September 1939.

26. PRO, FO 371/23753, R 7146/2613/67, no. 395, Knatchbull-Hugessen to Halifax, 5 Sep-

tember 1939, no. 795, Loraine to Halifax, 5 September 1939, R 7146/2613/67, no. 327, Halifax to Knatchbull-Hugessen, 7 September 1939, R 7241/2613/67, no. 411, Knatchbull-Hugessen to Halifax, 8 September 1939; PRO, FO 371/23819, R 7622/399/22, Greek views of Italian neutrality, Palairet to Halifax, 12 September 1939.

27. PRO, FO 371/23753, R 7151/2613/67, no. 795, Loraine to Halifax, 5 September 1939; PRO, CAC, PHPP 2/20, Loraine to Phipps, 8 September 1939; PRO, FO 371/23754, R 7556/2613/67, Halifax memorandum, WP(39)25, Position in the Balkans, 12 September 1939; Cadogan, *Diaries,* 15 September 1939, p. 217.

28. PRO, CAB 65/1, WM 7(39), War Cabinet meeting, 7 September 1939; PRO, CAB 80/2, Imlay memorandum, COS(39)34, 16 September 1939; PRO, CAB 79/1, COS(39) 21st meeting, 18 September 1939; PRO, CAB 79/1, COS(39) 22nd meeting, 19 September 1939.

29. PRO, WO 193/134, Ironside memorandum, British Strategy in the War, 7 September 1939; PRO, WO 193/134, Ironside memorandum, Note on Strategic Situation in Europe, 16 September 1939; Manuscript diaries of the late Field Marshall Lord Ironside—(copyright–The Lord Ironside), permission to quote from 1939/3, 7, 16, and 24 September 1939.

30. PRO, ADM 205/2, Minutes of Meetings in First Lord's Room, 18 September 1939; PRO, FO 371/23754, R 7981/2613/67, Churchill to Halifax, 20 September 1939, Halifax to Churchill, 22 September 1939; PRO, CAB 65/3, War Cabinet: Confidential Annex, 21 September 1939.

31. BUL, NC 18/1/1122, Neville to Ida, 23 September 1939; BUL, NC 18/1/1123, Neville to Hilda, 1 October 1939; CAC, HNKY 11/1, Hankey memorandum: War Policy, 12 September 1939.

32. PRO, CAB 99/3, SWC(39/40) 2d meeting, 22 September 1939; AN, 496AP, 17, Dr2, sdrb, Réunion du Conseil Suprême Interallié à Brighton, 22 September 1939; Cadogan, *Diaries,* 22 September 1939, p. 218; Butler, *Grand Strategy,* ii, p. 65.

33. SHAT, 27N, 5, 1, N 20/i, Réunion des Commandants en Chef, 28 September 1939; SHAT, 27N, 247, 1/1, Compte rendu des communications faites par le Général Gamelin, 24 October 1939.

34. PRO, FO 371/23754, R 8105/2613/67, no. 966, Loraine to Halifax, 26 September 1939; PRO, FO 1011/204, Loraine to Nichols, 27 September 1939; PRO, FO 1011/205, Loraine to Campbell Stuart, 9 October 1939; PRO, FO 371/23756, R 10958/2613/67, Loraine to Halifax, 29 November 1939, Noble minute, 3 December 1939.

35. PRO, FO 371/23753, R 7146/2613/67, no. 395, Knatchbull-Hugessen to Halifax, 5 September 1939; PRO, CAB 65/1, WM 61(39), War Cabinet meeting, 26 October 1939; Roskill, *The War at Sea,* 1: 49; Butler, *Grand Strategy,* 2: 66–67; Playfair, *The Mediterranean,* 1: 51–2.

36. MAE, P-40, Rochat, 6, Quai d'Orsay to Phipps, 1 November 1939; AN, 496AP, 19, Dr3, sdra, N 1325–27, Daladier to Massigli, 23 September 1939; MAE, P-40, Daladier, 4, Le Front d'orient, Daladier to Corbin and Massigli, 24 September 1939; MAE, P-40, Rochat, 10, N 1776–78, Daladier to Massigli, 6 November 1939.

37. MAE, Eur 30–40, Italie, 275, no. 3899–900, François-Poncet to Daladier, 23 September 1939; AN, 496AP, 18, Dr3, sdrb, François-Poncet to Daladier, 27 October 1939; MAE, P-40, Rochat, 10, N 2039, Massigli to Daladier, 30 October 1939, N 2070–79, Massigli to Daladier, 3 November 1939; AN, 496AP, 32, Dr2, N 267, Matériel de guerre pour la Turquie, Massigli to Daladier, 3 November 1939; SHM, Papiers Auphan, GG2, 162, 1, Odend'hal to Auphan, 30 October 1939; SHM, 1BB2, 208, 11, Darlan note, 11 October 1939; MAE, PA-AP, Hoppenot, 8, Hoppenot note, 23 September 1939; MAE, PA-AP, Dejean, 2, Projet de rapport pour le conseil des ministres, 10 November 1939.

38. MAE, P-40, Rochat, 6, N 3878, Corbin to Daladier, 7 November 1939.

39. PRO, FO 371/23823, R 7292/697/22, Foreign Office minute, 11 September 1939; Playfair, *The Mediterranean,* 1: 45–46.

40. PRO, ADM 116/4249, EWD 4/39, Contraband Control in the Mediterranean, Taylor to Burrough, 18 September 1939; PRO, ADM 205/2, Contraband Control, Burrough to Churchill, Pound, Phillips, 27 September 1939.

41. PRO, CAB 79/1, COS(39) 12th meeting, 11 September 1939; PRO, FO 371/23820, R

8104/399/22, Ingram to Nichols, 26 September 1939; PRO, ADM 205/4, Minutes of meeting in first lord's room, 26 September 1939; PRO, FO 800/276, Sargent to Ingram, 9 October 1939.

42. PRO, ADM 116/4173, ADC 1st meeting, 5 September 1939; PRO, ADM 116/4173, M 09006/39, Possibilities of war purchases from Italy, PAS(S) minute, 7 September 1939, D of C minute, 8 September 1939; PRO, CAB 65/1, WM 12(39), War Cabinet meeting, 11 September 1939; PRO, ADM 116/4173, M 09608/39, Ingram to Pound, 14 September 1939.

43. MAE, P-40, Daladier, 4, Procès-verbal d'une séance tenue au Ministère du Commerce, 20 September 1939; MAE, PA-AP, Dejean, 6, Procès-verbal sur la Commission mixte gouvernementale franco-italienne, 20 September 1939; MAE, Eur 30–40, Italie, 276, Leverve to Daladier, 9 October 1939; AN, 496AP, 18, Dr3, sdrb, N 4195–96, François-Poncet to Daladier, 10 October 1939.

44. DDI, 9/1, no. 328, p. 201; *Annuario Statistico Italiano,* 1939, p. 184; Raspin, *Italian War Economy,* pp. 131–33.

45. Guillen, "Le Coopération économique entre la France et l'Italie de septembre 1939 à juin 1940," in Duroselle, *L'Abîme,* pp. 123–24; ADAP, D/8, no. 542, pp. 526–27; PRO, ADM 116/4173, M 03597/40, Greene to Halifax and Cross, 14 February 1940.

46. ACS, MMG-AS, 75, Francia, 12 October—4 December 1939; ACS, MAG-1940, 152, 9; Guarneri, *Battaglie economiche,* 2: 430–40; Ciano, *Diario,* 14 January 1940, p. 386.

47. PRO, ADM 116/4173, M 011711/39, no. 17 ARFAR, Loraine to Halifax, 6 October 1939; PRO, FO 1011/206, Anglo-Italian protocol, 27 October 1939; PRO, FO 1011/206, Rodd memorandum, Report on contraband control talks with the Italians, 7 November 1939.

48. PRO, ADM 116/4249, M 010619/39, no. 1056/3, Admiralty to Cunningham and Contraband control bases in the Mediterranean, 3 October 1939; PRO, ADM 116/4249, M 011657/39, no. 2157–8/8, Admiralty to Cunningham and Contraband control bases in the Mediterranean, 8 October 1939; PRO, ADM 116/4249, no. 174 ARFAR, Halifax to Charles, 9 November 1939.

49. PRO, ADM 116/4249, M 012078/39, no. 1031, Loraine to Halifax, 10 October 1939, no. 1045, Loraine to Halifax, 14 October 1939; PRO, ADM 116/4177, M 013640/39, Loraine to Halifax, 27 October 1939.

50. PRO, ADM 116/4173, M 013002/39, no. 48 ARFAR, Loraine to Halifax, 12 October 1939; PRO, ADM 116/4177, M 011797/40, Record of meeting held at MEW, 15 October 1939; SHAT, 27N, 7, 1, N 172 S/CEMI, Odend'hal to Gamelin, 28 October 1939.

51. PRO, ADM 116/4249, R 9370/G, Halifax to Finlay, 2 November 1939, Admiralty to Cunningham and Contraband control bases in the Mediterranean, 13 November 1939; PRO, ADM 116/4177, M 013915/39, no. 674, Halifax to Charles, 18 November 1939.

52. SHM, 1BB2, 208, 11, Darlan journal, 30 September–10 October 1939; SHAT, 27N, 5, 1, N 22/i, Réunion des Commandants en Chef, 4 October 1939; PRO, ADM 205/4, L/204/39, Holland to Pound, 15 November 1939; Dreifort, *Myopic Grandeur,* p. 189.

53. PRO, ADM 199/1939, Phillips to Pound and Churchill, Daily Report no. 23, 27 September 1939, Daily Report no. 29, 3 October 1939, Daily Report no. 32, 6 October 1939, Daily Report no. 33, 7 October 1939, Daily Report no. 63, 6 November 1939; PRO, CAB 21/1317, Chalmers memorandum, 29 December 1939; BL, Cunningham Papers, 52558, Cunningham to Doodles, 29 October 1939, 52560, Pound to Cunningham, 7 January 1940.

54. PRO, CAB 65/1, WM 39(39), War Cabinet meeting, 6 October 1939; PRO, ADM 116/4177, M 09232/39, Phillips to Churchill, 6 October 1939, Danckwerts to Phillips, 6 October 1939, Churchill to Phillips and Danckwerts, 7 October 1939, Danckwerts minute, 12 October 1939, Phillips minute, 12 October 1939, Pound minute, 12 October 1939.

55. PRO, CAB 21/565, R 8534/577/G, Mediterranean entente, Halifax to Loraine, 10 October 1939; PRO, CAB 79/1, COS(39) 47th meeting, 13 October 1939; PRO, FO 371/23755, R 8843/2613/67, Noble minute, 12 October 1939; PRO, CAB 21/565, JP (39) 57, Cornwall-Jones memorandum, 13 October 1939; PRO, CAB 80/4, COS(39)80(JP), 16 October 1939; PRO, FO 371/23755, R 9380/2613/67, no. 1078, Loraine to Halifax, 26 October 1939; PRO, CAB 65/1, WM 46(39), War Cabinet meeting, 13 October 1939.

56. SHM, 1BB2, 208, 11, Darlan journal, 6 October 1939; Darlan, *Lettres et notes,* no. 55, p. 125; SHM, 1BB2, 208, 11, Darlan note, 11 October 1939; SHM, TTA, 56, Darlan to Pernot, 11

November 1939; SHM, 1BB2, 220, 3, N 42–FMF/SE, Darlan to Campinchi, 6 November 1939, N 1864 CAB.O, Campinchi to Daladier, 12 November 1939.

57. SHAT, 27N, 5, 1, N. 43/i, Réunion des Commandants en Chef, 13 November 1939; SHAT, 5N, 585, N 1794/DN, Daladier to Gamelin, 16 November 1939; SHM, 1BB2, 208, Darlan journal, 31 October–4 November 1939; Darlan, *Lettres et notes,* no. 51, p. 116; CAC, Churchill Papers, 20/15, Statement by the First Lord to the French Admiralty, 3 November 1939; Churchill, *War Papers,* 1: 325–29; Churchill, *Second World War,* 1: 87–88.

58. SHM, Papiers Auphan, GG2, 162, 1, Odend'hal to Auphan, 21 November 1939; MAE, Eur 30–40, Italie, 255, N 3096–97, François-Poncet to Daladier, 25 November 1939; SHM, 2BB7, L11, no. 41, Draft minutes of the 1st meeting of the Enemy Exports Committee, 30 November 1939; PRO, FO 371/23823, R 10634/700/22, German exports of coal to Italy, Morton to Sargent, 21 November 1939.

59. ASD, AP-I, 61, 2, B 13188, Cavagnari to Ciano, 3 October 1939; ASD, AP-I, 61, 2, Incontri con l'addetto navale inglese, Raineri Biscia to Cavagnari, 8, 13, 17, 20, 23 October 1939, 8 November 1939; PRO, ADM 116/4177, M 011797/40, Record of meeting held at MEW, 15 October 1939; ASD, AP-GB, 41, 2, Cattura di merci considerate di contrabando e destinate alla Germania, MAE to MMG, 14, 22 October 1939, 3 November 1939; ASD, RD-F, 286, 1, N. 238615, Ciano to Guaraglia, 9 November 1939; ASD, RD-L, 1077, 11, Condotta della Guerra Marittima, Pecori Giraldi to MMG, 6 November 1939; ASD, RD-L, 1077, 11, Gallina to Bastianini, 16 November 1939.

60. PRO, ADM 199, 330, M 016185/39, Halifax to Loraine, 23 November 1939; ASD, AP-I, 61, 2, N. 5241/2422, Contrabando assoluto e condizionale, Bastianini to Ciano, 24 November 1939; PRO, FO 371/23788, R 10817/1/22, Halifax to Ciano, 25 November 1939; MAE, Eur 30–40, Italie, 255, N 5086–87, François-Poncet to Daladier, 25 November 1939; SHM, 2BB7, L11, N 41, Draft minutes of the 1st meeting of Enemy Exports Committee, 30 November 1939; ASD, AP-I, 71, 3, Verbale del Comitato Interministeriale sul Blocco Marittimo, 1 December 1939; PRO, ADM 116/4249, no. 1191, Loraine to Halifax, 1 December 1939; ASD, AG, UC, 53, 2, N. 8311, Ciano to Halifax, 3 December 1939; Ciano, *L'Europa,* pp. 482–84; PRO, FO 1011/66, Loraine to Halifax, 4 December 1939; Ciano, *Diario,* 24 November 1939, 1, 2, 5, 6 December 1939, pp. 367–72.

61. PRO, CAB 66/3, WP(G)(39)131, Halifax memorandum, 4 December 1939; PRO, CAB 65/2, WM105(39), War Cabinet meeting, 6 December 1939; PRO, ADM 199/399, M 016312/39, Farquhar to MEW, 8 December 1939; Churchill, *War Papers,* 1: 468–69.

62. Ciano, *Diario,* 1, 2, 10 December 1939, pp. 370–73; ADAP, D/8, no. 410, pp. 374–76; ACS, SPD-CR, 32, 17, Foglio d'Ordini, Gran Consiglio del Fascismo, 7 December 1939.

63. ASD, AP-I, 71, 3, Verbali del Comitato Interministeriale sul Blocco Marittimo, 8, 29 December 1939; PRO, ADM 116/4177, M 015540/39, no. 1267, Loraine to Halifax, 22 December 1939; PRO, ADM 199/330, M 017323/39, Nicholls memorandum, Contraband control in the Mediterranean, 30 December 1939, M 0727/40, no. 16, Halifax to Loraine, 6 January 1940; Cadogan, *Diaries,* 29 December 1939, p. 241; PRO, FO 1011/210, Loraine to Halifax, 16 January 1940; Ciano, *Diario,* 20, 22, 29 December 1939, 13, 18 January 1940, pp. 375–88.

64. PRO, ADM 116/4177, M 03206/40, no. 31, Loraine to Halifax, 7 February 1940; Ciano, *Diario,* 3, 7, 8, 16 February 1940, pp. 393–96; Ciano, *L'Europa,* p. 505; Medlicott, *Economic Blockade,* 1: 296–302.

65. SHAT, 27N, 247, 2, N 1171/3, Weygand to Gamelin, 16 November 1939; SHAT, 1K, 130, 15/15, Weygand carnets, 30 November 1939; SHAT, 27N, 5, 1, N 53/i, Réunion des Commandants en Chef, 3 December 1939; SHAT, 5N, 580, 8/3, Weygand note, Note relative à une intervention alliée dans les Balkans, 9 December 1939.

66. SHAT, 27N, 5, 1, N 49/i, Réunion des Commandants en Chef, 27 November 1939, N 52/i, Réunion des Commandants en Chef, 2 December 1939, N 53/i, Réunion des Commandants en Chef, 3 December 1939, N 56/i, Réunion des Commandants en Chef, 5 December 1939; SHAT, 27N, 16, 2, N 336 AMG/TOE, Gamelin to Daladier, 5 December 1939.

67. MAE, P-40, Daladier, 6, Direction Politique, Note sur l'organisation du front d'Orient, 16 November 1939; AN, 496AP, 17, Dr2, sdrd, Direction Politique, Note sur la situation politique dans les Balkans, 17 December 1939; MAE, Eur 30–40, Italie, 276, De Lafonde to

François-Poncet, 6 November 1939; SHM, GG2, 162, Papiers Auphan, 5, Comment se pose le problème italien, Moysset to Auphan, 25 December 1939; MAE, PA-AP, Massigli, 99, Massigli to Léger, 16 December 1939; MAE, P-40, Rochat, 7, N, 73, Massigli to Daladier, 14 January 1940; SHAT, 1K, 130, 15/15, Weygand carnets, 6 December 1939.

68. AN, 496AP, 17, Dr2, sdrd, Aubert note, Le Front d'Orient, 8 December 1939; MAE, P-40, Rochat, 12, N 2965–70, Daladier to Corbin, 16 November 1939, N 3061–3, Daladier to Corbin, 25 November 1939; MAE, Eur 30–40, Italie, 277, Daladier to Corbin, 18 December 1939; MAE, PA-AP, Dejean, 2, Projet de rapport pour le conseil des ministres, 23 December 1939; SHAT, 1K, 130, 15/15, Weygand carnets, 5 December 1939.

69. Manuscript diaries of the late Field Marshal Lord Ironside (Copyright—The Lord Ironside), permission to quote from 1939/4, 3 December 1939; PRO, CAB 79/2, COS(39) 88th meeting, 25 November 1939; PRO, CAB 79/2, COS(39) 90th meeting, 27 November 1939; PRO, FO 371/23757, R 11066/2613/67, COS (39)142(JP), 3 December 1939, R 11347/2613/67, COS(39)146 and WP(39)148, 5 December 1939.

70. PRO, FO 1011/66, Halifax to Ciano, 25 November 1939; PRO, FO 371/23758, R 11701/2613/67, no. 1255, Loraine to Halifax, 18 December 1939; BUL, NC 18/1/1133A, Neville to Ida, 3 December 1939; PRO, CAB 65/2, WM 107(39), War Cabinet meeting, 7 December 1939.

71. MAE, P-40, Rochat, 12, N 154 Cab/DN, Gamelin to Daladier, 11 December 1939; SHAT, 27N, 5, 1, N 59/i, Réunion interalliée, 11 December 1939; PRO, FO 371/23758, R 11691/2613/67, Record of a meeting held at the headquarters of General Gamelin, 11 December 1939; Ironside Manuscript Diaries, 1939/4, 10–11 December 1939.

72. AN, 496AP, 17, Dr2, sdrd, Réunion du Conseil Suprême Interalliée, 19 December 1939; PRO, CAB 99/3, Supreme War Council, 19 December 1939; PRO, PREM 1/437, SWC 4th meeting, Bridges to Rucker, 19 December 1939; Bédarida, *Stratégie secrète*, pp. 202–13.

73. For Daladier's expression of frustration, specifically directed at Gamelin for not devising a *plan de guerre* that did not "run through your fingers," see SHAT, 5N, 580, 1, 8, Information du Président, Direction militaire de la guerre, 8 January 1940.

74. SHM, 1BB2, 208, 11, Darlan journal, 14 December 1939; SHAT, 5N, 580, 1/6, Note sur la conduite stratégique de la guerre, Darlan to Gamelin, 30 December 1939; AN, 496AP, 22, Dr1, sdra, Note sur la conduite de la guerre, Darlan to Daladier, 23 January 1940.

75. SHM, 1BB2, 207, 2/2, EMG note, 22 December 1939; AN, 496AP, 21, Dr7, sdrb, Amirauté note sur une opération navale dans l'Océan Glacial Artique, 14 January 1940.

76. SHM, 1BB2, 207, 2, 7, Situation actuelle en le Nord, Darlan to Daladier, 22 January 1940; AN, 496AP, 22, Dr1, sdrb, N 196–FMF/3, Note sur la Conduite de la Guerre, Darlan to Gamelin and Daladier, 27 January 1940, enclosing EMG note, Projet d'opération en Finlande et Scandinavie, 26 January 1940.

77. SHAT, 2N, 224, 2, CSDN, Note sur la situation actuelle, 15 January 1940; SHAT, 27N, 5, 1, N 73/i, Réunion des Commandants en Chef, 4 January 1940, N 81/i, Réunion des Commandants en Chef, 15 January 1940; AN, 496AP, 22, Dr1, sdra, Direction Politique note, Assistance à la Finlande: Conséquences sur le plan des relations Franco-Russes, 25 January 1940; MAE, P-40, Reynaud, 2, N 151–58, Action en Scandinavie, Daladier to Corbin, 17 January 1940; SHM, TTA, 92, Chronologie de la Marine; SHM, 1BB2, 207, 2, Réunion au Ministre de la Guerre, 24 January 1940.

78. PRO, CAB 66/4, WP(39)162, Churchill memorandum, 16 December 1939, WP(39)168, Halifax memorandum, 20 December 1939; PRO, ADM 199/1929, Churchill memorandum, A note on the war in 1940, 25 December 1939; Churchill, *War Papers*, pp. 522–70.

79. PRO, CAB 79/3, COS meeting, 31 December 1939; PRO, CAB 65/5, WM 2(40), War Cabinet meeting, 3 January 1940, WM 10(40), War Cabinet meeting, 12 January 1940; PRO, CAB 66/5, WP(40)35, 28 January 1940; Butler, *Grand Strategy*, 2: 96–106.

80. PRO, CAB 83/1, minutes of Military Co-ordination Committee meeting, 20 December 1939; PRO, CAB 79/3, COS(40) 15th meeting, 25 January 1940; PRO, FO 371/23758, R 11838/2613/67, Cadogan minute, 24 December 1939; Cadogan, *Diaries*, 25 December 1939, p. 240 (original emphasis); PRO, FO 371/23758, R 12185/2613/67, Nichols minute, 27 December 1939; PRO, CAB 21/1179, R 67/G, Foreign Office Aide-Mémoire, 5 January 1940; BUL, NC 7/11/32/132, Hoare to Chamberlain, 26 December 1939.

81. PRO, FO 371/24936, R 518/57/22, Loraine to Sargent, 7 January 1940; PRO, FO 800/320, Loraine to Halifax, 22 January 1940.

82. AN, 496AP, 22, Dr2, sdra, N 86/i, Réunion interalliée relative aux problèmes de Finlande et de Scandinavie, Première séance, 31 January 1940, N 88/i, Deuxième séance, 1 February 1940; AN, 496AP, 20, Dr3, Réunion du Conseil Suprême Interalliée, 5 February 1940; Bédarida, *Stratégie secrète,* pp. 215–64; PRO, ADM 205/4, Record of a meeting held at General Gamelin's Headquarters, 31 January 1940, Record of a meeting between French and British High Commands at Ministry of War, Paris, 5 February 1940.

Chapter 6

1. Ciano, *Diario,* 30 November 1939, 2, 4, 8, 9, 19 December 1939, 2, 27 January 1940, pp. 369–90; DDI, 9/2, nos. 290, 450, 538, 570, 579, 582, 588, 602, pp. 246–464; ADAP, D/8, no. 410, 518, pp. 374–502; Knox, *Mussolini Unleashed,* pp. 63–65.

2. ACS, SPD-CR, 32, 17, Foglio d'Ordini, Gran Consiglio del Fascismo, 7 December 1939; ASD, AP-I, 61, 1, Discorso pronunciato da S.E. il Conte Gaeazzo Ciano, 16 December 1939; Ciano, *Diario,* 16, 17 December 1939, 5 January 1940, pp. 374–84.

3. Bottai, *Diario,* 8 December 1939, pp. 169–71; Mussolini, *Opera Omnia,* 29: pp. 336–37; ASD, AG, UC, 12, N 10431, Attolico to Ciano, 27 December 1939; ASD, AG, UC, 13, Mussolini to Hitler, 5 January 1940.

4. Ciano, *Diario,* 24 December 1939, 9 January 1940, pp. 377, 385; AN, 496AP, 18, Dr3, sdrd, N 5737–46, François-Poncet to Daladier, 25 December 1939; PRO, FO 371/23758, R 12131/2613/67, no. 1282, Loraine to Halifax, 27 December 1939.

5. Ciano, *Diario,* 9, 21, 26 December 1939, 8, 22 January 1940, pp. 373–89; DDI, 9/3, no. 40, p. 28.

6. Graziani memorandum in Rossi, *Mussolini,* p. 153; Farinacci in Bottai, *Vent'anni,* pp. 150–51; Ciano, *Diario,* 31 December 1939, 2, 11 January 1940, pp. 380–85.

7. Favagrossa memorandum in Favagrossa, *Perché perdemmo,* pp. 247ff; USE, H-1, 8, 2, Stato Maggiore dell'Esercito memorandum, 10 January 1940; Ciano, *Diario,* 15, 29 January 1940, 1 February 1940, pp. 386–93.

8. ACS, MMG-AS, 107, 15, Copia di telegramma inglese cifrato, Parona to Sebastiani, 17 January 1940; USE, H-3, 35, 4, N Z/1921, Carboni to Graziani, 20 January 1940; Ciano, *Diario,* 20, 23 January 1940, pp. 388–90; Bottai, *Diario,* 20, 23 January 1940, pp. 174–75.

9. ACS, MMG-AS, 88, 1, Commissione Suprema di Difesa, Verbali della XVII Sessione, 14 February 1940; Ciano, *Diario,* 14 February 1940, p. 396; Bottai, *Diario,* p. 176.

10. Ciano, *Diario,* 12, 13 December 1959, 3, 8, 18, 21, 22, February 1940, pp. 374–98; ACS, MAG-1940, 182, 9/V/7, N 051, Teucci to MAG, 13 January 1940; ACS, MMG-AS, 104, 9/1, B 1613, Cavagnari to Maristat, 9 February 1940; ACS, MAG-1940, 182, 9/V/7, N 1471, MAG to Riccardi, 24 February 1940; ACS, MMG-AS, 104, 9/1, B 2679, Cavagnari to Maristat, 2 March 1940.

11. USE, H-9, 6, 4, N 5189, Scorte delle Forze Armate per la guerra, Badoglio to Mussolini, 19 February 1940; ACS, MMG-AS, 118, 17, N.B. 2648, Ispezione alle Forze Armate dell'Egeo, Cavagnari to De Bono, 29 Februry 1940; ASD, AG, UC, 85, 2, Primo Colloquio del Duce col Singor Sumner Welles, 26 February 1940, Verbale del colloquio svoltosi fra Ribbentrop e il Duce, 10–11 March 1940, Secondo Colloquio del Duce col Signor Sumner Welles, 16 March 1940; Ciano, *Diario,* 25, 28 February 1940, 10, 11, 13 March 1940, pp. 399–406; DDI, 9/3, nos. 512, 524, Appendix II/2, pp. 435–642; ADAP, D/8, nos. 663, 665, 669, pp. 685–714.

12. ASD, AG, UC, 15, 1, Resocontro sommario del colloquio avvenuto al Brennero, 18 March 1940; ADAP, D/9, no. 1; ASD, AG, UC, 85, 2, Verbali del colloqui svoltosi fra Ribbentrop e il Duce, 10–11 March 1940; ASD, AG, UC, 13, N 30, Intenzioni offensive Germaniche, Badini to Attolico, 15 March 1940; Ciano, *Diario,* 10, 11, 16, 18 March 1940, pp. 404–8; Schreiber, "The Mediterranean in Hilter's Strategy in 1940," in Deist, *The German Military in the Age of Total War,* pp. 240–81.

13. Ciano, *Diario*, 13, 17, 18 March 1940, pp. 406–8.

14. ACS, MMG-AS, 101, 9, N. 273, Caduta del Gabinetto Daladier, Nomis di Pollone to Guariglia, 21 March 1940; ASD, AG, UC, 62, N 220/1031, Missione Laval a Roma, Guariglia to Ciano, 1 April 1940; ASD, De Felice, Grandi, 66, 158/2, Dingli diary, pp. 101–76; ACS, MMG-AS, 107, 15, Copia di telegramma inglese cifrato, Cavagnari to Mussolini, 28 March 1940; DDI, 9/3, nos. 604, 636, pp. 526–48; Ciano, *Diario*, 19, 20, 27, 31 March 1940, 5, 7 April 1940, pp. 408–16.

15. Ciano, *Diario*, 23 March 1940, p. 409; USE, H-6, 20, N 3200, P.R. 12 edizione 1 marzo 1940, Direttive generali, Graziani to Italian army commanders, 28 March 1940; ACS, Carte Graziani, 72, 59/4, Mussolini memorandum (to Ciano, Badoglio, Soddu, Teruzzi, Graziani, Cavagnari, Pricolo, Muti, the King, and Sebastiani), Memoria Segretissima, 31 March 1940; USE, I-4, 6, 13, N. 5287, Piano di Guerra, Mussolini to Badoglio, 31 March 1940.

16. USE, I-4, 7, 5, N 5281, Badoglio to Mussolini, 4 April 1940; USE, I-4, 6, 13, N 5288, Badoglio to Mussolini, 6 April 1940; Ciano, *Diario*, 23 March 1940, 2, 6, 7 April 1940, pp. 409–16.

17. PRO, FO 371/24936, R 3419/57/22, no. 22, Osborne to Halifax, 15 March 1940, Sargent minute, 18 March 1940; PRO, FO 371/24938, R 3579/58/22, Loraine to Halifax, 14 March 1940, R 3428/58/22, no. 236 DIPP, Loraine to Halifax, 16 March 1940.

18. CAC, Churchill Papers, 91/6, Churchill to Pound, 1 March 1940; PRO, WO 106/2056, CR/ME/1015/G, Cairo Conference, 6 March 1940, CR/ME/1046/AQ, 8 March 1940; PRO, FO 1011/210, Loraine to Stanley, 20 March 1940; PRO, CAB 65/6, WM 70(40), War Cabinet meeting, 16 March 1940, WM 71(40), War Cabinet meeting, 18 March 1940; BUL, NC 18/1/1147, Neville to Ida, 16 March 1940, PRO, CAB 21/1293, 47/79/15, Marshall-Cornwall memorandum, Major Strategy of the War, 20 March 1940.

19. PRO, FO 371/24936, R 3661/57/22, no. 28 DIPP, Osborne to Halifax, 22 March 1940; PRO, FO 371/24937, R 3825/57/22, no. 31 DIPP, Osborne to Halifax, 27 March 1940, R 3919/57/22, no. 274 DIPP, Loraine to Halifax, 28 March 1940; PRO, CAB 21/978, no. 227 DIPP, Loraine to Halifax, 28 March 1940, R 3723/58/22, no. 255, Loraine to Halifax, 21 March 1940; Cadogan, *Diaries*, 18 March 1940, p. 264; PRO, CAB 21/978, Halifax to Chatfield, 31 March 1940.

20. MAE, P-40, Daladier, 7, N 296 Cab DN, Gamelin to Daladier, 7 March 1940; SHAT, 27N, 5, 3, N 103/i, Réunion des Commandants en Chef, 10 March 1940; MAE, P-40, Daladier, 7, Réunion du Comité de Guerre, 11 March 1940; SHAT, 27N, 5, 1, N 106/i, Réunion des Commandants en Chef, 15 March 1940; SHAT, 1K, 224, 9, 2, Churchill to Gamelin, 16 March 1940; SHAT, 27N, 9, 1, N 325 Cab/DN, Note sur la conduite de la guerre, Gamelin to Daladier, 16 March 1940; Villelume, *Journal*, pp. 41–42; Raphaël-Leygues, *Chronique*, p. 155; Réau, *Daladier*, p. 411; May, *Strange Victory*, pp. 324–36.

21. MAE, PA-AP, Dejean, 2, Projet de rapport pour le conseil des ministres, 9 March 1940; SHM, 2BB7, R1, CRR-1, Compte Rendu de Renseignements N 22, de Larosiere to Marine 2ème Bureau, 15 March 1940; SHM, 2BB7, R1, CRR-2, Compte Rendu de Renseignements N 26, de Larosiere to Marine 2ème Bureau, 29 March 1940; MAE, P-40, Dejean, 2, Ravitaillement de l'Italie en charbon allemand par la ligne Fribourg-Bâle, 26 March 1940; SHM, 2BB7, R1, CRR-2, Compte Rendu du Renseignements N 25, de Larosiere to Marine 2ème Bureau, 25 March 1940.

22. MAE, P-40, Reynaud, 3, Note sur les stocks de petrole italiens, March 1940; SHM, 2BB7, R1, CRR-1, Compte Rendu du Renseignements N 20, de Larosiere to Marine 2ème Bureau, 8 March 1940.

23. MAE, P-40, Dejean, 2, Dejean note, Les relations germano-italiennes, 27 March 1940; MAE, P-40, Charvériat, 3, Hoppenot note, Bilan et perspective de la guerre, 22 March 1940; MAE, PA-AP, Hoppenot, 8, Hoppenot note, L'Attitude de l'Italie, 6 April 1940; SHAT, 27N, 9, 1, N 692 FMF-3, Auphan to Gamelin, 19 March 1940; SHAT, 27N, 9, 1, N 337 Cab/DN, Gamelin to Darlan, Vuillemin, Bührer, 21 March 1940; SHM, TTA, 95, Conférence aux Affaires Etrangères, 23 March 1940.

24. SHAT, 27N, 5, 1, N 108/i, Réunion interalliée, 23 March 1940; MAE, P-40, Reynaud, 2, Reynaud to Phipps, 25 March 1940; MAE, P-40, Dejean, 2, Réunion du Conseil Supreme à Londres, 28 March 1940; PRO, CAB 99/3, SWC(39/40)6th meeting, 28 March 1940.

25. PRO, CAB 79/3, COS(40) 58th meeting, 26 March 1940; PRO, CAB 80/9, COS(40)270, 26 March 1940, COS(40)275, 27 March 1940; PRO, CAB 21/1317, The Major Strategy of the War, 28 March 1940.

26. PRO, CAB 21/978, Medhurst to Newall and Slessor, 29 March 1940; BL, Cunningham Papers, 52560, Pound to Cunningham, 30 March 1940; PRO, ADM 199/1940, Daily Report no. 210, Phillips to Pound, Churchill, 1 April 1940, Daily Report no. 213, Phillips to Pound, Churchill, 4 April 1940.

27. PRO, FO 371/24887, R 3940/5/67, Cadogan minute, 28 March 1940, no. 200 DIPP, Halifax to Knatchbull-Hugessen, 29 March 1940, WM 81 (40) War Cabinet meeting, 4 April 1940; PRO, CAB 65/6, WM 77(40), War Cabinet meeting, 29 March 1940; PRO, ADM 116/4153, M 06122/40, Planning conference at Aleppo, 23 March 1940, 2 April 1940; PRO, FO 371/22887, R 3574/5/67, no. 0921/17: Staff Talks at Aleppo, Cunningham to Admiralty, 17 March 1940, R 3863/5/67, Cadogan minute, 26 March 1940.

28. Ciano, *Diario,* 9 April 1940, p. 417; ASD, AG, UC, 16, 2, Hitler to Mussolini, 9 April 1940; Knox, *Mussolini Unleashed,* pp. 91–92.

29. Ciano, *Diario,* 10–11 April 1940, pp. 417–18; ASD, AG, UC, 16, 2, Mussolini to Hitler, 11 April 1940.

30. USE, *Verbali delle riunioni,* pp. 32–37; USE, *In Africa settentrionale,* pp. 166–71; Knox, *Mussolini Unleashed,* pp. 90–95.

31. USE, *Verbali delle riunioni,* pp. 38–42.

32. Faldella, *L'Italia,* pp. 150–51; Fioravanzo, *La marina italiana,* 21/1: 351–52; ACS, MMG-AS, 89, 5, N 1540, Pro-Memoria. Situazione delle unità in allestimento e collaudo, Farina to Cavagnari, 10 April 1940; ACS, MMG-AS, 120, Francia, Impressioni in Francia su operazioni navali anglo-francesi, Guariglia to Ciano and Cavagnari, 11 April 1940.

33. AN, 496AP, 20, Dr5, sdra, Reunion du Conseil Suprême à Londres, 9 April 1940; PRO, CAB 99/3, SWC meeting, 9 April 1940; PRO, ADM 199/1940, Daily Report no. 218, Phillips to Pound, Churchill, 9 April 1940; SHM, 2BB7, R1, départ, N 324, de Larosiere to Darlan, 1 April 1940, CRR-2, Compte Rendu de Renseignements N 20, de Larosiere to 2ème Bureau, 8 April 1940; MAE, P-40, Dejean, 3, Sous-Directeur d'Europe, Note: Attitude de l'Italie, 8 April 1940.

34. PRO, CAB 79/3, COS(40) 66th meeting, 6 April 1940; PRO, FO 371/24945, R 6147/58/22, COS(40)282(S), 8 April 1940; PRO, FO 371/24956, R 4721/173/22, no. 313 (20/36/40), Charles to Halifax, 11 April 1940; PRO, CAB 21/978, no. 355, Charles to Halifax, 11 April 1940; PRO, FO 371/24939, R 4766/58/22, no. 376 DIPP, Charles to Halifax, 15 April 1940.

35. PRO, FO 371/24954, R 4770/77/22, Jack Nicholls to Phil Nichols, 11 April 1940; PRO, CAB 21/978, Morton to Ismay, 11 April 1940; PRO, FO 371/24931, R 5404/48/22, Cross to Butler, 15 April 1940.

36. PRO, FO 371/24939, R 4698/58/22, Nichols minute, 12 April 1940, Sargent minute, 12 April 1940, R 4646/58/22, no. 233, Halifax to Charles, 15 April 1940; PRO, CAB 65/6, WM 92(40), War Cabinet meeting, 14 April 1940, WM 94(40), War Cabinet meeting, 16 April 1940; PRO, CAB 21/978, no. 247, Halifax to Charles, 17 April 1940.

37. SHM, Papiers Auphan, GG2, 162, 1, Odend'hal to Auphan, 11 April 1940, Odend'hal to Auphan, 16 April 1940; MAE, P-40, Dejean, 3, N 2239–41, François-Poncet to Reynaud, 12 April 1940, N 2257, François-Poncet to Reynaud, 14 April 1940; MAE, PA-AP, Hoppenot, 17, Corbin to Hoppenot, 13 April 1940; SHAT, 2N, 52, 4, N 30, Potentiel de guerre de l'Italie, Ministre du Blocus, 12 April 1940.

38. SHM, 1BB2, 207, 7, 5, N 37 FMF/0, Darlan to Daladier, 12 April 1940; SHAT, 5N, 583, 10, N 926 FMF/3, Darlan to Daladier, 13 April 1940; MAE, P-40, Daladier, 7, Réunion du Comité de Guerre, 13 April 1940, Réunion du Comité de Guerre, 16 April 1940; PRO, FO 371/24940, R 4826/58/22, no. 133 DIPP, Campbell to Halifax, 16 April 1940; PRO, CAB 21/1319, Interview with Admiral Darlan, Holland to Admiralty, 17 April 1940.

39. PRO, CAB 65/6, WM 95(40), War Cabinet meeting, 17 April 1940; BUL, NC 18/1/1151, Neville to Hilda, 20 April 1940; PRO, CAB 21/1319, Bevan to Cunningham, 17 April 1940; PRO, FO 371/24940, R 4986/58/22, MR(40)20, 18 April 1940; PRO, CAB 21/981, Clarke to Chalmers, 17 April 1940.

40. PRO, CAB 21/1319, Interview with Admiral Darlan, Holland to Admiralty, 17 April 1940; SHM, 1BB2, 207, 6, N 948 FMF/3, Darlan to Daladier, 17 April 1940.

41. SHAT, 27N, 9, 2, N 409 Cab/DN, Gamelin to Daladier, 18 April 1940; SHAT, 27N, 9, 3, N 2652 3/OS, Vuillemin to Gamelin, 17 April 1940; SHM, Papiers Auphan, GG2, 162, 1, Odend'hal to Auphan, 17 April 1940; AN, 496AP, 20, Dr5, sdrb, Sous-Direction d'Europe, Note: Italie et Balkans, 21 April 1940.

42. Ciano, *Diario,* 11, 20 April 1940, pp. 418–19; FRUS, 1940/2, Phillips to Hull, 19 April 1940, p. 686; Knox, "The Fascist Regime," p. 364.

43. ACS, MMG-AS, 107, 15, Copia di telegramma inglese cifrato, Cavagnari to Mussolini, 17 April 1940; ASD, AG, UC, 16, 2, Hitler to Mussolini, 18 April 1940; Mussolini, *Opera Omnia,* 29: 378–81; Ciano, *Diario,* 21, 22 April 1940, pp. 419–20.

44. Ciano, *Diario,* 22, 23, 24, 26 April 1940, pp. 419–22; MAE, P-40, Reynaud, 5, Reynaud to Mussolini, 22 April 1940; ASD, AG, UC, 62, N 2796/1330, Colloquio con Baudoin, Guariglia to Ciano, 25 April 1940, N 3058/1458, Guariglia to Ciano, 7 May 1940.

45. PRO, CAB 21/976, no. 310, Halifax to Charles, 19 April 1940; PRO, CAB 65/6, WM 96(40), WM 97(40), WM 98(40), War Cabinet meetings, 18–20 April 1940; PRO, CAB 107/2, IWB(40)1st meeting, 20 April 1940.

46. PRO, CAB 80/10, COS(40)304, 21 April 1940; PRO, CAB 79/3, COS(40) 90th meeting, 22 April 1940.

47. PRO, CAB 99/3, SWC 22–23 April 1940; MAE, P-40, Dejean, 3, Conseil Suprême à Paris, 22–23 April 1940.

48. PRO, CAB 79/3, COS(40) 95th meeting, 25 April 1940; PRO, CAB 65/6, WM 103(40), WM 104(40), WM 105(40), WM 106(40), WM 107(40), WM 108(40), War Cabinet meetings, 25–30 April 1940; PRO, FO 371/24902, R 5432/5413/67, Nichols minute, 28 April 1940; Cadogan, *Diaries,* 25–27 April 1940, p. 273; BL, Cunningham Papers, 52569, Cunningham to Darlan, 7 April 1940; PRO, CAB 21/1319, Fleet distribution, Bevan to Chalmers, 9 April 1940.

49. MAE, P-40, Daladier, 7, Réunion du Comité de Guerre, 26 April 1940; MAE, P-40, Reynaud, 3, S 50/16, British Record of an Anglo-French Meeting at 10 Downing Street at 9:30 P.M., 26 April 1940; PRO, CAB 99/3, SWC, 27 April 1940; MAE, P-40, Daladier, 7, Conseil Suprême à Londres, 27 April 1940.

50. SHAT, 27N, 6, 2, D.F.N. 151, Note relative aux precautions prises par l'Admiraute français contre l'entrée en guerre de l'Italie, 12 May 1940; SHAT, 27N, 6, 2, D.F.N. 158, Note relative aux precautions prises contre l'entrée en guerre de l'Italie, 14 May 1940; Coutau-Bégarie and Huan, *Darlan,* pp. 206–7; Darlan, *Lettres et notes,* no. 90, pp. 179–80; Masson, *La marine française,* pp. 61–62.

51. PRO, CAB 21/1319, Translation of French Appreciation: Plan of Operations in the Mediterranean, 25 April 1940; MAE, P-40, Daladier, 7, Gamelin note, Note sur la situation en Scandinavie, 26 April 1940; SHM, 1BB2, 207, 6, N 787/3FT, Renforcement des théâtres méditérranéens, Gamelin to Daladier, 30 April 1940; SHM, 1BB2, 207, 6, N 3041–3/OS/EMG, Vuillemin to Darlan, 30 April 1940; SHM, 1BB2, 207, 5, Darlan to Daladier, 2 May 1940; SHAT, 27N, 5, 1, N 128/i, Réunion des Commandants en Chef, 3 May 1940; MAE, P-40, Daladier, 7, Réunion du Comité de Guerre Restreint, 4 May 1940.

52. ASD, AG, UC, 17, 3, Hitler to Mussolini, 9 May 1940, Mussolini to Hitler, 10 May 1940; PRO, FO 371/24943, R 5152/58/22, no. 491 DIPP, Loraine to Halifax, 10 May 1940; Ciano, *Diario,* 10 May 1940, pp. 427–29.

53. Ciano, *Diario,* 3, 6, 9, 10, 11, 18, 29 May 1940, pp. 425–36; USE, H-9, 6, 3, C1/200.741, Balbo to Mussolini, 11 May 1940; USE, H-9, 6, 3, N 11, Efficienza dell'Esercito, Graziani to Mussolini, 25 May 1940; USE, *Verbali delle riunioni,* pp. 43–47.

54. ACS, MMG-AS, 107, 15, Copia di telegramma inglese in cifra, intercettato, Cavagnari to Mussolini, 7 May 1940, Copia di telegramma inglese inviato, Cavagnari to Mussolini, 15 May 1940; USMM, 3279, 9, N 383, Pontremoli to SIS, 8 May 1940; ACS, MMG-AS, 89, 5, N 2147: Pro-Memoria: situazione delle unità in allestimento e collaudo, Farina to Cavagnari, 22 May 1940; ACS, MMG-AS, 91, 7, B 6527, Ciano to Cavagnari, 20 May 1940.

55. Ciano, *Diario,* 10, 12, 13, 14, 15 May 1940, pp. 427–31; ASD, AG, UC, 17, 3, Hitler to Mussolini, 13 May 1940.

56. ASD, AG, UC, 17, 4, Alfieri to Ciano, 19 May 1940, pp. 430–33.

57. SHAT, 27N, 248, 1/2, N 1098–FMF/3, Auphan to Gamelin, 10 May 1940; SHAT, 27N, 6, 1/3, D.F.N. 152, 12 May 1940, D.F.N. 157, 14 May 1940, D.F.N. 158, 14 May 1940, D.F.N. 165, 15 May 1940; SHM, Papiers Auphan, GG2, 162, 1, Odend'hal to Auphan, 13 May 1940; SHAT, 27N, 82, 6, N 1029–3/FT, Opérations en Méditerranée, Gamelin to Darlan, 15 May 1940.

58. PRO, CAB 21/1319, Discussion with Weygand, Cunningham to Pound, 10 May 1940; PRO, CAB 79/4, COS(40) 129th meeting, 13 May 1940; PRO, CAB 85/16, MR(J)(40)(S)14, DF 165, 15 May 1940; PRO, CAB 79/4, COS(40) 135th meeting, 16 May 1940; PRO, CAB 65/7, WM 124(40), War Cabinet meeting, 16 May 1940; Cadogan, *Diaries*, 16 May 1940, p. 284.

59. PRO, CAB 21/978, no. 218 DIPP, Campbell to Cadogan, 16 May 1940; PRO, WO 208/4389, no. 38, Palairet to Halifax, 17 May 1940; PRO, WO 106/2065, 10875 cipher 21/5, Beirut conference, 20–21 May 1940.

60. PRO, CAB 79/4, COS(40) 153d meeting, 27 May 1940, COS(40) 154th meeting, 27 May 1940, COS(40) 159th meeting, 30 May 1940; PRO, CAB 21/1397, no. 227 DIPP, Halifax to Campbell, 28 May 1940; PRO, CAB 21/981, no. R 5992/G, Sargent to Ismay, 29 May 1940, no. 244 DIPP, Halifax to Palairet, 31 May 1940; PRO, WO 106/2065, CRME/1104/4/G, Minutes of Franco-Turkish-British conference at Haifa, 27 May–4 June 1940, no. 0131/7, Cunningham to Admiralty, 7 June 1940, Wavell to War Office, 9 June 1940.

61. Ironside Manuscript Diaries, 1940/2, 14 May 1940; PRO, CAB 79/4, COS(40) 131st meeting, 14 May 1940, COS(40) 138th meeting, 18 May 1940, COS(40) 147th meeting, 24 May 1940; PRO, CAB 21/1304, Medhurst to Rozoy, 19 May 1940.

62. SHAT, 27N, 6, 2, D.F.N. 167, 19 May 1940, D.F.N. 177, 28 May 1940; PRO, CAB 21/1304, N 240 MA/3, Note concernant les opérations aériennes contre l'Italie, Rozoy to Medhurst, 18 May 1940, N 2681 MA/3, Forces Aériennes disponsibles contre l'Italie, Rozoy to Medhurst, 21 May 1940, Medhurst to Slessor, 21 May 1940, Newall memorandum, 24 May 1940; PRO, AIR 75/8, Slessor memorandum, 2 June 1940; SHAT, 27N, 82, 4, N 1188/3–FT, Gamelin to Darlan, 26 May 1940, N 1215 FMF-3, Darlan to Gamelin, 29 May 1940.

63. Ciano, *Diario*, 15, 16, 18 May 1940, pp. 431–32; ASD, AG, UC, 17, 3, Hitler to Mussolini, 18 May 1940, Mussolini to Hitler, 19 May 1940.

64. PRO, FO 371/24931, R 5407/48/22, Relations with Italy: With Particular Reference to Contraband Control. Committee's Final Report, 26 April 1940; PRO, FO 371/24951, R 5919/60/22, Butler minute, 27 April 1940, R 5920/60/22, Sargent minute, 1 May 1940, Cadogan minute, 1 May 1940, Halifax minute, 2 May 1940, Butler minute, 3 May 1940; Cadogan, *Diaries*, 30 April 1940, p. 275; PRO, CAB 21/978, Sargent to Ismay, 13 May 1940, no. 0003/15, Admiralty to C-in-C Mediterranean and C-in-C East Indies, 15 May 1940; DDI, 9/4, nos. 451, 474, 475, 498, pp. 369–98; PRO, CAB 65/7, WM 129(40), War Cabinet meeting, 19 May 1940; PRO, FO 371/24945, R 6127/58/22, no. 406, Halifax to Loraine, 19 May 1940.

65. Ciano, *Diario*, 28 May 1940, p. 435; MAE, P-40, Reynaud, 3, N 3266–69, François-Poncet to Daladier, 28 May 1940; PRO, FO 371/24945, R 6113/58/22, no. 749, Loraine to Halifax, 29 May 1940; DDI, 9/4 nos. 616, 643, 696, pp. 479–538; Cadogan *Diaries*, 24, 29 May 1940, pp. 289, 292; PRO, CAB 65/7, WM 153(40), War Cabinet meeting, 3 June 1940; PRO, CAB 21/978, Ismay to Percival, 3 June 1940.

66. MAE, P-40, Rochat, 25, N 3090, François-Poncet to Daladier, 18 May 1940, N 3141–2, François-Poncet to Daladier, 21 May 1940; AN, 496AP, 24, Dr4, sdrb, François-Poncet to Daladier, 20 May 1940, Daladier note, 25 May 1940; MAE, PA-AP, Dejean, 5, réunion de le cabinet diplomatique, 23 May 1940, Churchill to Reynaud, 28 May 1940; Cadogan, *Diaries*, 26–27 May 1940, pp. 290–91; MAE, P-40, Reynaud, 6, Comité de Guerre, 25 May 1940.

67. MAE, P-40, Reynaud, 4, Saint-Quentin to Daladier, 29 May 1940; AN, 496AP, 24, Dr4, sdrb, N 946, Daladier to François-Poncet, 28 May 1940, N 1089–90, Daladier to Saint-Quentin, 30 May 1940, Reynaud note, 30 May 1940; MAE, P-40, Rochat, 23, N 966–967, Daladier to François-Poncet, 31 May 1940, N 968–71, Hoppenot to François-Poncet, 31 May 1940; ASD, AG, UC, 62, N 2272R, Guariglia to Ciano, 30 May 1940; DDI, 9/4, nos. 644, 652, 657, 659, 661, 664, 665, pp. 498–510.

68. Ciano, *Diario*, 27, 28, 31 May 1940, pp. 434–37; ASD, AG, UC, 85, 2, Colloquio con l'Am-

basciatore degli Stati Uniti, 27 May 1940; MAE, P-40, Reynaud, 5, N 3360–62, François-Poncet to Daladier, 1 June 1940; HL, Phillips Diary, 55M-69, 24, Phillips to Roosevelt, 31 May 1940.

69. USE, I-4, 6, 13, Riunione con il Duce e gli Stati Maggiori delle forze armate, 29 May 1940; Ciano, *Diario*, 26, 29, 30 May 1940, pp. 434–36; ASD, AG, UC, 18, 1, Mussolini to Hitler, 30 May 1940.

70. Fioravanzo, *La marina italiana*, 21/1: 353–55.

71. USE, *Verbali delle riunioni*, 1: 48–53; ASD, AG, UC, 18, 1, Badoglio to Cavagnari, Pricolo, Graziani, 30 May 1940.

72. ASD, AG, UC, 18, 1, Hitler to Mussolini, 31 May 1940, Mussolini to Hitler, 2 June 1940; Ciano, *Diario*, 1, 2 May 1940, pp. 438–39; Schreiber, "The Mediterranean in Hitler's Strategy in 1940," in Deist, *The German Military in the Age of Total War*, pp. 240–81.

73. Ciano, *Diario*, 4 June 1940, p. 440; USE, *Verbali delle riunioni*, 1: 54–58; ACS, Graziani, 51, Badoglio to Cavagnari, Pricolo and Graziani, 7 June 1940.

74. Ciano, *Diario*, 10 June 1940, p. 442; USMM, 2703, discorsi, L'entrata in guerra dell'Italia, Mussolini, 10 June 1940.

75. PRO, ADM 199/1940, Daily Operations Report no. 282, Harcourt to Pound and Churchill, 11 June 1940; Faldella, *L'Italia*, pp. 305–10; Gabriele, *Operazione C3*, pp. 56–59; Schreiber, "Italy and the Mediterranean," in Hattendorf, *Naval Strategy and Policy in the Mediterranean*, p. 125; Playfair, *The Mediterranean*, 1: 109–24; Knox, *Mussolini Unleashed*, pp. 125–33.

76. Cadogan, *Diaries*, 10 June 1940, p. 296; SHAT, 2N, 238, 1, 5, N 390 3/EM.DN, Etude sur le potential de guerre de l'Italie, CSDN note, 4 May 1940; PRO, FO 371/24944, R 6057/58/22, Notes on Italian Air Force since 1 March 1940, West to Loraine, 10 May 1940; PRO, FO 371/24903, R 6605/5413/67, British forces in Mediterranean as of 31 May 1940, Nichols memorandum, 31 May 1940; Ironside Manuscript Diaries, 1940/2, 15 May 1940.

77. PRO, CAB 80/12, COS(40)404, 28 May 1940; PRO, CAB 99/3, SWC, 31 May 1940; SHAT, 27N, 4, 1, Séance du Conseil Suprême, 31 May 1940; PRO, CAB 79/4, COS(40)157th meeting, 29 May 1940; Cadogan, *Diaries*, 12 June 1940, p. 297.

78. MAE, P-40, Rochat, 13, N 2017–25, Daladier to Corbin, 24 May 1940; SHAT, 5N, 580, 7, N 1212/3FT, Conduite à tenir en cas d'Italie hostile, Weygand to Reynaud, 27 May 1940, N 1213/3FT, Propositions en vue de l'adoption d'une politique militaire franco-britannique commune, au cas où l'Italie ouvrirait les hostilités en Méditerranée, 27 May 1940.

79. BL, Cunningham Papers, 52566, Pound to Cunningham, 6 June 1940, Cunningham to Pound, 7 June 1940; Cunningham, *Sailor's Odyssey*, pp. 227–42.

80. MAE, P-40, Reynaud, 2, Notes sur les Operations Scandinaves, Darlan to Reynaud, 9 May 1940; SHM, GG2, 162, Papiers Auphan, 1, Auphan mission à Douvres, 28 May 1940, Odend'hal to Auphan, 4 June 1940; SHM, 2BB7, L11, Odend'hal to Darlan, 5 June 1940; Coutau-Bégarie and Huan, *Darlan*, pp. 213–96.

Bibliography

Archival Sources

Britain

Birmingham University Library (BUL)
British Library, London (BL)
Centre for Kentish Studies, Maidstone, Kent (CKS)
Churchill Archives Centre, Churchill College, Cambridge (CAC)
National Maritime Museum, Greenwich (NMM)
Oxford University Library, Oxford (BOD)
Public Record Office, London (PRO)
Trinity College Library, Cambridge (TCL)

France

Archives Nationales (AN)
Ministère des Affaires Etrangères (MAE)
Service Historique de l'Armée de l'Air (SHAA)
Service Historique de l'Armée de la Terre (SHAT)
Service Historique de l'Armée de la Marine (SHM)

Italy

Archivio Centrale dello State (ACS)
Archivio dell'Ufficio Storico dell'Aeronautica (AUSA)
Archivio Storico Diplomatico al Ministero degli Affari Esteri (ASD)
Ufficio Storico dello Stato Maggiore dell'Esercito (USE)
Ufficio Storico della Marina Militare (USMM)

United States

Franklin D. Roosevelt Library, Hyde Park, N.Y. (FDRL)
Houghton Library, Harvard University, Cambridge, Mass. (HL)

Library of Congress, Washington, D.C. (LC)
National Archives and Records Administration, Washington, D.C. (NARA)

Canada

Trinity College Library, University of Toronto (TCUT)

Printed Sources

Abbazia, P. *Mr. Roosevelt's Navy: The Private War of the U.S. Atlantic Fleet, 1939–1942.* Annapolis, Md., 1975.

Adams, J. *The Doomed Expedition: The Norwegian Campaign of 1940.* London, 1989.

Adamthwaite, A. P. *France and the Coming of the Second World War, 1936–1939.* London, 1977.

——. "War Origins Again." *Journal of Modern History* 56 (1984).

Addison, P. *The Road to 1945: British Politics and the Second World War.* London, 1975.

Agar, A. *Footprints in the Sea.* London, 1959.

Ageron, C.-R. *France coloniale ou parti colonial?* Paris, 1978.

Akten zur Deutschen Auswartigen Politik, 1918–1945. Series C and D. Gottingen, 1973–81. *Documents on German Foreign Policy.* Series C and D. London, 1949–83.

Alexander, Martin S. "Did the Deuxième Bureau Work? The role of Intelligence in French Defence Policy and Strategy, 1919–39." *Intelligence and National Security* 6 (1991).

——. "The Fall of France, 1940." *Journal of Strategic Studies* 13 (1990).

——. "'Fighting to the Last Frenchman'? Reflections on the BEF Deployment to France and the Strains in the Franco-British Alliance, 1939–40." *Historical Reflections/Reflexions Historiques* 22 (1996).

——. *The Republic in Danger: General Maurice Gamelin and the Politics of French Defence, 1933–1940.* Cambridge, 1992.

——. "Safes and Houses: William C. Bullitt, Embassy Security and the Shortcomings of the US Foreign Service in Europe before the Second World War." *Diplomacy and Statecraft* 2 (1991).

——, ed. *Knowing Your Friends: Intelligence Inside Alliances and Coalitions from 1914 to the Cold War.* London, 1998.

Alfieri, Dino. *Due ditatori di fronte.* Milan, 1948.

Aloisi, Pompeo. *Journal (25 Juillet 1932–14 Juin 1936).* Ed. M. Toscano. Paris, 1957.

Alpert, M. *A New International History of the Spanish Civil War.* London, 1994.

Amé, C. *Guerra segreta in Italia, 1940–43.* Rome, 1954.

Andò, E., and E. Bagnasco. *Navi e marina italiani nella seconda guerra mondiale.* Parma, 1977.

Andrew, Christopher. *Her Majesty's Secret Service: The Making of the British Intelligence Community.* New York, 1986.

Andrew, C., and D. Dilks, eds. *The Missing Dimension: Governments and Intelligence Communities in the Twentieth Century.* London, 1984.

Anfuso, Filippo. *Dal Palazzo Venezia al Lago di Garda.* Bologna, 1957.

——. *Roma, Berlino, Salò (1936–1945).* Milan, 1950.

Angot, E., and R. de Lavergne. *Le Général Vuillemin.* Paris, 1965.

Annuaire officiel des officers de l'Armée Active. Paris, annual.

Annuario statistico italiano. Rome, 1926–42.

Araldi, V. *Dalla non belligeranza all'intervento. Come e perchè l'Italia entrò in guerra.* Bologna, 1965.

Ardereth, M. *The French Communist Party: A Critical History (1920–1984) From Comintern to "the Colours of France."* Manchester, 1984.

Arena, N. *Bandiera di combattimento: Storia della marina militare italiane (1924–1945).* Rome, 1974.

Arisi Rota, A. *La diplomazia del ventennio: Storia di una politica estera.* Milan, 1990.

——. "La politica del 'peso determinente': Nota su un concetto di Dino Grandi." *Il Politico* 53 (1988).

Armellini, Q. *Diario di guerra: Nove mesi al comando supremo.* Milan, 1946.

Arnold, W.V. *The Illusion of Victory: Fascist Propaganda and the Second World War.* New York, 1998.

Askew, W.C. "The Secret Agreement between France and Italy on Ethiopia, January 1935." *Journal of Modern History* 25 (1953).

Assemblé Nationale. *Les Événements survenus en France de 1933 à 1945: Témoignages et documents recueillies par la Commission d'Enquête Parlementaire.* 9 vols. Paris, 1947.

Atherton, L. "Lord Lloyd at the British Council and the Balkan Front, 1937–1940." *International History Review* 16 (1994).

Auphan, P. *L'Honneur de servir: Mémoires.* Paris, 1978.

——. *Mensonges et vérité: Essai sur la France.* Paris, 1949.

Auphan, P., and J. Mordal. *La Marine française dans la Seconde Guerre Mondiale.* Paris, 1976. *The French Navy in World War II.* Annapolis, 1959.

Badoglio, Pietro. *L'Italia nella seconda guerra mondiale: Memorie e documenti.* Milan, 1946. *Italy in the Second World War.* Trans. M. Currey. London, 1948.

Baer, George W. *The Coming of the Italian-Ethiopian War.* Cambridge, 1967.

Bailey, T.A., and P. Ryan. *Hitler vs. Roosevelt: The Undeclared Naval War.* New York, 1979.

Baldwin, S. *Service of Our Lives.* London, 1937.

Bandini, F. *Technica della sconfitta: Storia dei quaranta giorni che precedettero e seguirono l'entrata dell'Italia in guerra.* Milan, 1964.

Bankwitz, P. *Maxime Weygand and Civil-Military Relations in Modern France.* Cambridge, 1967.

Baptiste, F.A. "The British Grant of Air and Naval Facilities to the United States in Trinidad, St. Lucia, and Bermuda in 1939." *Caribbean Studies* 16 (1976).

Barclay, G. St. J. "Singapore Strategy: The Role of the United States in Imperial Defence." *Military Affairs* 39 (1975).

Bargoni, F. *Esploratori, fregate, corvette ed avvisi italiani 1861–1968.* Rome, 1968.

——. *L'Impegno navale italiano durante la guerra civile spagnola (1936–1939).* Rome, 1992.

Barker, A.H. *The Civilizing Mission.* London, 1961.

Barnett, Correlli. *The Collapse of British Power.* London, 1972.

——. *Engage the Enemy More Closely: The Royal Navy in the Second World War.* London, 1991.

Barron, G.J. *Leadership in Crisis: FDR and the Path to Intervention.* Port Washington, 1973.

Barros, J. *The Corfu Incident of 1923: Mussolini and the League of Nations.* Toronto, 1966.

Bartlett, C.J. *The Global Conflict: The International Rivalry of the Great Powers, 1880–1990.* London, 1994.

Basch, A. *The Danube Basin and the German Economic Sphere.* London, 1944.

Bastianini, Giuseppe. *Uomini, cose, fatti.* Milan, 1959.

Baudouin, Paul. *Neuf mois au gouvernement: Avril–décembre 1940.* Paris, 1948.

——. "Un voyage à Rome (fevrier 1939)." *Revue des Deux Mondes*, 1 May 1962.
Baum, W., and E. Weichold. *Der Krieg der 'Achsenmächte' in Mittelmeer-Raum: Die 'Strategie' der Diktatoren*. Göttingen, 1973.
Beaufre, A. *1940: The Fall of France*. Cassell, 1967. *Le Drame de 1940*. Paris, 1965.
Bédarida, F., ed. *La Stratégie secrète de la drôle de guerre: Le Conseil supréme interalliée, septembre 1939–avril 1940*. Paris, 1979.
Beesly, P. *Very Special Admiral: The Life of Admiral J.H. Godfrey C.B.* London, 1980.
——. *Very Special Intelligence: The Story of the Admiralty's Operational Intelligence Centre 1939–1945*. London, 1977.
Bell, C.M. *The Royal Navy, Seapower, and Strategy between the Wars*. Princeton, 2000.
Bell, P.M.H. *The Origins of the Second World War in Europe*. London, 1986.
Bentley, M., and J. Stevenson, eds. *High and Low Politics in Modern Britain*. Oxford, 1983.
Bérard, A. *Un ambassadeur se souvient*. Paris, 1976.
Bergougnoux, P. "Le réarmement de la marine nationale (1934–1939)." *Revue Historique des Armées* 4 (1985).
Bernardi, Giovanni. "La Dibattuta questione della parità navale tra Italia e Francia nel periodo tra le due guerre mondiali." *Revue Internationale d'Histoire Militaire* (1978).
——. *Il disarmo navale fra le due guerre mondiale (1919–1939)*. Rome, 1975.
Bernotti, Romeo. *Cinquant'anni nella Marina militare*. Milan, 1971.
——. *La Guerra sui mari conflitto mondiale*. 3 vols. Livorno, 1947–50.
——. "Italian Naval Policy under Fascism." *Naval Institute Proceedings* (1956).
——. "Il Mediterraneo nel prologo del secondo conflitto mondiale." *Nuova antologia* (1956).
——. *Storia della guerra nel Mediterraneo*. Rome, 1960.
Bertrand, M. *La Marine française au combat, 1939–1945*. 2 vols. Paris, 1982–83.
Beschloss, Michael R. *Kennedy and Roosevelt: The Uneasy Alliance*. New York, 1980.
Bessell, R., ed. *Fascist Italy and Nazi Germany: Comparisons and Contrasts*. Cambridge, 1996.
Biagini, A., and A. Gionfrida, eds. *Lo Stato Maggiore Generale tra le due guerre (verbali delle riunioni presiedute da Badoglio dal 1925 al 1937)*. Rome, 1997.
Birkenhead, L. *Halifax: The Life of Lord Halifax*. London, 1965.
Blatt, J. "The Parity That Meant Superiority: French Naval Policy towards Italy at the Washington Conference, 1921–22, and Interwar French Foreign Policy." *French Historical Studies* 2 (1981).
——. ed. *The French Defeat of 1940: Reassessments*. Providence, 1998.
Bloch, Marc. *Étrange défaite: Temoignage écrit en 1940*. Paris, 1946. *Strange Defeat: A Statement of Evidence Written in 1940*. Trans. G. Hopkins. London, 1949.
Blondel, Jules. *Au filière de la carrière: Récit d'un diplomate, 1911–1938*. Paris, 1960.
Blum, Leon. *L'Histoire jugera*. Montreal, 1945.
Bocca, G. *Storia d'Italia nella guerra fascista, 1940–1943*. Rome, 1973.
Bois, E.-J. *La malheur de la France*. London, 1941. *Truth on the Tragedy of France*. Trans. N.S. Wilson. London, 1941.
Bolech, D. "Le Relazioni fra Italia e Inghilterra dalla conclusione dell'accordo di Roma del 16 aprile 1938 alla crisi cecoslovacca del maggio 1938." *Politico* 40 (1975).
Bolech Cecchi, D. *L'Accordo di une imperi: L'accordo italo-inglese del 16 aprile 1938*. Milan, 1977.
——. *Non bruciare i ponti con Roma: Le relazioni fra l'Italia, la Gran Bretagna e la Francia dall'accordo di Monaco allo scoppio della seconda guerra mondiale*. Milan, 1986.
Bond, Brian J. *Britain, France, and Belgium, 1939–1940*. London, 1990.

——. *British Military Policy between Two World Wars.* Oxford, 1980.
——, ed. *Fallen Stars: Eleven Studies in Twentieth-Century Military Disaster.* Oxford, 1991.
Bonnet, Georges, *Dans la tourmente, 1938–1948.* Paris, 1971.
——. *Défense de la paix: De Washington au Quai d'Orsay.* Geneva, 1946.
——. *Fin d'une Europe.* 3 vols. Geneva, 1948.
——. *Le Quai d'Orsay sous trois républiques, 1870–1961.* Paris, 1961.
——. *Vingt ans de vie politique, 1918–1938: de Clemenceau à Daladier.* Paris, 1969.
Boothe, C. *Europe in the Spring.* New York, 1940.
Borgogni, M. "A Proposito della politica estera fascista negli anni trenta." *Il Politico,* 1982.
Bosworth, R.J. *Explaining Auschwitz and Hiroshima: History Writing and the Second World War, 1945–1990.* London, 1993.
——. *Italy: The Least of the Great Powers.* London, 1979.
Bosworth, R.J., and G. Rizzo, eds. *Altro Polo: Intellectuals and Their Ideas in Contemporary Italy.* Sydney, 1983.
Bosworth, R.J., and S. Romano, eds. *La politica estera italiana (1860–1985).* Bologna, 1991.
Bottai, Giuseppe. *Diario, 1935–1944.* Milan, 1994.
——. *Vent'anni e un giorno (24 luglio 1943).* Milan, 1949.
Botti, F., and V. Ilari. *Il pensiero militare italiano dal primo al secondo dopoguerra.* Rome, 1985.
Bourdé, G. *La Défaite du Front Populaire.* Paris, 1977.
Bourdin, J., ed. *Léon Blum, chef de gouvernement.* Paris, 1967.
Boyce, R., ed. *French Foreign and Defence Policy, 1918–1940: The Decline and Fall of a Great Power.* London, 1998.
Boyce, R., and E.M. Robertson, eds. *Paths to War: New Essays on the Origins of the Second World War.* London, 1989.
Bragadin, M. *Che ha fatto la marina? 1940–1945.* Milan, 1956.
Breyer, S. *Battleships and Battle Cruisers, 1905–1970.* Garden City, N.Y., 1973.
Brondi, A.M. *Un generale e "Otto milioni di baionette".* Rome, 1946.
Brundu Olla, P. *L'Equilibrio difficile: Gran Bretagna, Italia, e Francia nel Mediterraneo, 1930–1937.* Milan, 1980.
Buccianti, G. *Verso gli accordi Mussolini-Laval.* Milan, 1984.
Buchanan, T. *Britain and the Spanish Civil War.* New York, 1997.
Buffotot, P. "The French High Command and the Franco-Soviet Alliance, 1933–39." *Journal of Strategic Studies,* 1982.
——. *Histoire de l'Armée de l'Air, 1939–1945.* Paris, 1980.
Bullitt, W.C. *For the President Personal and Secret: Correspondence between Franklin D. Roosevelt and William C. Bullitt.* Ed. O.H. Bullitt, Boston, 1972.
Bullock, A. *Hitler and the Origins of the Second World War.* Oxford, 1967.
Burgwyn, H.J. *Italian Foreign Policy in the Interwar Period, 1918–1940.* Westport, Conn., 1997.
Butler, J.R.M. *Grand Strategy,* vol. 2, *September 1939–June 1941.* London, 1954.
Butterworth, S.B. "Daladier and the Munich Crisis: A Reappraisal." *Journal of Contemporary History* 9 (1974).
Cadogan, Alexander *The Diaries of Sir Alexander Cadogan, 1938–1945.* Ed. D. Dilks. New York, 1972.
Cairns, J.C. "A Nation of Shopkeepers in Search of a Suitable France, 1919–40." *American Historical Review* 79 (1974).
——. "Reflections on France, Britain, and the Winter War Prodrome, 1939–40." *Historical Reflections/Reflexions Historiques* 22 (1996).

Calamandrei, P. *Diario, 1939–1945*. Florence, 1982.
Callahan, R. "The Illusion of Security: Singapore, 1919–42." *Journal of Contemporary History* 9 (1974).
Canevari, E. *La guerra italiana: Retroscena della disfatta.* 2 vols. Rome, 1948–49.
Cannistraro, P.V., and B.R. Sullivan. *Il Duce's Other Woman.* New York, 1993.
Carboni, G. *Memorie segrete (1935–1948).* Florence, 1955.
Carley, M.J. *The Alliance That Never Was and the Coming of World War II.* Chicago, 1999.
Carlton, D. *Anthony Eden: A Biography.* London, 1981.
Carocci, G. *La politica estera dell'Italia fascista, 1925–1928.* Bari, 1969.
Caroff, M. *Le Théâfatre Méditerranéen,* vol. 1, *Du 2 septembre 1939 au 25 juin 1940.* Paris, 1960.
Casali, Alan., and M. Cattaruzza. *Sotto i mari del mondo: La Whitehead, 1875–1990.* Rome, 1990.
Cassels, Alan. *Mussolini's Early Diplomacy.* Princeton, 1970.
——. "Was There a Fascist Foreign Policy?" *International History Review* 5 (1983).
Cavagnari, Domenico. "La marina nella viglia e nel primo periodo della guerra." *Nuova Antologia* 440 (1947).
Cavallero, C. *Il dramma del maresciallo Cavallero.* Milan, 1952.
Cavallero, Ugo. *Comando supremo: Diario 1940–43 del Capo di S.M.G. Premessa di Carlo Cavallero.* Ed. G. Bucciante. Bologna, 1948.
——. *Gli avvenimenti militari nell'Impero dal 12 gennaio 1938–XVI al 12 gennaio 1939–XVII.* 2 vols. Addis Ababa, 1939.
Ceadel, M. *Pacifism in Britain, 1914–1945.* Oxford, 1980.
Ceva, Lucio. "Altre notizie sulle conversazioni militari italo-tedesche alla vigilia della seconda guerra mondiale." *Il Risorgimento* 4 (1978).
——. "Appunti per una storia della Stato Maggiore generale fino alla viglia della 'nonbelligerenza' (giugno 1925–lugio 1939)." *Storia Contemporanea* 10 (1979).
——. "Lo Sviluppo degli aerei militari in Italia (1938–1940)." *Il Risorgimento,* 1983.
——. Review of Knox's *Mussolini's Unleashed,* in *Storia Contemporanea* 14 (1983).
——. *Storia delle forze armate italiane.* Turin, 1981.
Ceva, L., and A. Curami. "Industria bellica e stato nell'imperialismo fascista degli anni '30." *Nuova Antologia,* 1988.
Ceva, L., and A. Curami. *Industria bellica anni trenta: Commesse militari, l'Ansaldo ed altri.* Milan, 1992.
Chabod, F. *A History of Italian Fascism.* London, 1963.
Chamberlain, N. *In Search of Peace.* London, 1939.
Chambrun, C. *Traditions e souvenirs.* Paris, 1952.
Chambrun, R. *Pierre Laval: Traitor or Patriot?* New York, 1984.
Charmley, John. *Chamberlain and the Lost Peace.* London, 1989.
——. *Churchill: The End of Glory.* London, 1993.
——. *Churchill's Grand Alliance.* New York, 1995.
Chatfield, L. *The Navy and Defence,* vol. 2, *It Might Happen Again.* London, 1947.
Chautemps, C. *Cahiers secrets de l'armistice, 1939–1940.* Paris, 1963.
Chauvel, J. *Commentaire,* vol. 1, *De Vienne à Alger, 1938–1944.* Paris, 1971.
Chiavarelli, E. *L'Opera della marina italiana nella guerra italo-etiopica.* Milan, 1980.
Chukumba, S.U. *The Big Powers against Ethiopia: Anglo-French-American Diplomatic Maneuvers during the Italo-Ethiopian Dispute, 1934–1938.* Washington, D.C., 1979.
Churchill, Winston *The Churchill War Papers,* vol. 1, *At the Admiralty, September 1939–May 1940.* Ed. M. Gilbert. New York, 1993.
——. *The Second World War.* 6 vols. Boston, 1948–53.

Ciano, Galeazzo. *Diario, 1937–1943.* Ed. R. DeFelice. Rome, 1990.
——. *L'Europa verso la catastrofe.* Milan, 1948.
Cienciala, A.M. *Poland and the Western Powers, 1938–1939: A Study in the Interdependence of Eastern and Western Europe.* London, 1968.
Cigliana, C. "I Precedenti della campagna di Grecia." *Rivista militare,* November–December 1973.
Ciocca, P., and G. Toniolo, eds. *L'Economia italiana nel periodo fascista.* Bologna, 1976.
Clarke, J.C. *Russia and Italy against Hitler: The Bolshevik-Fascist Rapprochement of the 1930s.* Westport, Conn., 1991.
Clayton, A. *The British Empire as a Superpower, 1919–39.* London, 1986.
Clidakis, H. "Neutrality and War in Italian Policy, 1939–40." *Journal of Contemporary History* 9 (1974).
Clifford, N.R. "Britain, America, and the Far East 1937–1940: A Failure in Cooperation." *Journal of British Studies* 3 (1963–64).
Clough, S.B. *The Economic History of Modern Italy.* New York, 1964.
Cohen, M.J. and M. Kolinsky, eds. *Britain and the Middle East in the 1930s: Security Problems, 1935–39.* London, 1992.
Colville, J. *The Fringes of Power.* London, 1985.
Colvin, I. *Vansittart in Office.* London, 1965.
Comité d'Histoire de la Deuxième Guerre Mondiale. *Français et britanniques dans la drôle de guerre.* Paris, 1979.
——. *La Guerre en Méditerranée, 1939–1945.* Paris, 1971.
——. *Les Relations franco-britanniques de 1935 à 1939.* Paris, 1975.
Conn, S. "Changing Concepts of National Defense in the United States, 1937–1941." *Military Affairs* 28 (1964).
Conti, C. *Servizio segreto: Cronache e documenti dei delitti di Stato.* Rome, 1945.
——, ed. *Il processo Roatta: I documenti.* Rome, 1945.
Cora, Giuliano. "Un diplomatico durante l'era fascista." *Storia e Politica* 5 (1966).
Couhat, J.L. *French Warships of World War II.* London, 1971.
Coulondre, R. *De Stalin à Hitler.* Paris, 1950.
Coutau-Bégarie, Henri. *Castex, le stratégie inconnu.* Paris, 1985.
——. "Comment les français se sont préparés à la guerre." *Revue d'Historie Diplomatique* 97 (1983).
——. *Le Désarmement naval.* Paris, 1995.
——. *L'Evolution de la pensée navale.* 3 vols. Paris, 1990–3.
Coutau-Bégarie, H., and C. Huan. *Darlan.* Paris, 1989.
Coverdale, J.F. *Italian Intervention in the Spanish Civil War.* Princeton, 1975.
Cowling, Maurice. *The Impact of Hitler: British Politics and British Policy, 1933–1940.* Cambridge, 1975.
Cowman, I. *Dominion or Decline: Anglo-American Naval Relations in the Pacific, 1937–1941.* Oxford, 1996.
Craig, G.A., and F. Gilbert, eds. *The Diplomats, 1919–1939.* Princeton, 1953.
Craigie, R. *Behind the Japanese Mask.* London, 1946.
Cras, H. *L'Armstice de juin 1940 et la crise franco-britanique.* Paris, 1959.
Crémieux-Brilhac, J.-L. *Les Français de l'an 40.* 2 vols. Paris, 1990.
Cross, J.A. *Sir Samuel Hoare: A Political Biography.* London, 1977.
Crouy-Chanel, E. *Alexis Léger, l'autre visage de Saint-John Perse.* Paris, 1989.
Crowson, N.J. *Facing Fascism: The Conservative Party and the European Dictators, 1935–1940.* London, 1997.

Cunningham, Andrew B. *A Sailor's Odyssey: The Autobiography of Admiral of the Fleet, Viscount Cunningham of Hyndhope.* New York, 1951.
Curami, A. "Piani e progetti dell'aeronautica italiana, 1939–1943: Stato maggiore e industrie." *Italia Contemporanea* 187 (1992).
Daladier, Edovard. *Défense du pays.* Paris, 1939.
Dallek, R. *Franklin D. Roosevelt and American Foreign Policy, 1932–1945.* New York, 1979.
Dalton, H. *Memoirs*, vol. 2, *The Fateful Years, 1931–1945.* London, 1957.
Dalton, H. *The Political Diary of Hugh Dalton, 1918–40.* Ed. B. Pimlott. London, 1986.
D'Amoja, F. *Declino e prima crisi dell'Europa di Versailles: Studio sulla diplomazia italiana ed europea, 1931–1933.* Milan, 1967.
——. *La politica estera dell'Impero.* Milan, 1967.
Daridan, J. *Le Chemin de la défaite, 1938–1940.* Paris, 1980.
Darlan, Alain. *L'Amiral Darlan parle.* Paris, 1952.
Darlan, François. *Lettres et notes de l'Amiral Darlan.* Ed. H. Coutau-Bégarie and C. Huan. Paris, 1992.
Davignon, V. J. *Berlin, 1936–1940: Souvenirs d'une mission.* Brussels, n.d.
Deakin, F. W. *The Brutal Friendship: Mussolini, Hitler, and the Fall of Italian Fascism.* London, 1962.
Decoux, J. *Adieu Marine.* Paris, 1957.
De Felice, Renzo. *Mussolini il Duce.* 2 vols. Turin, 1974–81.
——. *Mussolini il fascista.* 2 vols. Turin, 1966–8.
——. *Mussolini l'alleato.* 2 vols. Turin, 1990.
——. *Il problema dell'Alto Adige.* Bologna, 1973.
——. ed. *L'Italia fra tedeschi e alleati: La politica estera fascita e la seconda guerra mondiale.* Bologna, 1973.
De Risio, C. *Generali, servizi segreti e fascismo.* Milan, 1978.
Degli Esposti, F. "L'industria bellica italiana e le commesse tedesche (1937–43)." *Rivista di storia contemporanea* 2–3 (1993).
Deist, Wilhelm, ed. *The German Military in the Age of Total War.* New York, 1985.
Deist, Wilhelm, et al., eds. *Germany and the Second World War.* 6 vols. Oxford, 1990–94.
Del Boca, A. *Gli Italiani in Africa Orientale*, vol. 3. Bari, 1982.
——. ed. *Le guerre coloniali del fascismo.* Bari, 1991.
DeLuna, G. *Badoglio: Un militare al potere.* Milan, 1974.
DeMonte, M. *Uomini ombra: Ricordi di un addetto al servizio segreto navale, 1939–1943.* Rome, 1955.
Dennis, P. *Decision by Default: Peacetime Conscription and British Defence, 1919–1939.* London, 1972.
DeRisio, C. "Aspetti della crisi politico-militare nel 1939–40: La non belligeranza italiana e il blocco navale anglo-francese." *Rivista Marittima* 117 (1984).
Destremau, B. *Weygand.* Paris, 1989.
Dictionary of National Biography. Vols. 1931–1970. London, 1949–81.
Di Giovanni, M. *I paracadutisti italiani: Volontari, miti e memoria della seconda guerra mondiale.* Gorizia, 1991.
Dilks, David. *Neville Chamberlain*, vol. 1, *Pioneering and Reform, 1869–1929.* Cambridge, 1984.
——. ed. *Retreat from Power: Studies in Britain's Foreign Policy of the Twentieth Century.* 2 vols. London, 1981.
Di Nolfo, E. *Mussolini e la politica estera italiana, 1922–1933.* Padua, 1960.

Di Nolfo, E., R.H. Rainero, and B. Vigezzi, eds. *L'Italia e la politica di potenza in Europa (1938–1940).* Milan, 1985.

Divine, R.A. *The Reluctant Belligerent: American Entry into World War II.* New York, 1965.

Dizionario Biografico degli Italiani. 54 vols. Rome, 1960–99.

Dockrill, M. *British Establishment Perspectives on France, 1936–40.* New York, 1999.

Docteur, A. *Darlan, amiral de la flotte: La Grande Enigma de la guerre.* Paris, 1949.

Docteur, M. *La Vérité sur les amiraux.* Paris, 1949.

Documents Diplomatiques Français, 1932–1939. Second Series. Vols. 1–19. Paris, 1963–86.

Documents on British Foreign Policy, 1919–1939. Second Series. vols. 12–21; Third Series, vols. 1–7. London, 1954–73.

Doerr, P.W. *British Foreign Policy, 1919–1939: "Hope for the Best, Prepare for the Worst."* Manchester, 1998.

Domarus, Max. *Hitler, Reden und Proklamationen 1932–1945.* 3 vols. Wurzburg, 1962–63. *Hitler, Speeches and Proclamations, 1932–1945.* 3 vols. Wauconda, Ill., 1990.

Doughty, Robert A. *The Seeds of Disaster: The Development of French Army Doctrine, 1919–1939.* Hamden, 1985.

Douglas, R. "Chamberlain and Eden, 1937–38." *Journal of Contemporary History* 13 (1978).

Doumanis, N. *Myth and Memory in the Mediterranean: Remembering Fascism's Empire.* London, 1997.

Doumenc, J.-A. *Les Papiers secret du Général Doumenc: Un Autre Regard sur 39–40.* Ed. F. Delpla. Paris, 1992.

Dragnich, A.N. *Serbs and Croats: The Struggle in Yugoslavia.* New York, 1992.

Dreifort, John E. *Myopic Grandeur: The Ambivalence of French Foreign Policy toward the Far East, 1919–1945.* Kent, 1991.

——. *Yvon Delbos at the Quai d'Orsay: French Foreign Policy during the Popular Front, 1936–1938.* Lawrence, 1973.

Dubief, H. *Le Déclin de la Troisième République: 1929–1938.* Paris, 1979.

Duff Cooper, A. *Old Men Forget: The Autobiography of Viscount Norwich.* London, 1953.

Dülffer, J. *Weimar, Hitler, und die Marine: Reichspolitik und Flottenbau, 1920 bis 1939.* Düsseldorf, 1973.

Duroselle, J.-B. *L'Abîme, 1939–1945.* Paris, 1982.

——. *La Décadence, 1932–1939.* Paris, 1979.

Duroselle, J.-B., and E. Serra, eds. *Italia e Francia dal 1919 al 1939.* Milan, 1981.

——. eds. *Italia, Francia, e Mediterraneo.* Milan, 1990.

Dutailly, H. *Les Problemes de l'armée de terre française, 1935–1939.* Paris, 1980.

Dutter, G. "Doing Business with the Fascists: French Economic Relations with Italy under the Popular Front." *French History* 4 (1990).

Dutton, David. *Anthony Eden: A Life and Reputation.* London, 1997.

——. *Austen Chamberlain: Gentleman in Politics.* Bolton, 1985.

——. *Neville Chamberlain.* London, 2001.

——. *Simon: A Political Biography of Sir John Simon.* London, 1992.

Eden, A. *The Memoirs of Anthony Eden, Earl of Avon 2 vols.* Boston, 1962–65.

Edwards, K. *The Grey Diplomatists.* London, 1938.

——. *Uneasy Oceans.* London, 1939.

Edwards, P. "The Foreign Office and Fascism, 1924–1929." *Journal of Contemporary History* 5 (1970).

Emmerson, J.T. *The Rhineland Crisis.* London, 1977.

Facon, P. "Le Haut Commandement aérien français et la crise de Munich." *Revue Historique des Armées,* 1983.

——. "Le Haut Commandement aérien français et la problème du réarmement 1938–39." *Revue Historique des Armées*, 1980.

Faldella, E. *L'Italia nella seconda guerra mondiale. Rivisione di guidizi.* Bologna, 1960.

Favagrossa, C. *Perché perdemmo la guerra. Mussolini e la produzione bellica.* Milan, 1946.

Feiling, K. *The Life of Neville Chamberlain.* London, 1946.

Ferrante, E. *Il pensiero strategico navale in Italia.* Rome, 1988.

Ferrari, D. "Dalla divisione ternaria alla binaria: una pagina di storia dell'Escercito italiano." In *Memorie storiche militari.* Rome, 1983.

——. "Il Piano segreto di Balbo." *Studi Storico-Militari 1984*, 1985.

Ferretti, V. "La politica estera giapponese e I rapporti con l'Italia e la Germania (1935–1939)." *Storia Contemporanea* 7 (1976).

Ferris, J.R. *The Evolution of British Strategic Policy, 1919–26.* London, 1989.

Fink, C., I.V. Hull, and M. Knox, eds. *German Nationalism and the European Response, 1890–1945.* Norman, 1985.

Fioravanzo, Giuseppe. "Italian Strategy in the Mediterranean, 1940–43." *United States Naval Institute Proceedings* 84 (1958).

——. *La marina italiana nella seconda guerra mondiale*, vol. 21, *L'Oganizzazione della marina durante il conflitto*, bk. 1, *Efficienza all'aperatura delle ostilità.* Rome, 1972.

Flandin, P.-E. *Politique française, 1919–1940.* Paris, 1947.

Fonvielle-Alquier, F. *Les Français dans la drôle de guerre, 39–40.* Paris, 1971. *The French and the Phony War, 1939–40.* Garden City, N.Y., 1973.

Foot, M.R.D. ed. *Historical Essays in Honour and Memory of J.R. Western.* London, 1973.

Foreign Relations of the United States. Vols. 1937–1940. Washington, D.C., 1954–59.

Fraccaroli, A. *Italian Warships of World War II.* London, 1968.

François-Poncet, André. *Au Palais Farnèse: Souvenirs d'une ambassade à Rome, 1938–1940.* Paris, 1961.

——. *Souvenirs d'une ambassade à Berlin, septembre 1931–octobre 1938.* Paris, 1946.

Frank, Willard C. "Multinational Naval Cooperation in the Spanish Civil War, 1936." *Naval War College Review*, 1994.

——. "Naval Operations in the Spanish Civil War, 1936–1939." *Naval War College Review*, 1984.

Frankenstein, R. *Le Prix du réarmement français, 1935–1939.* Paris, 1982.

Fucci, F. *Emilio De Bono: Il maresciallo fucilato.* Milan, 1989.

Fuchser, L.W. *Neville Chamberlain and Appeasement: A Study in the Politics of History.* New York, 1982.

Funk, A.L. "Negotiating the Deal with Darlan." *Journal of Contemporary History* 8 (1973).

Funke, M. *Sanktionen und Kanonen: Hitler, Mussolini, und der internationale Abessinienkonflikt, 1934–36.* Düsseldorf, 1971.

Gabrié, J. *Les Marines de la guerre 1935–1945.* Paris, 1994.

Gabriele, Mariano. "1939: Viglia di guerra nel Mediterraneo." *Rivista Marittima* 17 (1984).

——. "I piani della marina francese contro l'Italia nel 1939." *Bolletino d'Archivio dell'Ufficio Storico della Marina Militare*, 1988.

——. "L'Italia nel Mediterraneo fra tedeschi e alleati, 1938–1940." *Rivista Marittima* 117 (1984).

——. *Operazione C3: Malta.* Rome, 1990.

Gamelin, Maurice. *Servir.* 3 vols. Paris, 1946–47.

Garder, M. *La Guerre secrète des services spéciaux français, 1935–1945.* Paris, 1967.

Garnier, J.-P. *Excellences et plumes blanches, 1922–1946.* Paris, 1961.

Gates, E.M. *End of the Affair: The Collapse of the Anglo-French Alliance, 1939–1940.* Berkeley, 1981.
Gatta, B. *Mussolini.* Milan, 1988.
Gatzke, H.W., ed. *European Diplomacy between Two Wars, 1919–39.* Chicago, 1972.
Gauché, M. *Le Deuxième Bureau au trauvail, 1935–1940.* Paris, 1953.
Gehl, J. *Austria, Germany, and the Anschluss, 1931–1938.* London, 1963.
Gemzell, C.-A. *Raeder, Hitler, und Skandanaview: Der Kampf für einen maritimen Operationsplan.* Lund, 1965.
Géraud, A. "France and the Anglo-German Naval Treaty." *Foreign Affairs* (1935).
——. *The Gravediggers of France.* New York, 1944.
Giambartolomei, A. "I Servizi segreti militari italiani." *Rivista Militare,* 1983.
Giannini, A. "L'accordo italo-germanico per il carbone (1940)." *Rivista di Studi Politici Internazionali* 21 (1954).
Giardana, G. *Il patto a quattro nella politica estera di Mussolini.* Correggio, 1976.
Gibbs, N.H. *Grand Strategy,* vol. 1, *Rearmament Policy.* London, 1976.
Gilbert, Martin. *Churchill: A Life.* London, 1991.
——. *Finest Hour: Winston S. Churchill, 1939–1941.* London, 1989.
——. *Prophet of Truth: Winston S. Churchill, 1922–1939.* London, 1990.
Gilbert, M., and R. Gott. *The Appeasers.* London, 1967.
Giorgerini, Giorgio. *La Battaglia dei convogli in Mediterraneo.* Milan, 1977.
——. *Da Matapan al Golfo Persico: La marina militare italiana dal fascismo alla Repubblica.* Milan, 1989.
Giorgerini, G., and A. Nani. *Almanacco storico delle navi militari italiane: La marina e le sue navi dal 1861 al 1975.* Rome, 1978.
Girault, R., and R. Frank, eds. *La Puissance en Europe, 1938–1940.* Paris, 1984.
Gladwyn, L. *The Memoirs of Lord Gladwyn.* London, 1972.
Goda, N.J.W. *Tomorrow the World: Hitler, Northwest Africa and the Path toward America.* College Station, 1998.
Goglia, L. "Il Mufti e Mussolini: Alcuni documenti italiani sui rapporti tra nazionalismo palestinese e fascismo negli anni trenta." *Storia Contemporanea* 17 (1986).
Goldman, A. "Sir Robert Vansittart's Search for Italian Cooperation against Hitler, 1933–36." *Journal of Contemporary History* 9 (1974).
Goldman, E.O. *Sunken Treaties: Naval Arms Control between the Wars.* University Park, 1994.
Goldrick, J., and J.B. Hattendorf, eds. *Mahan Is Not Enough: The Proceedings of a Conference on the Works of Sir Julian Corbett and Admiral Sir Herbert Richmond.* Newport, 1993.
Goldstein, E., and J. Maurer, eds. *The Washington Conference, 1921–22: Naval Rivalry, East Asian Stability, and the Road to Pearl Harbor.* London, 1994.
Gombin, R. *Les Socialistes et la guerre.* The Hague, 1970.
Gordon, G.A.H. "The Admiralty and Imperial Overstretch, 1902–1941." *Journal of Strategic Studies* 17 (1994).
——. *British Seapower and Procurement between the Wars: A Reappraisal of Rearmament.* Annapolis, 1988.
Grandi, Dino. *Il mio paese: Ricordi autobiografici.* Bologna, 1985.
Grange, D.J. "Structure et techniques d'ne propagande: Les Emissions arabes de Radio-Bari." *Relations internationales* 2 (1974).
Greene, N. *Crisis and Decline.* Ithaca, 1969.
Greenwood, S. "Caligula's Horse Revisted: Sir Thomas Inskip as Minister for the Coordination of Defence, 1936–39." *Journal of Strategic Studies,* 1994.

Gretton, P. "The Nyon Conference—The Naval Aspect." *English Historical Review* 90 (1975).

Guariglia, Raffaele. *Ricordi, 1922–1946*. Naples, 1949.

——. *Scritti 'storico-eruditi' e documenti diplomatici (1936–1940)*. Naples, 1981.

Guarneri, F. *Battaglie economiche tra le due grandi guerri*. Milan, 1953.

Guerri, G. B. *Galeazzo Ciano: Una vita, 1903–1944*. Milan, 1979.

Gunsburg, J. A. *Divided and Conquered: The French High Command and the Defeat of the West, 1940*. Westport, Conn., 1979.

Haggie, P. *Britannia at Bay: The Defence of the British Empire against Japan, 1931–1941*. Oxford, 1981.

Haight, J. M. *American Aid to France, 1938–1940*. New York, 1970.

——. "France, the United States, and the Munich Crisis." *Journal of Modern History* 32 (1960).

Haine, C. G. *The Origins and Background of the Second World War*. New York, 1943.

Halder, F. *Kriegstagebuch: Tägliche Aufzeichnungen des Chefs des Generalstabes des Heeres, 1939–1942*. 3 vols. Stuttgart, 1962–64. *The Halder Diaries, 1939–1942*. 2 vols. Trans. T. N. Dupuy. Boulder, 1975.

Halifax, L. *Fullness of Days*. London, 1957.

Halpern, Paul G. *The Mediterranean Naval Situation, 1908–1914*. Cambridge, 1971.

Haraszti, E. H. *Treaty-Breakers or Realpolitiker? The Anglo-German Naval Agreement of June 1935*. Trans. S. Simon. Boppard, 1973.

Hardie, F. *The Abyssinian Crisis*. London, 1974.

Harvey, O. *The Diplomatic Diaries of Oliver Harvey, 1937–1940*. Ed. J. Harvey. London, 1970.

Hattendorf, John B., ed. *Naval Policy and Strategy in the Mediterranean Sea, Past, Present, and Future*. London, 2000.

——, ed. *Ubi Sumus? The State of Naval and Maritime History*. Newport, 1994.

Hattendorf, J. B., and R. S. Jordan, eds. *Maritime Strategy and the Balance of Power: Britain and America in the Twentieth Century*. London, 1989.

Henderson, N. *Failure of a Mission: Berlin, 1937–1939*. London, 1940.

Herman, J. *The Paris Embassy of Sir Eric Phipps*. Brighton, 1998.

Herriot, E. *Etudes et témoignages*. Paris, 1975.

Herwig, Holger H. *The Politics of Frustration: The United States in German Naval Planning, 1889–1941*. Boston, 1976.

——. "Prelude to Weltblitzkrieg: Germany's Naval Policy towards the United States, 1939–41." *Journal of Modern History* 44 (1971).

Hibbert, C. *Benito Mussolini: The Rise and Fall of Il Duce*. Harmondsworth, 1975.

Higham, R. *Armed Forces in Peacetime*. London, 1972.

Hildebrand, K. *The Foreign Policy of the Third Reich*. Berkeley, 1973.

Hillgruber, Andreas. *Germany and the Two World Wars*. Cambridge, 1981.

——. *Hitlers Strategie: Politik und Kriegführung, 1940–1941*. Frankfurt, 1965.

Hilton, S. E. "The Welles Mission to Europe, February-March 1940: Illusion or Realism?" *Journal of American History* 58 (1971–72).

Hinsley, F. H. *British Intelligence in the Second World War: Its Influence on Strategy and Operations*. Vol. 1. London, 1979.

Hitler, Adolf. *Hitler: Reden und Proklamationen 1932–1945*. 2 vols. Ed. M. Domarus. Munich, 1963–65. *Hitler: Speeches and Proclamations, 1932–1945*. Trans. M. F. Gilbert. Wauconda, 1990–98.

——. *Hitlers Weisungen für die Kriegsführung, 1939–1945*. Ed. W. Hubatsch. Frankfurt, 1962. *Hitler's War Directives, 1939–1945*. Trans. H. R. Trevor-Roper. London, 1964.

Hitler, A., and B. Mussolini. *Hitler e Mussolini: Lettere e documenti.* Ed. V. Zincone. Milan, 1946.

Hoare, S. *Nine Troubled Years.* London, 1954.

Höhne, H. *Canaris: Patriot im Zwielicht.* Munich, 1976.

Hood, Ronald C. "The French Navy and Parliament between the Wars." *International History Review* 6 (1984).

——. *Royal Republicans: The French Naval Dynasties between the World Wars.* Baton Rouge, 1985.

Hopkins, J. *Into the Heart of the Fire: The British in the Spanish Civil War.* Stanford, 1998.

Hoptner, J.B. *Yugoslavia in Crisis, 1934–1941.* New York, 1964.

Hore-Belisha, L. *The Private Papers of Hore-Belisha.* Ed. R.J. Minney. London, 1960.

Horne, A. *The French Army and Politics, 1870–1970.* London, 1984.

House of Commons, Great Britain. *Parliamentary Debates.* Annual. London.

Howard, Michael E. *The Continental Commitment: The Dilemma of British Defense Policy on the Eve of the Two World Wars.* London, 1972.

——. *The Mediterranean Strategy in the Second World War.* New York, 1968.

——, ed. *The Theory and Practice of War: Essays in Honour of B.H. Liddell Hart.* London, 1966.

Howarth, S., ed. *Men of War: Great Naval Leaders of World War II.* London, 1992.

Howarth, S., and D. Law, eds. *The Battle of the Atlantic 1939–1945: The 50th Anniversary International Naval Conference.* Annapolis, 1994.

Hull, C. *The Memoirs of Cordell Hull.* London, 1948.

Humble, R. *Fraser of North Cape: The Life of Admiral of the Fleet Lord Fraser (1898–1981).* London, 1983.

Iachino, A. *La sorpresea di Matapan.* Verona, 1957.

——. *Tramonto di una grande marina.* Milan, 1960.

Ickes, Harold L. *The Secret Diary of Harold L. Ickes.* 2 vols. London, 1955.

I Documenti Diplomatici Italiani. Eighth Series. Vols. 1–13. Rome, 1950–1953.

Imlay, Talbot. "How to Win a War: British and French Strategies for War against Germany, 1938–1940." Ph.D. dissertation, Yale University, 1997.

Ion, A.H., and E.J. Errington, eds. *Great Powers and Little Wars: The Limits of Power.* Westport, Conn., 1993.

Iriye, A. *The Origins of the Second World War in Asia and the Pacific.* New York, 1987.

Ironside, L. *The Ironside Diaries, 1937–1940.* Ed. R. Macleod and D. Kelly. London, 1963.

Irvine, William D. "Domestic Politics and the Fall of France in 1940." *Historical Reflections Reflexions Historiques* 22 (1996).

——. *French Conservatism in Crisis: The Republican Federation of France in the 1930s.* Baton Rouge, 1979.

Ismay, L. *The Memoirs of General Lord Ismay.* London, 1960.

Israelyan, V.L., and L.V. Kutakov. *Diplomacy of Aggression: Berlin-Rome-Tokyo Axis—Its Rise and Fall.* Moscow, 1970.

Italy, Ministero del Tesoro, Ragioneria Generale dello Stato. *Il bilancio dello Stato negli esercizi finanziari dal 1930–31 al 1941–42.* Rome, 1951.

Jackson, J. *The Popular Front in France Defending Democracy.* Cambridge, 1988.

Jackson, Peter. "France and the Guarantee to Romania, April 1939." *Intelligence and National Security* 10 (1995).

——. *France and the Nazi Menace: Intelligence and Policy Making, 1933–1939.* Oxford, 2001.

Jacomet, R. *L'Armement de la France, 1936–1939*. Paris, 1945.
James, R.R. *Anthony Eden*. New York, 1987.
James, W. *The Sky Was Always Blue*. London, 1951.
Jenkins, R. *Baldwin*. London, 1987.
Jervis, Robert. *Perception and Misperception in International Politics*. Princeton, 1976.
Jordan, Nicole. "Maurice Gamelin, Italy, and the Eastern Alliances." *Journal of Strategic Studies*, 1991.
——. *The Popular Front and Central Europe: The Dilemmas of French Impotence, 1918–1940*. Cambridge, 1992.
——. "Strategy and Scapegoatism: Reflections on the French National Catastrophe, 1940." *Historical Reflections/Reflexions Historiques* 22 (1996).
Jouan, R. *Historie de la marine française*. Paris, 1950.
Journal Officiel de la République Française, Assemblée Nationale. *Débats Parlementaires*. Paris, annual.
Kaiser, David E. *Economic Diplomacy and the Origins of the Second World War*. Princeton, 1980.
Kaufman, R.G. *Arms Control during the Pre-Nuclear Era: The United States and Naval Limitation between the Two World Wars*. New York, 1990.
Kemp, T. *The French Economy, 1913–39*. London, 1972.
Kennedy, G., and K. Neilson, eds. *Butterfly Wings: Incidents and International Relations, 1795–1940*. New York, 2002.
Kennedy, Paul M. "Appeasement and British Defence Policy in the Inter-war Years." *British Journal of International Studies* 4 (1978).
——. *The Realities behind Diplomacy: Background Influences on British External Policy, 1865–1980*. London, 1981.
——. *The Rise and Fall of British Naval Mastery*. London, 1976.
——. *The Rise and Fall of the Great Powers: Economic Change and Military Conflict from 1500 to 2000*. London, 1987.
——. *Strategy and Diplomacy, 1870–1945*. London, 1983.
——. "Strategy versus Finance in Twentieth-Century Britain." *International History Review* 3 (1981).
——. "The Tradition of Appeasement in British Foreign Policy, 1865–1939." *British Journal of International Studies* 2 (1976).
Kersaudy, F. *1940: La Guerre du fer*. Paris, 1987. *Norway 1940*. London, 1990.
Kershaw, Ian. *Hitler*, 2 vols. New York, 1999, 2000.
Kettenacker, H.L., ed. *Das 'Andere Deutschland' im Zweiten Weltkrieg: Emigration und Widerstand in internationaler Perspektive*. Stuttgart, 1977.
Kier, E. *Imagining War: French and British Military Doctrine between the Wars*. Princeton, 1997.
Kiesling, E.C. *Arming against Hitler: France and the Limits of Military Planning*. Lawrence, 1996.
Kirkpatrick, I. *Mussolini: A Study in Power*. New York, 1964.
Knox, H. MacGregor. *Common Destiny: Dictatorship, Foreign Policy, and War in Fascist Italy and Nazi Germany*. New York, 2000.
——. "Conquest, Foreign and Domestic, in Fascist Italy and Nazi Germany." *Journal of Modern History* 56 (1984).
——. "The Fascist Regime, Its Foreign Policy and Its Wars: An 'Anti-Anti-Fascist Orthodoxy'?" *Contemporary European History*, 1995.
——. *Mussolini Unleashed: Politics and Strategy in Fascist Italy's Last War*. Cambridge, 1982.

Koburger, C. W. *The Cyrano Fleet: France and Its Navy, 1940–42*. New York, 1989.
Kordt, E. *Nicht aus den Akten*. Stuttgart, 1950.
Kupferman, F. *Laval*. Paris, 1987.
Lacouture, J. *Léon Blum*. Paris, 1977.
Lagardelle, H. de. *Mission à Rome*. Paris, 1955.
Langhorne, R., ed. *Diplomacy and Intelligence during the Second World War*. Cambridge, 1985.
Lanza, M. (L. Simoni). *Berlino: Ambasciata d'Italia, 1939–1943*. Rome, 1946.
Lash, J. P. *Roosevelt and Churchill, 1939–1941: The Partnership That Saved the West*. London, 1977.
Laurens, F. D. *France and the Italo-Ethiopian Crisis, 1935–1936*. Paris, 1967.
Laval, Pierre. *Laval parle*. Paris, 1948. *The Diary of Pierre Laval*. New York, 1948.
Lavine, M. F. *Count Ciano: Foreign Affairs and Policy Determination in Fascist Italy, January 1939–June 1940*. City? 1977.
Le Goyet, P. *Le Mystère Gamelin*. Paris, n.d.
——. *Munich: "Un traquenard"?* Paris, 1988.
Le leggi e i decreti reali secondo l'ordine della inserzione nella Gazzetta ufficiale. Rome, annual.
Leeds, S. B. *These Rule France*. New York, 1940.
Lefranc, G. *Le Front populaire: 1934–1938*. Paris, 1978.
——. *Le Mouvement socialiste sous la Troisième République*. Paris, 1963.
Lessona, A. *Memorie*. Rome, 1963.
Leto, G. *OVRA. Fascismo–Antifascismo*. Bologna, 1952.
Leutze, James R. *Bargaining for Supremacy: Anglo-American Naval Relations, 1937–1941*. Chapel Hill, 1977.
——. "The Secret of the Churchill-Roosevelt Correspondence: September 1939–May 1940." *Journal of Contemporary History* 10 (1975).
Lockhart, R. B. *The Diaries of Sir Robert Bruce Lockhart, 1915–1938*. Ed. K. Young. London, 1973.
Longo, L. E. *Franceso Saverio Grazioli*. Rome, 1989.
Louis, W. R. *British Strategy in the Far East 1919–1939*. Oxford, 1971.
Lowe, C., and F. Marzari. *Italian Foreign Policy, 1870–1940*. London, 1975.
Lowe, P. *Great Britain and the Origins of the Pacific War: A Study of British Policy in East Asia, 1937–1941*. Oxford, 1977.
Lowenthal, M. M. "Roosevelt and the Coming of the War: The Search for United States Policy, 1937–42." *Journal of Contemporary History* 16 (1981).
Luciolli, M. *Palazzo Chigi, anni roventi*. Milan, 1976.
Ludwig, E. *Talks with Mussolini*. London, 1933.
Lukacs, John. *Five Days in London: May 1940*. New Haven, 1999.
——. *The Last European War*. Garden City, N.Y., 1976.
Lytte, R. B. *Il Duce: The Rise and Fall of Benito Mussolini*. New York, 1987.
Lyttelton, A. *The Seizure of Power: Fascism in Italy, 1919–1929*. Princeton, 1987.
McBride, W., ed. *New Interpretations in Naval History: Selected Papers from the Thirteenth Naval History Symposium*. Annapolis, 1998.
McCarthy, J. M. "The Imperial Commitment, 1939–1941." *Australian Journal of Politics and History* 23 (1977).
MacDonald, C. A. "Britain, France, and the April Crisis of 1939." *European Studies Review* 2 (1972).
——. "Radio Bari: Italian Wireless Propaganda in the Middle East and British Countermeasures 1934–38." *Middle Eastern Studies* 13 (May 1977).

McIntyre, W. D. *The Rise and Fall of the Singapore Naval Base, 1919–1942*. London, 1979.
McKercher, B. J. C. *Transition of Power: Britain's Loss of Global Pre-eminence to the United States, 1930–1945*. New York, 1999.
Mack Smith, Denis. *Mussolini*. London, 1981.
——. "Mussolini, Artist in Propaganda: The Downfall of Italian Fascism." *History Today* 9 (1959).
——. *Mussolini's Roman Empire*. London, 1976.
McLachlan, D. *Room 39: Naval Intelligence in Action, 1939–45*. London, 1968.
Maiolo, Joseph A. *The Royal Navy and Nazi Germany, 1933–39: A Study in Appeasement and the Origins of the Second World War*. New York, 1998.
Mallett, Robert. "The Italian Naval High Command and the Mediterranean Crisis, January—October 1935," *Journal of Strategic Studies* 22 (1999).
——. *The Italian Navy and Fascist Expansionism 1935–1940*. London, 1998.
Marder, Arthur J. *Old Friends, New Enemies: The Royal Navy and the Imperial Japanese Navy. Strategic Illusions, 1936–1941*. Oxford, 1981.
——. "The Royal Navy and the Ethiopian Crisis of 1935–36." *American Historical Review* 75 (1970).
——. "Winston Is Back: Churchill at the Admiralty, 1939–40." In *From the Dardanelles to Oran: Studies of the Royal Navy in War and Peace, 1915–1940*. London, 1974.
Martel, G., ed. *The Origins of the Second World War Reconsidered: The A. J. P. Taylor Debate after Twenty-Five Years*. London, 1986.
Marzari, F. "Projects for an Italian-led Balkan Bloc of Neutrals, September-December 1939." *Historical Journal* 13 (1970).
——. "Western-Soviet Rivalry in Turkey, 1939." *Middle Eastern Studies* 7 (1971).
Massigli, R. *La Turquie devant la guerre: Mission à Ankara, 1939–1940*. Paris, 1964.
Masson, Philippe. *Histoire de la marine*. 2 vols. Paris, 1981–83.
——. "La Marine française en 1939–1940." *Revue Historique des Armées* (1979).
——. *La Marine française et la guerre 1939–1945*. Paris, 1991.
Maugeri, F. *Ricordi di un marinaio*. Milan, 1980.
May, Ernest R. *Strange Victory: Hitler's Conquest of France*. New York, 2000.
——, ed. *Knowing One's Enemies: Intelligence Assessment before the Two World Wars*. Princeton, 1984.
Mazzetti, M. *La politica militare italiana fra le due guerre mondiali (1918–1940)*. Salerno, 1974.
Medlicott, William N. *British Foreign Policy since Versailles 1919–1963*. London, 1968.
——. *The Coming of War in 1939*. London, 1963.
——. *The Economic Blockade*. Vol. 1. London, 1952.
Melograni, P. *Rapporti segreti della polizia fascista 1938/1940*. Milan, 1978.
Melton, G. E. *Darlan: Admiral and Statesman of France, 1881–1942*. Westport, Conn., 1998.
Merglen, A. *Histoire et avenir de troupes aéroporteés*. Paris, 1968.
Micaud, C. A. *The French Right and Nazi Germany, 1933–39*. New York, 1963.
Michel, H. *La Défaite de la France (septembre 1939–juin 1940)*. Paris, 1980.
Micheletti, B., and P. Paolo Poggio, eds. *L'Italia in guerra, 1940–43*. Brescia, 1991.
Middlemas, K. *Diplomacy of Illusion: The British Government and Germany, 1937–1939*. London, 1972.
Millman, Brock. *The Ill-Made Alliance: Anglo-Turkish Relations, 1934–1940*. Montreal, 1998.
——. "Toward War with Russia: British Naval and Air Planning for Conflict in the Near East, 1939–40." *Journal of Contemporary History* 29 (1994).
Mills, W. C. "The Nyon Conference: Neville Chamberlain, Anthony Eden, and the Appeasement of Italy in 1937." *International History Review* 15 (1993).

Milza, P., and S. Berstein. *Le Fascisme italien, 1919–1945*. Paris, 1980.
Minardi, S. "L'Accordo militare segreto Badoglio-Gamelin del 1935." *Clio*, 1987.
Minniti, Fortunato. "Aspetti organizzativi del controllo sulla produzione bellica in Italia (1923–1943)." *Clio*, 1977.
——. "Aspetti territoriali e politici del controllo sulla produzione bellica in Italia (1936–42)." *Clio*, 1979.
——. "Le materie prime nella preparazione bellica dell'Italia (1935–1943)." *Storia contemporanea* 17 (1986).
——. "Il problema degli armamenti nella preparazione militare italiana dal 1935 al 1943." *Storia Contemporanea* 9 (1978).
——. "La politica industriale del Ministero dell'Aeronautica: mercato, pianificazione, sviluppo (1935–1943)." *Storia Contemporanea* (1981).
Moch, J. *Rencontres avec Léon Blum*. Paris, 1970.
Mola, A. A., ed. *Dall'Italia giolittiana all' Italia repubblicana*. Turin, 1976.
Mommsen, W. J., and L. Kettenacker, eds. *The Fascist Challenge and the Policy of Appeasement*. London, 1983.
Montanari, M. *L'esercito italiano alla vigilia della seconda guerra mondiale*. Rome, 1982.
——. *Le truppe italiane in Albania (Anni 1914–20 e 1939)*. Rome, 1978.
Montanelli, I., and M. Cervio. *L'Italia dell'Asse (1936–1940)*. Milan, 1980.
Montgomery Hyde, H. *British Air Policy between the Wars, 1918–1939*. London, 1976.
Monzie, A. de. *Ci-devant*. Paris, 1941.
Moreau, J. *Les Derniers Jours de l'amiral Darlan*. Paris, 1985.
Mori, Renato. *Mussolini e la conquista dell'Etiopia*. Florence, 1978.
——. "Verso il riavvicinamento fra Hitler e Mussolini." *Storia e Politica* 15 (1976).
Morison, S. E. *History of the United Staes Naval Operations in World War II*, vol 1, *The Battle of the Atlantic: September 1939–May 1943*. London, 1948.
Mosley, R. *Mussolini's Shadow: The Double Life of Count Galeazzo Ciano*. New Haven, 1999.
Mourélos, Y. G. *Fictions et réalités: La France, la Grèce, et la stratégie des opérations périphériques dans le sud-est européen (1939–1940)*. Thessaloniki, 1990.
Murfett, Malcolm. *Fool-Proof Relations: The Search for Anglo-American Naval Cooperation during the Chamberlain Years*. Singapore, 1984.
——, ed. *The First Sea Lords: From Fisher to Mountbatten*. Westport, 1995.
Murray, Williamson. *The Change in the European Balance of Power, 1938–1939: The Path to Ruin*. Princeton, 1984.
——. "The Role of Italy in British Strategy, 1938–1939." *Journal of the Royal United Services Institute* 124 (1979).
Murray, W., and A. R. Millett, eds. *Calculations: Net Assessment and the Coming of World War II*. New York, 1992.
——, eds. *Military Effectiveness*, vol. 2, *The Interwar Period*. Boston, 1988.
Mussolini, Benito. *Four Speeches on the Corporate State*. New York, 1935.
——. *My Autobiography*. London, 1939.
——. *Opera Omnia di Benito Mussolini*. Vols. 1–44. Florence, 1951–80.
Mysyrowicz, L. *Autopsie d'une défaite*. Lausanne, 1973.
Namier, L. B. *Diplomatic Prelude, 1938–1939*. New York, 1971.
——. *Europe in Decay, 1936–1940*. London, 1950.
Naylor, J. F. *A Man and an Institution: Sir Maurice Hankey, the Cabinet Secretariat, and the Custody of Cabinet Secrecy*. Cambridge, 1984.

Neidpath, J.L. *The Singapore Naval Base and the Defence of Britain's Eastern Empire, 1919–1941.* Oxford, 1981.
Nello, Paolo. *Dino Grandi: La formazione di un leader fascista.* Bologna, 1987.
——. *Un fedele disubbiente: Dino Grandi da Palazzo Chigi al 25 luglio.* Bologna, 1993.
Néré, J. *The Foreign Policy of France from 1914–1945.* London, 1975.
Neustadt, Richard. *Alliance Politics.* New York, 1970.
Nöel, Leon. *Les Illusions de Stresa: L'Italie abandonnée à Hitler.* Paris, 1975.
——. *Munich et la Pologne: Souvenirs.* Paris, 1946.
O'Brien, E.D. "With the Duce in Libya." *English Review* 64 (May 1937).
Ollard, R.L. *Fisher and Cunningham: A Study in the Personalities of the Churchill Era.* London, 1991.
Ormos, M. "L'opinione del conte Stefano Bethlen sui rapporti italo-ungheresi (1927–31)." *Storia Contemporanea* 2 (1971).
——. "Sur les causes de l'échec du pacte danubian." *Acta Historica* 14 (1968).
Overy, Richard J. *The Air War, 1939–1945.* New York, 1980.
Overy, R.J., with A. Wheatcroft. *The Road to War.* London, 1989.
Paillole, P. *Services spéciaux, 1935–1945.* Paris, 1975.
Pariani, A. *Chiacchiere e realtà: Lettere agli amici.* Milan, 1949.
Parker, R.A.C. "Britain, France, and Scandanavia, 1939–1940." *History* 61 (1976).
——. *Chamberlain and Appeasement: British Policy and the Coming of the Second World War.* New York, 1993.
——. "Economics, Rearmament, and Foreign Policy: The United Kingdom before 1939—a Preliminary Study." *Journal of Contemporary History* 10 (1975).
——. "Great Britain, France and the Ethiopian Crisis 1935–1936." *English Historical Review* 89 (1974).
——. *Struggle for Survival: The History of the Second World War.* Oxford, 1989.
Parti républicain radical et radical-socialiste. *35e Congrès du Parti républicain radical et radical-socialiste tenu à Marseilles, France.* Paris, annual.
Pastorelli, P. *Italia e Albania, 1924–1927: Origini diplomatiche del Trattato di Tirana del 22 novembre 1927.* Florence, 1927.
Paul-Boncour, Joseph. *Entre deux guerres: Souvenirs sur la troisième république.* 3 vols. Paris, 1945–46.
Peden, G.C. *British Rearmament and the Treasury, 1932–1939.* Edinburgh, 1979.
Pedriali, F. *Guerra di Spagna e aviazione italiana.* Pinerolo, 1989.
Pelz, S. *Race to Pearl Harbor: The Failure of the Second Naval Conference and the Onset of World War II.* Cambridge, 1974.
Perett, W.G. "French Naval Policy and Foreign Affairs, 1930–1939." Ph.D. dissertation, Stanford University, 1977.
Perich, G. *Mussolini nei Balcani.* Milan, 1966.
Petacco, A. *Le Battaglie navali del Mediterraneo nella seconda guerra mondiale.* Milan, 1977.
Peters, A.R. *Anthony Eden at the Foreign Office, 1931–1938.* New York, 1986.
Petersen, J. *Hitler-Mussolini: Die Entstehung der Achse Berlin-Rom, 1933–1936.* Tübingen, 1973.
Petrie, C. *The Life and Letters of the Right Hon. Sir Austen Chamberlain.* Vol. 2. London, 1940.
Philpott, William and Martin Alexander, eds. *Anglo-French Defence Cooperation between the Wars.* London, forthcoming.
Pieri, P., and G. Rochat. *Pietro Badoglio.* Turin, 1974.
Pike, D.W. *Conjecture, Propaganda, and Deceit and the Spanish Civil War.* Stanford, 1968.

Pillon, G. *Spie per l'Italia.* Rome, 1968.

Pirelli, A. *Taccuini, 1922–1943.* Bologna, 1984.

Playfair, I. S. O. *The Mediterranean and the Middle East,* vol. 11, *The Early Successes against Italy.* London, 1954.

Polastro, W. "La Marina militare italiano nel primo dopoguerra (1918–1925)." *Il Risorgimento* 3 (1977).

Ponce de Leon, A. M. *L'Italia entra in guerra: Gli eventi diplomatici dal 1 gennaio 1939 al 10 giugno 1940.* Bologna, 1963.

Posen, B. R. *The Sources of Military Doctrine: France, Britain, and Germany between the World Wars.* Ithaca, 1984.

Post, G. *Dilemmas of Appeasement: British Deterrence and Defense, 1934–37.* London, 1993.

Pownall, H. *Chief of Staff: The Diaries of Lt. Gen. Sir Henry Pownall.* Vol. 1, *1933–1940.* Ed. B. Bond. London, 1970.

Pratt, Lawrence R. "The Anglo-American Naval Conversations on the Far East of January 1938." *International Affairs* 47 (1971).

——. *East of Malta, West of Suez: Britain's Mediterranean Crisis, 1936–1939.* Cambridge, 1975.

Preston, A., ed. *General Staffs and Diplomacy before the Second World War.* London, 1978.

Preston, P. *Franco: A Biography.* New York, 1994.

Pricolo, F. *La Regia Aeronautica nella seconda guerra mondiale.* Milan, 1971.

Pritchard, R. J. *Far Eastern Influences upon British Strategy towards the Great Powers, 1937–1939.* London, 1979.

Quartararo, Rosaria. "Il 'Canale' segreto di Chamberlain." *Storia contemporanea* 7 (1976).

——. "Imperial Defence in the Mediterranean on the Eve of the Ethiopian Crisis, July–October 1935." *Historical Journal* 20 (1977).

——. "Inghilterra e Italia: dal patto di Pasqua a Monaco." *Storia Contemporanea* 7 (1976).

——. "La crisi mediterranea nel 1935–36." *Storia contemporanea* 6 (1975).

——. *Roma tra Londra e Berlino: Politica estera fascista dal 1930 al 1940.* Rome, 1980.

Raeder, Erich. *Mein Leben.* 2 vols. Tübingen, 1956–57.

——. *Struggle for the Sea.* London, 1959.

Rainero, R. H., and A. Biagini, eds. *L'Italia in guerra: Il primo anno—1940.* Rome, 1991.

Ranger, R. *The Naval Arms Control Record, 1919–1939: Axis Violations versus Democratic Compliance Policy Failures.* Fairfax, 1987.

Raphaël-Leygues, J. *Chronique des années incertaines 1935–1945.* Paris, 1977.

——. *Darlan, Laborde: L'Inimitie de deux amiraux.* Brest, 1990.

Raphaël-Leygues, J., and F. Flohic. *Darlan.* Paris, 1986.

Raspin, A. *The Italian War Economy, 1940–1943.* New York, 1986.

Ratliff, A. "Les Relations diplomatiques entre la France et les Etats-Unis (1938–40)." *Revue d'Histoire de la Deuxième Guerre Mondiale* 75 (1969).

Réau, Elisabeth du. "Edouard Daladier: La conduite de la guerre et les prémices de la défaite." *Historical Reflections/Réflexions Historiques* 22 (1996).

——. *Edouard Daladier, 1884–1970.* Paris, 1993.

——. "Enjeux stratégiques et redéploiement diplomatique français: Novembre 1938–septembre 1939." *Relations internationales* 35 (1983).

Rémond, R. *The Right Wing in France from 1815 to de Gaulle.* Philadelphia, 1969.

Rémond, R. and J. Bourdin, eds. *Édouard Daladier: Chef de gouvernement, avril 1938–septembre 1939.* Paris, 1977.

Renouvin, P. "La Politique extérieure de la France de 1933 à 1939: Progrès et lacunes de l'information historique." *Bulletin de la Classe des Lettres et des Sciences Morales et Politiques* 49 (1963).

Reussner, A. *La Puissance navale dans l'historie.* 3 vols. Paris, 1964–71.

Reussner, M. A. *Les Conversations franco-britanniques d'Etat-Major, 1935–1939.* Paris, 1969.

Reynaud, Paul. *Au coeur de la mêlée.* Paris, 1951. *In the Midst of the Fight.* Trans. J. D. Lambert. New York, 1955.

——. *Mémoires.* 2 vols. Paris, 1960–63.

Reynolds, David. *The Creation of the Anglo-American Alliance, 1937–1941.* London, 1981.

Ribbentrop, Joachim von. *The Ribbentrop Memoirs.* Trans. O. Watson. London, 1954.

Rich, Norman. *Hitler's War Aims.* 2 vols. New York, 1973–74.

Richardson, C. "French Plans for Allied Attacks on the Caucasus Oil Fields, 1940." *French Historical Studies* 8 (1974).

Richardson, D., and G. Stone, eds. *Decisions and Diplomacy: Essays in Twentieth-Century International History.* London, 1995.

Rintelen, E. *Mussolini als Bundesgenosse: Erinnerungen des deutschen Militärattachés in Rom, 1936–1943.* Tübingen, 1951. *Mussolini l'alleato.* Rome, 1952.

Roatta, Mario. *Otto milioni di baionette.* Verona, 1946.

——. *Sciacalli adosso SIM.* Rome, 1955.

Roberts, A. *"The Holy Fox": A Biography of Lord Halifax.* London, 1991.

Robertson, Esmonde M. "Hitler and Sanctions: Mussolini and the Rhineland." *European Studies Review* 7 (1977).

——. *Hitler's Pre-War Policy and Military Plans, 1933–1939.* London, 1963.

——. *Mussolini as Empire-Builder: Europe and Africa, 1932–1936.* London, 1977.

Robertson, J. C. "The Hoare-Laval Plan." *Journal of Contemporary History* 10 (1975).

Rochat, Giorgio. "L'Esercito e il fascismo." In *Fascismo e società italiana.* Turin, 1973.

——. *L'Esercito italiano da Vittorio Veneto a Mussolini.* Bari, 1967.

——. *Militari e politici nella preparazione della campagna d'Etiopia: Studio e documenti, 1932–36.* Milan, 1971.

——. "Mussolini, chef de guerre (1940–43)." *Revue d'histoire de la deuxième guerre mondiale* 25 (1975).

——. "Mussolini e le forze armate." *Il Movimento di Liberazione in Italia* 95 (1969).

Rochat, G., and G. Massobrio. *Breve storia dell'esercito italiano dal 1861 al 1943.* Turin, 1978.

Roi, Michael L. *Alternative to Appeasement: Sir Robert Vansittart and Alliance Diplomacy, 1934–1937.* Westport, Conn., 1997.

Romano, S. "Diplomazia nazionale e diplomazia fascista: continuità e rottura." *Affari esteri* 16 (1984).

Roosevelt, Franklin D. *Churchill and Roosevelt: The Complete Correspondence.* 3 vols. Ed. W. F. Kimball. Princeton, 1984.

——. *F.D.R.: His Personal Letters, 1928–1945.* 2 vols. Ed. E. Roosevelt and J. P. Lash. New York, 1950.

Rose, Norman. "The Resignation of Anthony Eden." *Historical Journal* 25 (1982).

——. *Vansittart: Study of a Diplomat.* London, 1978.

Roskill, Stephen W. *Churchill and the Admirals.* London, 1977.

——. *Hankey, Man of Secrets,* vol. 3, *1931–1963.* London, 1974.

——. *Naval Policy between the Wars.* 2 vols. London, 1968–76.

——. *The War at Sea, 1939–1945,* vol. 1, *The Defensive.* London, 1954.

Rossi, F. *Mussolini e lo stato maggiore: Avvenimenti del 1940.* Rome, 1951.

Rossi-Landi, G. *La Drôle de Guerre: La Vie politique en France, 2 septembre 1939–10 mai 1940.* Paris, 1971.

——. *Hommes Politique*. Paris, 1973.
Rossiter, A. "Popular Front Economic Policy and the Matignon Negotiations." *Historical Journal* 30 (1987).
Rostow, N. *Anglo-French Relations, 1934–1936*. London, 1984.
Rota, A. A. *La diplomazia del ventennio. Storia di una politica estera*. Milan, 1990.
Rovighi, A., and F. Stefani. *La participazione italiana alla guerra civile spagnola (1936–1939)*. 2 vols. Rome, 1992–93.
Rumi, G. *Alle orgini della politica estera fascista (1918–1923)*. Bari, 1968.
Sabatier de Lachadenède, R. *La Marine française et la guerre civile d'Espagne 1936–1939*. Paris, 1993.
Sadkovich, James J. "The Development of the Italian Air Force Prior to World War II." *Military Affairs*, 1987.
——. *The Italian Navy in World War II*. Westport, Conn., 1994.
Sala, T., and G. Vaccarino, eds. *L'Italia nell'Europa danubiana durante la seconda guerra mondiale*. Florence, 1967.
Salerno, Reynolds M. "The French Navy and the Appeasement of Italy, 1937–39," *English Historical Review* 112 (1997).
——. "Multilateral Strategy and Diplomacy: The Anglo-German Naval Agreement and the Mediterranean Crisis, 1935–36." *Journal of Strategic Studies* 17 (1994).
Salewski, M. *Die deutsche Seekriegsleitung, 1935–1945*. 3 vols. Frankfurt, 1970–75.
Salmon, P., ed. *Britain and Norway in the Second World War*. London, 1995.
Salvemini, Gaetano. *Mussolini diplomatico*. Rome, 1945.
——. *Prelude to World War II*. London, 1953.
Santoni, Alberto. "Italian Naval Policy from 1930–1941." *Revue Internationale d'histoire Militaire* 73 (1991).
——. *Storia e politica navale dell'età contemporanea*. Rome, 1993.
Santoro, G. *L'Aeronautica italiana nella seconda guerra mondiale*. Vol. 1. Rome, 1957.
Sartre, Jean Paul. *Les Carnets de la drôle de guerre (novembre 1939–mars 1940)*. Paris, 1983. *War Diaries: Notebooks from a Phony War, November 1939–March 1940*. Trans. Q. Hoare. London, 1984.
——. *Les Chemins de la liberté*, vol. 2, *Le Sursis*. Paris, 1945.
Sauvy, A. "The Economic Crisis of the 1930s in France." *Journal of Contemporary History* 4 (1969).
Sbacchi, A. *Ethiopia under Mussolini: Fascism and the Colonial Experience*. London, 1985.
Schmidt, C. T. *The Corproate State in Action: Italy under Fascism*. New York, 1939.
Schofield, B. B. *British Sea Power: Naval Policy in the Twentieth Century*. London, 1967.
——. "Die Rolle Frankreichs im strategischen und operativen Denken der deutschen Marine," *Beihefte der Francia*, 10 (1981).
Schreiber, Gerhard. *Das Deutsche Reich und der Zweite Weltkrieg*, Vol. 3, *Der Mittelmeeraum und Südosteuropa*. Stuttgart, 1984.
——. *Revisionismus und Weltmachtstreben: Marineführung und deutsch-italienische Beziehungen, 1919–1945*. Stuttgart, 1978.
——. "Les Structures stratégiques de la conduite de la guerre italo-allemande au cours de la deuxième guerre mondiale." *Revue d'Histoire de la Deuxième Guerre Mondiale*, (1980).
——. "Sul teatro mediterraneo nella seconda guerra mondiale: Inediti punti di vista della marina germanica del tempo." *Rivista Marittima* 120 (1987).
——. "Zur Kontinuität des Gross-und Weltmachtstrebens der deutschen Marineführung." *Militärgeschichtliche Mitteilungen* 26 (1979).

Schreiber, G., B. Stegemann, and D. Vogel. *Germany and the Second World War,* vol. 3, *The Mediterranean, Southeast Europe, and North Africa, 1939–1941.* Oxford, 1995.

Schuker, S. A. "France and the Remilitarization of the Rhineland, 1936." *French Historical Studies* (1986).

Segrè, C. G. *Italo Balbo: A Fascist Life.* Berkeley, 1987.

Serra, E. "La questione italo-etiopica alla conferenza di Stresa." *Affari Esteri* 9 (1977).

Serrano, C. *L'Enjeu espagnol: PCF et guerre d'Espagne.* Paris, 1987.

Sforza, C. *Illusions et réalités de l'Europe.* Neuchâtel, 1944.

Shakespeare, G. *Let Candles Be Brought In.* London, 1949.

Shay, R. P. *British Rearmament in the 1930s: Politics and Profits.* Princeton, 1977.

Shorrock, William. *From Ally to Enemy: The Enigma of Fascist Italy in French Diplomacy, 1920–1940.* Kent, 1988.

Siebert, F. *Italiens Weg in den Zweiten Weltkrieg.* Frankfurt, 1962.

Simon, Viscount. *Retrospect: The Memoirs of the Rt. Hon. Viscount Simon.* London, 1952.

Simone, A. *J'accuse: The Men Who Betrayed France.* New York, 1940.

Slessor, J. *The Central Blue.* New York, 1957.

Smith, M. S. *British Air Strategy between the Wars.* Oxford, 1984.

Soutou, G.-H. "L'Alliance franco-polonaise (1925–1933) ou comment s'en débarrasser?" *Revue d'historie Diplomatique* (1981).

——. "La Perception de la puissance française par René Massigli en 1938." *Relations internationales,* 1983.

Spertini, M., and E. Bagnasco. *I Mezzi d'assalto della Xa Flottiglia MAS, 1940–1945.* Parma, 1991.

Squadrilli, E. *Politica marinara e impero fascista.* Rome, 1937.

Stafford, Paul R. "The Chamberlain-Halifax visit to Rome: A reappraisal." *English Historical Review* 98 (1983).

——. "The French Government and the Danzig Crisis: The Italian Dimension." *International History Review* 6 (1984).

——. "Italy in Anglo-French Strategy and Diplomacy, October 1938–September 1939." Ph.D. disertation, Oxford University, 1984.

Starhemberg, E. R. *Between Hitler and Mussolini.* New York, 1942.

Stato Maggiore dell'Esercito Ufficio Storico. *L'Esercito italiano tra la prima e la seconda guerra mondiale (novembre 1918–giugno 1940).* Rome, 1954.

——. *In Africa settentrionale: La preparazione al conflitto. L'avanzata su Sidi el Barrani.* Rome, 1955.

——. *Memorie storiche militari.* Rome, annual.

——. *Verbali delle riunioni tenute dal capo di stato maggiore generale,* vol. 1 (26 gennaio 1939–29 dicembre 1940). Rome, 1983.

Steinberg, Jonathan. *All or Nothing: The Axis and the Holocaust, 1941–43.* London, 1990.

Stephen, M. *The Fighting Admirals: British Admirals of the Second World War.* London, 1991.

Strang, L. *Home and Abroad.* London, 1956.

Suarez, G. *Briand.* Vol. 4 Paris, 1952.

Sullivan, Brian R. "A Deal with the Devil: Italian Military Intelligence under the Fascist Regime, 1922–1943." Unpublished article.

——. "Fascist Italy's Military Involvement in the Spanish Civil War: A Review Essay." *Journal of Military History* 59 (1995).

——. "A Fleet in Being: The Rise and Fall of Italian Sea Power, 1861–1943." *International History Review* 10 (1988).

——. "Italian Naval Power and the Washington Disarmament Conference of 1921–22." *Diplomacy and Statecraft* 4 (1993).
——. "A Thirst for Glory: Mussolini, the Italian Military and the Fascist Regime, 1922–1936." Ph.D. dissertation, Columbia University, 1984.
Suvich, Fulvio *Memorie, 1932–36.* Milan, 1984.
Sweet, J. *Iron Arm: The Mechanization of Mussolini's Army, 1920–1940.* Westport, Conn., 1980.
Tamaro, A. *Venti anni di storia.* Rome, 1953.
Tamchina, R. "In Search of Common Causes: The Imperial Conference of 1937." *Journal of Imperial and Commonwealth History* 1 (1972).
Tardieu, A. *Notes de semaine, 1938: L'Année de Munich.* Paris, 1939.
Tasso, A. *Italia e Croazia,* vol. 1, *1918–1940.* Macerate, 1967.
Taylor, A. J. P. *The Origins of the Second World War.* London, 1961.
Templewood, V. [Sir Samuel Hoare]. *Nine Troubled Years.* London, 1954.
Thomas, Hugh *The Spanish Civil War.* London, 1965.
Thomas, Martin *Britain, France, and Appeasement: Anglo-French Relations in the Popular Front Era.* Washington, D.C.: 1996.
Thompson, G. *Front-Line Diplomat.* London, 1959.
Thorne, Christopher. *The Approach of War, 1938–1939.* London, 1967.
——. *The Limits of Foreign Policy: The West, the League, and the Far Eastern Crisis of 1931–1933.* London, 1972.
Till, G. *Air Power and the Royal Navy, 1914–1945.* London, 1979.
Toscano, Mario. "Le conversazioni militari italo-tedesche alla viglia della seconda guerra mondiale." *Rivista Storica italiana,* 1952.
——. *Designs in Dipolmacy: Pages from European Diplomatic History in the Twentieth Century.* Baltimore, 1970.
——. *The Origins of the Pact of Steel.* Baltimore, 1967.
——. *Storia dei trattati e relazioni internazionali.* 2 vols. Turin, 1958–63.
——. *Storia diplomatica della questione dell'Alto Adige.* Bari, 1969.
Tosi, F. F., G. Grassi, and M. Legnani, eds. *L'Italia nella seconda guerra mondiale e nella resistenza.* Milan, 1988.
Tosti, A. *Da Versailles a Cassabile: Lo sforzo militare nel venticinquennio, 1918–1943.* Rocca San Casciano, 1954.
Tuleja, T. V. *Statesmen and Admirals: The Search for a Far Eastern Naval Policy.* New York, 1963.
Vaïsse, Maurice. *Sécurité d'abord: La Politique française en matière de désarmement.* Paris, 1981.
——. ed. *Ardennes 1940.* Paris, 1991.
Valle, Giuseppe. *Uomini nei cieli: Storia dell'aeronautica italiana.* Rome, 1958.
Van Evera, S. *Causes of War: Power and Roots of Conflict.* Ithaca, 1999.
Vansittart, Robert *The Mist Procession: The Autobiography of Lord Vansittart.* London, 1958.
Vigezzi, B. *L'Italia neutrale.* Milan, 1966.
Villari, L. *Storia Diplomatica del Conflitto Italo-Ethiopico.* Bologna, 1943.
Villelume, P. de. *Journal d'une défaite, août 1939–juin 1940.* Ed. R. Rémond. Paris, 1976.
Visconti-Prasca, S. *Io ho aggredito la Grecia.* Milan, 1946.
Von Hassell, U. *The Von Hassell Diaries, 1938–44.* Trans. F. H. von Gaetringen and K. P. Reiss. Garden City, 1947.
Wagner, G., ed. *Lagevorträge des Oberbefehlshabers der Kriegsmarine vor Hitler, 1939–1945.* Munich, 1972.

Waites, N., ed. *Troubled Neighbors: Franco-British Relations in the Twentieth Century.* London, 1971.

Waley, D. P. *British Public Opinion and the Abyssinian War, 1935–1936.* London, 1975.

Wallace, W. V. "Roosevelt and British Appeasement in 1938." *Bulletin of the British Association for American Studies* 5 (1962).

Walt, S. M. *The Origins of Alliances.* Ithaca, 1987.

Wandycz, P. S. *The Twilight of French Eastern Alliances 1926–1936: French-Czechoslovak-Polish Relations from Locarno to the Remilitarization of the Rhineland.* Princeton, 1988.

Wark, Wesley K. *The Ultimate Enemy: British Intelligence and Nazi Germany, 1933–1939.* Ithaca, 1985.

Warner, O. *Cunningham of Hyndhope: Admiral of the Fleet.* London, 1967.

Watkins, K. W. *Britain Divided: The Effect of the Spanish Civil War on British Public Opinion.* London, 1963.

Watt, Donald C. "The Anglo-German Naval Agreement of 1935: An Interim Judgement." *Journal of Modern History* 18 (1956).

——. "Anglo-German Naval Negotiations on the Eve of the Second World War." *Journal of the Royal United Services Institute* 610–611 (1958).

——. "Gli Accordi mediterranei anglo-italiani del 16 aprile 1938." *Rivista di Studi Politici Internazionali* 26 (1959).

——. "Hitler's Visit to Rome and the May Weekend Crisis: A Study in Hitler's Responses to External Stimuli." *Journal of Contemporary History* 9 (1974).

——. *How War Came: The Immediate Origins of the Second World War, 1938–1939.* New York, 1989.

——. "The Rome-Berlin Axis, 1936–1940: Myth and Reality." *Review of Politics* 22 (1960).

——. "The Secret Laval-Mussolini Agreement of 1935 on Ethiopia." *Middle East Journal* 15 (1961).

——. *Too Serious a Business: European Armed Forces and the Approach of the Second World War.* London, 1975.

Webster, R. A. "Autarky, Expansion, and the Underlying Continuity of the Italian State." *Italian Quarterly* (1964).

Weinberg, Gehard L. *The Foreign Policy of Hitler's Germany.* 2 vols. Chicago, 1970–80.

——. *A World at Arms: A Global History of World War II.* Cambridge, 1994.

Weiss, S. *Allies in Conflict: Anglo-American Strategic Negotiations, 1938–1944.* London, 1996.

Weygand, Maxime "How France is Defended." *International Affairs* 18 (July–August 1939).

——. *Mémoires.* 3 vols. Paris, 1950–57.

Whealey, R. H. *Hitler and Spain: The Nazi Role in the Spanish Civil War, 1936–1939.* Lexington, 1989.

Wheatley, R. H. "Mussolini's Ideological Diplomacy: An Unpublished Document." *Journal of Modern History* 39 (1967).

Winkler, H. R. *Paths Not Taken: British Labour and International Policy in the 1920s.* Chapel Hill, 1994.

Wiskemann, E. *The Rome-Berlin Axis: A History of the Relations between Hitler and Mussolini.* London, 1949.

Wolfe, M. *The French Franc between the Wars, 1919–39.* New York, 1951.

Wolfers, A. *Britain and France between Two Wars.* New York, 1966.

Woodward, L. *British Policy in the Second World War.* Vol. 1. London, 1970.

Woolf, S. J. "Inghilterra, Francia, e Italia: Settembre 1939–giugno 1940." *Rivista di Storia Contemporanea* 3 (1972).

Wright, Jonathan, and Paul Stafford. "Hitler, Britain, and Ho;gbbach Memorandum." *Militärgeschichtliche Mitteilungen* 42 (1987).

Young, Robert J. "The Aftermath of Munich: The Course of French Diplomacy, October 1938 to March 1939." *French Historical Studies* 8 (1973).

——. *France and the Origins of the Second World War.* New York, 1996.

——. "French Military Intelligence and the Franco-Italian Alliance, 1933–1939." *Historical Journal* 28 (1985).

——. *In Command of France: French Foreign Policy and Military Planning, 1933–1940.* Cambridge, 1978.

——. "Preparations for Defeat: French War Doctrine in the Inter-War Period." *Journal of European Studies* 2 (1972).

——. "Soldiers and Diplomats: The French Embassy and Franco-Italian Relations, 1935–1936." *Journal of Strategic Studies* 7 (1984).

Zamagni, V. *The Economic History of Italy, 1860–1990.* Oxford, 1993.

Zamboni, G. *Mussolinis Expansionspolitik auf dem Balkan.* Hamburg, 1970.

Zay, J. *Carnets secrets.* Ed. P. Henriot. Paris, 1942.

Index

Abyssinia. *See* Ethiopia
Adriatic Sea, 3, 17, 21–22, 53, 105, 115–116, 130, 160, 165, 180, 194
Aegean Sea, 3, 89, 130, 135, 156, 160, 185, 191, 202–203, 209
Albania, 44, 105, 114–117, 125, 127, 130, 137, 178, 214, 216, 217, 219
Aleppo Conference (1940), 189
Alexandretta, 64, 119
Alexandria, 67, 123, 148, 189, 198, 203–204
Algeria, 5, 94, 124, 132, 206
Aloisi, Pompeo, 15
Alphand, Hervé, 161
Alsace-Lorraine, 5, 186
Alto Adige (South Tyrol), 3, 12, 55, 59, 146–147, 178
Ambrosio, Vittorio, 90
Anfuso, Filippo, 186
Ansaldo, Giovanni, 195
Anschluss. *See* Germany
Anti-Comintern Pact, 30, 36
Aosta, Duke of, 81
Aregai, Abebe, 80
Atlantic Ocean, 35, 71–72, 89, 91, 93, 106, 121, 123–125, 128, 132–133, 148, 151, 160, 164–165, 191, 195
Attolico, Bernardo, 50, 124, 132, 135, 146, 179
Aubert, Louis, 92–93, 128, 170
Australia, 103, 109–110, 138
Austria, 3, 6, 10, 12, 15, 40–42, 44, 55, 63, 214, 216, 219
  Austro-German accords. *See* Germany
Axis. *See* Italy; Rome-Berlin Axis
Backhouse, Roger, 97–102, 120, 122, 137
Badoglio, Pietro, 19, 55, 88–90, 125, 135–136, 144, 181, 183, 185, 190–191, 200, 206–209
Baistrocchi, Federico, 19–20
Balbo, Italo, 78, 176, 200, 208
Baldwin, Stanley, 14
Balearic Islands, 17–18, 29, 32–33, 36, 46, 74, 89, 132, 204, 211
Bastianini, Giuseppe, 184
Baudouin, Paul, 104–105, 113–114
Belgium, 33, 49, 199, 205–206, 210
Berthod, Aimé, 92
Black Sea, 24, 64, 130–131, 141, 156, 160
Blondel, Jules-François, 42, 55–57, 70
Bloomberg, Werner von, 40
Blum, Léon, 13, 16, 31, 35, 44, 52, 58, 91, 153
Bonnet, Georges, 52, 54–56, 58–59, 70, 73–74, 90, 92–93, 96, 103–104, 109, 112–113, 119, 150, 153–154, 161, 219
Bottai, Giuseppe, 30, 79, 143, 179, 185
Bourragué, Admiral, 46, 121
Bracken, Brendan, 76
Briand, Aristide, 31
Bridges, Edward, 172
Brinon, Fernand de, 104
Brivonesi, Bruto, 62
Bruce, Stanley, 48
Bührer, General, 70–71, 90, 94
Buisson, Louis, 45
Bulgaria, 33, 63. 72, 159
Bullitt, William, 26, 44, 142
Buti, Gino, 113
Butler, Robert A., 48, 51, 189, 193, 205
Bywater, Hector C., 61

Cadogan, Alexander, 48, 53, 77, 102, 108–109, 117, 131, 157, 175, 186, 189, 202, 205, 210–211, 218
Cambon, Roger, 27
Canaris, Wilhem, 18, 124, 133, 145
Carboni, Giacomo, 124, 143
Castex, Raoul, 164
Caucasus, 173, 186, 188–189, 203
Cavagnari, Domenico, 19, 31, 61–62, 66–67, 86–89, 116, 124–125, 132–134, 136, 144, 146, 166, 181–183, 185, 191, 200–201, 206–209
Cavallero, Ugo, 43, 80
Cerruti, Vittorio, 32
Chalmers, William, 98
Chamberlain, Austen, 49
Chamberlain, Lady, 49–50
Chamberlain, Neville, 13–14, 24, 26–27, 36–37, 39–40, 47, 49–50, 52–53, 60, 63–64, 68–69, 75, 77–78, 81–82, 84–85, 92, 95, 99–100, 108–110, 115, 117–120, 129–131, 137–139, 148–149, 157–158, 171–172, 175–176, 184, 186, 193–194, 197–198, 205, 214, 217
Charles, Noel, 69, 197
Charles-Roux, François, 57, 70, 206
Charvériat, Emile, 153
Chatfield, Ernle, 14, 27, 36–38, 102–103, 109, 122, 131, 141, 149, 164
Chautemps, Camille, 32, 44
China, 6, 11
  Reformed Government of the Republic of China. *See* Japan
  Sino-Japanese war. *See* Japan
  Tientsin crisis, 131, 139
Churchill, Winston, 76, 117, 148, 150, 156–157, 164–165, 174, 186, 198, 205–206, 210
Ciano, Costanzo, 15, 87
Ciano, Galeazzo, 14–20, 26–27, 30–31, 42, 49–51, 55–57, 60, 62, 64–65, 67, 75, 79, 82–85, 90, 104–106, 114–116, 123–126, 131–132, 134–136, 143–147, 149, 153, 163, 166–168, 176, 178–184, 190, 195–196, 199–201, 205–206, 209–210, 215
Clodius, Karl, 145–146, 183
Collier, Laurence, 77
Colson, Louis, 91, 141
Comert, Paul, 70
Contraband control in the Mediterranean, 159–168, 205, 215–217, 219
Corbin, Charles, 56, 83, 174, 193
Corfu, 6, 116, 130, 192
Corsica, 58, 70, 89, 94, 96, 100, 113, 124, 150, 180, 185, 207
Coulondre, Robert, 74
Craigie, Robert, 109, 131
Crete, 123, 130, 194–195, 199, 202–204, 211–212
Cristich, Bosko, 105
Croatia, 114–115, 126–127, 135, 180–181, 199
Crolla, Guido, 26–27
Crookshank, Walter, 76
Cunningham, Andrew, 28, 137, 139, 148, 164, 166, 169, 189, 203, 211–212
Czechoslovakia, 5, 21–22, 44–45, 52, 54, 58, 60, 80, 85, 214, 216, 219
  Czechoslovak crisis (1938), 56, 60, 62–72

Daily Herald, 137
Daladier, Edouard, 35, 45, 52–54, 57–58, 70–71, 73, 81–82, 84, 91–94, 96–97, 99, 104, 110, 112–114, 116, 118–119, 124, 128, 130, 138–142, 152–154, 157, 161, 170, 172–174, 176, 187, 206, 211, 219–220
Dalton, Hugh, 48
Danckwerts, V. H., 53, 103, 109, 120, 122, 164
D'Annunzio, Gabriele, 4
Dardanelles, 64, 118, 159
Darlan, François, 28, 33–34, 46, 52, 54, 70–72, 90–91, 93–97, 111, 128, 139–142, 151–152, 164–165, 169, 172–173, 175, 194–195, 198–199, 202, 204, 211–212, 219
De Bono, Emilio, 10, 78, 83, 144
De Courten, Raffaele, 86
Dejean, Maurice, 159
Delbos, Yvon, 16, 22, 26, 31–32, 38, 44
Denmark, 189, 191, 195
Dickens, Gerald, 98
Dingli, Adrian, 50, 184
Djibouti, 84, 94, 96, 105, 113, 119, 135, 141, 185
Djibouti-Addis Ababa railway, 74, 104–105, 119
Docteur, Jules, 141
Dodecanese, 17, 89, 125, 130, 132, 155, 158, 202–204
Dollfuss, Engelbert, 12
Donegani, Guido, 168
Drax, Ernle, 98–99, 101, 120, 122
Duff Cooper, Alfred, 26, 51, 68, 75
Dulantry, Walter, 48

Eden, Anthony, 13, 16, 23, 26, 36, 38–40, 48, 51
Egypt, 23, 36, 63, 65, 82, 87, 96, 102, 109, 121–122, 132, 135, 139, 165, 171, 192, 198, 200, 203
Enemy Exports Committee, 166
Esteva, Jean-Pierre, 28, 164

Ethiopia (Abyssinia), 11–15, 17, 19–20, 43, 53, 55, 60, 65, 80, 94, 96, 122, 129, 178, 188, 200, 213, 215, 219

Farinacci, Roberto, 144, 180
Fagiuoli, Vicenzo, 104, 114–115
Favagrossa, Carlo, 143–144, 181
Federzoni, Luigi, 78
Finland, 1, 171, 173–175, 178, 191
  Soviet-Finnish war (1939–40). *See* Soviet Union
Fiume, 3–4
Flandin, Pierre-Etienne, 44
France
  Air Force, 34–35, 111
  Albanian invasion, reaction to, 116–120
  Anglo-French staff talks. *See* Great Britain
  Anglo-French-Turkish mutual assistance treaty (1939). *See* Great Britain
  Anglo-German naval agreement, reaction to, 11
  Anglo-Italian Easter Accords, reaction to, 51–54
  Anschluss, reaction to, 44–47
  Army, 34–35, 57, 111, 198, 200
  Comité de Guerre, 194
  Comité Permanent de la Défense Nationale (CPDN), 22, 46, 94, 96
  Conseil Supérieur de la Défense Nationale (CSDN), 57, 174
  Council of Ministers, 110
  Deuxième Bureau, 80, 96, 100, 111–113, 140–141, 152, 173, 187–188, 192
  État-major général de la Marine (EMM). *See* France: Marine Nationale
  Franco-Italian agreement (1935), 10–11, 74, 83, 86ß
  Franco-Italian economic protocol (1939), 161
  Franco-Italian military talks (1935). *See* Italy
  Franco-Romanian treaty (1939), 112
  Franco-Turkish friendship treaty and military accord (1938), 64
  Franco-Turkish mutual defense treaty (1939), 119
  French Indochina, 33–34
  French Somaliland, 94, 184
  General Staff, 112, 117, 119, 128–129, 169, 188, 204, 219
  Guarantee to Poland (1939), 112, 123
  Guarantee to Greece (1939), 117, 123
  Guarantee to Romania (1939), 118, 123
  Marine Nationale, 14, 28, 34, 46–47, 54, 57–58, 69, 71–72, 91, 93, 95–97, 101–102, 111, 116, 123, 128, 130–131, 133, 139, 160, 162, 164, 173, 195, 198, 210, 212
  Maginot Line, 5, 183–184, 200
  Ministry of Blockade, 193
  Ministry of Finance, 57–58
  Munich, reactions to, 73–76
  Nyon conference. *See* Spanish civil war
  Pirate submarine campaign. *See* Italy
  Popular Front, 13, 15–16, 214
  Prague coup, reaction to, 110–114
  Quai d'Orsay, 22, 29, 32–34, 58, 70, 83, 103–104, 119, 127, 152, 154, 158–159, 169, 174, 195, 197, 219
  Radical Party, 54, 92, 104, 153, 187
Franco, Francisco, 16–18, 20, 22, 24, 27, 43
François-Poncet, André, 74–75, 83, 90, 92, 103–105, 112–113, 119, 124–125, 128, 135, 153–154, 159, 166, 179–180, 184, 206, 219
Fritsch, Werner von, 40

Gambara, Gastone, 81, 199
Gamelin, Maurice, 34, 38, 46, 52, 54, 70, 91, 94–97, 113, 128–131, 139–142, 151–152, 157–158, 165, 169, 171–174, 188, 195, 198, 202, 211
Garibaldi, Giuseppe, 2
Gauché, Maurice, 45, 141
George VI, King, 205
Géraud, André (Pertinax), 104
Germany
  Abwehr, 17–18
  Anglo-German naval agreement. *See* Great Britain
  Anschluss, 15, 41–49, 60, 63, 217
  Austrian coup d'etat (1934), failed, 12
  Austro-German accords (1936), 15
  Belgium, defeat of, 205
  Bohemia and Moravia, invasion of (Prague coup), 108
  Coal exports to Italy, 165–168, 182–183, 187, 215
  Condor Legion, 18
  Danzig crisis. *See* Poland
  Dutch army, defeat of, 203
  Friedrichshaven talks (1939), 132–133
  German-Polish nonaggression pact, 124
  German-Romanian treaty (1939), 112
  Intervention in Spanish civil war. *See* Spanish civil war
  Italian-German alliance. *See* Italy, Pact of Steel
  Italian-German intelligence collaboration, 17–18, 124, 133, 145
  Kriegsmarine, 10, 79, 86, 125, 132–133

Germany (*continued*)
  Kristallnacht, 79–81
  Luftwaffe, 9, 94, 208
  Munich conference and agreement. *See* Czechoslovakia: Czechoslovak crisis
  Pact of Steel. *See* Italy
  Rome-Berlin Axis. *See* Italy
  Seekriegsleitung. *See* Germany: Kriegsmarine
  Soviet-German nonaggression pact (1939). *See* Soviet Union
  Spanish civil war, intervention in, 17–19
  Versailles, reactions to, 7, 10
  Wehrmacht, 9, 95, 134, 199
Ghigi, Pellegrino, 42
Giannini, Alberto, 145, 182–183
Gibraltar Straits, 17, 52, 67, 100, 113, 125, 148, 150, 160, 163–164, 186, 191, 198–199, 206, 211
Giorgini, Schiff, 150
Goebbels, Joseph, 81, 136
Göring, Hermann, 18, 50, 124
Gort, Lord, 100, 102, 131, 139
Grandi, Dino, 40, 42, 49–50, 116, 149, 176, 185, 201
Graziani, Rodolfo, 144, 180, 190, 200, 206–208
Great Britain
  Admiralty. *See* Great Britain: Royal Navy
  Albanian invasion, reaction to, 116–120
  Anglo-French staff talks, 120–123, 188–189
  Anglo-French-Turkish mutual assistance treaty (1939), 158, 203
  Anglo-German naval agreement (1935), 10–11, 124
  Anglo-Italian commercial agreement (1939), 162
  Anglo-Italian Easter Accords (1938), 49–51, 56, 58–59, 62, 65, 77, 82–83, 117, 123, 214, 216–217
  Anglo-Italian Gentlemen's Agreement (1937), 20, 22
  Anglo-Italian Joint Standing Committee, 162
  Anglo-Turkish agreement (1939), 118
  Anglo-Turkish guarantee and armaments credit agreement (1938), 64
  Anschluss, reactions to, 47–49
  Balkan bloc, interest in, 155–159
  British Council, 63
  British Expeditionary Force (BEF), 76, 108, 120, 172, 212
  Chiefs of Staff (COS), 14, 19–20, 37, 47, 50, 53–54, 81, 84, 99–100, 103, 109–110, 118, 122, 129, 131, 138, 154–156, 164, 171, 175, 189, 192–194, 197–198, 203–204, 210–211, 217
  Colonial Office, 65
  Committee of Imperial Defence (CID), 20, 24, 50, 52–54, 99–100, 122, 131, 136, 138, 140
  Committee on Coordination of Departmental Action (Italy), 197
  Committee on Defence Programs and Their Acceleration, 76
  Ethiopia, recognition of, 24, 36
  "European Appreciation, 1939–40," 100–101
  Foreign Office (FO), 19, 23, 26, 76–78, 81, 83–84, 101–102, 110, 130–131, 148, 150, 154–155, 158, 160, 171, 186, 189, 193, 198, 205, 218
  Foreign Policy Committee (FPC), 51, 82, 100, 117, 131
  Guarantee to France (1939), 95
  Guarantee to Greece (1939), 117–118, 123
  Guarantee to Poland (1939), 108, 123
  Guarantee to Romania (1939), 118, 123
  Imperial Conference (1937), 22
  Joint Planning Committee (JPC), 100, 103, 137
  Military Coordination Committee, 175
  Ministry of Economic Warfare (MEW), 160–161, 163, 166–167, 189, 193, 198
  Munich, reactions to, 76–78
  Nyon conference. *See* Spanish civil war
  Palestinian rebellion (1936), 13
  Pirate submarine campaign. *See* Italy
  Prague coup, reactions to, 108–110, 129
  Royal Air Force (RAF), 76, 122, 161, 204
  Royal Navy, 10, 14, 22, 26–27, 33, 37, 53–54, 67–69, 76, 97–99, 101–102, 109, 118, 120, 123, 129, 133, 137, 139–141, 148, 160–161, 163–164, 183, 194, 196, 199, 210, 217, 219
  Strategical Appreciation Subcommittee (SAC), 102, 122
  Treasury, 3, 84
Greece, 6, 19, 32, 49, 63, 72, 82, 89, 91, 116–118, 123, 128, 130–131, 134–135, 151, 154–155, 159–160, 171–172, 192, 194–195, 202–203, 211
Guariglia, Raffaello, 75, 132, 196
Guarneri, Felice, 61, 135–136, 143
Guillen, Pierre, 161

Haifa, 17, 67, 198, 203
Halifax, Lord, 40–41, 48, 51–52, 59, 63, 69, 77, 82, 84, 92, 100, 102, 109–110,

118–119, 131, 138, 149, 155, 163, 166–167, 171, 186, 193, 197, 205
Hankey, Maurice, 24, 36, 75, 157
Hart, Liddell, 101
Hassell, Ulrich von, 12
Herriot, Edouard, 44, 58, 153
Himmler, Heinrich, 146, 180
Hitler, Adolf, 7–8, 12, 15–19, 29–30, 40, 42, 50, 55–56, 59–60, 65, 75, 78, 81, 107, 124, 134, 136, 145–146, 152–153, 156, 179, 183, 185–186, 188–190, 196, 199, 201, 205, 207–208, 213–214, 219
Hoare-Laval pact, 12
Hoare, Samuel, 68–69, 175
Hong Kong, 98, 101–102
Hoppenot, Henri, 103, 159
Hore-Belisha, Leslie, 100, 102, 140
Hungary, 33, 63–64, 80, 107, 114, 180
Huntziger, Charles, 64

India, 6, 65, 110, 122
Indian Ocean, 61, 101, 106, 121, 132–133
Ingram, Maurice, 26, 68
Inskip, Thomas, 39, 68
Ironside, Edmund, 136–137, 156, 170, 175
Ismay, Hastings, 69, 100, 140–141, 198
Italy
  Albania, invasion of, 114–116
  Anglo-Italian commercial agreement (1939). *See* Great Britain
  Anglo-Italian Easter Accords (1938). *See* Great Britain
  Anglo-Italian Gentlemen's Agreement (1937). *See* Great Britain
  Anglo-Italian Joint Standing Committee. *See* Great Britain
  Anschluss, reactions to, 41–43
  Balkans, aspirations in, 43–44, 105, 123, 127, 147
  Claims on France, 81–86
  Corpo Truppe Volontarie (CTV), 43
  Economic Warfare Committee, 167
  Franco-Italian agreement (1935). *See* France
  Franco-Italian economic protocol (1939). *See* France
  Franco-Italian military talks (1935), 10
  General Staff, 19, 20–21, 31, 61, 135–136, 144, 181–182, 185, 195, 200, 207
  Gran Consiglio del Fascismo, 20, 43, 83, 86, 106, 115, 167, 179
  Istituto per la Ricostruzione Industriale (IRI), 61
  Italian-German alliance. *See* Italy: Pact of Steel
  Italian intelligence services, 17–18, 60, 62, 66, 75, 88–89, 124, 145, 196, 200
  Italo-Yugoslav friendship treaty (1937), 21–22
  "Jewish problem," Manifesto of Race, and race laws, 65–66, 78–79, 217
  Ministry of Italian Africa, 134
  Munich, reactions to, 78–81
  National Congress for the Study of Foreign Questions, 57
  Nonbelligerence, 136, 143–147
  Nyon conference. *See* Spanish civil war
  Order of the Annunziata, 126
  Pact of Steel, 60–61, 79–80, 105–106, 123–127, 131, 145–146, 214, 216–217
  Pirate submarine campaign (1937), 24–29, 31, 217
  Prague coup, reaction to, 114–115
  Regia Aeronautica, 9, 137, 210
  Regia Marina, 9, 61–62, 66–67, 86–90, 94, 102, 123, 132–134, 137, 140, 162, 166, 184, 190–191, 207, 209–210
  Regio Esercito, 209–210
  Rome-Berlin Axis, 18, 20, 65, 83, 106, 126, 138
  Spanish civil war, intervention in, 16–18
  Stato Maggiore della Marina (SMM). *See* Italy: Regia Marina
  Supreme Defense Commission, 182
  World War II, entry into, 209–210

Jacomet, Robert, 93
Japan, 6, 11, 128
  Reformed Government of the Republic of China, 52
  "New Order" in East Asia, 77
  Sino-Japanese war, 6, 24, 30, 33, 36, 77, 101
Jebb, Gladwyn, 49, 109

Keitel, Wilhelm, 124
Kennedy, John Noble, 121
Kennedy, Joseph, 110, 131
Knatchbull-Hugessen, Hughe, 155
Knox, MacGregor, 146

Laborde, Jean de, 164
La Chambre, Guy, 45, 141
Larosiere, Robert de, 187–188
Laval-Mussolini agreement. *See* France: Franco-Italian agreement (1935)
Laval, Pierre, 10–11, 115, 184
League of Nations, 3–4, 11, 14, 30, 36, 55–56
  Non-Intervention Committee, 16, 22, 27
Léger, Alexis, 31, 55, 58, 70, 73, 103, 109, 152, 169

Lelong, Albert, 121
Le Luc, Admiral, 142
Levant, 91, 94, 131
Libya, 3, 20, 23, 29, 36, 53, 64–65, 72, 82, 87–88, 90, 94, 96, 104, 121–123, 125, 129, 132, 134–135, 137, 140, 144, 150, 152, 165, 171, 181, 185, 188, 190–192, 199–200, 206, 208–209, 211
Lindsay, Ronald, 110
Little Entente, 21–22, 33
  Meeting at Bled, Slovenia, 65
Lloyd, Lord of Dolobran, 63
Locarno Agreements (1925), 5–6, 13
Loraine, Percy, 63, 123–125, 130, 135, 140, 148–149, 155, 158, 162, 166, 168, 171, 176, 179, 185, 205, 218
Lyons, J. A., 110

Macek, Vladimir, 114, 126
Mackensen, Hans Georg von, 85, 104, 115, 167, 178, 189–190, 201
Macmillan, Harold, 76
Malta, 67, 85, 87, 113, 121, 123, 129, 189, 191, 198, 207, 209, 212
Mandel, Georges, 150
Marchandeau, Paul, 57
Margottini, Carlo, 61, 133–134
Marin, Louis, 44
Massigli, René, 29, 58, 70, 119, 159, 169, 170
Masson, Philippe, 71
Mazzini, Giuseppe, 2
Mediterranean crisis (1935–36), 10–16
Mediterranean Locarno, 6, 13
Menzies, Robert, 138
Milch, Erhard, 124
Montigny, Jean, 44
Montreux conference (1936), 64
Monzie, Anatole de, 150
Morocco, 5, 12, 124
Morton, Desmond, 193
Munich conference and agreement. *See* Czechoslovakia: Czechoslovak crisis
Mussolini, Benito, 4, 7–8, 10–13, 15–17, 19–20, 24–26, 29–30, 41–43, 49–51, 56, 59–60, 62, 65, 74–75, 78–79, 82–83, 85, 90, 104–107, 112–116, 123–126, 134–136, 143–147, 149–150, 161, 167, 176, 178–186, 188–191, 195–196, 199, 201, 205–209, 213–215, 219
Mussolini, Edda, 15, 201
Mussolini, Rachele, 17
Muti, Ettore, 185

Neurath, Konstantin von, 40
Newall, Cyril, 69, 100, 122, 141
New Zealand, 103, 109–110, 138
Nicholls, John, 101
Noble, Andrew, 102
Noble, Percy, 98
Noël, Léon, 74
Noguès, Auguste, 95
Non-Intervention Committee. *See* League of Nations
North Sea, 11, 125, 133, 165, 194
Norway, 174–177, 186, 188–192, 194–199, 204

Odend'hal, Admiral, 122, 193, 195, 202
Ollive, Emmanuel, 139
Osborne, Francis, 186
Ottoman Empire, 3, 6

Pacific Ocean, 34, 101, 103, 110
Pact of Steel. *See* Italy
Palestine, 3, 13, 17, 63, 65, 122, 203
Pariani, Alberto, 20, 31, 60, 65, 87–89, 124, 144
Paul, Prince, 105
Paul-Boncour, Joseph, 44, 46, 52
Pavelic, Ante, 21, 199
Pecori Giraldi, Corso, 166
Perth, Earl of, 40, 42, 48–51, 56–57, 59, 68, 82, 84, 119, 125
Pétain, Henri, 152
Philip of Hesse, Prince, 182
Phillips, Tom, 164, 197
Phillips, William, 195
Phipps, Eric, 48, 58, 73, 77, 119, 130
Poland, 1, 5, 49, 55, 80, 85, 112, 114, 128, 134, 141, 150, 154, 165
  Danzig crisis, 127, 132, 140
  German-Polish nonaggression pact. *See* Germany
Pope Pius XII, 176, 182, 201
Pound, Dudley, 26, 67–68, 99, 121, 129, 137, 139, 141, 148, 164, 189, 198–199
Pricolo, Francesco, 144, 191, 206–207
Pyrenees frontier, 16, 32, 45, 58

Raeder, Erich, 86, 132–133, 145
Raineri Biscia, Giuseppe, 86, 166
Raphaël-Leygues, Jacques, 73
Red Sea, 7, 94, 96, 129, 134, 189, 198, 200
Revue Universelle, 45
Reynaud, Paul, 93, 111, 187–189, 192, 196–198, 206
Rhineland, 5, 10, 12–15
Ribbentrop, Joachim von, 40–42, 56, 79, 82, 85, 93, 105, 115, 125–126, 132, 134, 167, 179, 183, 201, 207
Riccardi, Raffaelo, 168, 181–182, 185

Ricci, Renato, 167, 182, 185
Roatta, Mario, 18, 134
Rochat, Charles, 74, 103
Rodd, Francis, 160
Romania, 5, 21–22, 33, 63–64, 72, 112, 128, 141, 151, 154, 156, 180, 186, 190, 195
  Franco-Romanian treaty (1939). *See* France
  German-Romanian treaty (1939). *See* Germany
Rome-Berlin Axis, 18, 22
Ronco, Colonel, 61
Roosevelt, Franklin, 36, 110, 205–206

Salonika, 89, 116, 130, 139–140, 150–152, 154–157, 169, 176, 194–195, 199, 211, 215
Sardinia, 132, 152
Sargent, Orme, 49, 185
Scandinavia, Allied strategy in, 168–177, 215, 218, 220
Schusschnigg, Kurt, 40, 42
Sforza, Carlo, 150
Simon, John, 39, 68–69, 137, 149
Singapore, 6, 23–24, 36, 109, 121–122, 171
Sino-Japanese war. *See* Japan
Soddu, Ubaldo, 144, 181, 191, 200
Somalia (Somaliland), 3, 94, 134–135
South Tyrol. *See* Alto Adige
Soviet Union, 1, 5, 33, 49, 112, 121, 127–128, 130, 150, 154, 156, 170, 174–176, 179–180, 183, 188, 208, 219
  Pirate submarine campaign. *See* Italy
  Nyon conference. *See* Spanish civil war
  Soviet-Finnish war (1939–40), 171, 178–179, 186
  Soviet-German nonaggression pact (1939), 136, 141, 146, 150, 157
Spain, 124, 128, 132, 140
Spanish Morocco, 33, 52, 72, 89, 140
Spanish civil war, 16–20, 22–23, 53, 81–82, 104, 116, 216, 219
  Non-Intervention Committee. *See* League of Nations
  Nyon conference (1937), 27–29
  Pirate submarine campaign. *See* Italy
Stanhope, Lord, 100, 102
Stanley, Oliver, 75, 117
Strang, William, 38, 77
Stresa front, 10–12, 14–15, 55
Stoyadinovich, Milan, 21, 105
Strunk, Roland, 15
Suez Canal, 7, 11, 52, 64, 74, 87, 104–105, 109, 113, 119, 121, 132, 141, 160, 166, 186, 191, 195, 199, 211
Supreme War Council (SWC), 154, 170–172, 188–189, 192, 197, 202, 210

Suvich, Fulvio, 15
Sweden, 173–177, 186
Syria, 3, 5, 63, 119–120, 139, 151, 158, 169, 195
Szabó, Lászlo, 195

Taylor, A. H., 160
Thaon di Revel, Paolo, 182, 185
Thrace, 130, 170, 176, 203
Tunisia, 5, 23, 84, 88, 94, 96, 105, 113, 119, 121–122, 124, 132, 135, 165, 180, 189, 192. 200, 206, 211
Turkey, 3, 19, 32, 49, 63–64, 82, 89, 91, 117–119, 123, 128, 130–131, 134, 151, 155–159, 169–170–172, 188–189, 194–195, 202–203
  Anglo-French-Turkish mutual assistance treaty (1939). *See* Great Britain
  Anglo-Turkish agreement (1939). *See* Great Britain
  Anglo-Turkish guarantee and armaments credit agreement (1938). *See* Great Britain
  Franco-Turkish friendship treaty and military accord (1938). *See* France
  Franco-Turkish mutual defense treaty (1939). *See* France

United States, 1, 36–39, 60, 82, 103, 110, 121, 131, 134, 138, 142, 153, 181, 200

Valle, Giuseppe, 43, 88–89, 124, 144
Vansittart, Robert, 23, 36, 40, 48, 84
Vittorio Emanuele III, King, 74, 135–136, 149, 176, 182, 195–196, 201, 206
Vuillemin, Joseph, 34, 45–46, 90, 95, 128, 141, 195, 204

Water, Te, 48
Wavell, Archibald, 137, 169
Welles, Sumner, 183
Weygand, Maxime, 130, 150, 154, 156, 169–170, 172, 195, 202, 211
Wilhelm II, King, 182
Wood, Kingsley, 102, 197
World War I (Great War), 3–7
  Paris Peace Conference (1919), 3–4, 6–7, 10–11
  Treaty of London (1915), 3

Yugoslavia, 4–6, 21–22, 43, 63, 72, 112, 114, 135, 154, 160, 172, 186, 190, 192–194, 199–200
  Italo-Yugoslav friendship treaty. *See* Italy

Zog, King, 115–116

Cornell Studies in Security Affairs

A series edited by

Robert J. Art, Robert Jervis, *and* Stephen M. Walt

Political Institutions and Military Change: Lessons from Peripheral Wars, by Deborah D. Avant
Japan Prepares for Total War: The Search for Economic Security, 1919–1941, by Michael A. Barnhart
Flying Blind: The Politics of the U.S. Strategic Bomber Program, by Michael E. Brown
Citizens and Soldiers: The Dilemmas of Military Service, by Eliot A. Cohen
The Origins of Major War, by Dale C. Copeland
Military Organization, Complex Machines: Modernization in the U.S. Armed Forces, by Chris C. Demchak
Innovation and the Arms Race: How the United States and the Soviet Union Develop New Military Technologies, by Matthew Evangelista
A Substitute for Victory: The Politics of Peacemaking at the Korean Armistice Talks, by Rosemary Foot
The Wrong War: American Policy and the Dimensions of the Korean Conflict, 1950–1953, by Rosemary Foot
The Best Defense: Policy Alternatives for U.S. Nuclear Security from the 1950s to the 1990s, by David Goldfischer
The Meaning of the Nuclear Revolution: Statecraft and the Prospect of Armageddon, by Robert Jervis
Fast Tanks and Heavy Bombers: Innovation in the U.S. Army, 1917–1945, by David E. Johnson
Modern Hatreds: The Symbolic Politics of Ethnic War, by Stuart J. Kaufman
The Vulnerability of Empire, by Charles A. Kupchan
The Transformation of American Air Power, by Benjamin S. Lambeth
Anatomy of Mistrust: U.S.–Soviet Relations during the Cold War, by Deborah Welch Larson
Planning the Unthinkable: How New Powers Will Use Nuclear, Biological, and Chemical Weapons, edited by Peter R. Lavoy, Scott D. Sagan, and James J. Wirtz
Cooperation under Fire: Anglo-German Restraint during World War II, by Jeffrey W. Legro
No Exit: America and the German Problem, 1943–1954, by James McAllister
Liddell Hart and the Weight of History, by John J. Mearsheimer
Reputation and International Politics, by Jonathan Mercer
Undermining the Kremlin: America's Strategy to Subvert the Soviet Bloc, 1947–1956, by Gregory Mitrovich
Report to JFK: The Skybolt Crisis in Perspective, by Richard E. Neustadt
The Sacred Cause: Civil-Military Conflict over Soviet National Security, 1917–1992, by Thomas M. Nichols
Liberal Peace, Liberal War: American Politics and International Security, by John M. Owen IV

Bombing to Win: Air Power and Coercion in War, by Robert A. Pape
A Question of Loyalty: Military Manpower in Multiethnic States, by Alon Peled
Inadvertent Escalation: Conventional War and Nuclear Risks, by Barry R. Posen
The Sources of Military Doctrine: France, Britain, and Germany between the World Wars, by Barry Posen
Dilemmas of Appeasement: British Deterrence and Defense, 1934–1937, by Gaines Post Jr.
Crucible of Beliefs: Learning, Alliances, and World Wars, by Dan Reiter
Eisenhower and the Missile Gap, by Peter J. Roman
The Domestic Bases of Grand Strategy, edited by Richard Rosecrance and Arthur Stein
Societies and Military Power: India and Its Armies, by Stephen Peter Rosen
Winning the Next War: Innovation and the Modern Military, by Stephen Peter Rosen
Vital Crossroads: Mediterranean Origins of the Second World War, 1935–1940, by Reynolds Salerno
Fighting to a Finish: The Politics of War Termination in the United States and Japan, 1945, by Leon V. Sigal
Alliance Politics, by Glenn H. Snyder
The Ideology of the Offensive: Military Decision Making and the Disasters of 1914, by Jack Snyder
Myths of Empire: Domestic Politics and International Ambition, by Jack Snyder
The Militarization of Space: U.S. Policy, 1945–1984, by Paul B. Stares
The Nixon Administration and the Making of U.S. Nuclear Strategy, by Terry Terriff
The Ethics of Destruction: Norms and Force in International Relations, by Ward Thomas
Causes of War: Power and the Roots of Conflict, by Stephen Van Evera
Mortal Friends, Best Enemies: German-Russian Cooperation after the Cold War, by Celeste A. Wallander
The Origins of Alliances, by Stephen M. Walt
Revolution and War, by Stephen M. Walt
The Tet Offensive: Intelligence Failure in War, by James J. Wirtz
The Elusive Balance: Power and Perceptions during the Cold War, by William Curti Wohlforth
Deterrence and Strategic Culture: Chinese-American Confrontations, 1949–1958, by Shu Guang Zhang